Objects Unencapsulated

Java, Eiffel, and C++??

Ian Joyner

Object and Component Technology Series

Prentice Hall PTR
Upper Saddle River, NJ 07458
http://www.phptr.com

Library of Congress Cataloging-In-Publication Data

Joyner, Ian.
    Objects unencapsulated: Java, Eiffel, and C++?? / Ian Joyner.
      p. cm. -- (Object and component technology series)
    Includes bibliographical references and index.
    ISBN 0-13-014269-7
    1. Object-oriented programming (Computer science) 2. Java
(Computer program language) 3. Eiffel (Computer program language)
4. C++ (Computer program language)   I. Title.   II. Series.
QA76.64.J69   1999
005.1'17--dc21   99-15199
                                       CIP

Editorial/production supervision: BooksCraft, Inc., Indianapolis, IN
Acquisitions Editor: Jeffrey Pepper
Editorial Assistant: Linda Ramagnano
Marketing Manager: Dan Rush
Manufacturing Manager: Alexis R. Heydt
Cover Design Director: Jerry Votta
Cover Production Artist: Talar Agasyan
Cover Designer: Wee Design
Project Coordinator: Anne Trowbridge
Typeset by the author on a Power Macintosh G3 using Adobe FrameMaker software

                         Object and Component Technology Series
                               Editor: Bertrand Meyer

© 1999 by Prentice Hall PTR
Prentice-Hall, Inc.
Upper Saddle River, New Jersey 07458

The publisher offers discounts on this book when ordered in bulk quantities. For more information contact:
Corporate Sales Department
Phone: 800-382-3419 Fax: 201-236-7141
E-mail: corpsales@prenhall.com

Or write:
Prentice Hall PTR
Corp. Sales Dept.
One Lake Street
Upper Saddle River, NJ 07458

All rights reserved. No part of this book may be reproduced, in any form or by any means, without permission in writing from the publis

All product names mentioned herein are the trademarks of their respective owners.

Printed in the United States of America
10 9 8 7 6 5 4 3 2 1

ISBN 0-13-014269-7

Prentice-Hall International (UK) Limited, *London*
Prentice-Hall of Australia Pty. Limited, *Sydney*
Prentice-Hall Canada Inc., *Toronto*
Prentice-Hall Hispanoamericana, S.A., *Mexico*
Prentice-Hall of India Private Limited, *New Delhi*
Prentice-Hall of Japan Inc., *Tokyo*
Prentice-Hall (Singapore) Pte. Ltd.., *Singapore*
Editora Prentice-Hall do Brasil, Ltda., *Rio de Janeiro*

Contents

Preface xi

    Structure of the Book xv
    About C++ Code Examples xvi
    Acknowledgments xviii
    Why Should We Be Concerned? xx

Chapter 1

Language Principles 1

    1.1 Programming 3
    1.2 Communication, Abstraction, and Precision 6
    1.3 Notation 8
    1.4 Tool Integration 9
    1.5 Correctness 9
    1.6 Types 14
    1.7 Flexibility, Correctness, and Reuse 16
    1.8 Redundancy and Checking 19
    1.9 Encapsulation and Implementation Hiding 21
    1.10 Safety and Courtesy Concerns 25
    1.11 Implementation and Deployment Concerns 26

1.12 Why OO? 27
1.13 On Programming Language Evolution 27
1.14 The Usefulness of Mathematics 28
1.15 Legacy Systems 28

Chapter 2

Entities and Types 31

2.1 From Bits to Semantics 31
2.2 Basic Structures: The Class 37
2.3 Usefulness of Grammars 45
2.4 Classes and Types 48
2.5 Structs (C++) 49
2.6 Typedefs (C++) 49
2.7 Global Environments 50
2.8 Class Metadata 51
2.9 Obsolete (Eiffel) 54
2.10 Invariants (Eiffel) 56
2.11 Components 58

Chapter 3

Modules and Imports 63

3.1 Namespaces (C++) 64
3.2 Clusters (Eiffel) 67
3.3 Packages (Java) 68
3.4 Header Files (C++) 68
3.5 Import (Java) 72
3.6 ACE Specification (Eiffel) 72
3.7 Separate or Integrate? 73

Chapter 4

Members and Features 77

4.1 Basic Structures 77
4.2 Members (C++ and Java) 88
4.3 Anonymous Parameters in Class Definitions (C++) 88

Contents

4.4 Default Arguments (C++) 90
4.5 Local Entity Declarations (Java and C++) 92
4.6 Inlines (C++) 93
4.7 Pointers and References (C++) 98
4.8 Declarations and Definitions (C++) 98
4.9 Scope 100
4.10 Constants 100
4.11 Static (C++) 103
4.12 Once Routines 104
4.13 Class Variables and Redefinition 105

Chapter 5

Type Extension: Inheritance and Virtuals *107*

5.1 Basic Structures: Inheritance and Derived Classes 109
5.2 The Nature of Inheritance 116
5.3 Multiple Inheritance 121
5.4 Virtual Classes (C++) 129
5.5 Nested Classes (Java and C++) 132
5.6 Polymorphism and Inheritance 138
5.7 Union 139
5.8 Enumeration Types 143
5.9 Name Overloading 146
5.10 Virtual Functions (C++) 152
5.11 Pure Virtual Functions (C++) 159
5.12 Function Overloading (C++ and Java) 162
5.13 Virtuals and Inlining 168

Chapter 6

Type Extension: Generics and Templates *171*

6.1 Basic Structures 173
6.2 C++ Syntax 176
6.3 Constrained Genericity 176
6.4 Genericity and Code Bloat 177

6.5 An Alternative Form of Genericity.................. 178
6.6 Java and Genericity 182
6.7 Some Theory on Genericity 186
6.8 Genericity and Covariance........................ 189

Chapter 7

Interfaces and Access Control *191*

7.1 Basic Structures 191
7.2 Friends (C++)..................................... 193
7.3 Controlled Exports vs. Friends..................... 195
7.4 Multiple Interfaces 200
7.5 External Assignment (C++ and Java)................ 201
7.6 Export Controls and Nesting 202
7.7 Mutable Const (C++).............................. 204
7.8 Generalization 205

Chapter 8

Constructors, Destructors, and Other Operators .. *207*

8.1 Nameless Constructors (C++) 207
8.2 Default Constructors (C++ and Java)................ 208
8.3 Constructor Inheritance 208
8.4 Expanded Initialization (Eiffel) 209
8.5 Constructor Initialization (C++).................... 209
8.6 Destructors (C++) 211
8.7 Dispose (Eiffel) 211
8.8 Operator = (C++) 211
8.9 . and -> (C++) 212
8.10 Delete and Delete [] (C++)........................ 215
8.11 Prefix and Postfix Operators (C++) 216
8.12 || and && (C++)................................. 217
8.13 Operator Overloading (C++ and Eiffel).............. 218
8.14 Implicit Conversions and Overloading (C++) 219
8.15 Calling Parent Features 220
8.16 Calling Descendant Features 223
8.17 Conditional Expressions.......................... 224

Contents

Chapter 9

Casts..................................225

9.1 Type Casts (C++)..............................225
9.2 RTTI and Type Casts (C++) 228
9.3 New Type Casts (C++) 232
9.4 Type Inference.................................232
9.5 Java and Casts.................................233
9.6 Signature Variance (Eiffel) 233

Chapter 10

Compile Time 247

10.1 Global Analysis...............................247
10.2 Type-Safe Linkage (C++) 249
10.3 Class Interfaces...............................251

Chapter 11

Run Time..............................253

11.1 Concurrency — It's about Time!..................253
11.2 Garbage Collection 266
11.3 Constructors and Temporaries (C++) 273
11.4 Bad Deletions (C++)...........................274
11.5 Slicing (C++).................................275
11.6 Program Execution 276
11.7 Dynamic Linking..............................277
11.8 Exception Handling............................279
11.9 LinkageError (Java)...........................283

Chapter 12

Other Details...........................285

12.1 Comments 285
12.2 Hexadecimal Literals (Eiffel) 287
12.3 Double, double toil and trouble...................288
12.4 Class Header Declarations (C++) 290

Chapter 13

Projects, Design, and Other Factors 293

13.1 Design by Contract. 293
13.2 Preconditions, Types, and Invariants 296
13.3 The Software Life Cycle 297
13.4 CASE Tools 301
13.5 Reusability and Communication 303
13.6 Reusability and Trust 304
13.7 Reusability and Compatibility 305
13.8 Reusability and Portability........................ 307
13.9 Reusability and Size............................. 308
13.10 Idiomatic Programming 308
13.11 Low-Level Coding 309
13.12 Knowing the Correct Construct 310
13.13 Efficiency and Optimization. 310
13.14 Standardization, Stability, and Maturity............. 312
13.15 Complexity................................... 314
13.16 C++: The Overwhelming OOL of Choice? 318

Chapter 14

General Issues 321

14.1 Pointers...................................... 322
14.2 Booleans..................................... 324
14.3 Logical and Bitwise Operators..................... 326
14.4 Arrays....................................... 327
14.5 Function Arguments............................. 331
14.6 void and void* 332
14.7 NULL vs. 0................................... 338
14.8 char; signed and unsigned 339
14.9 void fn ().................................... 340
14.10 fn ()....................................... 341
14.11 fn (void) 344
14.12 return 344
14.13 Switch Statements 346
14.14 Metadata in Strings 347

Contents

14.15 ++, -- **348**
14.16 Assignment Operator............................ **350**
14.17 Assignment Expressions **352**
14.18 Defines.. **354**
14.19 Case Sensitivity................................. **356**
14.20 Semicolons **359**
14.21 Comments **361**
14.22 Cpaghe++i.................................... **362**

Bibliography.................................*365*

WEBliography................................*375*

Bibliographic Index..........................*379*

Index.......................................*381*

Copyrights and Trademarks

Macintosh and Mac OS are trademarks of Apple Computer.
Design by Contract is a trademark of Interactive Software Engineering Inc.
Java is a trademark of Sun Microsystems.

Quotes from *The Unix Hater's Handbook* by Simson Garfinkel, Daniel Weise, and Steven Strassmann, Copyright 1994, IDG Books Worldwide, Inc. All rights reserved. Reproduced by permission.

Quotes from James Bach *The Hard Road from Methods to Practice* © 1997 IEEE.

Quotes from Palsberg and Schwartzbach *Object-Oriented Type Systems*. Copyright John Wiley and Sons Limited. Reproduced with permission.

Quotes from M Ellis/B Stroustrup, THE ANNOTATED C++ REFERENCE MANUAL, © 1990 AT&T Bell Telephone Laboratories. Reprinted by permission of Addison Wesley Longman.

Quotes from S Meyers, EFFECTIVE C++, © 1992 Addison Wesley Longman Company Inc. Reprinted by permission of Addison Wesley Longman.

Quotes from S Meyers, MORE EFFECTIVE C++, © 1996 Addison Wesley Longman Company Inc. Reprinted by permission of Addison Wesley Longman.

Quotes from J Gosling et al., THE JAVA LANGUAGE SPECIFICATION, © 1996 Addison Wesley Longman Company Inc. Reprinted by permission of Addison Wesley Longman.

Quotes from B Stroustrup, THE DESIGN AND EVOLUTION OF C++, © 1994 AT&T Bell Labs. Reprinted by permission of Addison Wesley Longman.

Quotes from B Stroustrup, THE C++ PROGRAMMING LANGUAGE – 3rd ed. © 1997 AT&T. Reprinted by permission of Addison Wesley Longman.

Preface

No doubt, right now you are standing in a bookshop deciding why you would want to buy this book instead of the plethora of other books you see on the shelf in front of you on C++, Java, and, to a lesser extent, Eiffel. Or you might have already bought it and wonder why you should read on. But this is just the preface, right? And nobody reads the preface unless they are standing in a bookstore, so you can probably buy it now and save reading the rest of the preface! This book gives you three books in one, and it is no longer—and probably even shorter—than many of the single books. I share with many readers the experience that we don't very often make it through one of those 500-page megavolumes. This book also tells you about the commonalities, differences, strengths, and pitfalls of these languages and gives you an honest appraisal of how they measure up to what you need to write quality software.

This book is a *critical look* because it is critical that we address the issues that continue to make programming an unnecessarily difficult task; that is, a look into aspects of current programming practice that ensure the continuation of the "software crisis." In doing so, it is critical of many aspects of popular programming languages, and as such it delivers a message that will not be well received in some quarters. However, we must realize that no technology is absolute. We must throw down the gauntlet in order to progress.

This book will not teach you any of these languages in themselves, as it concentrates on features they have in common or how they are different. This book will give you a deeper understanding, as I have gained over the years of developing it, of programming language features, not only of the languages presented here, but of many others as well, and of the many controversies and arguments, mostly bogus, that programming languages give rise to.

Many books on programming languages are guides of how to avoid the traps and pitfalls of the language. Of course, many new programmers want to learn these secrets in order to enter the ranks of expert programmers, and there is no shortage of books to capitalize on this desire. Warnings of potential traps is particularly the case with C++ literature, where Bjarne Stroustrup's books give many warnings, and Scott Meyers' books give even more, but they tend to justify C++ in that, if you know about these problems, everything will be all right. This book takes a different and perhaps less popular view, that warnings are not enough; languages must be designed from the ground up to be more solid. Car purchasers would not be impressed if the dealer warned that a car occasionally violently jerks to the left: if driving on the road from Amalfi to Sorrento, they would suddenly meet their doom. This book seeks to cut through the language and object-oriented (OO) hype and get to the truth about both.

One way hype becomes established is that people tend to fall in love with technology too quickly. We love our computers for the power we perceive they can give us. We particularly fall in love with the first technology we use. It is natural to love our first car, but the time comes when we must move on or be stuck with something that costs a fortune to maintain. This is of course what the enthusiast wants, but it is not appropriate for those who want a car just as a practical means of transport. The computer industry is already paying heavily to retain technologies well beyond their use-by date, an example being the year 2000 (Y2K) problem.

People also like to follow technologies that become well established, because they give a sense of belonging to a larger cultural group. This is not necessarily a bad phenomenon, except where the larger cultures overrun smaller groups, and where adherence to one technology damages new technologies and stifles innovation. This has often been a problem in science where protection of established false beliefs has often been used protect a power base. In computing, these power bases are particularly strong and financially lucrative. One thinks of Galileo as the quintessential victim of this phenomenon; the perpetrators of Galileo's suffering were the most respected and "wise" people of the time.

This book takes the approach that technology must be constantly reevaluated in order to be improved; we must see and admit the flaws in our current technologies no matter how passionate we feel about them. Observed flaws, of course, come as a bitter pill to some who will throw up no end of smoke screens to cover the fact. Such defense is the basis of the religious wars that have become common in the industry, and these religious wars undermine the professionalism of the industry. This book focuses on the technology of programming languages and takes three well-known languages as a basis for its comments. Other technologies, as well as the hype that is present in the industry, also need reevaluation.

Hype is very valuable to marketeers in raising the public's consciousness of a particular product. I recently heard a fashion industry marketeer state, "A white shirt is a white shirt; but a hyped white shirt is a white shirt you want to buy." We should not condemn those who use hype, since it is natural to resort to hype in a market where some products dominate due to strongly held loyalties, but we should not allow these loyalties or hype to prevent proper evaluation of technologies. The computer industry is an industry where the most strongly held loyalties can be observed; as consumers it is our responsibility to beware that hype is often used to create the illusion that something is what it is not.

The main goal of this book is to compare three languages: C++, Java, and Eiffel. To my knowledge, no other book compares languages in this way, although I can appreciate why as it is not a simple exercise. Originally, this was a paper only on C++, but when Java appeared it addressed many of the problems of C++, so a direct comparison of Java and C++ seemed like a good idea. Since I had started on Java, comparisons to other languages also seemed like a good idea. Eiffel was an obvious choice, since in many ways it is comparable to C++ and Java. I wanted to do others like Smalltalk, Beta, and Oberon, but these languages are somewhat different again, and three languages already provided more than enough material.

Another unique aspect of this book is that it takes a practical look at language features and how they relate to productivity on a software project. My purpose has not been to produce an academic treatise or thesis on the theoretical aspects of languages, but to give practical reasons as to why certain language features are good or bad, or may lead to problems. Sometimes this ties in with theory, and it is my opinion that theory exists only to make practice easier and to enable things we have not previously thought of. Theory is not a straightjacket to constrain us; rather theory enables new things.

Many people are starting to feel burnt by the overenthusiastic adoption of what is known as object-oriented technology. My own start in OO was at Sydney University where we had an honors class presented by Professor Jan Hext on data abstraction, and in part of this class we learnt Simula. I was impressed by this language, as many others have been, including Bjarne Stroustrup and Alan Kay. Several years later I went on to do several large projects using Object Pascal. It was during one of these projects that C++ came to my attention, so I enthusiastically bought Bjarne Stroustrup's first edition of *The C++ Programming Language*. As I read this I felt somewhat ill at ease, as concepts that I was very familiar with seemed to be buried somewhat beneath complexities that I, as an experienced OO practitioner of several years, had difficulty understanding. At this stage C++ was very simple compared to the C++ of today. Originally, C++ offered no real advantages over Object Pascal, as it then did not have multiple inheritance, templates, and so on. I did not want to judge a language without practical experience, as I reasoned that practical experience would probably make sense of some of the obscurities very quickly.

It was also around this time that Brian Henderson-Sellers recommended to me a book called *Object-Oriented Software Construction* by Bertrand Meyer. I found this book a very enjoyable read because it examined what the real objectives of software engineering are and then gave solutions. It explained much about what had gone right and wrong in my previous projects. One thing annoyed me about the book—it introduced yet another programming language that Meyer called Eiffel. I really wanted something that explained OO like this, but that applied it to languages I knew, like Object Pascal and the newer C++. I thought Eiffel was a bit like Knuth's Mix assembler language in his *Art of Computer Programming* series. I did not like having to cope with yet another language. However, as I progressed through the book, I discovered that Eiffel was so clean and simple that it did not prove a distraction at all. Even though I made no real effort to learn it, by the end of the book, I felt it was quite familiar; not only that, but I had learned new advanced OO concepts like multiple inheritance, genericity, and garbage collection, which neither Object Pascal nor C++ offered at that time.

The opportunity to use C++ for real came while I was working for Unisys Corporation. A large project, UNIX X.500, had been done in C++. Even then, C++ was still quite primitive, with no multiple inheritance, templates, and such, and compilation was done with the CFront preprocessor. My colleagues had little experience with OO other than C++, but were enthusiastic that C++ was the ultimate language and said that I had not really done OO until I had done C++. It was not long before I found out why I had been ill at ease reading Stroustrup's first edition. Practical experience did not explain the previously noted obscurities but turned up many pitfalls. After just a few weeks, I had two pages full of point notes of problems I had found. After a few months I wrote this up as a report and submitted it to an internal Unisys newsgroup. A few people who had been pushing C++ in their own departments came out in defense of C++. They really prompted me to find more flaws, and the paper became quite long. I then submitted it to Internet news groups in early 1992. Again this went through the test by fire, which gave me many more ideas. So I completely revised it into a second edition and resubmitted it to Newsnet in late 1992.

After 1992 I decided that I had spent enough time on this project and that I wanted to stick to software engineering. However, in 1996 I started to examine Java, which claimed to avoid the problems of C++, and, as mentioned earlier, this inspired me to reexamine my earlier evaluation of C++ in comparison to other languages. Thus the third edition of this critique was published on the Internet in late 1996.

After the third edition was published, many people commented that I didn't really go far enough; there were many other problems in C++. They gave me lectures on some of the other problems and pointed me in other directions to research. They were right, and I found several sources of new material and things I hadn't thought about before. I began adding this material to what was to become the fourth edition, but the paper was getting very long. When I restructured it into book format, I found it was over 150 pages, so I decided it could be possible material for a book. If you have read the previous three editions, you will find that the book preserves a lot of the original material, but rearranges it into a more logical learning order, and it adds a lot of fresh material—I hope you like the result. So it is worth buying, or at least borrowing from a friend.

Structure of the Book

Throughout this book we will follow a top-down course through the object-oriented paradigm, examining each of the languages in turn, drawing attention to their differences, strengths, weaknesses, and problems.

In chapter 1, we examine some principles and concepts that will be useful in coming to some conclusions as to how our languages are suited to the task: without knowing what to expect of modern-day programming languages, we won't be able to form any opinions.

Chapter 2 starts at the top of object-oriented languages, looking at objects, classes, and the basic entities in OO languages. Chapter 3 looks at the concept of modules, or how the basic entities are grouped in our languages, and how groups of classes can be packaged together. Chapter 4 examines the insides of these entities: the features.

Chapters 5 and 6 examine how to use the basic entities to construct larger systems; that is, how to compose the entities with inheritance in chapter 5 and genericity in chapter 6.

Chapter 7 covers the features providing exports and access control, how interfaces are defined, and how access to the implementations of classes is prevented.

Chapter 8 examines how objects are initialized and destroyed, and looks at various other operators as well.

Chapter 9 deals with casts and how they are not needed in well-defined type systems.

Chapters 10 and 11 look at some compile-time and run-time issues. Chapter 12 contains some miscellaneous issues that do not fit in other chapters.

Chapter 13 draws many threads together and looks at project organization, design, and other factors, and how our languages provide these features.

Chapter 14 looks at specific issues from C that affect C++, or have been discarded from C++, and how Java and Eiffel do not suffer from these problems.

About C++ Code Examples

It is very difficult to develop examples in C++ to conform to how C++ can and should be written. By "can be written," I mean can it be compiled by most compilers on the market today. By "should be written," I mean, is it written to be conformant with the latest draft standard and the way the gurus say it should be written, which might not be accepted by any compiler on the market. (By the way, the International Standards Organization [ISO] points out that a draft standard is *not* a standard!). By including C++ examples, one is wide open to criticism that the examples are not good examples.

This sounds like a pathetic excuse on my part, but Al Stevens, a well-known writer about C++, including one of the *Teach Yourself C++* books, says in a recent Dr. Dobb's article:

> We C++ writers have been in a quandary for some time now. The problem is rapid language evolution. If you write about the language the way that current compilers support it, your work is obsolete even as you write. If you write about the language the way the committee has defined it, few, if any, contemporary compilers can compile the programs in your work (because virtually no compiler compiles with the current proposed standard).

[Stevens 97]

And further:

> All the C++ books in my bookcase, including some fairly recent ones, use this style of code. However, if a brand new book uses this style of code, that book is labelled "old fashioned" before it goes out the door.

Also:

> Listing Four is a fully compliant (with the proposed Standard) C++ program that a legacy C++ compiler would not compile but that a

compliant compiler—if one was available—would compile. Herb and I have been told by a reputable authority that this is how C++ programmers should be taught to program. Listing Four is politically correct.

Thus I am sure you will have no problem finding detractors who will say this book is not valid because the examples do not conform to one compiler or another (at one time or another), or to the standard, or to someone's notion of politically correct. So I make no apology for this—it is something that no one can get right! I do include the examples because they help illustrate what I am talking about, in the spirit of a picture is worth a thousand words.

Acknowledgments

Around 1996 I had an inkling that my Internet paper might grow into a reasonable book project, but did not take the idea too seriously until Geoff Eldridge voiced the idea and was encouraging after that. Geoff runs a well-respected Internet site disseminating much useful information on OO technology, and has also been instrumental in getting wide circulation for my original paper examining C++.

Soon after that Bertrand Meyer also expressed interest in publishing such a work in the Object-Technology Series. He has been very encouraging, but has not unduly influenced the project as the designer of one of the languages this book examines. I am not always complementary of his language, and the freedom to perform this work and yet to have an outlet is much appreciated.

John Potter has also been most encouraging and arranged part-time employment in his Object Technology Group with the Microsoft Research Institute at Macquarie University (MRI). He has given me many projects to do that have provided insights documented here, and helped test others. The frequent discussions at MRI have been most illuminating, and have certainly helped straighten out some areas of this book, although any areas of inaccuracy are my responsibility only. In this group is David Clarke, with whom I have shared an office, many type-related discussions, and an absurd sense of humor; David Holmes, who is a leading expert on concurrency in Java, and who provided many detailed and helpful comments on an early draft; James Noble, who knows much about prototyping languages and patterns; Jon Tidswell, who offered much support and taught me a lot about computer security in a very short conversation; Ryan Shelswell, who we lost to higher callings in Scotland, but who also contributed many insights. Although this group is being disbanded mid-1999, I'm sure you will hear a lot from these talented young people in the next millennium (if we survive the millennium bug catastrophe that is!).

I should also mention Professor Jan Hext who, as I mentioned, I first knew at Sydney University where he taught me Simula in an honors course, and so set my sights on OO, even before the term was known, and who gave some good advice on the pitfalls of publishing a book. Paul Greenfield has also been a common factor in my continuing education, from being a tutor at Sydney University to one who I have continually worked with in several different jobs. He showed how you can be a practical engineer with high-level concepts. Don Gregory has also been a good friend, encouraged several endeavors, and published an early form of this book as a paper in his A Series Journal. Owen Reddecliffe was another person who proved to me that high-level languages were practical and could be extremely efficient, and the fact that he wrote a compiler for an ALGOL-like language in 4,000 lines of Basic is an education in itself.

That being said, during the preparation of this book, my mother unexpectedly passed away from complications after heart bypass surgery, and like anyone who has lost a parent, I wish there were a way I could express my thanks to her more directly and regret the many missed opportunities. She was the epitome of love and would find great distress in how modern technology is used to amplify mankind's greed and hatred. This book is therefore dedicated to:

Lois Nellie Joyner

She gave me life
My passage into the world
But more than organic fact
   we are here for a higher purpose
She was a channel of love
Bringing everyone together
   and back together again
In this broken world love is silly and feeble-minded
   but where she is now love reigns in strength
If all could grasp her love beyond reason
   the world would be beyond war, guns and aggression
   beyond the hate of those less fortunate or different
The world should learn from her love, her compassion
These she has left us
   and let us pray that they shall never be gone.

—Ian Joyner
30 July 1998

Why Should We Be Concerned?

One lesson I learned from this is that professions can afford to be far more self-critical. It seems that doctors are very willing to submit patients to procedures that they themselves might be reluctant to undergo. Many medical practices are inherently dangerous, and yet research is very slow to investigate alternatives. Many medical practices are based around fixing problems after they have happened rather than assessing a patient's whole lifestyle to effect prevention in the first place. No wonder so many are turning to alternative medicine. The problem with this is that there is never a shortage of charlatans hoping to cash in. But there is truth behind such alternatives, which old professions too readily deny.

Unfortunately, the computing profession is also involved with safety and with enterprises that are critical, and yet too many computer professionals are unwilling to explore and encourage alternatives. If the human race is to continue to improve, then we need more resources spent on research, and everyday practitioners should become far more open-minded than they are now.

Professions are also overburdened with rules; unfortunately they are for the most part not the right ones. An example of this is *secondary rules* that make up for some deficiency in another rule or process, instead of addressing the root cause. Of course, this does not mean that we don't need safeguards against fraud in professions and against those whose prime motive is to make money for very little effort.

The fact that many in computing defend the status quo with deeply flawed arguments shows that we have still very far to go.

> It is not enough that you should understand about applied science in order that your work may increase man's blessings. Concern for man himself and his fate must always form the chief interest of all technical endeavours, concern for the great unsolved problems of the organization of labor and the distribution of goods—in order that the creations of our mind shall be a blessing and not a curse to Mankind. Never forget this in the midst of your diagrams and equations.
>
> —ALBERT EINSTEIN
> Address, California Institute of Technology, 1931

1

Language Principles

A programming language functions at many different levels and has many roles; it should be evaluated with respect to those levels and roles. Historically, programming languages have had a limited role—that of writing executable programs. While this is the real purpose of programs, which should not be forgotten, as programs have grown in complexity, this role alone has proved insufficient. Many analysis and design techniques have arisen to support other necessary roles.

Object-oriented (OO) techniques help in the analysis and design phases; OO languages support the implementation phase, but in many cases these lack uniformity of concepts, integration with the development environment, and commonality of purpose. Traditional problematic software practices are infiltrating the OO world with little thought. Often these approaches appeal to management because the techniques are outwardly organized: people are assigned organizational roles such as project manager, team leader, analyst, designer, and programmer. Unfortunately these approaches are simplistic and insufficient and result in demotivated and uncreative environments.

OO, however, offers a better, rational approach to software development. The complementary roles of analysis, design, implementation, and project organization should be better integrated in the OO scheme. This results in economical software production and more creative and motivated environments. We should not assume that this will fix all our problems: a tool is only as good as the person using it.

An OO language should support not only implementation but analysis and design factors as well. This is the point of all high-level languages but one which has been missed by those who still insist that software development is two separate processes of design and implementation, with design notations separate from programming languages. High-level languages are not just assemblers with fancy syntax but arise from integrating both design and implementation concepts and notations. Unfortunately, some OO languages are not as faithful to this principle as they should be. It is also widely acknowledged that C is an assembler language with fancy syntax.

The organization of projects also requires tools external to the language and compiler, like *make*. A reevaluation of these tools shows that often the division of labor between them has not been along optimal lines—first, programmers need to do extra *bookkeeping* work that could be automated; second, inadequate *separation of concerns* has resulted in inflexible software systems.

This unfortunate state of affairs has arisen because compromises were made to fit program development systems to the technology of the day, rather than the systems being designed around the problem domain of software development. This might have been necessary at the time, but it is no longer appropriate, especially as computer users become more sophisticated and demanding and as software becomes more complex. The state of the art in software development today carries too many compromises from the past, compromises that are no longer necessary or valid.

C++ is an interesting experiment in adapting the advantages of OO to a traditional programming language and development environment. Bjarne Stroustrup should be recognized for having the insight to put the two technologies together; he ventured into OO not only before solutions to many issues were known, but before the issues were even widely recognized. He deserves better than a back full of arrows—much careful thought has gone into C++. But, in retrospect, we can see that C++ is not an elegant fulfilment of OO concepts and realize that the UNIX development environment with limited linker support does not provide enough compiler support for many of the features that should be in a high-level language.

There are solutions to the problems that C++ uncovered. C++ has gone down a path in research, but now we know what the problems are and how to solve them. We should adopt or develop such languages. Fortunately, such languages have been developed—industrial-strength languages that are meant for commercial projects, which are not just academic research projects. It is now up to the industry to adopt them on a wider scale.

Java is an interesting development taking a different approach to C++: strict compatibility with C is not seen as a relevant goal. Java is not the only C-based alternative to C++ in the OO world. There has also been Objective-C from Brad Cox, mainly used in NeXT's OpenStep environment; Objective-C will be prominent in Apple's new-generation operating system, Rhapsody. Objective-C is more like Smalltalk, in that all binding is done dynamically at run time.

Java and C++ are both based on C syntax, Java not as closely as C++. While this syntax has proven popular due to its conciseness, it is not the most regular nor readable of syntaxes. We should not reject languages just because they are not based on the familiar C syntax. Syntax is actually only a small part of a language, most often learned in days as opposed to the months and years it takes to learn how to actually produce good programs. We should feel free to adopt clearer syntaxes.

A language should not only be evaluated from a technical point of view, considering its syntactic and semantic features; it should also be analyzed from the viewpoint of its contribution to the entire software development process. A language should enable communication between project members acting at different levels, from management, who set enterprise-level policies, to testers, who must test the result. All these people are involved in the general activity of programming, so a language should enable communication between project members separated in space and time. A single programmer is not often responsible for a task over its entire lifetime.

Most important of all is the user: software that does not satisfy a user need is worthless. This is not to say, however, that the best software has the most users, or that software with few users is worth less than software with many users. This reasoning is used too often in this industry, by those who cannot judge products on technical merits. In all our advances to make programs easier to produce, we must not lose sight of making software useful and useable.

1.1 Programming

[Morgan 90]
(1.2)

Programming and specification are now seen as the same task. One man's specification is another's program. Eventually you get to the point of processing a specification with a compiler, which generates a program that actually runs on a computer. Morgan banishes the distinction between specifications and programs: "To us they are all programs." Programming is a term that refers not only to implementation but to the whole process of analysis, design, and implementation.

Reade gives this explanation of programming and languages.

> One, rather narrow, view is that a program is a sequence of instructions for a machine. We hope to show that there is much to be gained from taking the much broader view that programs are descriptions of values, properties, methods, problems, and solutions. The role of the machine is to speed up the manipulation of these descriptions to provide solutions to particular problems. A programming language is a convention for writing descriptions that can be evaluated.
>
> [Reade 89] (1.1)

Reade also describes programming as being a "separation of concerns."

> The programmer is having to do several things at the same time, namely,
>
> (1) describe what is to be computed;
>
> (2) organize the computation sequencing into small steps;
>
> (3) organize memory management during the computation.
>
> [Reade 89] (1.1.1)

Reade continues:

> Ideally, the programmer should be able to concentrate on the first of the three tasks (describing what is to be computed) without being distracted by the other two, more administrative, tasks. Clearly, administration is important but by separating it from the main task we are likely to get more reliable results and we can ease the programming problem by automating much of the administration.
>
> The separation of concerns has other advantages as well. For example, program proving becomes much more feasible when details of sequencing and memory management are absent from the program. Furthermore, descriptions of what is to be computed should be free of such detailed step-by-step descriptions of how to do it if they are to be evaluated with different machine architectures. Sequences of small changes to a data object held in a store may be an inappropriate description of how to compute something when a highly parallel machine is being used with thousands of processors distributed throughout the machine and local rather than global storage facilities.
>
> Automating the administrative aspects means that the language implementer has to deal with them, but he/she has far more opportunity to
>
> [Reade 89] (1.1.2)

make use of very different computation mechanisms with different machine architectures.

Bookkeeping Tasks

These quotes from Reade are a good summary of the principles used in this book to analyze and compare languages. What Reade calls administrative tasks, I call *bookkeeping*. Bookkeeping adds to the cost of software production and reduces flexibility, which in turn adds more to the cost. C and C++ are often criticized for being cryptic because C concentrates on points 2 and 3, while the description of what is to be computed is obscured.

High-level languages describe what is to be computed; that is, the problem domain. How a computation is achieved is in the low-level machine-oriented deployment domain. Automating the bookkeeping tasks enhances correctness, compatibility, portability, and efficiency. Bookkeeping tasks arise from having to specify how a computation is done. Specifying how things are done in one environment hinders portability to other platforms.

One of the most important language principles is to make the task simpler for the programmer. Removing bookkeeping tasks cannot be underestimated in accomplishing this. We should distinguish between high-level languages that remove bookkeeping tasks and languages that have high-level syntax but expose the bookkeeping tasks of the underlying system—these are really assemblers with fancy syntax.

A way to judge if a language construct is worth the trouble is: does it eliminate bookkeeping? For example, we will see in this book that genericity, or some equivalent, is worth it because it removes the need for the bookkeeping of type casts. Java does not have genericity, which results in programmers having to do many type casts when retrieving objects from collections. Genericity is an example of the *declarative approach*.

Declarative Approach

The most significant way high-level languages replace bookkeeping is that they use a declarative approach, whereas low-level languages use operators, which make them more like assemblers. The declarative approach centralizes decisions and lets the compiler generate the underlying machine operators. With the operator approach, the bookkeeping is the programmer's responsibility to use the correct operator to access an entity: if a decision changes, the programmer will have to change all operators, rather than changing the single declaration and simply recompiling. C and C++ provide operators rather than adopting the declarative approach; thus the programmer is often concerned with low-level mechanisms.

High-level languages hide the implementation detail, making program development and maintenance far more flexible.

We shall see that this is one of the greatest differences between Eiffel and C++: Eiffel is more declarative, rather than having a plethora of operators. Having more operators in a language might give it the appearance of being more powerful, but the declarative approach provides equivalent power in a more subtle form, producing programs that are easier to understand. Java is somewhere between Eiffel and C++.

While C and C++ syntax is similar to high-level language syntax, C and C++ cannot be considered high-level because they do not remove bookkeeping from the programmer the way high-level languages should, requiring the compiler to take care of these details.

The most important quality of a high-level language is that it removes the bookkeeping burden from the programmer in order to enhance speed of development, maintainability, and flexibility. This attribute is more important than OO itself and should be intrinsic to any modern programming paradigm.

The industry should be moving toward these ideals, which will help in the economic production of software, rather than using the costly techniques of today. We should consider what we need and assess the problems of what we have against that. OO provides one solution to these problems. The effectiveness of OO, however, depends on the quality of its implementation.

1.2 Communication, Abstraction, and Precision

The primary purpose of any language is communication. A specification is communication from one person to another entity of a task to be fulfilled. (We shall describe later the notion of contract, a part of which is the description of what is to be fulfilled.) At the lowest level, the task is that a computer executes a program. At the next level it is the compilation of a program by a compiler. At higher levels, specifications communicate to other people what the programming task must accomplish.

At the lowest level, instructions must be precisely executed, but there is no understanding; it is purely mechanical. At higher levels, understanding is important because human intelligence is involved, which is why enlightened management practices emphasize training rather than forced processes. This is not to say that precision is not important; precision at the higher levels is of utmost importance, or the rest of the endeavor will fail. Many projects fail due to lack of precision in the requirements and other early stages.

[Adams 96]   Unfortunately, often those who are least skilled in programming work at the higher levels, so specifications lack the desirable properties of abstraction and precision. Just as in the *Dilbert Principle*, the least effective programmers are promoted to where they will seemingly do the least damage. This is not quite the winning strategy that it seems, since that is where they actually do the most damage, and teams of confused programmers are then left to straighten out their specifications while the so-called analysts move onto the next project or company to sow further seeds of disaster.

[Deming 82]
[Latzko and Saunders 95]
[DeMarco and Lister 87]

(Indeed, since many managers have not read or understood the works of Deming, De Marco, and Lister, as well as Tom Peters' later works, the message that the physical environment and attitudes of the workplace lead to quality has been lost or at least ignored. Perhaps the humor of Scott Adams is now the only way this message will have impact.)

At higher levels, abstraction facilitates understanding. Abstraction and precision are both important qualities of high-level specifications. Abstraction does not mean vagueness, nor the abandonment of precision. Abstraction means the removal of irrelevant detail from a certain viewpoint. With an abstract specification, you are left with a precise specification—precisely the properties of the system that are relevant. Abstraction and precision are really two sides of the same coin.

I have heard it said that abstraction is the enemy of efficiency. This is a completely wrong characterization of abstraction; correct abstraction in fact results in efficiency. It is not creating layers of software, hiding lower levels from application programs, although this approach has other advantages such as making software platform independent.

[Aho 92]
(Chapter 1)

Abstraction is a fundamental concept in computing. Aho and Ullman say, "An important part of the field [computer science] deals with how to make programming easier and software more reliable. But fundamentally, computer science is a science of *abstraction*—creating the right model for a problem and devising the appropriate mechanizable techniques to solve it." Furthermore, "Abstraction in the sense we use it often implies simplification, the replacement of a complex and detailed real-world situation by an understandable model within which we can solve the problem."

A well-known example that exhibits both abstraction and precision is the London Underground map designed by Harold Beck. This is a diagrammatic map that has abstracted irrelevant details from the real London geography to result in a conveniently sized and more readable map. Yet the map precisely shows the underground lines, stations, and interchanges, and the precision means that no stations are missing and that they are all in the correct order. Many other city transport systems have adopted the principles of Beck's map. Using this model passengers can easily solve such problems as "How do I get from Knightsbridge to Baker Street?"

Beck's abstraction has proven popular because it has enabled passengers to find their way around transport systems efficiently. This efficiency results only from good abstraction; abstraction is certainly not the enemy of efficiency.

1.3 Notation

A programming language should support the exchange of ideas, intentions, and decisions between project members; it should provide a formal, yet readable, notation to support consistent descriptions of systems that satisfy the requirements of diverse problems. A language should also provide methods for automated project tracking. This ensures that modules (classes and functionality) that satisfy project requirements are completed in a timely and economic fashion. A programming language aids reasoning about the design, implementation, extension, correction, and optimization of a system.

During requirements, analysis, and design phases, formal and semiformal notations are desirable. Notations used in analysis, design, and implementation phases should be complementary, rather than contradictory. Currently, analysis, design, and modeling notations are too far removed from implementation, while programming languages are in general too low level. Both designers and programmers must compromise to fill the gap. Many current notations provide difficult transition paths between stages. This semantic gap contributes to errors and omissions between the requirements, design, and implementation phases.

Better programming languages are an implementation extension of the high-level notations used for requirements analysis and design, which will lead to improved consistency between analysis, design, and implementation. OO techniques emphasize the importance of this, as abstract definition and concrete implementation can be separate, yet provided in the same notation.

Programming languages also provide notations to formally document a system. Program source is the only reliable documentation of a system, so a language should explicitly support documentation, not just in the form of comments. As with all language, the effectiveness of communication is dependent upon the skill of the writer. Good program writers require languages that support the role of documentation; they also require that the language notation is perspicuous and easy to learn. Those not trained in the skill of writing programs can read them to gain understanding of the system. After all, it is not necessary for newspaper readers to be journalists.

1.4 Tool Integration

A language definition should enable the development of integrated automated tools—for example, browsers, editors, and debuggers—to support software development. The compiler is just another tool having a twofold role, the first of which is code generation for the target machine. The role of the machine is to execute the produced programs. A compiler has to check that a program conforms to the language syntax and grammar so that it can understand the program in order to translate it into an executable form. Second, and more important, the compiler should check that the programmer's expression of the system is valid, complete, and consistent; i.e., that it performs semantics checks to see if a program is internally consistent. Generating a system that has detectable inconsistencies is pointless.

There is a trade-off in the issue of tool integration: that is, should the development environment support multiple languages with a set of generic tools, which might not suit all languages well, or be biased toward one language; or should a language have its own development environment with tools that are better suited to its own needs, but which make integration with other languages more difficult?

1.5 Correctness

Deciding what constitutes an inconsistency and how to detect it often raises passionate debate. The discord arises because the detectable inconsistencies do not exactly match real inconsistencies. There are two opposing views. The first is that languages that overcompensate are restrictive; you should trust your programmers. The second is that programmers are human and make mistakes and that program crashes at run time are intolerable.

Both of these views have merit and there should not be the amount of argument between the two sides that we see. Modern programming languages must be designed so that common errors are detected, but not in such a way that they are overly restrictive and prevent programmers doing what needs to be done to solve any particular problem. This section provides some diagrams that will help you understand what the correct balance is and that the two seemingly opposed ideals can both be satisfied.

Figures 1-1 to 1-5 present some of these trade-offs, considering undercompensation and overcompensation, and what the ideal should look like. Figure 1-1 shows the key. Here we see four categories: correct software, software with inconsistencies that result in failure at run time, software that is overcautious resulting in false alarms at compile time, and software that is inefficient because extra checks are required at run time.

Language Principles

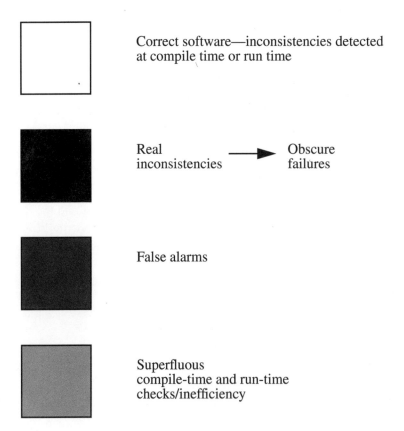

Figure 1-1. Key to consistency diagrams

In figure 1-2 the black box represents the real inconsistencies, which must be covered by either compile-time checks or run-time checks. In the scenario of figure 1-2, checks are insufficient, so obscure failures occur at run time, varying from obscure run-time crashes to strangely wrong results to being lucky and getting away with it. Currently too much software development is based on programming until you are in the lucky state, known as hacking. This sorry situation in the industry must change by the adoption of better languages to remove the ad hoc nature of development.

The view presented in this book is that a language and run-time environment should be sufficiently designed so that no obscure errors of this nature can occur. It is these errors that substantially increase the cost of software development, while seriously decreasing the quality of the end result.

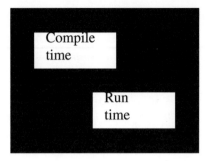

Figure 1-2. Obscure errors left undetected

Some feel that compiler checks are restrictive and that run-time checks are not efficient, so they passionately defend this model, since programmers are supposedly trustworthy enough to remove the rest of the real inconsistencies. Although most programmers are conscientious and trustworthy people, this leaves too much to chance. You can produce defect-free software this way, as long as the programmer does not introduce the inconsistencies in the first place, but this becomes much more difficult as the size and complexity of a software system increases and as many programmers become involved. The real inconsistencies are often removed by hacking until the program works, with a resultant dependency on testing to find the errors in the first place. Sometimes companies depend

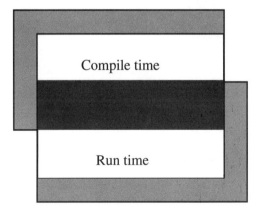

Figure 1-3. Language too restrictive

on the customers to actually do the testing and provide feedback about the problems. While fault reporting is an essential path of communication from the customer, it must be regarded as the last and most costly line of defense.

It is the expertise, techniques, and patterns that good programmers have developed to avoid the pitfalls of these environments that should be integrated into modern languages.

Figure 1-3 shows that the language detects inconsistencies beyond the real inconsistency box. Here we can see false alarms. The run-time environment also doubles up on inconsistencies that the compiler has detected and removed, resulting in run-time inefficiency. The language will be seen as restrictive and the run time as inefficient. You won't get any obscure crashes, but the language will get in the way of some useful computations. Pascal is often (somewhat unfairly) criticized for being too restrictive.

Figure 1-4 shows an even worse situation, where the compiler generates false alarms on fictional inconsistencies and does superfluous checks at run time, but fails to detect real inconsistencies.

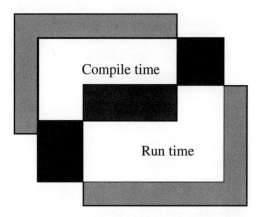

Figure 1-4. Language too restrictive and too loose

The best situation would be for a compiler to statically detect all inconsistencies without false alarms, as shown in figure 1-5.

In this ideal situation, once a program is compiled, it is correct and guaranteed to work. Furthermore, it will run efficiently since run-time checks are minimized. However, it is not possible to statically detect all errors with the current state of technology because a significant class of inconsistencies—such as divide by zero; array index out of bounds; and a class of type checks that are discussed in the section on RTTI and type casts—can be detected only at run time.

Correctness

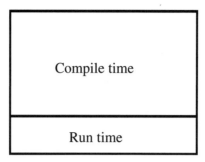

Figure 1-5. Ideally designed language

The current ideal is to have the detectable and real inconsistency domains coincide exactly, with as few checks left to run time as possible. This has two advantages—first, your run-time environment will be a lot more likely to work without exceptions, so your software is safer; second, your software is more efficient because you don't need so many run-time checks. A good language will correctly classify inconsistencies that can be detected at compile time as well as those that must be left until run time.

The price for this ideal is that compilers of such languages must do a lot more work, and hence compile times can be frustratingly longer. However, this increase in development time is more than offset by the decrease in time and frustration of chasing obscure defects and in the cost of relying on a large testing group to find such problems. Deming states that we should cease dependence on inspection, a form of which is having a testing department. If we are to implement this Deming quality principle, we must expect our compilers to do more. [Deming 82] (Point 3)

This analysis shows that, due to the fact that some inconsistencies can be detected only at run time and that such detection results in exceptions, exception handling is an exceedingly important part of software. Unfortunately, exception handling has not received serious enough attention in most programming languages.

This section naturally leads to the question of types, as type soundness directly relates to the absence of obscure failures, or conversely a type system can be sound only if obscure failures cannot occur. Cardelli gives a good explanation of this correspondence. The next section looks at type systems and how well-designed type systems will help resolve the problems illustrated in this section. [Cardelli 97]

1.6 Types

The previous section examined the conditions of correctness in programming. Ascertaining that a program is correct before it is run leads naturally to the topic of types. As Cardelli says, "The fundamental purpose of a **type system** is to prevent the occurrence of *execution errors* during the running of a program." A program is *type safe* if all type errors are caught by checks. Type safety is *static* if all the checks are at compile time and none are during program execution.

[Cardelli 97]

In order to produce correct programs, syntax checks for conformance to a language grammar are not sufficient. We should also check semantics. Some semantics can be built into the language, but mostly this must be specified by the programmer about the system being developed.

Semantics checking is done by ensuring that a specification conforms to some schema. For example, the sentence, "The boy drank the computer and switched on the glass of water" is grammatically correct, but nonsense: it does not conform to the mental schema we have of computers and glasses of water. A programming language should include techniques for the detection of similar nonsense. The technique that enables detection of the above nonsense is types. We know from the computer's type that it does not have the property drinkable. Types define an entity's properties and behavior.

Programming languages can be either typed or untyped; typed languages can be statically typed or dynamically typed. Static typing ensures at compile time that only valid operations are applied to an entity. In dynamically typed languages, type inconsistencies are not detected until run time. Smalltalk is a dynamically typed language, not an untyped language. Eiffel is statically typed. While dynamically typed languages are more flexible, the disadvantage is that, since the compiler does not detect a whole class of errors, testing becomes very much more complicated, because it is even more important to ensure that every possible path in the program is covered by some test.

C++ is statically typed, but there are many mechanisms that allow the programmer to render it effectively untyped, which means errors are not detected until a serious failure occurs. Some argue that sometimes you might want to force someone to drink a computer, so, without these facilities, the language is not flexible enough. The correct solution though is to modify the design, so that now the computer has the property drinkable. Undermining the type system is not needed, as the type system is where the flexibility should be, not in the ability to undermine the type system. Providing and modifying declarations is declarative programming. Eiffel tends to be declarative with a simple operational syntax, whereas C++ provides a plethora of operators.

Types

Defining complex types is a central concept of OO programming.

[Bruce 96] Perhaps the most important development [in programming languages] has been the introduction of features that support abstract data types (ADTs). These features allow programmers to add new types to languages that can be treated as though they were primitive types of the language. The programmer can define a type and a collection of constants, functions, and procedures on the type, while prohibiting any program using this type from gaining access to the implementation of the type. In particular, access to values of the type is available only through the provided constants, functions, and procedures.

[Ege 96] OO programming also provides two specific ways to assemble new and complex types: "objects can be combined with other types in expressive and efficient ways (composition and hierarchy) to define new, more complex types."

Probably the most significant factor in OO programming is its type orientedness. In fact the next step beyond OO should be type orientation, or perhaps type oriented is what OO should have been all along. The important thing about type orientation is how to specify new types; how to use those types to derive more types, for which OO offers the orthogonal mechanisms of inheritance and genericity; and how to specify and derive relationships between types. In a type-oriented system, you will have a type notation for specifying basic types and a type calculus for combining preexisting types into new types.

Once the type-oriented mindset and culture replace the OO mindset and culture, type orientation will enable formal specification techniques to become more widely used; this is the next step beyond the OO analysis (OOA) and OO design (OOD) methodologies. Then we will move beyond the OO hype, and OO will have grown up into what it should always have been; then perhaps programming will finally become a true industrial-strength engineering discipline.

An early type-oriented language was Pascal, which, while not perfect (in fact frustrating in many ways for the serious programmer), did not deserve the scorn that was heaped on it by the C community, which very much missed the point of types until Bjarne Stroustrup came on the scene. Niklaus Wirth, the designer of Pascal, has moved on through several languages and has now designed Oberon, the central concept of which is type extension.

The conclusion of this section is that it is not objects or classes or inheritance that deliver the real benefits; it has been types all along, but most of us missed it in the anti-Pascal hysteria. Types are a most important area of research that benefit real-world software, not only in ensuring type correctness, but also in ensuring optimized systems that avoid superfluous run-time checks.

1.7 Flexibility, Correctness, and Reuse

Perhaps you are now convinced that types are very useful to ensure correctness. Types introduce semantic information, but also the danger of reducing flexibility and thereby opportunities for reuse. We need to consider what flexibility we get from a typeless language, and then we should consider how such flexibility can be built into type systems while removing the undesirable flexibility of typeless systems that results in system failures. This section therefore examines flexibility, correctness, and reuse together.

A typeless language allows us to build patterns of code into which you can plug any other entities. One such pattern could be to relate two entities and return some other entity

$$x, y \bullet \textbf{if } x \circledR y \textbf{ then } a \textbf{ else } b$$

without any form of typing in the x, y part (the declaration part for those who are programmers). This means that any entity x can be related to any other entity y. $\circledR$ itself is generic and stands for any real relation. This is a very good pattern, and many more complex patterns can be written in such a way that you can plug in arguments of any type. Since any type can be used in the function, you never have to rewrite this pattern, and so you have the ultimate reusability. Since the entities are typeless, we have great flexibility.

However, as discussed previously, such flexibility can result in absurd actions such as switching on glasses of water and drinking computers. It is not hard to think of entities and relations where the resulting pattern does not make sense. The challenge is to specify patterns in such a way as to preclude such nonsensical combinations that would probably result in system failure. For a more mathematical view of this (actually this is based on lambda calculus, but I want to give you a gentle introduction without scaring you off with the entire notation), we should consider a particular relation. A function to return the maximum of two entities can be defined using the pattern introduced in the previous paragraph.

$$max \triangleq x, y \bullet \textbf{if } x \geq y \textbf{ then } x \textbf{ else } y$$

(The $\triangleq$ character denotes *is the name of*. That is, I name the function $x, y \bullet \textbf{if } x \geq y$ **then** x **else** y to be *max*. $\triangleq$ is also often read *is defined as*, but you should probably think of it the other way of just attaching a name to an otherwise anonymous entity; in lambda calculus you do not actually give the functions names, but just treat them as anonymous entities.) Now there are many entities in the universe that have no ordering, so rather than being flexible, we are being less flexible, insisting that everything must be ordered. For example, we could invoke *max* as follows:

$$max\ (pen, sword)$$

which expands to

$$\{x, y \bullet \textbf{if}\ x \geq y\ \textbf{then}\ x\ \textbf{else}\ y\}(pen, sword)$$

and substituting *pen* and *sword* into x and y finally becomes

if $pen \geq sword$ **then** pen **else** $sword$

which is nonsensical (at least without some defined ordering relation between pens and swords, such as "the pen is mightier than the sword," but the point is that in order to write programs, such relationships must be precisely defined.) Another point of mathematical explanation here: x and y are known as bound entities. That is because they are abstract and must be bound to an actual entity to make any sense. This is in contrast to free entities such as a and b in the first expression above.

In order to bring some sense to *max*, we need to introduce some types:

$$max \triangleq x, y: ORDERED \bullet \textbf{if}\ x \geq y\ \textbf{then}\ x\ \textbf{else}\ y$$

but we still have a problem here, as we can relate any types that are *ORDERED*, even if they are of unlike types. Supposing that we could rate a pen by the number of words it has written and a sword by the number of people killed. The above function definition would allow us to relate pens and swords since they now have some kind of ordering, but it is still nonsense. Either we need a canonical attribute that we can compare the entities on, or we must have a further restriction that the entities must not only be ordered, but they must also be like entities. Hence we finally have

$max \triangleq x: ORDERED; y: \text{like } x \bullet \text{if } x \geq y \text{ then } x \text{ else } y$

This is a pattern that can be reused, without having to rewrite the function for every different type. We have introduced some flexibility back into the system, with the right kind of constraints with types. The idea so far is that we must introduce some type over which the relations that can be plugged into the pattern can be applied, and then we must say how the types of the entity arguments must be related.

We can still do more: we can provide general patterns where the types are left abstract and must be plugged in later. This is still better than having to rewrite functions for each different type. For example, we might define a generic process for driving, where we teach the driver about accelerators, brakes, and steering wheels. In order to drive any particular vehicle, we have to specialize certain functions, but the overall principles remain the same. So we define the function as follows:

$drive \triangleq V: VEHICLE \bullet \ldots$

Now we can plug any vehicle such as car, truck, or bus into V. Unfortunately, we can also plug in a train or a ship, which are entities for which this pattern has no use. Thus we must constrain this scheme further to say what general types this pattern is useful for.

$drive \triangleq V: VEHICLE \rightarrow ROAD\_VEHICLE \bullet \ldots$

Given that we have defined *ROAD_VEHICLE* as any vehicle that is driven using accelerators, brakes, and steering wheels (which excludes such things as bulldozers), then this is a good solution, as we now can drive as follows:

$drive\ [V \leftarrow CAR]$

but not

> *drive* [*V* ← *SPACE_SHUTTLE*]

We are not licensed for that.

This section has been a partially theoretical introduction to themes that we will come across again later. We have seen that typing is desirable to disallow nonsense that will cause problems in our run-time software, but the flexibility that we have lost from typeless languages can be put back by using well-defined mechanisms. These mechanisms also mean that you do not have to rewrite a well-defined function for all different types, so these mechanisms put into a typed language are the basis of reusability. If you are really interested in the theory of all this, you should consult Cardelli.

[Cardelli 96]

Another small note on lambda calculus: it is a calculus in which all the entities themselves are functions, so it is a calculus of functions. For example, if you see the symbol "4" in lambda calculus, you should not think of it as a constant 4 (although it is), but as a function that represents the value 4. When we write programs, we are combining functions, and thus lambda calculus serves as a basis for a formal study of programming. This is of practical value, because lambda calculus shows how the composition of some functions can be simplified to other functions; therefore lambda calculus can help optimize programs, either manually or by automatic optimizer.

An industry observation that comes out of this section is that flexibility and reuse versus correctness with type restrictions is an argument that raises great passion from both sides. The people against typing correctly see that they are often forced to rewrite a general pattern based on different types. The typed people correctly argue that software that fails at run time due to easily preventable causes is unacceptable. As in many things in computing, you can have your cake and eat it where the design is elegant. Type systems have made great progress in the last ten years, and hopefully this section, while not being too formal, has given you a flavor of how type systems have been improved so that flexibility and reuse are not sacrificed.

1.8   Redundancy and Checking

Redundant information is often needed to enable correctness checking. Type definitions define the kinds of elements in a systems universe and the properties governing the valid combinations and interactions of the elements; for example, stars, planets, moons, and gravitational force. Declarations define the entities in a systems universe; for example, the sun, Jupiter, and Europa. The compiler uses redundant information for consistency checking and strips it away to produce efficient executable systems. Types are redundant information. You can program in an entirely typeless language, but this would be to deny the progress that has been made in making programming a disciplined craft that produces correct programs economically.

It is a misconception that consistency checks are training wheels for student programmers and that syntax errors are a hindrance to professional programmers. Languages that exploit techniques of schema checking are often criticized as being restrictive and therefore unusable for real-world software. This is nonsense and misunderstands the power of these languages. It is an immature conception; the best programmers realize that programming is difficult. As a whole, the computing profession is still learning to program.

While C++ is a step in this direction, it is hindered by its C base, importing such mechanisms as pointers with which you can undermine the logic of the type system. Java has abandoned these C mechanisms where they hinder. "The Java compiler employs stringent compile-time checking so that syntax-related errors can be detected early, before a program is deployed in service." The programming community has matured in the last few years, and, while there was vehement argument against such checking in the past by those who saw it as restrictive and disciplinarian, the majority of the industry now accepts and even demands it. [Sun 95]

No Silver Bullet

Checking has also been criticized from another point of view. This point of view says that checking cannot guarantee software quality, so why bother? The premise is correct, but the conclusion is wrong. Checking is neither necessary, nor sufficient to produce quality software. However, it is helpful and useful, and is a piece in a complicated jigsaw puzzle that should not be ignored.

In fact there are few things that are necessary for quality software production. Mainly, software quality is dependent on the skill and dedication of the people involved, not methodologies or techniques. There is nothing that is sufficient. As Brooks has pointed out, there is no *silver bullet*. Good craftsmen choose the right tools and techniques, but the result is dependent on the skill used in applying the tools. Any tool is worthless in itself. But the *silver bullet* rationale is not a valid rationale against adopting better programming languages, tools, and environments; unfortunately, Brooks's article has been misused. [Brooks 95] (Chapter 16)

Another example of consistency checking comes from the user interface world. Instead of correcting a user after an erroneous action, a good user interface will not offer the action as a possibility in the first place. For example, if a menu item cannot be done, it is greyed out. It is cheaper to avoid error than to fix it. Most people drive their cars with this principle in mind—smash repair is time consuming and expensive.

Program development is a dynamic process; program descriptions are constantly modified during the development and maintenance phases. The problem is how to make sure that parts of the program that previously worked continue to function correctly; modifications often lead to inconsistencies and error. Consistency checks help prevent such bugs, which can creep into a previously working system. These checks help verify that, as a program is modified, previous decisions and work are not invalidated.

It is interesting to consider how much checking could be integrated in an editor. The focus of many current-generation editors is text. What happens if we change this focus from text to program components? Such editors might check not only syntax, but semantics. Signaling potential errors earlier and interactively will shorten development times, alerting programmers to problems rather than wasting hours on changes which later have to be undone. Future languages should be defined very cleanly in order to enable such editor technology.

1.9 Encapsulation and Implementation Hiding

[Macquarie 81]

There is much confusion about encapsulation, mostly arising from C++ equating encapsulation with *data hiding*. The Macquarie dictionary defines the verb *to encapsulate* as "*to enclose in or as in a capsule.*" The OO meaning of encapsulation is to enclose related data, routines, and definitions in a class capsule. This does not necessarily mean hiding, but rather protection from undesirable forces.

[Stroustrup 97]
(2.4)

The C++ literature states this as the *principle of data hiding*, which Stroustrup states as follows: "Decide which modules you want; partition the data so that data is hidden within modules." However, there is really no such principle, or at least it mis-states the real principle, as it confuses several factors. The purpose of storing data is exactly so that it may be accessed, not hidden.

Many seem to promote the idea that with OO programming you hide, or are hidden from, the details of the underlying system. My view is quite different: in fact, OO programming should give you access to the underlying system; since the interfaces are now better grouped and designed, this becomes simpler, and you have access to far more than you did with obscure low-level interfaces. As we saw earlier, abstraction is not adding layers to software to protect it from lower levels; abstraction does result in clean design of interfaces.

The mistaken promotion of hiding has meant that many programmers have stuck with assembler or low-level languages such as C. The systematic design of system interfaces results in more open systems. You might want some items of information to be generally public, but others to be accessible only by a restricted set of external entities. For any data to be completely hidden means it is lost, and that is pointless. The whole point of designing good interfaces is to make the facilities of the underlying system—be it a single-user graphical user interface (GUI) system, a centralized transaction processing server, or a global network such as the Internet—more easily accessible. What becomes *hidden* is the implementation behind the interface.

Security

The first issue that seems to arise out of this is security. Does such openness mean a field day for hackers? The opposite is true, as obscure interfaces are the very opportunity that hackers are looking for. General security, however, is at a different level of abstraction to the interfaces we are talking about. Security is mostly object based, not class based. For example, a bank system will have a basic class representing *ACCOUNT*. Security is not based on the *ACCOUNT* class, but on each individual account object: customers may access only their own account, not that of other customers. Some security is class based and you can determine the privileges of an object based on its more general class.

In our planetary example, we have planets and moons as classes, but this does not express the relationships between the real entities, except in the metacase to say that a planet can have moons. The class model does not express that Europa is actually a moon of Jupiter. Such relationships and security relationships cannot be expressed in the class model. Thus, class-based encapsulation is something different to security.

Such security issues are outside of the scope of static determination in a programming language. The mechanisms that provide such security are external to your program. Security considerations are mostly dynamic, and policies will change without the need to recompile programs.

Implementation Hiding

The second, and more important, factor when considering programming is implementation hiding; you do want to hide implementation. Included in implementation, however, are both data and routines. The separation of implementation and interface is a most important consideration in OO languages. Implementation hiding is an orthogonal concept to encapsulation that is possible because of encapsulation. Don't confuse the two—because a data item or routine is encapsulated does not mean it is hidden. Both data and routines in a class are classified according to their role in the class as interface or implementation.

To put this another way, first you encapsulate information and operations together in a module; then you decide what is visible and what is hidden because it is implementation detail. Most often only the interface routines and data should appear at design time, the implementation details appearing later. (We shall see in chapter 7 that the relationship between interface and implementation is not even this close, since you should be able to export different interfaces to different clients.)

One factor in implementation hiding is hiding the particular algorithms used. If the algorithms need to change for some reason such as efficiency considerations, then this should not affect the rest of the system. Another important aspect of implementation hiding is the hiding of the physical structure of data, which is significantly different to hiding the data itself.

Exposing physical structure is most likely COBOL's Achilles' heel. Don't underestimate this one—it is currently costing the industry billions of dollars in the form of the Y2K problem. COBOL's record structure has proven to be an extremely useful way of developing commercial applications, but along with lack of real procedures and arguments, exposing the structure of the data is one of COBOL's greatest weaknesses. Unfortunately, some of the so-called modern languages in fact make no improvement in terms of physical data structure hiding; for example, C's pointer mechanism exposes physical data structure because you must know the structure of the data you are accessing via the pointer.

Procrustean Structures

This reminds me of a story told by Wayne Wilner on the architecture of the Burroughs B1000 computer (an extremely flexible machine that had no fixed architecture. In fact all languages were run on a virtual machine long before virtual machines became widely known as with the Java virtual machine [JVM]). That was a story of Procrustes, an ancient Attican malefactor. Procrustes would wait by the side of the road and force unfortunate wayfarers to lie on an iron bed. If the wayfarer was too big for the bed, Procrustes would cut his legs to fit; if the wayfarer was too small for the bed he would stretch him to fit. In the end, Theseus forced Procrustes to lie in his own bed. Modern computing is full of such Procrustean structures, forcing clients to be exposed to dangers they shouldn't be, which should be centralized in one place.

Encapsulation provides the means to separate the abstract interface of a class from its implementation: the interface is the visible surface of the capsule; the implementation is hidden in the capsule. The interface describes the essential characteristics of objects of the class that are visible to the exterior world. Like routines, data in a class can also be divided into characteristic interface data, which should be visible, and implementation data, which should be hidden. Interface data are any characteristics that might be of interest to the outside world. For example, when buying a car, the purchaser might want to know data such as the engine capacity and horsepower. However, the fact that it took John Engineer six days to design the engine block is of no interest.

Implementation hiding means that data can be manipulated, that is updated, only within the class, but it does not mean hiding interface data. If the data were hidden, you could never read it, in which case classes would perform no useful function as you could only put data into objects, but never get information out. As we shall see, data should be accessed functionally, but in this context we mean the mathematical notion of function, not the common misuse of the term function in programming languages to mean "value returning subroutine."

In order to provide implementation hiding in C++ it is recommended that you access your data through C functions. This is a simplistic solution, which places the bookkeeping burden on the programmer. While C++ calls this the data hiding principle, it is not the data that is actually being hidden, but the access mechanism to the data. The access mechanism is the implementation detail that you are hiding. C++ has visible differences between the access mechanisms of constants, variables, and functions. There is even a typographic convention of uppercase constant names, which makes the differences between constants and variables visible. The fact that an item is implemented as a constant should also be hidden. Most non-C languages provide uniform functional access to constants, variables, and value returning routines. In the case of variables, functional access means they can be read from the outside, but not updated. An important principle is that updates are centralized within the class.

Above I indicated that encapsulation was grouping operations and information together. Where do functions fit into this? The wrong answer is that functions are operations. Functions are actually part of the information, as a function returns information derived from an object's data to the outside world.

This theme and its adverse consequences that place the burden of encapsulation on the programmer rather than being transparent recur throughout this book.

Meyer calls the previous discussion *Information Hiding*. "The designer of every module must select a subset of the module's properties as the official information about the module, to be made available to authors of client modules." This again is implementation hiding, but Meyer makes it clear what information is being talked about; that is, information about the program itself, not the information or data that the program manages. So it is now clear that what we are talking about is *metadata*. Data is data in the module; metadata is data about the module, i.e., descriptive data.

[Meyer 97]
(3.2)

Now we have one more point to clarify. Since we are talking about hiding the implementation, or information about certain aspects of the program, what we are really talking about is abstraction, which is a topic we have already covered and you will remember is the suppression of irrelevant detail. Cardelli puts this eloquently. *"Abstract types* come from the desire to hide irrelevant program information and to protect internal program invariants from external intervention. An abstract type is an ordinary type along with a set of operations; the structure of the type is hidden and the provided operations are the only ones authorized to manipulate objects of that type."

[Cardelli 93]

1.10 Safety and Courtesy Concerns

This book makes two general types of criticism about safety concerns and courtesy concerns. Safety concerns affect the *external* perception of the quality of the program; failure to meet them results in unfulfilled requirements, unsatisfied customers, and program failures.

Courtesy concerns affect the *internal* view of the quality of a program in the development and maintenance process. Courtesy concerns are usually stylistic and syntactic, whereas safety concerns are semantic. The two often go together. It is a courtesy concern for an airline to keep its fleet clean and well maintained, which is also very much a safety concern (not getting to your destination due to delay or crash is extremely rude—so courtesy concerns and safety concerns are often interrelated).

Courtesy issues are even more important in the context of reusable software. Reusability depends on the clear communication of the purpose of a module. Courtesy is important to establish social interactions, such as communication. Courtesy implies inconvenience to the provider, but provides convenience to others. Courtesy issues include choosing meaningful identifiers, consistent layout and typography, meaningful and nonredundant commentary, etc. Courtesy issues are more than just a style consideration: a language design should directly support courtesy issues. A language, however, cannot enforce courtesy issues, and it is often pointed out that poor, discourteous programs can be written in any language. But this is no reason for being careless about the languages that we develop and choose for software development.

Programmers fulfilling their obligations in regard to courtesy and safety concerns provide a high-quality service that benefits other programmers who must read, reuse, and maintain the code; they also produce programs that delight the end user.

The *design by contract* model has been advocated in the last few years as a [Meyer 97]
model for programming by which safety and courtesy concerns can be formally [Kilov and Ross]
documented. Programming by contract documents the obligations of a client and
the benefits to a provider in preconditions; it documents the benefits to the client
and obligations of the provider in postconditions.

Unfortunately, courtesy is becoming a decreasing commodity these days, and
it is particularly manifest on the Internet, where aggression and contempt for others abound. On programming projects, too many programmers are now leaving
these considerations up to others, while they get on with what they deem to be
more important things. Courtesy concerns are very much tied up with the concept
of *egoless programming*.

Programmers should not be entirely egoless; they should have enough ego in
order to take pride in doing a good job, thereby making sure that safety and courtesy concerns are satisfied.

1.11 Implementation and Deployment Concerns

Class implementers are concerned with the implementation of the class. Clients of
the class need to know only as much information about the class as is documented
in the abstract interface. The implementation is otherwise hidden.

Another aspect that is just as important is to shield programmers from
deployment concerns. Deployment is how a system is installed on the underlying
technology. If deployment issues are built into a program, then the program lacks
portability and flexibility. One kind of deployment concern involves how a system
is mapped to the available computing resources. For example, in a distributed system, this means what parts of the system run at which location. Since things can
move around a distributed system, programmers should not build into their code
location knowledge of other entities. Locations should be looked up in a directory.

Another deployment issue is how individual units of a system are plugged
together to form an integrated whole. This is particularly important in OO, where
several libraries can come from different vendors, but their combination results in
conflicts. A solution to this is some kind of language that binds the units. Thus, if
you purchase two OO libraries and they have clashes of any kind, you can resolve
this deployment issue without having to change the libraries, which you will not
be able to do if you don't have access to the source.

Programmers should not only be separated from implementation concerns of
other units, but separated from deployment concerns as well.

1.12 Why OO?

A question you should consider is when is OO applicable? OO is a universal paradigm. It is very general and powerful. There is nothing that you could not program in it. But is this always appropriate? Lower-level programmers have tended to keep writing such things as device drivers in C. It is not lower levels that I am interested in, but the higher levels. Remember I said before that high-level languages were developed not just as implementation languages with fancy syntax, but as design notations as well. However, OO might still be too low level for a number of applications. A recent book suggests that software engineers are too busy designing systems in terms of stacks, lists, queues, etc., instead of adopting higher-level, domain-oriented architectures. Shaw offers some hope to the industry that we are learning how to architect to solve problems, rather than distorting problems to fit particular technologies and solutions.

[Shaw 96]

For instance, commercial and business programming might be faster using a paradigm involving business objects. While these could be provided in an OO framework, the generality is not needed in commercial processing and will slow and limit the flexibility of the development process. By analogy, walking is a fine mode of transport, but do I choose to walk everywhere? There seems to be a potentially large market for specialized paradigms that support rapid application development (RAD) techniques. These paradigms may be based on some OO language, framework, and libraries in the background. In anything, though, we should be cautious, as this is an industry particularly prone to buzzwords and fads.

1.13 On Programming Language Evolution

It is interesting to note that the evolution of many languages has gone from complexity to more simple forms. Java is a notable example of a language where features have been dropped in order to end up with a better language. One of programming languages' most notable designers, Niklaus Wirth, discarded much from his Modula language and added a few simple concepts to produce his latest language, Oberon.

Wirth warns that

[Wirth 90]

> The definition of a language must be coherent and concise. This can only be achieved by a careful choice of the underlying abstraction and an appropriate structure combining them. The language manual must be reasonably short, avoiding the explanation of individual cases derivable from the general rules. The power of a formalism must not be measured by the length of its description. To the contrary, an overly

lengthy definition is a sure symptom of inadequacy. In this respect, not complexity but simplicity must be the goal.

1.14 The Usefulness of Mathematics

Being able to make software more mathematically based is indeed a laudable goal, and it is theoretically desirable. The outcome of being theoretically desirable means that, in practice, programming would be simplified. Languages should apply mathematics wherever useful and where it makes the concepts simpler.

The relationship between mathematics and programming is not as clear as many would hope, and this relationship keeps the research community very active. For example, sets were a good start to developing type theories, but after a point the mathematics of sets is not applicable, and it is found that type theory needs its own mathematics. A controversial mathematical argument is the argument of covariant and contravariant arguments, an argument we shall deal with in greater detail in a later chapter.

Another view of mathematics is that objects are distinguished by their state; if the state is different, you have a different object. Now this is clearly not the case in the real world—you are the same person, whether you are in Sydney or London; your position is irrelevant to your identity. You could say that position is external state, and perhaps it is internal state that distinguishes objects. However, internal state is also not identity distinguishing. Even though, when you are ill, you might say, "I am not feeling myself today," whether you are sick or well, you are still the same person.

Now we can make a connection between mathematics and design abstraction: if an item of information does not affect an object's mathematical identity, it should be abstracted out. This is good design and results in smaller, more manageable classes that can be better reused in other contexts. This is a similar process to the normalization that occurs in the design of relational databases.

Mathematics has been very helpful in developing computing: without it, we would not have computers or the software industry of today. However, many of the issues are still to be worked out, and new styles of mathematics will need to be developed in order to deal with the complexities of today's software systems.

1.15 Legacy Systems

The term *legacy code* has been bandied about as some kind of insult and as an excuse to rewrite systems in the latest technology. As C. S. Lewis (the main character in the biographical motion picture *Shadowlands* starring Joss Ackland and Anthony Hopkins in a later version) pointed out, because something is old does not mean it is bad. In fact this is even more true about software: software does not degrade with time, it remains exactly as it was written. Some excellent software has been written in the past—it is not out of date, just out of fashion. One thing is certain, much very poor software will continue to be produced in the future unless fundamental changes are made to the software industry, but much current prejudice dictates against that.

Undoubtedly, the most famous software defect due to *legacy code* is the so-called millennium, or Y2K, bug. In fact there are several errors in this terminology. First of all, it is really a *turn-of-the-century* defect, as it would have occurred at the turn of any century (nursing homes already report errors with age of residents who were born in the nineteenth century); millennium sounds so much more ominous however. Second, as E. W. Dijkstra pointed out, the term *bug* is itself fraudulent. Bugs do not creep into the system unbeknown to the programmer; they are written in from the start. The more precise term should be *software defect*.

What is it then that makes a system a legacy system? A system is legacy if it cannot be moved from one environment to another when that move is mandated. For example, with the turn-of-the-century defect, the environment that is changing is the century. The environment must change—we have no choice according to the progress of time. All code that used two digits for the year instead of four is therefore legacy code because it does not adapt to the environment of the new century. This problem also arises from ambiguity: any two-digit date is ambiguous as to which century it belongs in.

Another use of the legacy insult has been about mainframe systems. This has been used as a reason for moving mainframe systems to UNIX or NT, which are seen as *modern* operating systems. The benefits of such a move are actually far from clear, as the world has suddenly discovered (as Bertrand Meyer has said) the obvious: you need centralized servers. This all has to do with distribution economics. Instead of being shipped physical artifacts, you now download the artifacts over a network, whether it is data or software updates.

The main problem with the legacy insult is that often the replacement proposed is sure to become tomorrow's legacy. We need to be far clearer about what the benefits are, and in fact build systems that exhibit far less context dependencies on their environment. In other words, what software systems need to be is *future proof*.

2
Entities and Types

We begin our journey in this chapter with a look at how we progressed from the earliest programming languages that concentrated on bits and bytes to the latest languages of today that concentrate on the semantics of entities and types. We then continue to look at entities and types in our languages introducing the basic structures. We take a closer look at some of the various details of our languages. Finally, we look at the topic of components that provide coarser grained building blocks and are the focus of large-scale system assembly.

2.1 From Bits to Semantics

Probably the most fundamental property of any programming language is which entities you can define and manipulate and how you characterize these entities. In machine coding and assembly languages, one is concerned with memory cells, be it bits, bytes, words, or some other machine-oriented unit. Structured programming languages were built around higher-level entities and introduced basic types such as *INTEGER*, *REAL*, *CHARACTER*, etc., and other structured types such as *ARRAY* and maybe *STRING*. Structured programming languages used as their basic building units procedures and functions, also known as routines or subroutines. One of the earliest such languages was FORTRAN, the original version having been developed in the late 1950s.

COBOL was another language developed in the late 1950s; it was and continues to be a highly paradigmatic language designed for building large business software systems. COBOL was a great contrast to FORTRAN, which served scientific applications. Perhaps these established the prolonged language wars that we still have today, as COBOL was not suited to scientific applications, but was a language more suitable for business applications. COBOL's paradigm was to allow the programmer to define business records and then a series of *paragraphs* that could be *performed* to process those records. Neither language was intrinsically superior to the other, just better suited to its own problem domain.

Records were a significant advance because programmers could define entity layouts. Being able to define such entity layouts was seen as significant in Pascal, with its own version of records, and in C with its `structs`.

Following FORTRAN and COBOL in the late 1950s was ALGOL (*algo*rithmic *l*anguage). This was the first formally designed language with a formal syntax notation known as *BNF*, or Backus-Naur Form, after its developers. Even though ALGOL was formally designed, how to implement it proved beyond the ability of most compiler writers and techniques of the time. That is, except for one college kid contracted for $5,000 by Burroughs Corporation during his summer break of 1960 to write an ALGOL 58 compiler for the Burroughs B205. He claimed he could do it in the three and a half months of his summer vacation. Most compilers up to that time had taken about 25 man-years to develop, so it seemed that some Burroughs manager had taken leave of his senses—except for the fact that the student was Don Knuth, and he indeed did have a working ALGOL compiler by the end of his summer vacation. [Waychoff 79]

Burroughs later went on to develop the B5000 computer which used ALGOL as its systems programming language. All system software was developed in ALGOL; there was no assembler. This was very significant in 1963, and in fact is still very advanced. The B5000 ALGOL heritage still lives on in the Unisys ClearPath A Series line of computers. While much system software is now written in C, C is not as high-level as the ALGOL-based languages, and most machines still need an assembler. The B5000 was a truly unique machine in its day, and its descendant the Unisys ClearPath A Series is also unique today, in that it has no assembler. The B5000 did systems programming exclusively in a high-level language long before UNIX was written in C, although still not exclusively, even though C is more of a stylized assembler rather than a high-level language like ALGOL. The B5000 showed that high-level languages can be very effective for systems programming.

The B5000 also introduced another unique feature, being the first commercial implementation of virtual memory. Virtual memory was regarded by most of the industry with suspicion, in much the same way as garbage collection has been regarded in the recent past.

Even though ALGOL was a very advanced language at the time, it still offered only very primitive entities, such as integers, reals, etc., and arrays. Interestingly, ALGOL's arrays were a significant improvement on its successor languages of Pascal and C, both of which have significantly damaged and primitive arrays. ALGOL arrays could be sized dynamically. In fact, the B5000 implementation of arrays also included index bounds checking in hardware, which was the precursor of triggering exceptions based on a precondition. This feature was most significant in the early detection of run-time errors, before other memory blocks could be corrupted.

Hoare noted that ALGOL 60 was a significant improvement over most of its *successors*.

[Hoare 89]   The more I ponder the principles of language design, and the techniques that put them into practice, the more is my amazement at and admiration of ALGOL 60. Here is a language so far ahead of its time that it was not only an improvement on its predecessors but also on nearly all its successors.

The fundamental structuring entity in ALGOL is the *block*. A block contains some data definitions followed by the code that manipulates that data. Blocks enable the definition of activation records by declaring locals in the block. An *activation record* containing memory space for its locals is automatically created on the run-time stack when a block is entered. Unfortunately, this has one large drawback—the record and its locals with their values are deleted when the block is exited.

This deficiency was recognized, and another language, one that generalized the structuring concept of procedure with locals into a record that could be activated independently of procedure entries and exits, was developed as a superset of ALGOL. That language was Simula, and it has been a most influential language, with other languages such as Smalltalk, Eiffel, and C++ drawing inspiration from the concepts of Simula. The Simula people themselves have gone on to develop another language called BETA, which generalizes everything into *patterns*.

The generalized structure invented in Simula was the class, and hence Simula is the ancestor of all OO languages. It was the direct inspiration for C with classes, which was the parent of C++.

Simula also influenced Smalltalk. When Alan Kay, one of Smalltalk's designers, was a new postgraduate student, he was given the job of installing a new ALGOL compiler that the computer science department had just received. A not-very-interesting job turned out to be most interesting, as the compiler turned out to be not just ALGOL, but Simula.

One unfortunate aspect of Simula was its name. "Simula" gives the impression that it is a specialized simulation language rather than a general-purpose language. It has since been suggested that SIMULA should be an acronym for SIMple Universal LAnguage. However, the basic idea of simulation—building programs based on real-world entities—is the basis of OO programming.

Of course classes allow a programmer to define the entities that are present in a system, in much the same way COBOL records do. An advantage to classes, though, is that you can not only define the data in the entity, but also the behavior of the entity, because the routines that define an entity's processing are defined within the class. COBOL is now being extended into Object-COBOL. Some 4GLs package code and data together—for example, Unisys LINC, where an ISPEC represents a business object, and so it is a kind of object-based COBOL.

C also is descended from ALGOL. The first language based on ALGOL from which C derives was Combined Programming Language (CPL). This was the result of collaboration between the University of London Institute of Computer Science and the Cambridge University Mathematical Laboratory. The basic philosophy of CPL was that, while ALGOL was ideal for expressing algorithms, it was too far removed from the realities of computer hardware. This philosophy is certainly key in its descendants.

CPL provided the basic types `integer`, `real`, `complex`, and `index`. The structure of CPL is essentially the same as ALGOL, being based on a nested block structure. CPL also blurred the distinction between variable and function, introducing *function variables*. Function variables, in contrast to ordinary variables, could be parameterized. CPL also had routine variables that, like function variables, could be passed around. CPL arrays were also very flexible; an array declaration declared the type and the dimensionality, but the actual bounds of the array were not determined until the array was actually initialized.

Basic CPL (BCPL) was a much lower-level language than CPL, being mainly typeless, its one type being the word. BCPL also introduced the notion of *static* variables, although this could properly be traced back to *own variables* in ALGOL. BCPL was also designed to enable separate compilation much as exists in C today.

Another feature introduced in BCPL was the concept of *left values*. This meant that programmers could manipulate not only the values stored in variables, but also the references to the variables themselves. This feature did not appear in CPL, as it is inherently dangerous. A real-world analogy is being able to manipulate a person's name so that it refers to a different person. The real world has laws to prevent this kind of deception and fraud, and, while it might not be this serious in computing, it is dangerous, since a reference made to one entity could be changed to refer elsewhere (which might be the basis for computer fraud itself). C and C++ obviously still have the ability to manipulate references, but most languages now discard this ability, as it adds nothing to the computational ability of a language, but has many problems.

B was a language that Dennis Ritchie and Ken Thompson developed at Bell Laboratories. It was also typeless like BCPL and, due to the typelessness, the compilers could be simple. B introduced such operators as +=, ++, the address of operator &, and contents operator, *. BCPL had a form of goto where the target could be a general left value expression, but B and C could only take simple labels as the target. BCPL's generalized goto could be extremely difficult to debug, so this is a reasonable restriction in B.

[Emery 86] Ritchie then designed C as the programming language to implement UNIX. C, however, is a typed language, introducing the basic types `char`, `int`, `float`, and `double`, but its typing facilities do not go much further, and it is the typing facilities that distinguish most modern languages. You can find further details and comparisons between CPL, BCPL, B, and C in [Emery 86].

Other languages have used different concepts for their basic structure. While basic data types, procedures, classes, etc., provide fine-grained ways to structure programs, it was felt that there was a need for more coarse-grained structures. Hence languages such as Modula introduced structuring around modules. C has a form of primitive modules based around header files and implementation files. The design of a language is a careful balance, deciding when to integrate and when to separate. Separation of fine-grained from coarse-grained structuring provides separation of concerns. As we shall see consistently throughout this book, C and C++ have many different levels of structure defined into the language, and this adds to the complexity of the task of programming in C and C++. We shall see that clean separation of issues is the basis to build the best integrated development environments.

Another significant class of languages is used for functional programming. Here functions provide the basic structuring entities. Generally in functional programming, there are no variables or procedures; everything is a function and, yet, functional programming is a very powerful paradigm.

Other languages are rule based, such as PROLOG. Some languages like Z (pronounced *zed*) are schema based and are used for system specification. In the commercial world, business rules are now becoming popular for the basis of specification and programming.

The main points of heredity of the languages discussed in this book look as shown in figure 2-1.

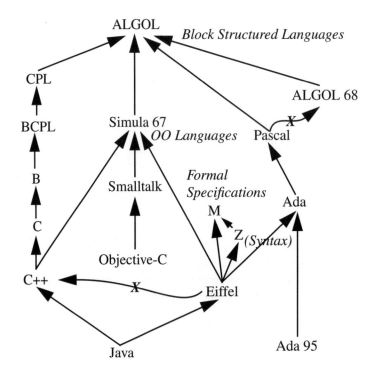

Figure 2-1. Language heredity

Note that descendance does not necessarily mean a more advanced language. ALGOL 68 was influential on Niklaus Wirth in that it showed him what he did not want Pascal to be; C++ had a similar influence on the design of Eiffel. The other significant influences on Eiffel were Ada for its syntax and Z and M for their formalisms in software specifications, which was where ideas for Eiffel assertions came from. Bertrand Meyer had worked on the early definitions of both M and Z.

We can program with many different kinds of entities, but how do we characterize the entities we are building? The answer is with types. Most languages have basic types, but most significantly records and classes enable you to define your own types. These types allow you to instantiate entities of those types and to define new types in terms of preexisting types.

With so many options for entities and types, what is the poor programmer to do? Perhaps the answer is to look for a language that provides a mix of paradigms and entities from those paradigms. As it turns out, this is not an effective strategy. The purpose of different entities tends to overlap, if not duplicate each other. This has been tried in hybrid languages such as PL/I, which was a mixture of ALGOL, FORTRAN, and COBOL. Simula gave the clue that very few concepts are needed. In OO languages, all you need is classes to define all the types you need to build complex entities.

Now we can see where we are in contrast to the early programming languages, FORTRAN, COBOL, and ALGOL. The early approaches to improve programming languages involved inventing new languages to handle different kinds of entities that were in the problem domain. For example, SNOBOL was invented for specialized string processing. However, with paradigms such as OO programming, you actually define your own entities, so, for new entities, you don't need a new language since these programming languages provide the mechanisms to extend the entities that are in the language. In OO languages, the basic structure to define new entities is the class.

2.2 Basic Structures: The Class

The fundamental structuring entity in OO languages is the class. A class is a semantic entity that allows the definition of an interface and operations on objects that are instantiated from types derived from the class. A class forms a template from which types can be derived, and a type forms a template for objects to be created. Some people might already be objecting to this description, and I should point out that this is not the only way that class-oriented systems could be built. However, it does adequately describe the way our observed languages construct systems. If you are familiar with the basic constructs of classes and grammars you could skim or skip the next few sections.

In many cases, classes correspond directly to types, but this need not always be the case, as further modifications can be made to classes in order to define specific types. We will see this later in the chapter on *genericity*. Since Java does not have genericity, classes and types directly correspond, but as we shall see the lack of genericity is a major drawback to the flexibility of systems that can be described in Java, and it limits reuse in Java.

When you define a class, you not only define a template for entities the class describes, but you also define a *calculus* of operations that are valid on objects of that class; that is, not only have you defined a set of entities, but also you have defined how those entities can be manipulated and combined.

The syntactical definitions for classes and examples in our three languages follow.

Eiffel

```
┌─EIFFEL──────────────────────────────────────────────┐
│                                                     │
│   Class_declaration    ≜      [Indexing]            │
│                               Class_header          │
│                               [Formal_generics]     │
│                               [Obsolete]            │
│                               [Inheritance]         │
│                               [Creators]            │
│                               [Features]            │
│                               [Invariant]           │
│                               end ["--" class Class_name] │
│                                                     │
└─────────────────────────────────────────────────────┘
```

The Eiffel grammar is presented in Extended Backus-Naur Form (EBNF), standardized by Niklaus Wirth. This is a clear and concise grammar notation for describing programming languages. In this example, Class_declaration is the language element being defined (≜). The elements of the declaration are given in the order in which they appear in real programs. Optional elements are marked by enclosing them in brackets, for example [Indexing]. Thus the only required elements here are Class_header and **end**. So the smallest possible class can be given by the example

Eiffel

    class C
    end

You can define an almost infinite number of such trivial classes, so long as they all have different names (or until you get extremely bored!). Although all such classes are trivially equivalent, they are not equivalent from the type point of view, and objects generated from them would not be type compatible. This trivial non-equivalence of structurally equivalent types is important. For example, a *REAL* can be used to store a temperature and a water level. Although the internal computer structure of these data is the same, they are different types of quantity and therefore should not be interchanged.

Eiffel style conventions are that all text is set in a proportional font; keywords are shown in **bold**; identifiers follow the mathematical typographical con-

Basic Structures: The Class

vention of being in *italics*, with classes and types in uppercase *ITALICS*. Programmers do not have to worry about these conventions since they are automatically done by formatting tools.

Keywords in the grammar are given in bold, and other literals that appear in the program text are given in double quotes, for example "--"; these are known as *terminals* in the grammar and are the elements that actually appear in your programs. Other terms in plain type require further definition in another grammar production; these are known as *non-terminals* and appear only in the grammar, not in your programs. The terminals are of most interest when considering the syntax of the language, and the non-terminals are of interest most in considering the semantics. Thus Class_header is further defined as

---
EIFFEL

Class_header	≜	[Header_mark] **class** Class_name
Header_mark	≜	**deferred** | **expanded**
Class_name	≜	Identifier

Here, Header_mark is shown as optional, but when it is present it is either the keyword **deferred** or **expanded**. Such alternatives are separated by the | character.

The only element of EBNF we have not seen yet is repetition, where elements enclosed in braces, {...}, are repeated zero or more times. If a repeated element must appear at least once, a superscript + appears after the braces, $\{...\}^+$. An example of repetition is

---
EIFFEL

| Compound | ≜ | { Instruction ";" ... } |

This syntax also shows a semicolon as separator between Instructions; it should be thought of as a sequential composition operator of instructions. In fact, syntactically, the semicolon as separator in Eiffel is optional, so strictly it should be shown in brackets, but a textual note about this in the Eiffel specification keeps the grammar easier to read, even though the brackets would be needed if you were developing a parser with an automatic parser generator.

As you can see, keywords are distinguished from further production rules by the typographic convention of being bold. This enhances human readability. Input to a parser generator would need to quote the keywords as with other literals.

A more elaborate example of a class declaration in Eiffel is

Eiffel

```
class
    ELEVATOR_DOOR
inherit
    DOOR
creation
    make
feature
    make (e: ELEVATOR) is
        do
            ...
            opened := true
        end

    open is
        do
            ...
            opened := true
        end

    close is
        do
            ...
            opened := false
        end

    is_open: BOOLEAN is
        do
            Result := opened
        end

feature { NONE }
    opened: BOOLEAN
end
```

C++

The specifications of C++ and Java do not use EBNF, but rather are based on a notation used to define C. A C++ class is defined as

---
C++

class-name:
    identifier
    template-id

C++

class-specifier:
    class-head { *member-specification*$_{opt}$ }

class-head:
    class-key identifier$_{opt}$ *base-clause*$_{opt}$
    class-key nested-name-specifier identifier base-clause$_{opt}$

class-key:
    `class`
    `struct`
    `union`

The simplest possible classes in C++ are

C++

```
class C {};
struct C {};
union C {};
```

The elevator door example in C++ looks like

```cpp
// File: elevatordoor.h                                    C++

#include "Elevator.h"
#include "Door.h"

class ElevatorDoor : public Door
{
public:
    void ElevatorDoor(Elevator e);

    void open();
    void close();
    int is_open();

private:
    int opened;
};

// File: elevatordoor.cpp

#include "elevatordoor.h"

void ElevatorDoor::ElevatorDoor (Elevator e)
{
    ...
    opened = 1;
}

void ElevatorDoor::open()
{
    ...
    opened = 1;
}

void ElevatorDoor::close()
{
    ...
    opened = 0;
}

int ElevatorDoor::is_open()
{
```

Basic Structures: The Class

```
        return opened;
}
```

Now C++ has added classes to the base C language. Classes are a welcome addition, but C++ has not removed the entities that the class concept subsumes. C++ inherits all of these structures from C, but in addition adds more in order to overcome the problems. Such concepts are `struct`, `union`, `typedef`, globals and `namespace`, and header files. In the rest of this chapter, we will have a closer look at these structuring entities, except for union, which in type theory is more closely related to type extension. We postpone our look at union until the chapter on type extension with inheritance.

Java

A Java class is defined as

Java

ClassDeclaration:
    ClassModifiers$_{opt}$ `class` *Identifier Super$_{opt}$ Interfaces$_{opt}$ ClassBody*

ClassModifiers:
    ClassModifier
    ClassModifiers ClassModifier

ClassModifier: one of
    `public abstract final`

And the simplest possible class in Java is

Java
```
class C {}
```

In C++ and Java, as with Eiffel, structural equivalence of classes does not imply type equivalence.

The elevator door example in Java looks like

```java
public class ElevatorDoor extends Door                    Java
{
    public void ElevatorDoor (Elevator e)
    {
        ...
        opened = true;
    }

    public void open()
    {
        ...
        opened = true;
    }

    public void close()
    {
        ...
        opened = false;
    }

    public boolean is_open()
    {
        return opened;
    }

    private boolean opened;
}
```

These examples in our three languages already illustrate some marked differences. Syntactically, the Java example looks similar to C++, but in terms of length and detail looks closer to the Eiffel example. C++ has considerably more syntactic noise, with `#includes`, and the class interface is separated from its implementation which is in a different file. Java has the one class definition as does Eiffel. With Java, you could write a separate interface if required.

Java also requires an access modifier on each member, which makes member definition a little more cluttered. C++ and Eiffel prefer to group blocks of feature or members together with one access specifier, although you could put one per member if you wanted to. Whichever is more readable is to some extent a matter of personal taste, but the ease of readability will be based on how easy it is to pick out the significant items, and this is easier if there is less syntactic noise.

Java also has interfaces that are like classes with no implementation details at all.

Java

InterfaceDeclaration:
  InterfaceModifiers$_{opt}$ `interface` *Identifier*
      ExtendsInterfaces$_{opt}$ InterfaceBody

InterfaceModifiers:
  InterfaceModifier
  InterfaceModifiers InterfaceModifier

ClassModifier: one of
  `public (abstract **obsolete**)`

Interfaces introduce new reference types whose members are only constants and abstract methods. An interface can extend multiple other interfaces, and a class can implement multiple interfaces. The `abstract` keyword applied to interfaces is superfluous and is obsolete in Java.

2.3 Usefulness of Grammars

Language grammars have several roles. First, and important to the vast majority of people, is that a grammar will help you determine reasonably precisely what you can write in the language. If, for example, you forget exactly how to order the constructs in a class declaration, you can consult the grammar to find out where things should go. Another use is if you get a syntax error and can't quite determine what the real syntax should be, you can consult the grammar to find the exact form that compilers should accept (and if they don't, you can be certain that you can submit it as a compiler defect because the compiler does not conform to its specification).

The ability to read grammars is a skill that any good programmer should develop. Programmers who don't develop this skill will not be able to read the *road map* of a language precisely in order to get the best out of the language as a tool, and they will find it difficult to predict exactly what a compiler will accept and reject, slowing down a programmer's productivity. They will also find it difficult to be adaptable and learn new languages. As you can see, reading grammars is pretty straightforward, at least compared to programming itself. Being able to read a grammar is like being able to read a map to find your way around town. Trying to understand a whole grammar at once is rather daunting, so, just like driving around town, you will need to study only a small part of a grammar to work out specific points of syntax.

The second important use of grammars is as input to language processing tool generators, such as compilers. Not as many people will use a grammar for this purpose, but it should not be misunderstood that grammars are only for this "elite" class of programmers. Grammars should be useful to all programmers of a language to make the best use of the language's syntactic features, which are the visible manifestation of the underlying concepts.

A well-defined grammar will also allow tools such as editors to do smarter things. For example, when you start a new class, a smart program editor will be able to generate the framework of a class for you. Thus grammars are useful for the class of programs known as *acceptors*, such as compilers, and *generators*, which output elements of the language. These tools are very convenient, but you should not rely on such clever tools to do your programming for you; programming will always require your brain power.

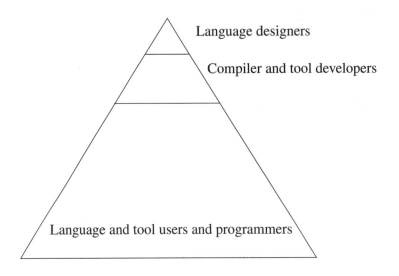

Figure 2-2. Grammar users

A third and even more elite use of grammars is applied by the language designers themselves; they actually write the grammar. Using a grammar with an automatic checker can help remove all of the language's syntactic irregularities that would plague its users. It is a mistake to think that language designers design the language and then leave it to tool and compiler developers to define the grammar to build compilers. By the way, grammars and languages are not one-to-one, but many-to-one: many grammars can define the same language, and this fact helps to simplify a grammar. A simpler grammar not only may be easier to read, but may generate faster parsers if they are being used to automatically generate a parser.

Thus grammars should be much more widely used than they currently are. figure 2-2 represents the users of grammars.

Grammars may also be useful in another way—in general system design. A grammar is a formalized way of breaking syntactic elements into their subcomponents. This is exactly what is done in general systems design, so EBNF could be used in design, or better still an abstract grammar that omits such concrete details as ordering and keywords. Such a use of a grammar notation helps identify the entities in a system, which is the subject of this chapter.

As with language design, other formalisms complement the use of EBNF. Language designers should also use techniques such as denotational semantics to help formally model the static acceptability of programs and their dynamic properties. Other formalisms such as Z should also be used. However, such formalisms are often ignored, and software projects go on for far longer than expected due to their ad hoc foundations. (For a further introduction to formalisms, consult [Meyer 90], and for Z, consult [PST 91].)

However, it must be appreciated that adoption of one or another tool or method will not solve your problems. Good software is developed only by skillful practitioners who will choose the right tools and apply them correctly.

[TTW 61]

You might also come across grammars done in BNF and a more graphical form called *Syntax Charts*, *Syntax Diagrams*, or *Railroad Diagrams*. Niklaus Wirth introduced this graphical form of BNF in the definition of Pascal. However, predating Wirth is a syntactical chart of ALGOL 60 produced by Taylor, Turner, and Waychoff of Burroughs Corporation in 1961. For an example of syntax charts see appendix J of [Meyer 92].

If you know BNF, then you will agree that EBNF is an improvement, as it simplifies grammar descriptions and thus is an advance in this important attribute of readability. The BNF form of the above Eiffel EBNF representations is

```
<class_declaration>   ::=   <indexing><class_header> <formal_generics>
                            <obsolete> <inheritance> <creators>
                            <features> <invariant>
                            "end" <class_end_comment>
```

<indexing>	::=	... | <empty>
<class_header>	::=	<header_mark> "class" <class_name>
<header_mark>	::=	"deferred" | "expanded" | <empty>
<class_name>	::=	<identifier>
<compound>	::=	<instruction> |
		<instruction>";" <compound>

The visual form of BNF turns many people off (which shows that syntax really is important). It is not as convenient as EBNF, since many more productions need to be introduced to handle optional parts and repeated parts. The visual strangeness of putting non-terminals in angle brackets and the define operator being ::= detracts from BNF's readability. You should note, however, that EBNF is strictly equivalent to BNF, as the optional construct [P] is shorthand for <p> ::= ... | <empty>, and the repeated construct {P} is shorthand for <p> ::= ... | ... <p>. Note that repetition in BNF relies on recursion for the production.

The form of grammar used for Java and C++ has several drawbacks. A major drawback is that it is not free format—that is, a white space character affects the semantic interpretation. In this case alternatives are given on separate lines instead of having the alternative separator | as in EBNF. This means that, when constructs are ordered, they must be placed on one line, and, if they will not fit on one line, you have to introduce artificial productions. Conversely, if you want to put more than one alternative on a line, you must use the rather informal annotation "one of", as shown in the Java example.

Optionals are also flagged by the subscript $_{opt}$. This will not do for input to most automatic parser generators and will have to be transposed in some way.

Also, with the Eiffel grammar, the grammar starts out with the top-level construct Class_declaration (in [Meyer 92] all constructs are also given in alphabetical order). The Java and C++ grammars start off with the minute details of lexical conventions, and you have to wade through a lot of grammar to get to the starting point. This tends to make grammars less useful for the working programmer.

The C grammar style also has the drawback of BNF that repeated constructs must be written using the longhand recursive notation.

2.4 Classes and Types

A fundamental question is: are classes types? The answer to this question helps characterize our languages. According to Stroustrup, in C++ "a class is a user-defined type." In Java, a type can be a primitive type or a reference type based on

[Stroustrup 97 (1.7, 10.1)

a class, an interface, or an array. It is important to note the correspondence between interfaces and types in Java. Eiffel does not so closely equate the two concepts. "Every type should be based on a class." In Eiffel all types, even primitive types and arrays, are derived from classes. While a user can define types as classes, the two are not directly equated due to being able to derive multiple types from one class because of genericity.

[Meyer 97]
(2.2)

2.5 Structs (C++)

`Struct` is in C++ only as a compatibility mechanism to C. When you have classes you don't need structs. In fact, in C++ the `struct` and `class` keywords are almost synonymous. "The Java language has no structures or unions as complex data types. You don't need structures and unions when you have classes—you can achieve the same effect simply by using instance variables of a class."

[Sun 95]

`Struct` and `class` are not strict synonyms in C++, however. The difference is that, in `structs`, members are by default `public`, whereas in a class members are by default `private`. According to Stroustrup, "Which style you use depends on circumstances and taste. I usually prefer to use `struct` for classes that have all data public. I think of such classes as 'not quite proper types, just data structures.' Constructors and access functions can be quite useful even for such structures, but as a shorthand rather than generators of properties of the type."

[Stroustrup 97]
(10.2.8)

Eiffel and Java similarly have no equivalents to `struct`.

2.6 Typedefs (C++)

Typedef is yet another mechanism not needed. In C and C++ a typedef merely introduces a synonym for a type; it does not define a new type (despite the highly suggestive terminology). Thus you can freely interchange the types of the next example.

C++

```
typedef int weight;
typedef int length;
weight w;
length l;

l = w;
```

2.7 Global Environments

There are two important properties of globals. First, a global is visible to the whole program—its scope, which is a compile-time view. Second, a global is active for the entire execution of a program—its duration, which is a run-time property. Scope and duration are often interdependent, but this is not always necessarily the case. Global scope is not generally desirable in the OO paradigm, as will be explained later. Permanent duration is desirable and can easily be provided without globals. The life of any entity is the life of the enclosing object, so to have entities that are active for the whole execution of the program, you create some objects when the program starts that don't get deallocated until the program completes.

The global environment provides a special case of nested classes. When classes are nested in a global environment, dependencies can arise that make the classes difficult to decouple from the original program and, therefore, not reusable by themselves. You might be forced to relocate a large amount of the global environment as well. There are also problems with the related mechanisms of header files and namespaces. Even if a class is not intended for use in another context, it will benefit from the discipline of OO design. Each class is designed independently of the surrounding environment, and relationships and dependencies between classes are explicitly stated.

In C++ functions can change the global environment beyond the object in which they are encapsulated. Such changes are side effects that limit the opportunity to produce loosely coupled objects, which is essential to enable reusable software. This is a drawback of both global and nested environments. A good OO language will only permit routines in an object to change its state.

While C++ cannot do without globals due to its C heritage, the use of globals is certainly discouraged. "Maybe 'just one little global variable' isn't too unmanageable, but that style leads to code that is useless except to its original programmer. It should be avoided." [Stroustrup 97 (10.2.4)]

Removing the global environment is trivial: simply encapsulate it in an object or set of objects. The previously global entities are then subject to the discipline of OOD; globals circumvent OOD. Objects can also provide a clean interface to the external environment, or operating system, without loss of generality for a negligible performance penalty. Classes are independent of the surrounding environment as well as the project for which they were first developed, and they are more easily adaptable to new environments and projects.

Scott Meyers' item 28 also recommends this approach, using structs (which are much the same as classes in C++) to partition the global namespace. This [Meyers 92] (item 28) helps manage the namespace on a project with many programmers, and it also helps in the combination of libraries from different programmers or vendors. C++ has since added the explicit namespace mechanism to its definition to solve this problem. Eiffel and Java use classes exclusively to define this partitioning, whereas C++ provides several mechanisms, all of which, except class itself, are to solve problems due to backwards compatibility with C; thus they are not necessary in other languages.

Java has removed globals from the language altogether. Eiffel is another example of a language where there are no globals. Both these languages show that globals are not needed for the development of large computer systems. Java has backed down a little from this position with the introduction of nested classes. We will have a more detailed look at these in a later section.

In concurrent and distributed environments, you are better off without globals. In a distributed environment, the global state of the system may be impossible to determine. In order to develop distributed systems, you cannot have globals. Similarly with concurrent environments—problems arise when two or more process threads access shared resources at the same time. Shared resources should be accessed only via the object that manages the resource and prevents contention for the shared resource. Such a resource should not be a global.

You might recall that we have two kinds of variables, *free* and *bound*. Global variables are the programming equivalent of free variables, and manipulating free variables can lead to undesirable consequences.

2.8 Class Metadata

One of the major considerations about reusability is that, in order to use a service, you must be able to find the service that matches your requirements. At a fine-grained level, you might want functional services; that is, to be able to find a function that will transform some data into another value. For example, you might want to find the square root of numbers, or you might want to find out what tomorrow's weather will be like.

Even calculating something relatively simple like a square root can be quite complex, and it is time consuming to write your own algorithm. If we needed to develop such an algorithm in every application we wrote, software construction would be extremely slow and tedious. In most situations, a programmer will find a square root function in a library of functions. Many other functions can be found in such libraries.

A function to calculate tomorrow's weather will be quite a bit more complex; in fact, it is so large that many people would call it an application. Viewed in this way, applications are really just large functions, and you can explore this further by looking at the functional programming paradigm.

Given a library of functions, or a set of libraries, we have a problem—how do we find the functions we need? In a small library, programmers can probably easily find the functions they want. When you have many complex libraries, though, the problem becomes extremely difficult. Many times, you might even code functions that you never knew existed beforehand.

The problem of finding functions is partially solved by self-documenting software. Given the kind of service that you want, you can search on the function's name, return type, arguments, and their types. A single function name might not suffice, as different users might think of different aliases; it might be a good idea to provide other information. This information could be in the form of keywords or, perhaps more informally, a text description of the function. Such information about a function is called *metadata*.

Functional and Nonfunctional (QoS) Information

Information about a function is also of two kinds: functional information and nonfunctional information. Functional information describes what the function does. (Don't confuse the terminology of *function* with *functional* here.) Nonfunctional information describes other qualities about the function, things like accuracy and speed of the algorithm for example. A client programmer can use this information as well as the functional information to determine the suitability of the function. If the accuracy or speed is not sufficient, a function with a better algorithm needs to be found, or a special function might have to be written. The nonfunctional information describes the *quality of service* or QoS of a function and, while secondary to what the function does, can be very important in determining the usability of a function in a certain context.

The information about a function must be provided by the function's programmer. This is only one side of the story. The other side of the story is when client programmers search for functions that satisfy their needs. In this case, the development environment must provide the facilities so that the client can determine the suitability of functions. Currently, programmers use directory searches and text processors like editors or *grep* to search for such information. While tools like grep are extremely useful, and almost indispensable, these facilities are fairly primitive, and it can be seen that facilities such as grep make no use of in-built semantics. In order to build large systems successfully, we need more sophisticated environments, where such information is known about and manipulated by the environment.

We have now seen how information can be used in the case of finding single functions. Often we need information about how these functions should be called, in what order. For example, file processing should progress in the order of opening, reading and writing, and closing the file. Closing the file first would generally lead to some sort of error. Just having an environment that will find us functions gives no information about the ordering of these routines.

Classes are collections of routines that operate on a single object. So, in a file object, we will have the routines to open, read and write, and close. Information can be added to the routines of a class to express such ordering. For example, the read, write, and close routines might test a flag to check that the file is open, which the open routine set.

Indexing

Just as metadata can be used on functions, metadata can also be supplied about classes. Development environments can use this information to simplify searching for possible classes to use, either as parents or as service providers. For this purpose, Eiffel provides the *Index* clause. Here the class programmer can enter metadata such as keywords and other information that could be of help to a client programmer in finding the class out of a large set of libraries. An example of the *Index* clause is

Eiffel
        indexing
            sentence, clause, grammar; -- keywords
            author: Enid Blyton;
            date: 1/9/31
        class *GRAMMAR* ....

Unfortunately, this information has no set format, so different library vendors will use their own schemes. Also, this information does not affect the semantics of the class at all, and in some ways it should not really be a part of the text of a class. It would perhaps be better as a part of the development environment, but since no two development environments provide the same treatment of such data, perhaps the Eiffel scheme suffices for now. However, while it is a step in the right direction, better facilities will be needed.

With the advent of code repositories, such metadata will probably be better kept in the repository, which will then link to the class text. This scheme will preserve the separation of concerns, while providing good integration. Interactive Software Engineering's (ISE) Eiffel compiler and development environment make a good attempt to use the class index metadata within the development environment.

In Java the equivalent of providing an index clause is to use documentation comments. These comments can be processed with the javadoc tool, which extracts the comments into html files. Thus a client can search the WEB for Java libraries. ISE's Eiffel environment also provides a documentation tool that will generate html for this purpose and that will generate many other formats as well.

The balance between integration and separation of metadata is in fact a complex one. At one extreme is the old commercial programming way, where programs were only code and you had filing cabinets full of paper documentation (and there are still process managers insisting on keeping things in the stone age). This hardly made good use of a computer's capabilities in document handling, but it was the scheme mandated by many a company's quality department. You also don't want to unnecessarily complicate a class text with metadata, even though you do want a degree of integration. Here the capabilities of computers should be put to good use in the development environments of the future.

2.9 Obsolete (Eiffel)

As we saw in the last section, metadata conveys useful information about a class. The OO paradigm is meant to be for large-scale software engineering projects, and a key feature of the reusability attribute is that, once a given functionality has been developed, it remains useful over a long period of time. If a software artifact does not exhibit longevity, then it can hardly be considered reusable.

Unfortunately, software elements don't often remain stable for long, so an important feature of any programming system must be to allow evolution of developed software. Thus we take a more lenient approach than the ideal of "design once and use forever." Once you have designed a class, chances are that you will be forced to make modifications either because errors need to be corrected or because you have learned more about the problem domain and would like to make improvements to the service.

One advantage with OO programming is that many such changes can be hidden behind the class interface. However, again in practice this ideal often cannot be met, and a class interface will have to be changed. If you are adding features, then you have no problem, apart from advertising the new interfaces. If you are changing signatures, deleting features, or replacing features, then you must not only communicate the changes, but make your changes as easy for your users as possible.

Eiffel offers a mechanism for evolving class libraries and their interfaces—**obsolete**. With this you can mark a class or any of its routines as obsolete.

Eiffel

    class *A*
        obsolete
            "Class A is obsolete, use class B instead."
        ...
    end

A client might have already built a substantial piece of software around class *A*. When they install the updated library, ordinarily, the library vendor will have just replaced class *A* with class *B*, and perhaps the new library documentation might note to now use *B* instead of *A*. Clients will then be forced to upgrade all of their software to make it work again. The Eiffel **obsolete** mechanism is much more helpful and gives the client a grace period. When the client tries to use *A*, the compiler prints out the obsolete message, which advises what needs to be done. As class *A* has not actually been removed, the client can continue to use *A* until it is convenient to make the changes.

Routines can similarly be flagged.

Eiffel

    oldr (...) **is**
        obsolete "Use *newr* instead."
        ...
    end

Thus if an entire class is not obsolete, but only certain aspects of its interface, a client programmer is not left stranded.

Java provides the `@deprecated` documentation comment tag, which can be used similarly to Eiffel's **obsolete** on classes and functions. A Java compiler will issue a warning if an `@deprecated` entity is used. Such metadata about class evolution is an important facility in real world programming. While it might be argued that such information would be better kept in a repository rather than in the syntax of the *programming* language, the fact that Java and Eiffel compilers make use of these clauses shows that there is a correct balance between separation and integration.

Obsolete in Eiffel and `@deprecated` in Java show how languages can include features that support project organization and allow for changing requirements and designs.

2.10 Invariants (Eiffel)

In designing a class it is very important to capture the semantics of the class. In fact, Meyer sees invariants as one of the most important concepts of the OO method. "To me the notion of the invariant is one of the most illuminating concepts that can be learned from the object-oriented method. Only when I have derived the invariant (for a class that I write) or read and understood it (from someone else's class) do I feel that I know what the class is about."

[Meyer 97] (11.8)

The class invariant in Eiffel describes constraints that object states must satisfy at all times. In practice this means that every routine in a class must leave the class in a consistent state, and it is of critical importance that each routine satisfy the class invariant. During the execution of a routine, however, the object state may be in an inconsistent state, which breaks the invariant. This does not matter as long as the routine leaves the object in a consistent state.

A simple example of a class invariant is a date class.

> **class** *DATE* *Eiffel*
> **feature**
>   *day, month*: *INTEGER*
>
>   ...
>
> **invariant**
>   *valid_date*: 1 <= *day* **and** *day* <= 31 **and** 1 <= *month* **and** *month* <= 12
> **end** -- *DATE*

As I said, this is a simple example, and real date validity is a bit more complicated; in fact, you might want to write the invariant as a *BOOLEAN* function.

> **class** *DATE* *Eiffel*
> **feature**
>   *day, month*: *INTEGER*
>
>   ...
>
>   *valid*: *BOOLEAN* **is**
>   **do**
>   ...
>   **end**

>   **invariant**
>   *valid_date*: *valid*
>   **end** -- *DATE*

Valid_date is an optional invariant label that will be used at run time for debugging. Class invariants must also hold in subclasses. If we have a subclass for twentieth-century dates, we do not need to repeat the class invariant—it is reused; we simply add a further constraint to the invariant.

Eiffel

>   **class** *TWENTIETH_CENTURY_DATE*
>   **inherit**
>   *DATE*
>   **feature**
>
>   ...
>
>   **invariant**
>   *valid_year*: 1901 <= *year* **and** *year* <= 2000
>   **end** -- *TWENTIETH_CENTURY_DATE*

The validity on days and months is automatically inherited from *DATE*, and both invariant expressions are anded together in the subclass. If day or month validity is broken in the subclass, the invariant label *valid_date* will be used to identify the exception at run time.

Since invariants must be checked at run time at the exit of each routine in the class, run-time overheads can become significant. As part of the Eiffel environment, invariants can be turned on and off for separate modules within the program being compiled.

Since routines must satisfy the class invariant when the execution thread exits an object, class creation routines become even more significant, because a creation routine must make sure that objects are initialized in a state that satisfies the class invariant.

Invariants and Formal Techniques

The concept of invariants comes from formal design techniques, and this is one factor that sets Eiffel apart as not just a programming language, but as a design language. Eiffel invariants do not have all the operators of predicate logic such as the existential and quantification operators, but what it has is appropriate for the design of most classes. The notion of invariants also comes from ADTs; of the languages examined here, Eiffel best supports the concept of ADTs.

The relationship of invariants to design is important, as invariants give programmers the constraints within which to work when writing or adapting routines in the class or subclasses. Invariants succinctly document the expected behavior of a class and its routines.

C++ and Java have no direct support for invariants, although invariant-like mechanisms can of course be provided. [Stroustrup 97] recognizes the importance of invariants and suggests how programmers might go about writing them in C++, but the result is not particularly integrated or pretty. Even so, this is a good deal of extra work, and it does not provide documentation as clearly as the Eiffel mechanism. It is precisely this direct support for design concepts that sets Eiffel apart as a more sophisticated language. It is also the fact that Eiffel produces running programs that sets it apart from other design methodology notations (not that all of these even support design concepts such as invariants.)

Design entails more than just invariants, which express only constraints on object states. Dynamic considerations, which express allowable state changes, are subject to invariants. We will see how Eiffel supports this factor in design in the precondition and postcondition specifications on routines.

2.11 Components

A major industry trend over the last few years has been components. Components are coarse-grained entities that are distributed in binary form and dynamically, rather than statically, linked into client applications. A system architecture can be seen as components and the connections between them, together with a description of the properties and constraints.

The connections between the components are made at run time rather than at compile time or design time. This means that components can be dynamically configured and reconfigured. Thus component architectures give the advantages of availability, reliability, and performance. You get availability because components can be dynamically configured, so upgrading components does not need recompiling or bringing down any part of the system. You have reliability since faulty components can be restarted or replaced. And you have performance—components can be dynamically balanced to adjust to different system loads.

Components give the consumer some flexibility. For example, a word processor user can buy a spell checker separately. All spell checker components would have the same interface, which could be used in all applications. Therefore, word processor users could use a single spell checker in all the word processing programs they use, which would save having to enter a word specific to the user, but uncommon in regular usage, into several dictionaries.

The idea of components is not exactly new. For example, MS-DOS's dynamically linked libraries (dlls) are a simple forerunner. Apple jumped the gun slightly on a more sophisticated concept—OpenDoc—only to find the market was not ready for components in this form. Given this fact, Apple dropped further development on OpenDoc to concentrate on its core businesses. OpenDoc is not completely dead; Apple still supports it, and it has been adopted as the component technology of the Object Management Group (OMG).

The lesson of OpenDoc is that the industry has no agreed understanding as to what components are. Microsoft has certainly been very active, defining such technologies as Visual Basic controls (VBXs), ActiveX, object linking and embedding (OLE) controls (OCXs), COM, DCOM, etc. Even Microsoft has had problems setting the direction, with rereleases of technology under different names. The other major player is Sun with Java technology. It has defined its component strategy as JavaBeans.

Components must also become the basis of more than just simple PC style concepts like spell checkers; they must establish themselves as the basis for corporate transaction processing. For this market Microsoft has defined Microsoft Transaction Server (MTS), and Sun's equivalent is Enterprise JavaBeans (EJB).

The idea of using components for transaction processing is hardly new. Burroughs A Series transaction servers (now Unisys ClearPath NX) started on this idea in the mid-1970s, when it was decided a dynamically linked library system was just what was needed to structure its database system, DMSII. A Series libraries now form the basis of much of the software on these machines and are an excellent example of what components should be.

First, A Series libraries are language independent and can be written in a variety of languages—ALGOL, COBOL, etc.—as well as called from a variety of languages; the calling language does not have to be the same as the library language. Thus, A Series libraries give a level of language interoperability. This is extremely important in interworking of diverse components, but such a fundamental requirement seems to be missing from many recent developments, since they mainly guide language use to a single language, mostly C++.

Second, A Series libraries export a fixed interface, and clients import this interface. Third, the libraries are dynamically linked, at which time the importing interface and exporting interface must match. The one essential ingredient that A Series libraries lack is that they are proprietary and not cross platform.

Components vs. Objects

A misunderstanding current in the industry is that objects have failed, and components are the next great hope. In his book on component software, Szyperski quotes that an International Data Corporation (IDC) White Paper on "*Component Technology* (Steel, 1996) explains why software components are succeeding where objects so far have failed: objects are too fine-grained and their deployment requires too much understanding of an object's working." For an excellent discussion of the many issues around components, and a clarification on the many misunderstood issues, Szyperski's is the book to read.

[Szyperski 98] (2.3.4)

As is frequent in this industry, we set up two technologies as competitors, assuming that they provide much the same function and that one is bound to replace the other. This is due to the bandwagon effect, where many technologists and marketers want to advantageously position themselves at what might be the crest of the next wave. Another factor is industry hype, which appeals to people's passions, rather than their technical assessment. What can be said about objects vs. components is that objects are now reasonably understood and that components are very little understood.

The fact is that components and objects are orthogonal—that is, independent. As the IDC quote admits, objects are fine grained and, in contrast, components are coarse grained. When we use the term *coarse grained* here, we mean entire units of execution, whereas *fine grained* refers to the units that are internal to an execution unit, be it an application or component. Object code is statically linked at compile time to form the execution units, and components are linked dynamically at run time.

Components are loosely coupled, and objects are tightly coupled. You cannot express many of the connections between components on a design diagram—this would be like trying to capture every possible connection between telephones to establish every possible telephone call between telephones in the world. You could use OO programming to program your components, but by no means is this necessary as observed in a recent article in *IEEE Software*. An example of this is again A Series libraries, which use non-OO languages.

[Brown 98]

Apart from components not being objects, components are also not libraries, clusters (as in Eiffel), or packages (as in Java). These entities provide common classes that can be used in other applications or components. An application or component will typically use classes out of many class libraries. This import of classes from libraries is a static compile-time operation, whereas the usage of a component and the import of a component interface is a dynamic run-time operation.

[Stroustrup 97] (23.4.3)

[Stroustrup 97] (24.1)

[Stroustrup 97] (24.4)

Unfortunately, the component confusion is perpetuated in the very highest levels of the C++ world: "Typically, one works on a set of related classes. Such a set is often called a *class library* or a *component*." As you can see from the above, along with other notable authors on the subject of components, I disagree that components are class libraries. This view just adds to the confusion and means that components are nothing different. Furthermore, "The notion of component, which is the basic unit of design..." comes from the chapter on design and programming, and, since the notion of component has previously been defined as *class library*, this statement seems curious. Continuing, "The unit of design is a collection of classes, functions, etc., rather than an individual class." However, this describes a composition, and a composition is made up of more fundamental design units. These quotes lead to the conclusion that C++ has a poor concept of design and a confused notion of what components are.

Components and Design by Contract

Essential in the use of components is the question of how to integrate them. Commonly, interfaces mean that a set of procedure entry points with their formal arguments and types are given. However, this is not enough to express what conditions must be in effect for the procedure to run successfully, and what conditions will be satisfied after the procedure has run, that is, what exactly the procedure accomplishes. As Szyperski says, a component "needs to come with clear specifications of what it requires and provides."

[Szyperski 98]

In objects, this extra information has been shown by Bertrand Meyer and others to be very important in the composition of objects and in documenting for client programmers what a service class provides. Not only is this a benefit for documentation purposes, but during run-time testing when it helps in determining that the system is working correctly. This way, defects are detected earlier in testing, rather than later in production when it is a more serious and costly problem.

Objects, of course, have static binding, and the usage of object interfaces is programming in the small. It is even more important in programming in the large, with dynamic binding as with components, that the advantages of design by contract are utilized. With components, it is more likely that you are linking only to a binary module with only the interface description, whereas, with objects, you are more likely to have the class source available. Thus an abstract description of what an interface does is even more important.

[Digre 98]

Unfortunately, the common interface definition languages (IDLs), such as CORBA/ODP IDL and Microsoft IDL, do not incorporate the idea of design by contract. The components world can only be seen as immature without it. A *component definition language* (CDL) has been defined that includes the notion of contracts for the Business Object Component Architecture (Boca).

3

Modules and Imports

A fundamental consideration in the structuring of any system is how to break the system down into modules and how those modules will interact and gain access to each other's information and services. Not only must you consider this question, which is analysis, but you must also determine how new modules can be built out of existing modules, which is synthesis. Synthesis provides interesting problems because there can be clashes between the modules you are trying to assemble into a system. Therefore, we need a *module calculus* that gives the programmer the needed facilities. This chapter looks at how each of our languages views modules.

The classes of most OO languages are very much the same. However, OO languages differ sharply when it comes to modules. C++ inherits C's modules, which are based on header and implementation files, but now adds namespaces in order to provide more control over modules.

In Eiffel, the basic unit of modularization is the class itself. Eiffel defines no other kinds of modules within the language. Most Eiffel implementations provide *clusters* as a way to package classes together. Eiffel thus considers packaging to be a part of the development environment, not of the language.

Java is quite similar to Eiffel in that it has *packages* that are similar to clusters. Unlike Eiffel where clusters are not defined as part of the language, packages *are* defined as part of the Java language.

3.1 Namespaces (C++)

Namespaces are a new concept in C++ introduced in July 1993. Namespaces address the problem of clashing between global names imported from different header (.h) files. The C++ solution is namespaces, where globals are put in a namespace. Access to these entities must be qualified with the namespace name. For example, A::x means access entity x in namespace A. Another namespace B might also have an entity named x, but these names will not clash. Entities not in a namespace are considered to be in the *global* namespace.

Namespaces provide a mechanism for modular programming in C++. A namespace can be used to encapsulate everything in a .h file. Namespaces can also be used in a manner similar to classes. In fact, a namespace is a named scope, and local scopes, global scopes, and classes are namespaces. Namespaces are open, but classes are closed; that is, you can add to namespaces anywhere in the program, but you can't do this with classes. For example:

```
namespace A                                                    C++
{
    f ();  // Add function f () to namespace A
}
```

elsewhere:

```
namespace A                                                    C++
{
    g ();  // Add function g () to namespace A
}
```

In the assembled system, the namespace A has both functions f and g.

You could develop such data types as *STACK* and *LIST* in namespaces: the drawback is that you get only one instantiation of the namespace in your program, so such entities are better handled by classes.

At a very high level, programs are often divided into a number of phases. For example, a compiler can be divided into parser phase, pass 1, 2...n phases, and code generation phase. Only one of these will exist in an execution of the program, so namespaces can be used to implement such modules.

Namespaces (C++)

Namespaces address the problem of name clashing entities. However, the names of the namespaces themselves can clash. For example, if two header files have namespaces called MY_NS, you have a clash, but, since namespaces are open, you will get a single namespace in which both sets of definitions are included, and this might not be what you want.

You can also compose namespaces with *using-directives* as follows:

C++
```
namespace My_lib
{
    f ();
}

namespace Your_lib
{
    g ();
}

namespace Our_lib
{
    using namespace My_lib;    // Using directive
    using namespace Your_lib;
    h ();
}
```

If any clashes occur between My_lib and Your_lib, you can use *using-declarations* to select the entity you want. If you want both, C++ has no mechanism such as renames; it is one or the other

C++
```
namespace My_lib
{
    f ();
    g ();
}

namespace Your_lib
{
    f ();
    g ();
}

namespace Our_lib
```

```
{
    using namespace My_lib;    // Using directive
    using namespace Your_lib;
    using My_lib::f;
    using Your_lib::g;
    h ();
}
```

A further problem arises because of overloaded names, since one using-declaration makes them all active; you cannot select some from one namespace and others from other namespaces

```
namespace My_lib                                                            C++
{
    f ();
    T operator+ (const T&, const T&);
    T operator+ (const S&, const T&);
}

namespace Your_lib
{
    g ();
    T operator+ (const T&, const T&);
    R operator+ (const S&, const R&);
}

namespace Our_lib
{
    using namespace My_lib;    // Using directive
    using namespace Your_lib;
    using My_lib::operator+;
    h ();
}
```

Thus you can get only the + operators from My_lib.

According to the C++ syntax, you can apply templates to any declaration, which means you can apply templates to namespaces. However [Stroustrup 97] contains no discussion of this possibility. It does seem entirely reasonable that namespaces should be able to be generic.

[Stroustrup 97]

3.2 Clusters (Eiffel)

As previously discussed, Eiffel classes provide the modularization features you need. External to the language facilities of classes is a way to organize your projects, keep files of related classes together, and package classes together for release as a library. This facility is a *cluster*. Clusters are not the equivalent of modules in other languages, such as namespaces in C++ or packages in Java or Ada. In Eiffel, "Classes should be the only modules" and, because of this view, clusters are not a part of the language definition itself. As a result, various Eiffel vendors might have slightly different ways of Assembling Classes in Eiffel (ACE) and its specification language (LACE) is not used in all Eiffel implementations.

[Meyer 97]
(2.2)

When compiling an Eiffel system, clusters (and their equivalents) are important to the compiler in finding the classes that it must compile. This allows Eiffel to do away with facilities such as *make*.

Mapping classes into clusters is very natural: considering our compiler example, each phase contains a group of related classes. These classes will be put together in a cluster. Thus the important part is finding the classes themselves, and clusters will merely reflect the class design of the entire system. Hence, in the Eiffel view, clusters are not an important mechanism at all.

The cluster will somehow relate to the particular system environment you are using. For example, systems with hierarchical file system directories will keep the files of one cluster in a single directory. Other systems may not work this way, so clusters will need to be mapped onto the underlying system using different means.

Eiffel separates the concerns of the language from the development environment by allowing the programmer to define the mapping of the class name to the entity where the class definition is stored separately. As with Java it is important not to assume that a class definition is stored in a file; it could be stored as an entity in a database, in which case you must map the class name to some database key.

Clusters may contain classes and other clusters, but, usually, your structuring should have a cluster containing only other clusters—a *supercluster*—or classes—a *basic cluster*—but not both.

Clusters also provide a means of hiding classes that are not of interest outside the cluster. This means that classes outside the cluster will not be able to reference or create entities of these classes. Only the specific classes that need to be available outside the cluster have to be made visible.

So one of the most important differences to note between C++ namespaces and Eiffel's mechanisms is that Eiffel classes provide most of the modularization facilities of C++ namespaces. In Eiffel, you simply use a class that has a single object instance. As far as grouping related classes together, you do this using clusters, but clusters are not a part of the Eiffel language itself; they are merely a way of organizing projects onto an underlying system.

3.3 Packages (Java)

Packages are Java's way of creating modules. Like C++ namespaces, but unlike Eiffel's clusters, Java packages are a part of the language itself. Like Eiffel clusters, packages can contain subpackages and classes. Unlike C++ namespaces, Java packages contain no data. Java packages are actually closer to Eiffel's clustering mechanism for packaging libraries than to anything in C++.

Java packages provide a natural way of grouping together classes that logically belong together. They also provide the means for compilers to find classes, removing the need for *make*-like facilities.

Packages also provide the means to hide some classes—`private`—or to make them visible and usable outside the package—`public`.

The major difference between Java's packages and Eiffel's clusters is that packages define *friendly* visibility between classes within the Java package. Thus classes within a Java package can see each other's protected and private members. In the case of Eiffel, the fact that classes are included together in a cluster implies no special relationship between the classes; any visibility provisions must be made with the standard feature export mechanism. Thus, even within a cluster, Eiffel classes are loosely coupled, whereas in Java packages classes are more tightly coupled.

Java also provides a scheme of how packages and class names map onto the file system. While Java is not tied to any one particular file system, it will map best to a hierarchical structure. Furthermore, Java packages may be stored in other entities such as databases.

3.4 Header Files (C++)

In C++ a class interface must be maintained separately from its body. An abstract class interface is simply the class with the implementation detail suppressed, so the interface and implementation can both be maintained in one source. In C++ though, programmers must maintain the two sets of information. This is because of the C/UNIX style of programming with separate modules but little or no global analysis. Replicated information has the well-known drawback that, in the event of change, both copies must be updated. Sun calls this "The Fragile Superclass [Sun 95]

Problem." This can lead to inconsistencies that must be detected and corrected. Classes that depend on another class must be recompiled if the layout of that class changes. Tools can automatically extract abstract class descriptions from class implementations and guarantee consistency.

Splitting C and C++ programs into a myriad of small, separately compiled files turns out not to be a good way to organize projects; nor is it a good way to program, because you must maintain many header files. Some people now find it more convenient to keep an entire large system in one file as it solves many maintenance problems and also makes it easier to find things during editing. Unfortunately, while on many systems this scheme allows for global analysis, it still does not solve the problems arising from lack of global analysis in C++.

The programmer must also use #include to manually import class headers. #include is an old and unsophisticated mechanism to provide modularity and is a weak form of inheritance and import. C++ still uses this 30-year-old technique for modularization, while other languages have adopted more sophisticated approaches—for example, Pascal with Units, Modula with modules, and Ada with packages. In Eiffel the unit of modularization is the class itself, and includes are handled automatically. The OOP class is a more sophisticated way to modularize programs. Inheritance implements reusability and modularization, so #include is superfluous.

#includes also mean that a compiler compiles all definitions immediately, whether the definitions are needed in the module or not. By contrast, Eiffel and Java need to retrieve definitions of entities only when they are actually used in a module.

Another problem is that, if header A includes header B, and header B includes header A, a circular dependency occurs. The same problem occurs if header A includes headers B and C, and header B also includes header C. A simple but messy fix in all headers solves this problem

C++

```
#ifndef thismod
#define thismod
... rest of header
#endif
```

This is a manual implementation of cycle detection. The general algorithm is to have a list of places already visited. When you visit a node, just add it to the list. This is the effect of the #define thismod in the previous example. The define just adds the token into the define list. Of course this list is not exclusive to cycle detection entities, so the possibility of name clashes with other defines arises. So usually cycle detection define identifiers will be chosen according to some convention. Java and Eiffel relieve the programmer of this burden on two counts: first, the compiler works out modules that must be visited automatically from the program text; second, the cycle detection algorithm is built into the compiler itself.

Headers show how C++ addresses the problem of independent modules with a non-OO approach that is suboptimal; the programmer must supply this bookkeeping information manually. `#include` relates to the organization and administration of a project. Modern language design enables such manual bookkeeping mechanisms to be eliminated.

According to Stroustrup, C++ would be a better language without the C preprocessor. Most uses of `#define` are now covered by other mechanisms. Removing `#include` would require some other import mechanism. Stroustrup says, "I'd like to see Cpp abolished."

[Stroustrup 94 (18.1)

A Problem of Dependency

The major problem with the `#include` mechanism is that it sets up transitive dependencies; that is, if you `#include` one module, you are naturally dependent on that module, but you are also dependent on all other modules included by that header, and so forth. This means the effects of changes are not localized, but can affect large areas of the system. With Java imports and Eiffel's more subtle form of being dependent on something only if you use it, the dependencies are nontransitive; that is, changes in a module affect only modules that directly use the module. The dependency does not transfer to other modules that use the dependent module. Transitive dependency is a major factor in the brittleness of C++ software.

A class interface is equivalent to a module header. A module header contains data and routines exported to other modules. This is exactly the purpose of the class interface.

A class definition contains all knowledge of accessed classes and their dependencies (inheritance and client) in the class text. Dependency analysis is derivable from the class text, and much of the functionality of tools like make can be integrated into the compiler, so the errors and tedium encountered in the use of make are avoided. Dependency analysis also implements a level of *dead code elimination*.

A traditional system is assembled by combining modules; an OO system is assembled by combining classes. The classes may be obtained from different libraries, but the class should be the basic mechanism and the library reasonably unimportant, since it is only a packaging mechanism and does not affect the semantics of a system. You might observe that the module mechanisms described in this chapter are a lot more vague than the notion of class. Modules are a primitive form of class. Classes express more precisely relationships with other classes. C++ `#include` and modules have problems—the arising dependencies are not clear. Java packages confuse the situation somewhat by making classes within a package more interdependent than classes in different packages. This complicates the notion of class relationships, as you have to take these different visibility rules into account in design.

Standard C Libraries Deprecated

[CD2 96] Preserving this old technology is not just a case of keeping the `#include` mechanism. The C++ standard now "deprecates" the standard C libraries, which have been used for many years, in favor of standard C++ library headers. Instead of using

C
```
#include <stdlib.h>
```

you should now use

C++
```
#include <cstdlib>
```

This is more than just a slight syntactic difference, though, as the C definitions from `<stdlib.h>` belong to the global namespace, and the definitions from `<cstdlib>` belong to the `std` namespace. So, to make this change, wherever you use one of these definitions, you must qualify it with `std::`. This change has not proven popular with compiler vendors, so, while it is in the standard today, who knows whether it will actually become part of "in use" C++. Since the C++ standard has been so disruptive, the committee could have used the opportunity to introduce a more modern and convenient mechanism than `#include`.

Neither Java nor Eiffel needs header files or the `#include` mechanism. As already mentioned, this is no mere syntactic difference, but is a fundamental factor in reducing the brittleness of software by making module dependency nontransitive.

[Wirth 90] In Java and Eiffel, programmers do not have to maintain headers separately. Oberon, which is Wirth's successor to Modula, has also merged the definition and implementation parts of a module, and names that are to be visible from client modules are explicitly marked as exported. Eiffel and Java also merge definition and implementations, from which class interfaces may automatically be derived.

Dependence on other modules is also derived automatically; when Eiffel sees any declaration

c: C *Eiffel*

it knows the current class has a dependency on the class *C*. *C* is implicitly imported, so there is no `#include` mechanism—Eiffel has done the dependency analysis for you. If you add a new declaration to a class that hasn't been used before, the dependency is automatically generated the next time the class is compiled.

Eiffel provides a utility *short* that extracts class interface definitions from the class implementation. However, the function of this is for human readability, not to provide the compiler with class definitions as in a C header file.

Eiffel also separates the bookkeeping concerns from the language. These functions are provided by the LACE language. LACE is used separately from the Eiffel language, but it is processed by the compiler to map class names to their location (directory and file name in UNIX-style systems).

3.5 Import (Java)

Instead of raw `#include`, Java uses `import` to import definitions from other packages. You can import the package as a whole, or just selected entities from the package. Import is far better integrated with the Java environment than `#include`. Import also sets up only an immediate dependency; the dependencies are not transitive.

3.6 ACE Specification (Eiffel)

Specifying dependencies on external classes has no place in the Eiffel language itself, so Eiffel has no equivalent to C++'s `#include` for headers or to Java's imports for packages. Instead you separately tell the Eiffel environment which clusters you want to include in the application being built; when a class refers to another class, importing the definition is implicit. This allows you to put the usage specification in one place only, and you do not have to repeat `#includes` or `imports` in every file or compilation unit that the compiler processes. Since there is no real mechanism to describe here, this section is mainly to make the differences clear for comparison purposes.

An advantage with this approach is that you can have several different versions of clusters active at one time; to change to a different version, you need to make only one modification.

Because LACE is not standard, the details will differ between Eiffel system vendors. However, a typical LACE specification will be 20–30 lines, and very large ones might be 50–100 lines (which would probably be hundreds of classes and hundreds of thousands of lines). If you consider a Java or C++ system with a few hundred classes, each including several other packages or classes, then you have hundreds of lines (all in different files) to modify for one change, so Eiffel represents a considerable benefit to reducing maintenance.

The Eiffel ACE mechanism also offers several other advantages. Java imports offer no way to remove clashes if classes with the same name are imported from two or more different packages. If such a clash occurs, you must remove the ambiguity by fully qualifying each name with the package hierarchy it comes from. This is similar to the use of the C++ scope resolution operator, ::. Where you need to put the path of a class in the Java code, this exposes the organization of the library. If this organization changes, every explicit path to the class must also be changed and this means brittleness of code. Since making such changes is undesirable, you probably won't want to make such changes in the first place, which means including explicit class paths in the code is inflexible.

Furthermore, Eiffel ACE allows you to specify the location of clusters. Typically this gives a file path to the directory where the cluster files can be found. As Internet programming becomes more popular, in the future this could be extended to give an Internet location or other network location of a cluster. Java package names can include some form of Internet domain name identification; however, this name is not meant to imply anything about where the package is stored on the Internet. This might be just as well because, as noted above, any change in location would lead to changes to `import` statements in what has the potential to be many compilation units. Java has yet to provide a good way to connect packages to network locations, and such a location mechanism should be defined separately of any particular network or file system standard.

3.7 Separate or Integrate?

Despite the advantages for the programmer of maintaining both interface and implementation in one place, in C++

[Stroustrup 97] (8.2)
> An alternative to relying on separately specified interfaces is to provide a tool that extracts an interface from a module that includes implementation details. I don't consider that a good solution. Specifying interfaces is a fundamental design activity, a module can provide different interfaces to different users, and often an interface is designed long before the implementation details are made concrete.

This logic is seriously flawed and misleading on several levels. The premise that "specifying interfaces is a fundamental design activity" is correct, but the assumption that you must then physically keep interface and implementation separate to do this is wrong. This does not mean that you develop a class in some ad hoc fashion, only to find out what the interface is after the fact. In fact, Stroustrup is being critical of the Eiffel philosophy, which very much encourages interface design as separate from developing the implementation. This approach is far more intrinsic to the Eiffel approach than the C++ approach.

Using Tools for Separation and Integration

If you use ISE's environment, a separate tool is not even needed to extract the interface—you just click on a button in the IDE and the interface is automatically displayed for you. Better still, you can click on several buttons in order to give you the interface in several forms. The short form gives you the interface that is declared in the current class, but the flat/short form gives you the entire interface for the class, which includes all features inherited from ancestors. The flat/short form also tells you from which particular ancestor class the feature was inherited. This is an extremely useful form that is not present in C++ interfaces, where you would need an automatic tool to do this anyway. Visual Eiffel from Object Tools also has such facilities built into their IDE.

Stroustrup's next point, "a module can provide different interfaces to different users," is far better supported in Eiffel than C++. This point is such an important difference and has so many ramifications that we take a whole chapter to look at it (chapter 7). C++ does not really implement the multiple interface paradigm for classes, although it does for namespaces. Unfortunately, C++ does not even do a very good job of separating interface from implementation—you must put private members in the class definition, and inline functions must at least be put in the header file.

Stroustrup's final point, that "often an interface is designed long before the implementation details are made concrete," is not precluded by the approach that he is attacking; his whole argument is wrong.

Taking a further look at the premise that interfaces and implementation must be separated, I agree that users of a module should have to look at only the interface. However, does C++ do even this well? The answer is no on at least two counts. First, if you want to make use of the potential to inline functions, you must put the implementation in the header file. Second, class definitions include a private section that exposes the class's private implementation details to the user. Thus C++ is extremely weak in providing the interface/implementation separation that is being advocated.

Separate or Integrate?

The interface extraction tool strategy does not preclude design first, implement later; in fact, it encourages it. It also gives the user a better interface definition, while making life easier for the programmer by not requiring the maintenance of two separate sets of the same information in slightly different syntactic forms. Conceptually, the interface and implementation are distinct, but they are both facets of the same entity and there is no need to separate them—rather like a person having a mind and a body. Insisting that interfaces and implementations must be maintained separately is like suggesting, because an architect designs a building's exterior separate from the interior layout, that the building facade be built on a different block of land from the interior. We have no trouble in separating these two concepts in real life, and it is no different for computing entities—every object built implicitly has an interface.

Conceptual vs. Physical Separation

We should also note here that *separation of concerns* means conceptual separation, not physical separation. Physical separation leads to inconsistency. An architect is able to separate his concerns for the external look of a building from the details of interior layout; however, if the two are kept too separate, interior walls will not match up with the outside windows, and other such design errors will eventuate. Thus separate design of interfaces does not mean maintaining interfaces separate from implementation.

Java also takes the approach that interface and implementation are physically distinct, providing interfaces and classes that represent the implementation. Again this confuses the point that a single entity has aspects of both interface and implementation. The interface aspect can certainly be designed up front and the implementation completed later; then the interface should be extractable from the single entity. In Java, though, if you restrict yourself to single inheritance there is really no need for interfaces; in this case, each class still implicitly has an interface, without the need to actually declare a Java interface. Even Stroustrup admits [Stroustrup 97] that "naturally, every class presents an interface to users."
(12.5)

The other point to consider is that a class can have multiple interfaces. This is the same as considering that our building is multifaceted and that different people use the building in different ways. It is important to recognize this multifacetedness and to conceptually separate the facets, but this does not mean that we end up having to maintain multiple artifacts. In fact OO programming is based on the fact that multiple facets have been brought together into a single artifact; that is, data and processing are part of a single object.

It is a backwards step to now artificially separate interfaces and specification semantics from the implementation, especially as this means more manual work in support of some misguided purist notion that is a misinterpretation of the concept of separation of concerns. Too many things are built into computing based on oversimplistic interpretations of what are otherwise good principles.

Interfaces can certainly change after the implementation is done. The simplest case is to add extra entries to the interface. Changing existing entries is more difficult, since modules that use those routines might also have to change. However, only real purists insist that interfaces are complete and closed before implementation takes place. As a module matures, the interfaces will stabilize. The ability to change interfaces provides greater flexibility, and such iterative development is the way things happen in the real world.

It is also strange that Dr. Stroustrup does not consider the automatic tool solution to be a good solution, considering his description of the hoops the programmer must jump through in order to maintain separate interfaces—the problems, the extra work, and the potential for error.

4

Members and Features

In the previous chapters, we looked at factors in the definition of the outer-level entities in our three languages. In this chapter we look at what is encapsulated in those entities. In Java and C++ these are called class *members*, and in Eiffel they are called *features*.

4.1 Basic Structures

As you may well know, one of the defining traits of OO languages is that not only do classes act as record definitions for storing data, but also encapsulated within the class are the subprogram units that act upon that data. However, if we stop with this definition, we have not really captured the essence of the OO method. Many bad classes can be designed with the feature of combining data and routines, and systems of such classes might look perfectly sensible in class diagrams. What is really important in the design of a good OO system is the design of the operations that manipulate the data in an object, and the functions that return information from an object. In other words, it is the design of the routines and data together that define the class interface. Thus the thought that a class is merely data + routines is too primitive, and we should think of a class as a higher-level semantic entity with a coherent set of operations. It is the design of such coherent classes that is the hallmark of good OO design.

To set the scene of the structures provided in our languages, we will look at the syntactical definition of elements within classes in this section. If you are already familiar with these languages, you can skim or skip to the next section. (Remember the difference between our grammars, EBNF, and the C-style, grammar—in EBNF elements appearing one after the other must appear that way in the program, whether separated by a new line or not; in C-style, grammar elements appearing on different lines are alternatives.)

Eiffel

The Eiffel syntax for class features looks like

```
EIFFEL
        Features              ≜   feature { Feature_clause feature ... }⁺
        Feature_clause        ≜   [Clients]
                                  [Header_comment]
                                  Feature_declaration_list
        Feature_declaration_list ≜ {Feature_declaration ";" ... }
        Header_comment        ≜   Comment
```

This gives the general layout for defining groups of features. The features in a **feature** clause are most likely grouped because of some similar property, or they may be exported to the same clients, or some other property documented in the Header_comment.

The definition of a single feature is as follows:

```
EIFFEL
        Feature_declaration   ≜   New_feature_list Declaration_body
        Declaration_body      ≜   [Formal_arguments]
                                  [Type_mark]
                                  [Constant_or_routine]
        Constant_or_routine   ≜   is Feature_value
        Feature_value         ≜   Manifest_constant | Unique | Routine
```

Basic Structures

Not all combinations of the elements of Declaration_body are possible, particularly the simple case where they are all optionally omitted. However, this grammatical presentation simplifies the grammar for the reader. If a compiler uses the grammar as given, it must check for valid combinations; otherwise, a more complex grammar must be devised.

Multiple features can be defined in one declaration, attaching each feature name to the same definition.

EIFFEL

New_feature_list	≜	{New_feature "," ...}⁺
New_feature	≜	[**frozen**] Feature_name
Type_mark	≜	":" Type

If the declared feature is a routine or constant, the feature names refer to the same routine or constant (as we shall see later, a constant is a special case of a function). The feature names associated to a routine definition may later be independently redefined in descendant classes. However, definitions of data elements result in different data elements, not multiple names to the same element (known as *aliases* or *synonyms*).

Frozen means that the feature cannot be changed in descendants. However, because this applies to only one feature and not the whole list, you can use it to declare a name that can refer only to the entity in this declaration, as well as a name that can polymorphically refer to other entities.

A Type_mark must be given for variables and constants, but this is optional for routines. A routine without a type is a *procedure*, and a routine with a type is a *function*. The Type_mark is not really optional—its absence is semantically significant. A type is given by a class name or, if the class has generics, a class name with the actual types of its generics.

Now we can give a fuller example of a class.

Eiffel

    class BANK_ACCOUNT
    creation
        make
    feature {BANK_MANAGER, AUTOMATIC_TELLER}
        make (*initial_balance*: INTEGER) **is**

```
        local
                t: TRANSACTION
        do
                balance := initial_balance
                !! transactions.make    -- Create a transaction ledger.
                -- Create a transaction record
                !! t.make ("Open", initial_balance)
                transactions.extend (t)
        end

    balance: INTEGER

    deposit (amount: INTEGER) is
        local
                t: TRANSACTION
        do
                balance := balance + amount
                !! t.make ("Deposit", amount)
                transactions.extend (t)
        end

    withdraw (amount: INTEGER) is
        local
                t: TRANSACTION
        do
                balance := balance - amount
                !! t.make ("Withdraw", amount)
                transactions.extend (t)
        end

    close (reason: STRING) is
        local
                t: TRANSACTION
        do
                balance := 0
                !! t.make (reason, 0)
                transactions.extend (t)
        end

feature {BANK_MANAGER}
    transactions: LIST [TRANSACTION]
end
```

Basic Structures

You should read the above generic definition of *transactions* as "*transactions* is a *LIST* **of** *TRANSACTION*(s)."

C++

The definitions of C++ class members looks like

C++

member-specification:
    member-declaration   member-specification$_{opt}$
    access-specifier : *member-specification$_{opt}$*

member-declaration:
    decl-specifier-seq$_{opt}$ member-declarator-list$_{opt}$;
    function-definition ;$_{opt}$
    qualified-id ;
    using-declaration
    template-declaration

member-declarator-list:
    member-declarator
    member-declarator-list , *member-declarator*

member-declarator:
    declarator pure-specifier$_{opt}$
    declarator constant-initializer$_{opt}$
    identifier$_{opt}$: *constant-expression*

pure-specifier:
    = 0

constant-initializer:
    = *constant-expression*

Groups of members are generally divided according to their access specifier. The access specifiers are `public`, `protected`, and `private`. These are C++'s equivalent to the clients list grouping sets of features in Eiffel. We will look at these in more detail in chapter 7.

Members are specified as a series of *declarations* and *declarators*. Declarations specify how names are to be interpreted. A declarator declares a single object, function, or type within a declaration. A declaration does not necessarily reserve storage; if it does, it is called a *definition*. Be careful not to be confused by this terminology. In many languages, a definition defines something abstract, like a class definition (which is also C++ terminology), and a declaration is more likely to refer to a run-time structure, such as setting aside storage. Also this use of *definition* has nothing to do with #defines.

The concepts of declaration and declarator are much in line with C and in C++ can be used in their normal C setting. Members are much the same as such C declarations, with certain constraints.

The account example given above in Eiffel would look as follows in C++:

```
class BankAccount                                                  C++
{
public:
    // Constructor declaration
    BankAccount (int initialBalance);
    int GetBalance ();

    void deposit (int amount);
    void withdraw (int amount);
    void close (char *reason);
    List<Transaction>* GetTransactions ();

    ~BankAccount ();   // Destructor declaration

private:
    int balance;
    List<Transaction> *transactions;
};


BankAccount::BankAccount (int initialBalance)
{   // Constructor definition
    Transaction *t;

    balance = initialBalance;
```

Basic Structures

```
        transactions = new List<Transaction> ();
        t = new Transaction ("Open", initialBalance);
        // Create a transaction
        transactions->extend (t);
    }

    int BankAccount::GetBalance ()
    {
        return balance;
    }

    void BankAccount::deposit (int amount)
    {
        Transaction *t;

        balance = balance + amount;
        t = new Transaction ("Deposit", amount);
        transactions->extend (t);
    }

    void BankAccount::withdraw (int amount)
    {
        Transaction *t;

        balance = balance - amount;
        t = new Transaction ("Withdraw", amount);
        transactions->extend (t);
    }

    void BankAccount::close (char *reason)
    {
        Transaction *t;

        balance = 0;
        t = new Transaction (reason, 0);
        transactions->extend (t);
    }

    List<Transaction>* BankAccount::GetTransactions ()
    {
        return transactions;
    }
```

```
BankAccount::~BankAccount ()
{
    Transaction *t =
            new Transaction ("destruct", 0);
    transactions->extend (t);
}
```

Java

The syntax for a Java class body looks like

Java

ClassBody:
    { *ClassBodyDeclarations$_{opt}$* }

ClassBodyDeclarations:
    ClassBodyDeclaration
    ClassBodyDeclarations ClassBodyDeclaration

ClassBodyDeclaration:
    ClassMemberDeclaration
    StaticInitializer
    ConstructorDeclaration

ClassMemberDeclaration:
    FieldDeclaration
    MethodDeclaration

This is the general layout for defining members in a Java class. We can see that Java has two kinds of members: fields and methods. But we also have two other entities we can declare in the class body: static initializers and constructors. You might observe that there is no grouping as in C++ and Eiffel—each member is individually given its own access modifier. This makes the syntax for Java a little simpler, but each declaration in a Java class looks a little more complicated. Often you will find that a more complex grammar actually results in a simpler language, and one that is easier for writing programs. A language designer should design a simple language, and then devise a simple grammatical description of that language.

Basic Structures

The syntax for field declarations is given as

Java

FieldDeclaration:
  FieldModifiers$_{opt}$ *Type* *VariableDeclarators* ;

VariableDeclarators:
  VariableDeclarator
  VariableDeclarators , *VariableDeclarator*

VariableDeclarator:
  VariableDeclaratorID
  VariableDeclaratorID = *VariableInitializer*

VariableDeclaratorID:
  Identifier
  VariableDeclaratorID [ ]

VariableInitializer:
  Expression
  ArrayInitializer

FieldModifiers:
  FieldModifier
  FieldModifiers *FieldModifier*

FieldModifier: one of
```
    public   protected   private
    final    static   transient   volatile
```

The syntax of *FieldModifier* is not strictly correct and in reality would need extra productions. This is because you can have more than *one of* the modifiers, as in `final public`, but you cannot have more than one of `public`, `protected`, and `private` (although there was an access category of `private protected` in an older version of the Java specification). In EBNF, it is easier to express alternatives more accurately and formally.

The syntax for method declarations is given as

> *Java*
>
> *MethodDeclaration*:
>   *MethodHeader MethodBody*
>
> *MethodHeader*:
>   *MethodModifiers$_{opt}$ ResultType MethodDeclarator Throws$_{opt}$*
>
> *ResultType*:
>   *Type*
>   `void`
>
> *MethodDeclarator*:
>   *Identifier* (*FormalParameterList$_{opt}$*)
>
> *MethodModifiers*:
>   *MethodModifier*
>   *MethodModifiers MethodModifier*
>
> *MethodModifier*: *one of*
>   `public    protected    private`
>   `abstract    static    final    synchronized    native`

The Java version of our accounts class is

```
class BankAccount                                              Java
{
    private int balance;
    private List transactions;

    public void BankAccount (int initialBalance)
    {
        Transaction t;

        balance = initialBalance;
        transactions = new List ();
        // Create a transaction
```

```
            t = new Transaction
                    ("Open", initialBalance);
            transactions.extend (t);
        }

        public int GetBalance ()
        {
            return balance;
        }

        public void deposit (int amount)
        {
            Transaction t;

            balance = balance + amount;
            t = new Transaction ("Deposit", amount);
            transactions.extend (t);
        }

        public void withdraw (int amount)
        {
            Transaction t;

            balance = balance - amount;
            t = new Transaction ("Withdraw", amount);
            transactions.extend (t);
        }

        public void close (String reason)
        {
            Transaction t;

            balance = 0;
            t = new Transaction (reason, 0);
            transactions.extend (t);
        }

        public List GetTransactions ()
        {
                return transactions;
        }
    }
```

4.2 Members (C++ and Java)

Care should be taken with the meaning of the C++ and Java term *member*. The term is confusing because member is also used another way—as in, an object is a member of a class—but this is not in the sense of being a data item of the class. For example, a squirrel is a member of the class animal, or set of animals, and is also a member of the set of squirrels, but is not part of the data description of *ANIMAL* or *SQUIRREL*. We must take care to distinguish metadata from data.

This usage corresponds to the concept of member in set theory. A person can be a member of a club, but this does not make him or her part of the description of the club, which will remain the same whether that particular person is a member or not. But in C++, the term *member* means a data item or function of the class. If you add, delete, or change these members, you have changed the metadescription of the class. Take care not to confuse these meanings.

Some people might say that set theory is one thing, but programming is another, so there is no problem with using the terminology. However, set theory underpins the theory of computation and programming, and sets, classes, and types are related. Sets are a means of describing groups of entities that have some similarity. Supersets group entities according to broad concepts; subsets group entities according to narrower concepts—that is, more restrictive criteria. So sets also underpin our understanding of classes and subclasses.

In set theory we say $3 \in N$, or 3 is a member of the set of natural numbers. In objects we would say that Fred is a member of the class *PERSON*. But in C++, a data item in the description of the class is known as a member of the class. This is not mathematically correct, and the confusion could have been avoided.

Eiffel uses the term *feature* to refer to entities that are in a class description.

4.3 Anonymous Parameters in Class Definitions (C++)

C++ does not require parameters in function declarations to be named; the type alone can be specified. For example a function `f` in a class header can be declared as `f (int, int, char)`. This gives the client no clue to the purpose of the parameters without referring to the implementation of the function. Meaningful identifiers are essential in this situation because this is the abstract definition of a routine; a client of the class and routine must know that the first `int` represents a count of apples, etc. It is true that well-known routines might not require a name—for example, `sqrt (int)`—but this is not appropriate for large-scale software development.

The use of anonymous parameters handicaps the purpose of abstract descriptions of classes and members to facilitate the reusability of software, which we cover in more detail in section 13.5. Program text captures the meaning of the system for some future activity, such as extension or maintenance. To achieve reusability, communication of intent of a software element is essential.

Naming exists to help the human reader identify different entities within the program and to help reason about their function. For this reason naming is essential; without it, development of sophisticated systems would be nearly impossible. Some languages access parameters by their address (position) in the parameter list ($1, $2, etc). Positional parameters are a kind of name, since they refer to the entities "first," "second," etc., but this is unsatisfactory, even for shell scripts. Anonymous parameters can save typing in a function template, but then programming is not a matter of convenience because it is inconvenient for later readers (unless it is a write-once, run-once program, but we are considering only large-scale development). The redundancy is beneficial and saves later programmers having to look up the information in another place. A real convenience in function templates would be that abstract function templates could be automatically generated from the implementation text (see header files for more details).

This covers positional parameters when they are used in the called routine. In a routine invocation, the usual convention is position, where the order of the actual parameters must match the declared order in the receiving routine. This can also lose the meaning of the parameters being passed. An alternative is to have invocations as follows. For a declaration of *output*

output (*action*: *ACT*; *repeat*: *INTEGER*;
         message: *STRING*) **is** ...

a call would be

output (*repeat* := 3; *message* := "hello";
         action := *sneeze*)

It is convenient for the reader of the call that the integer 3 is the number of times the action and message are repeated. It is also convenient for the writer that the exact order of parameters need not be remembered; however, the parameter names must be remembered, and you have the added inconvenience of having to type them.

Anonymous parameters illustrate the link between courtesy and safety issues in programming. Due to pressure of work, a client programmer might wrongly guess the purpose of a parameter from the type. The failure of the original programmer to provide a courtesy has caused a client programmer to breach safety. However, the client programmer will probably be blamed for not taking due care. An interface client must know the intention of the interface for it to be used effectively.

Both Java and Eiffel do away with the distinction between a function definition and declaration. The first reason for this is that you don't need forward declarations because entities can be referenced before they are declared. The second reason is that Java and Eiffel have tools to extract abstract interface definitions from the main code automatically.

4.4 Default Arguments (C++)

Default arguments that assume a default value according to the routines declaration are supposed to provide a shorthand notation. Shorthand notations are intended to speed up software development. Such shorthand notations can be convenient in shell scripts and interactive systems. In large-scale software production, however, precision is mandatory, and defaults can lead to ambiguities and mistakes. With default arguments, the programmer could assume the wrong default for an argument. More importantly, default arguments undermine type safety. The type of a function is defined by the composition of its input types and its output type

$$f: T1 \times T2 \times T3... \to T4$$

The entire signature determines the type of the function, not just the return type. Default arguments mean that C++ is not type safe and that the compiler cannot check that the arguments in the call exactly match the function signature.

Furthermore, default arguments do not provide a great deal of convenience, as Stroustrup admits "Given general function overloading, default arguments are logically redundant and at best a minor notational convenience." If a function has five arguments, the last three of which are optional, and the caller wants to assume the defaults for parameters 3 and 4 but must specify parameter 5, then all five parameters must be specified. A better scheme would be to have a default keyword in function calls

[Stroustrup 9 (2.12.2)]

```
void f (a, b, default, default, e);
```

Default Arguments (C++)

or perhaps to omit it altogether

```
void f (a, b,,, e);
```

Other means, already in the language, can easily provide this mechanism. For example, a call to another (possibly inline) function could provide the defaults for the default arguments

```
void g(int a, b, e)    // the function definition
    {f(a, b, 0, 0, e);}

g(1, 2, 3);       // the call
```

This not only provides the convenience of default arguments, but is more powerful. Any argument or combination can be filled in with any combination of defaults, not just the last arguments. Multiple intermediate routines can provide multiple sets of defaults.

This is very close to overloading, and, in C++, default arguments can also be achieved by overloaded routines, so the above can actually be

```
void g(int a, b, c, d, e) {...}   // g defined with
                                  // 5 arguments
void g(int a, b, e)    // the function
    {g(a, b, 0, 0, e);}

g(1, 2, 3);       // the call
```

A more specific problem with default arguments is that, if a function is virtual and redefined, calls to the function will be dynamic, but defaults for the arguments will be inserted statically. That is, if a default argument is given in a base class and the default is changed in a derived class, if the function of an object of the derived class is invoked via a pointer of the base class, the defaults of the base class and not those of the derived class will be passed to the function.

Also watch for nesting: an inner routine will hide an outer routine with its defaults

```
    void f(int a = 777);                                            C++

    void inner()
    {
       void f(int a = 666);   // Hides outer f, defaults
                              // don't have to match.
    }
```

Default arguments also have a syntax peculiarity when supplying a pointer default

```
    void bad_default(char*=0);
```

gives a syntax error because the compiler interprets *= as an assignment operator. In this case the space is significant: * =.

Neither Java nor Eiffel has default arguments, although Java can use the overloading scheme we saw with C++. Strong typing is enforced so that the arguments of a call must match the routine signature.

4.5 Local Entity Declarations (Java and C++)

Declaring an entity close to where it is used has advantages and disadvantages—it is convenient, but it can make a routine appear more complex and cluttered. A problem is that an identifier can be mistakenly overloaded within a nested block in a function, with the resultant problems covered in the section on name overloading. ALGOL and C have this simple form of name overloading. (A block in the ALGOL sense contains both declarations and instructions.)

In-code declarations have other problems apart from mere stylistic considerations. The *Annotated C++ Reference Manual* (*ARM*) explains problems of local declarations with branching, which shows the complications in intermingling declarations and instructions. The question is what happens if you have a goto around a statement that contains a declaration, or a goto out of a block with a declaration. Fortunately, in C++ such jumps are illegal, but even so, this makes the language and programming more complicated.   [C++ ARM] (6.7)

In well-written OO software, routines will be small, typically performing one atomic operation per routine, so localized declarations will not be of much value. Small routines that implement atomic operations are fundamental to loose coupling. For example, a base class that provides a single routine that logically performs operations A and B is not useful to a subclass that needs to provide its own implementation of B, but does not want to change A. The descendant must reimplement the logic of both A and B, missing an opportunity to reuse the logic of A. Splitting A and B into different routines accomplishes loose coupling and, therefore, flexibility. Tight coupling reduces flexibility.

Efficiency is also attained without the complication of local entity declarations. Good design and clean modularization achieve efficiency, since the entities that would be locals to a block in C++ are created only when the routine is entered. Furthermore, small routines can be inlined, and, in this case, the locals will be created only when the expanded inline block is entered, which has the same effect as the programmer including the block manually.

Java implements locals the same way C++ does. In Eiffel the philosophy is to use good design to make routines sufficiently small and atomic—that is, one operation, one routine. With this approach, having local declarations in only one place in the routine and not throughout is sufficient. If you find a place where you want to introduce local variables within the code, this is an indication that you should write it as a separate routine. An objection could be that small routines with lots of overhead calling them is not efficient. Eiffel compilers solve this by automatically inlining routines. Thus the integrity of a design is preserved in the program text, but efficiency is retained. In C++ you could manually inline such functions.

4.6 Inlines (C++)

The problems described in this section are a consequence of placing the burden of encapsulation on the programmer. We covered encapsulation in chapter 1 if you wish to review it.

[Stroustrup 94] (2.4.1)   The main reason inlines were introduced in C++ was to alleviate the cost of crossing the protection barrier. The protection barrier in C++ is data hiding. When accessing a data item in C++, it is recommended not to do it directly, but via a class member function. For example, given an object reference *c,* you should not access the data member *di* directly.

C++
```
i = c.di; // Not recommended C++ style.
```

Instead di should be private and accessed as follows:

C++
```
i = c.get_di();
```

where `get_di` is

```
    int C::get_di() {return di;}                                     C++
```

However, Stroustrup found that some programmers were not using an access function because of the overhead of a function call. So inlines were introduced—any function that is defined in the class body, not just declared, is also an inline function. It is not always desirable to put function definitions in the class body itself (since C++ is not intended to have tools to automatically extract the interface), so an `inline` keyword is provided where a function is defined outside of the class body.

```
    inline int C::get_di() {return di;}                              C++
```

The inline function must be defined in the header file with the class body. The style of data hiding where an extra function must be written to access the value of a data item clutters the namespace and text of a class.

Inlines are merely an optimization, not a semantic concept. However, inlining does negatively impact the semantics of functions, because inlined functions cannot be redefined or used for dynamic binding. The inline mechanism has two conceptual mistakes and several practical mistakes. First, data hiding and implementation hiding are not the same. Implementation hiding has more to do with hiding the mechanics of the access mechanism so that you can't tell whether it is a constant, variable, or function you are accessing. Inlines are the wrong solution to this problem; the correct solution is uniform access. The OO concept is to hide implementation; data need not be private, but may be exported functionally from a class.

This leads to the second conceptual mistake—that functional access and C functions are different things. Functional access hides the access mechanism. C functions, however, make the access mechanism visible; you know you are invoking a piece of code that will be jumped to. Functional access by contrast is any entity name that can occur in the context of an expression. This entity could be a constant, variable, or value returning routine, but you can't and don't need to tell which it is if the implementation of the access mechanism is hidden. The statement `i = c.di` is functional access. C++ has solved this problem in exactly the wrong way in order to stay compatible with the flawed concept of function in C.

The programmer is required to bear this burden, which in turn makes software development more costly for every company using C++. Again flexibility is reduced. In order to restore information hiding—that is, access transparency between constants, variables, and C functions—programmers must as a matter of style hide constants and variables behind a C function, as is the case with `get_di()`. A fix to the language would have been better, but not possible to keep compatibility with C.

[CD2 96] (7.1.2)

The practical mistake is that a compiler can automatically generate inlines. Requiring a programmer to specify `inline` is a manual bookkeeping task. It is not hard for a compiler or optimizer to work out that `C::get_di() {return di;}` or even more complex routines could be inlined. In fact, `inline` is only a hint to a C++ compiler, and a compiler will use certain heuristics to determine whether to inline or not. This shows that a compiler can determine whether to automatically inline and is exactly the kind of optimization that Eiffel and other sophisticated languages perform. The reasons you might want to use inline functions are complex and platform dependent, so when porting an application from one platform to another, your optimizations are not necessarily portable. This is another good reason to leave such optimizations up to a compiler, as it will choose optimizations that are applicable to the target platform. It is important that applications as a whole are portable, not optimizations. What is optimal on one platform can be expensive on another.

The C++ approach—of having the programmer specify which functions are candidates for inlining—has one advantage. It is probably worth considering which functions should be inlined only after a nearly complete system has been profiled to find out which functions are called the most. In this case, the programmer marks for inlining only those functions which are in the 10 percent of functions which do 90 percent of the work, (or 20 percent/80 percent, as the case may be). Without systems that perform this kind of profiling and optimization automatically, it seems that this is a good argument for programmer-specified inlining.

However, an explicit inline specification should still not be part of the language definition. Inlines have nothing to do with the problem definition. Eiffel provides a natural place to put such manual inline specifications, and that is in the ACE specification, but this is correctly not mandated as part of LACE. If you want certain routines to be potentially inlined, put such optimizations in a separate specification, not in the program code. This means that extra optimization information such as hints to the compiler should not be placed in the program itself, but in a separate specification. This is also good *separation of concerns*. The Eiffel specification actually makes no statements about this, so the exact mechanics of such optimizations would be implementation dependent.

Performance Profiling

Probably the ultimate method for determining which functions should be inlined is to do a preliminary compilation of a system, with an option to make the compiler produce performance-monitoring code. You then run the program, which generates a machine-readable report with a performance profile including information such as how often each routine is invoked and how much time is spent in each routine. You then recompile your system turning off performance profiling, but this time the compiler automatically picks up the performance output of the program's previous run and applies appropriate optimizations for the target platform. You could also specify in your ACE high-level information as to whether you want to optimize for memory space or processor speed so that, when the compiler is faced with a trade-off, it knows what to do.

Another thing you should consider about accessor and update functions is that, in C++, you should of course read data members of external classes via their `get_ ()` function. However, what should you do for data members in the same class? To be consistent, you should probably use the accessor functions for your own data members. This means that, if you make changes to the class, it is somewhat protected from itself. In Eiffel, however, since access is uniform, you don't have to even think about this kind of problem.

Must Be in Header Files

Another practical problem with inline functions in C++ is that, if they are accessed from other translation units, they must be put in header files because, when the function is invoked from another module, the compiler must have access to the code in order to place it inline. Now, if the compiler decides not to inline the code after all, you will get a duplicate routine compiled in each source file that includes the header. This could cause the linker to complain about duplicate definitions; to get around that problem, the noninlined inline functions are treated as static.

Since an inline function usually must be in the header file, flagging a function as inline is not as easy as simply adding the inline keyword; you will have to move the whole function declaration from the implementation file to the header file if it is not already there. Once the inline function is in the header file, any changes to the inline function will cause all dependent modules to be recompiled whether they use the inline function or not.

Then suppose you need to make the function virtual. In this case, you must remove the inline function from the header file and put it back into the implementation file. All this is a maintenance nightmare.

Of course, since you typically use inlines to implement accessor functions, your header files, instead of being a simple definition of the class interface, become very messy. Eiffel does not have these problems because it gives you an accessor function to exported data for free—the accessor function is the data item itself. Thus Eiffel's interfaces are much cleaner, and you also reduce implementation since you don't need to duplicate public accessor functions with private data.

A further problem is that, if you refer a pointer to an inline function, then the compiler must generate a real function for it.

Inlines in Java and Eiffel

[Flanagan 96] Flanagan says, "A good Java compiler should automatically be able to 'inline' short Java methods where appropriate." An article in *Byte* (September 1996) suggests that, to optimize Java method calls, "you should make liberal use of the `final` keyword." *Byte* also suggests that instead of using small functions, pro-

[Wayner 96] grammers should inline small methods by hand. *Byte* further says, "The trade-off, then, is either better performance or code flexibility. You must decide which is most important to the program's operation in that situation."

In this respect, Eiffel again provides a better approach. An Eiffel compiler automatically determines that a routine is `final` or, in C++'s terminology, that a routine is not `virtual`. Also Eiffel automatically inlines. Therefore the Eiffel programmer does not need to bend the code to gain performance or consider trade-offs—you do not have to trade off flexibility to gain performance.

Eiffel has a further advantage—it understands the difference between implementation hiding and data hiding and provides implementation hiding (although called *information hiding*, it means information about the class, not information in the objects). Eiffel also accesses data and constants functionally, so in the instruction

Eiffel $i := c.di$

you can't tell and don't need to know whether *di* is implemented as a constant, variable, or routine function. The implementation is hidden: access is uniform since access to a constant or variable looks the same as a value-returning routine. The different access mechanisms behind these is hidden and automatically generated by the compiler. And since this implementation distinction is hidden, the need is greatly reduced for either the programmer to manually inline or for the compiler to automatically inline. In this case, Eiffel provides the maximum flexibility.

Since C functions are poor cousins to mathematical functions, and since C++ also confuses data hiding and implementation hiding, the language includes otherwise unnecessary mechanisms like inline.

Functional Naming

A subtle point on naming can also be mentioned here. In Eiffel, the value of an entity is returned by just invoking the name as a noun. This is like functional programming. In contrast the `get_` scheme of C++ and Java are imperative; that is, you use a verb as a command to actually do something. As mentioned, the implementation of how a value is actually obtained should be hidden, and therefore functional naming is preferred.

4.7 Pointers and References (C++)

References look like they have been added to C++ like object references in other OO languages, in order to restrict arbitrary manipulation that you have with pointers, which is meaningless when a pointer refers to an object. However, this turns out not to be the case. You cannot actually assign to a reference, and you certainly can't assign `null` to a reference. You can attach an object to a reference only at the reference declaration. You can perform some dirty tricks to undermine a reference, like initializing a pointer to `null` and then initializing a reference to the `null` pointer. C++ references do not replace most of the need for pointers, so you have an added complexity in the language in having to choose between where it is appropriate to use pointers or references. Java and Eiffel have only references, which provide functionality somewhere between C++ pointers and references.

4.8 Declarations and Definitions (C++)

In C++ a definition fully defines an entity, whereas a declaration only introduces the name of the entity. Each entity can have only one definition, but may have many declarations. The reason for this is that, if you use an entity, it must at least be introduced by a declaration before you use it. Don't expect this to solve all problems, though; you will need the full definition if, for example, you statically allocate a structure, in which case the size is needed from the definition, or you need to access any members of a class or struct.

"It is the programmer's task to ensure that every namespace, class, function, etc. is properly declared in every translation unit in which it appears and that all declarations referring to the same entity are consistent." Unfortunately, this is more bookkeeping. Even worse, if any declaration differs from an entity's definition, the compiler will probably not detect this—it will be left up to the linker, and linkers always give much more obscure errors. Fortunately, header files mean that you need only one textual description of most declarations, which are then repeated everywhere the header file is included. To get around the size problem, [Stroustrup 9 (9.2)]

Declarations and Definitions (C++)

[Stroustrup 97] (9.2.1) class definitions are put in header files. Stroustrup says, "One imperfect but simple method of achieving consistency for declarations in different translation units is to *#include header files* containing interface information in source files containing executable code and/or data definitions."

[Stroustrup 97] (9.2.3) Unfortunately, it is not as simple as having a single definition; in fact the rule is called the *one definition rule* (ODR). This rule means that an entity can be defined multiple times, but all the definitions must match. But this leads to subtle errors that are hard for a compiler to detect. Stroustrup warns, "Checking against inconsistent class definitions in separate translation units is beyond the ability of most C++ implementations. Consequently, declarations that violate the ODR can be a source of subtle errors. Unfortunately, the technique of placing shared definitions in headers and *#including* them doesn't protect against this last form of ODR violation." The last example mentioned here is

C++

```
// file1.c:
typedef int X;
struct S3 { X a; char b };

// file2.c:
typedef char X;
struct S3 { X a; char b; };    // error
```

[Stroustrup 97] (9.2.3) Splitting this up into #includes Stroustrup gives the following example of why you get obscure errors

C++

```
// file s.h
struct S { Point a; char b; };

// file1.c:
#define Point int
#include "s.h"
// ...

// file2.c:
class Point { /* ... */ };
#include "s.h"
// ...
```

In Eiffel and Java, you have no such complications. A single definition (although the terminology is *declaration*) suffices, which releases the programmer from the tedium of making sure that either entities—such as classes, routines, and methods—or variables and fields occur in a certain order. Thus, in Java and Eiffel, you have less work, less worry, and less error; the added complication of C++ adds absolutely no extra flexibility or other advantage.

The fundamental difference between Eiffel and Java compilers and C++ compilers is that Eiffel and Java compilers implement a multipass scheme to save the programmer extra work. C compilers and therefore C++ compilers do not do this, so the language is designed to make things easier for compilers, not for programmers. C/C++ has the attitude of "that's the way the compiler works; you must do things this way to make the compiler work." Thus C compilation strategies are exposed in the language definition of both C and C++, so many C++ books are instructions on how to drive a C++ compiler more than how to write programs in this language. This is a major reason it takes so long to learn C++—much longer than either Eiffel or Java—without even mastering programming or OO design and techniques, and why so many books are available on C++, while Eiffel and Java require relatively few.

4.9 Scope

The reason for the above complication in C++, vs. simplicity in Eiffel and Java is the definition of scope in the languages. In C++, the scope of an entity extends from its point of declaration to the end of the enclosing block. In Java and Eiffel, the scope of an entity is its entire enclosing environment. C++ does have an exception because a member function defined within a class body (which as we have seen applies to inline functions) is able to refer to every other member of the class. Such a function can refer to a member that is textually defined after it. Stroustrup claims this can confuse human readers. However, the liberation from ordering considerations is essential for sophisticated languages. [Stroustrup 9

While the scope rules of Java and Eiffel make life easier for the programmer since he or she no longer needs to be concerned with declaration order or with introducing superfluous declarations, it does make life harder for compilers which need to implement a multipass scheme. The scope rules of C++ show the adverse legacy of C, which dates back to the 1960s when building simpler compilers was a necessity. It is no longer necessary to burden programmers with these problems.

4.10 Constants

You can declare constants as class members in all of our languages, but the details vary.

Constants

Eiffel

In Eiffel, constants are declared with much the same syntax as variables and functions

Eiffel

    int_const: *INTEGER* **is** 37
    str_const: *STRING* **is** "a string"

In Eiffel, such constants can be defined only in terms of simple constants; you cannot define constants in terms of constant expressions

    three_K: *INTEGER* **is** 3 * 1024 -- not valid

A further generalization of this would be to allow any kind of expression to define a cheap function

    i: *INTEGER*
    three_i: *INTEGER* **is** 3 * *i* -- not valid

If a more sophisticated form of constant is needed than the simple form, you can use a **once** function

Eiffel

    three_K: *INTEGER* **is**
        once
            Result := 3 * 1024
        end

This is slightly heavy syntax for this simple example, but any complex calculation can be included in the body of the **once** function.

Another form of constant is the **unique** constant. With uniques, the programmer does not have to supply a value, but relies on the compiler to assign an integer number to each constant

Eiffel

    red, *green*, *blue*: *INTEGER* **is unique**

This form guarantees that the values are positive and unique within a class. Furthermore, if they are part of one declaration as in the last example, they are also guaranteed to be consecutive.

In Eiffel, arrays cannot be constant, but they can be initialized from a *manifest array*

> *a*: ARRAY [*T*] *Eiffel*
>
> ...
>
> *a* := <<*t1, t2, ... tn*>>

Here each element of the manifest array must conform to the actual element type of the array, *T*. Manifest arrays can also be passed as actual parameters where the formal argument is an array type. This can be used to pass variable numbers of arguments to a routine.

C++

C has a very primitive way of defining constants—the `#define`. Defining constants in this way means they are in scope from the point of definition to the end of the compilation unit, which is not a very useful way of defining constants that are class members. C++ defines constants better as part of the language, so you should avoid using `#define`s for constants

```
int const_int = 37;   // Not const, just initialized        C++
const int const_int = 37; // This is a constant
const char* str_const = "a string";
```

The last example raises the question as to whether it is the pointer or the string that is constant. This depends on where you put the `const` specification

```
// pointer to constant                                      C++
const char* str_const = "a string";
// constant pointer to variable
char* const ptr_const = "a string";
// pointer and object const
const char* const str_const = "a string";
// also pointer to const
char const* str_const = "a string";
```

You can also initialize constant arrays

C++

```
const int v[] = {1, 2, 3, 4};
```

Java

To declare constants in Java classes, you use the `final` modifier

Java

```
int const_int = 37;   // Not const, just initialized
final int const_int = 37; // This is a constant
final String str_const = "a string";
```

You can also declare constants in interfaces, but in this case you do not need the `final` modifier

Java

```
interface myIf
{
    int const_int = 37; // This is a constant
    String str_const = "a string";
}
```

You can also initialize constant references to objects:

Java

```
class Point
{
    final static Point origin = new Point (0, 0);
}
```

In this case the member origin always refers to the same Point object. That object, however, may be changed from another reference. This mechanism is similar to Eiffel **once** routines, where a **once** routine can be used to return a constant reference to a common object, but the state of that object may change.

4.11 Static (C++)

[C++ ARM] (7.1.1)

[Stroustrup 97] (9.2)

The word static is confusing in C++. The C++ ARM mentions this confusion and gives two meanings. First, a class can have static members, and a function can have static entities. The second meaning comes from C, where a static entity is local in scope to the current file. More recently, Stroustrup notes, "In C and older C++ programs, the keyword *static* is (confusingly) used to mean 'use internal linkage.' Don't use *static* except inside functions and classes."

The choice of different keywords would easily solve this confusing use of the same keyword for several meanings. There is also a third, more general meaning—that objects are statically or automatically allocated and deallocated on the stack when a block is entered and exited, as opposed to dynamically allocated in free space. Another general use of the word static is in static type checking, which obviously has no relation to the C uses, but overloads the language even further.

Static class members are useful. The ARM states that statics reduce the need for global variables, which is a good thing, but the C syntax obscures the purpose. [C++ ARM] (9.4)

Locals declared in functions can also be static. These are not needed in an OO language. The reason and history is that ALGOL has the notion of OWN locals in blocks. The semantics of an OWN entity is that, when a block is exited, the value of the OWN is preserved for the next entry to the block, i.e., the value is persistent. The implementation is that, at compile time, the OWN entity is limited in scope to the block, but at run time it is located in the global stack frame. The same instance of the variable is used in all invocations of the procedure, rather than each invocation using separate local storage on the stack. This causes complications in recursion.

Simula's designers generalized the ALGOL notion of block into class, thus giving birth to OO. Instead of discarding a class block on exit, it is made persistent. Declarations within the class block are persistent and, therefore, provide the functionality of static and OWN, which Simula discarded from its ALGOL base. Classes are more flexible than statics. Statics are persistent in the same way as globals, i.e., for the duration of the program. (This is not the undesirable property of globals, since statics are limited in scope—it is the fact that globals are accessible from everywhere that is the problem.) Class member lifetime is governed by the lifetime of the object, so OO languages do not need globals, OWNs, or statics.

Java implements class variables and methods with `static`. Note that the Java terminology is slightly inconsistent since "class member" refers to per-object members, whereas "class variable" and "class method" refer to static per-class entities.

Eiffel abolishes globals with **once** routines, which are described in the next section.

4.12 Once Routines

Eiffel has no globals, but does provide an essential mechanism to access widely available data and routines, akin to class variables and methods. This mechanism is the **once** function, which is a variant of **once** routines. If a routine is a procedure, then it will be executed only once in the execution of the program. **Once** functions are more interesting, as they can return immutable references to objects. These objects may themselves change, but every call to the **once** function will return the same result. An interesting property of such objects is that, since they have a permanent reference to them, they will never be garbage collected.

Once routines are applied on a class basis, so any object accessing the same routine in a class will get the same result. This makes **once** routines similar to the static class members of C++, except that static class members can be changed during the execution of the program. The syntax of a **once** routine is simple—you simply replace **do** with **once**

Eiffel

$f(p: P): R$ **is**
    require <precondA>
    once
        ...
        $Result := ...$
    ensure <postcondA>
end

Once routines can also be used to define constants. Therefore the constant syntax for features in Eiffel is superfluous, but provides a handy shorthand. The constant syntax can be applied only to basic types, so **once** routines provide a necessary mechanism for general constants.

4.13 Class Variables and Redefinition

In any language, it is interesting to consider the combined effect of features. The less traps and rules you have to learn because of the combinations the better. Prohibited combinations should be so only because they do not make semantic sense, not because they are too hard to implement, giving you maximum flexibility. If a combination is prohibited, it is usually for some complex reason, which you will have to understand in order to use the language effectively. If the prohibition is for some arbitrary implementation reason, this makes the language itself difficult to understand. Considering what happens to class variables in the presence of inheritance is an interesting case.

In Eiffel, **once** routines can freely be redefined as non-once routines and vice versa.

In Java, instance variables may be redefined as class variables and vice versa. However, instance methods may not be redefined as class methods, and class methods may not be redefined as instance methods.

In C++, static member functions cannot be overloaded or virtual.

5

Type Extension: Inheritance and Virtuals

T ype extension can be done with two mechanisms: inheritance and genericity. In general inheritance implements *subtype polymorphism* and genericity implements *parametric polymorphism*. Together, these form the major mechanisms for reuse in OO. In this chapter we look at inheritance and how our different languages support it (chapter 6 will look at genericity).

When designing a system you are concerned with two ways of building things, *synthesis* and *analysis*. Analysis allows you to break a system down into its component parts. Synthesis allows you to construct a system from preexisting components.

Analysis is a top-down exercise, starting with the system as a whole and dividing it into its entities. Each of these entities may be further subdivided, and you continue until you have elements that are low level enough to run on your computer.

Synthesis is bottom up, allowing you to start with the low-level entities and assemble them until you have completed the entire system. Hopefully in the synthesis case, you will have higher-level elements to deal with than the lowest-level element; often these will be in the form of libraries, and libraries may be built on top of other libraries. Reuse is accomplished by synthesis and so is a bottom-up exercise—thus a significant aspect of OO design is bottom up.

The ideas of analysis and synthesis are borrowed from general philosophy, where one can make analytic and synthetic statements. The Monadology of Leibnitz states

> When a truth is necessary its reason can be found by analysis, by resolving it into simpler ideas and truths until you reach those which are primitive. It is in this way that mathematicians reduce speculative theorems and rules of practice by analysis to definitions, axioms, and postulates. In the end one has simple ideas which are indefinable. There are also axioms and postulates—in a word, primary principles—which cannot be proved and do not need to be either.

[Flew 89]

Frequently, arguments break out between those who believe that top down is the correct *pure* way to design systems and those who more pragmatically use some degree of bottom-up assembly. As with so many arguments in the computer industry, the arguments are spurious and often pushed with a degree of religious fervor—conflicts without cause. It should be realized that analysis and synthesis are two sides of the same coin. A good designer will know when each is applicable. This further shows that the division of the process into analysis and design is also wrong, as analysis is just a design technique.

Another important concept—abstraction—clarifies where analysis and synthesis should be used. Abstraction is the suppression of detail at any stage of the design process. In the early stages of a project, you are interested in looking at the broad picture to get an understanding of what a system will do overall. You do not want to be concerned with low-level data structures, let alone bits and bytes. It is also important to note that languages and compilers provide abstraction at a particular level. In the OO world, the concept of the library also provides an important level of abstraction. You should note that bits and bytes are themselves abstractions, albeit at a very low level. Abstraction is a very important technique in the specification of systems, and programmers should be well trained in the art of abstraction.

Abstraction is also an important element in the communication skills of technical people. A designer should be able to present information about a system in the abstract terms that the customers understand. Where abstractions must be introduced that the customer does not understand, the designer should be able to present a concise and accurate definition of the concept in question.

In the previous chapters, we saw how the elements of an OO system are defined. We also saw how, in designing a class, you define a calculus of operations for objects of that class. The current section examines some of the mechanisms that OO provides to manipulate those entities to define new entities. This in fact is synthesis of existing entities and should be defined by some kind of class or type

[PST 91] calculus. An example of such a calculus is the schema calculus of the Z specification language.

The main operations provided for class calculus are inheritance, aggregation, and genericity. As you can see these operations enable synthesis, but it is only because of this that a system can be analyzed into manageable pieces. Hence the reason for the earlier comment that analysis and synthesis and, therefore, top-down and bottom-up design are really the two sides of the same coin. Some authors would argue that more than just a simple form of relation is required and that this should be specialized into aggregation and association, aggregation being a strong relationship and association being a weaker relationship. The Unified Modeling Language (UML) is such a notation that makes distinctions, but no such complication is necessary, although it may be useful to bear in mind that, in the real world, the relations could be described as such. However, the distinction is best discarded as soon as it is discovered.

5.1 Basic Structures: Inheritance and Derived Classes

New classes can extend existing classes by inheritance. This is also known as class specialization, since the new facilities in the class apply only to a restricted set of members (in the set theory sense) of the original class. If you are familiar with the basic concepts of inheritance, you may skim or skip the next few sections.

Eiffel

The Eiffel syntax for inheritance is as follows:

```
EIFFEL
         Inheritance        ≜    inherit Parent_list
         Parent_list        ≜    { Parent ";" ... }
              Parent        ≜    Class_type [Feature_adaptation]
    Feature_adaptation      ≜    [Rename]
                                 [New_exports]
                                 [Undefine]
                                 [Redefine]
                                 [Select]
                                 end
```

As you can see, the Eiffel definition of inheritance is quite complex, giving the programmer a great deal of control over how a parent class is inherited. In contrast, as we shall see, inheritance is relatively simple in C++ and Java; however, the basic complexity of inheritance is still there and must be accommodated in other ways, which we shall soon see. As a preview, basically C++ introduces the complexity in extra operators in the executable statements themselves to remove ambiguity. Java avoids the whole issue by having only single inheritance for classes.

The examination of these differences is the main topic of this chapter. The discussion of the Eiffel inheritance mechanism will thus be proportionately longer in this section, but most of the rest of the chapter is devoted to an explanation of the C++ mechanisms for partially achieving the same effect. Java does not have these same mechanisms, and, if you accept that only single inheritance is necessary, then it does not need them. (I don't take this view; from my experience, the restriction to single inheritance significantly reduces some opportunities for reuse.)

First, you will notice that Eiffel has multiple inheritance because multiple parents can be inherited in the inheritance clause. For each parent you can optionally adapt each feature that you inherit in the Feature_adaptation part. The adaptations are renaming, changing export status, undefining, redefining, and selecting. A slight problem exists with the grammar here for compiler writers: since the feature adaptation is optional, and every part within the Feature_adaptation is optional except the **end**, a parser generator finds it difficult to determine whether an **end** at this point is the end of Feature_adaptation or the end of the surrounding class. For example, both of the following are valid according to the grammar:

    class *C*   *Eiffel*
        inherit
               P
    end

and

    class *C*   *Eiffel*
        inherit
               P
        end
    end

Basic Structures: Inheritance and Derived Classes

The grammar of the rename clause is as follows:

```
EIFFEL
         Rename        ≜   rename Rename_list
         Rename_list   ≜   { Rename_pair ";" ... }
         Rename_pair   ≜   Feature_name as Feature_name
```

You can use the rename clause to remove name clashes, or just to give a feature a more appropriate name in its new class. (In lambda calculus, renaming is known as alpha-abstraction).

The grammar of the New_exports clause is:

```
EIFFEL
         New_exports      ≜   export New_export_list
         New_export_list  ≜   { New_export_item ";" ... }
         New_export_item  ≜   Clients Feature_set
         Feature_set      ≜   Feature_list | all
         Feature_list     ≜   { Feature_name ";" ... }
         Clients          ≜   "{" { Class_name ";" ... } "}"
```

Basically, this syntax allows you to group a set of features inherited from the parent and reexport them to a set of classes. You must be careful with new exports if you make them more restrictive because this opens up a way to make invalid calls through a parent reference. Compilers can restrict this, though. We will discuss this in greater detail in section 9.6.

The grammar of the undefine clause is:

```
EIFFEL
         Undefine      ≜   undefine Feature_list
```

The undefine clause allows one or more inherited effective—that is, not deferred—features to be made deferred.

The grammar of the redefine clause is:

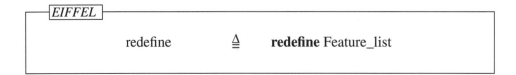

The redefine clause allows one or more inherited effective features to be redefined in the new class. It is Eiffel's way of flagging features as virtual except, unlike C++ where the designer of the base class must guess at virtual, Eiffel leaves this responsibility up to the designer of the new class. Java uses the final clause to flag that a member can no longer be virtual from that point in the inheritance chain down. This is an important point of difference, and the virtues are discussed later in this chapter in the section on virtual functions.

The grammar of the select clause is:

The select clause is a rather advanced feature, which allows the disambiguation of two distinct features from parent classes with the same name. Of course, one or both of them must have been renamed to remove the static ambiguity. This still leaves a dynamic ambiguity in that, if you call that feature via a parent reference attached to an object of the current class, the call must be directed to one or the other feature. The select clause allows the descendant class to decide which feature will be called.

Now, having made you wade through all that, it is time for an example to see how simple all this is, although we show a very complicated case, so you should not be scared off by this example.

Basic Structures: Inheritance and Derived Classes

Eiffel

```
class D
inherit
    A
        rename
            f1 as g1
        export
            {X, Y} p
            {NONE} h
        end
    B
        rename
            f1 as h1  -- f1 called via A or B will be ambiguous.
        export
            {ANY} all
        undefine
            u, v
        redefine
            r1, r2, r3
        select
            h1  -- call f1 from B
        end
    C
feature
    ...
end
```

Eiffel also allows direct repeated inheritance. For example:

Eiffel

```
class D
inherit
    A
        ...
    A
        ...
feature
    ...
end
```

C++

C++ uses the terms base class and derived class, whereas Eiffel uses the terms parent class and descendant class. The C++ grammar to specify inheritance is

---

C++

base-clause:
    : *base-specifier-list*

base-specifier-list:
    base-specifier
    base-specifier-list , *base-specifier*

base-specifier:
    ::$_{opt}$ *nested-name-specifier$_{opt}$ class-name*
    `virtual` *access-specifier$_{opt}$* ::$_{opt}$ *nested-name-specifier$_{opt}$ class-name*
    access-specifier `virtual`$_{opt}$ ::$_{opt}$ *nested-name-specifier$_{opt}$ class-name*

access-specifier:
    `private`
    `protected`
    `public`

As with Eiffel, C++ can inherit from multiple classes. C++ does not have so many options available for its *base-specifier*s. Some of the facilities available in Eiffel are done in other ways in C++, but there are things that you can do in Eiffel that you can't do at all in C++, for example, direct repeated inheritance. Eiffel also allows you to adapt things in the inheritance clause on a feature-by-feature basis, but you can't do this in C++. We will be saying more on this later in this chapter. As with Eiffel, C++ allows you to change the accessibility or export status of the members inherited from the base class. However, whereas Eiffel allows a fine-grained approach for each feature, C++ allows you to specify only `private`, `protected`, or `public`, which applies to every member of the base class.

Note that C++ uses the terminology of *base* class and *derived* class. The C++ ARM claims that the subclass and superclass were confusing. However, the terminology of base class is just as bad, as it could mean a class at the top of an inherit-

[C++ ARM] (chapter 10)

Basic Structures: Inheritance and Derived Classes

ance hierarchy. In fact, base class means any class that is inherited by a derived class, so a base class can itself be a derived class.

An example of C++ inheritance is:

C++

```
class D : public A, virtual public B {};
```

Java

Java inheritance is defined as:

Java

Super:
    `extends` *ClassType*

ClassType:
    TypeName

Interfaces:
    `implements` *InterfaceTypeList*

InterfaceTypeList:
    InterfaceType
    InterfaceTypeList , *InterfaceType*

InterfaceType:
    TypeName

An example of Java inheritance is

Java

```
class D extends A implements I, J {}
```

In Java, you can inherit from only one other class; however, you can implement multiple interfaces. Classes may have `abstract` methods, but interfaces are entities where all the methods are abstract.

A Java interface can also extend other interfaces.

Java

ExtendsInterfaces:
    `extends` *InterfaceType*
    ExtendsInterfaces , *InterfaceType*

InterfaceType:
    TypeName

5.2 The Nature of Inheritance

This section explains one of the key issues in our OO languages—the issue of inheritance. Inheritance seems a very simple idea—easy to understand at first—but turns out to have many subtleties. It is particularly important to use inheritance correctly to arrive at clean designs that are easy to modify and, if necessary, correct. Designs should not only be satisfying to the designer in some abstract sense, but must satisfy the pragmatic considerations of production code—that is modifiability.

You should particularly understand the issues in this section, and probably reread it after you have read other sections of this book. Understanding these issues will help you understand when to use inheritance for subtyping, or the *is-a* relationship; when to use inheritance for implementation, or a *non-is-a* relationship; when to prefer delegation to another object and when genericity is appropriate. This will help you arrive at good designs while maximizing reusability.

Maintaining Consistency

Inheritance is a close relationship providing a fundamental OO way to assemble software components, along with composition and genericity. Objects that are instances of a class are also instances of all ancestors of that class. For effective OO design, the consistency of this relationship should—for the most part—be preserved. Each redefinition in a subclass should be checked for consistency with the original definition in ancestor classes. A subclass should preserve the requirements of an ancestor class. Requirements that cannot be preserved indicate that there is a design error and that inheritance probably is not appropriate. Consistency due to inheritance is fundamental to OO design.

Implementation vs. Type Inheritance

We have two considerations when using inheritance: how do we relate types and how do we organize our classes to reuse code. The former is *type inheritance* and the latter *implementation inheritance*. Type inheritance is also known as interface, semantic, or behavioral inheritance. Implementation inheritance is also known as syntactic or code inheritance. It would be very satisfying if these two kinds of inheritance directly corresponded—unfortunately they don't.

An important property of type inheritance is *subsumption*. Subsumption means that if type B is a subtype of type A then an object of type B can be assigned to not only references of type B but also references of type A. You might also notice that here I have used the terminology type rather than class. This is because if a class B is a subclass of class A it is not necessarily a subtype of A and in that case an object of class B cannot be assigned by subsumption to a reference of class A.

Frequently, classes and types do correspond and features that are given an implementation in type A are reusable in a subtype B. This correspondence is very convenient and agrees with our first intuitions about the meaning of inheritance. However, types and classes don't always correspond and it is the cases where they don't correspond that cause the problems. As we mentioned, subtyping preserves our consistency constraints, but implementation inheritance does not necessarily preserve consistency and this is where the problems, and the many debates, arise.

Let us first look at a few views of what type and implementation inheritance are. Saake et al. classify implementation or syntactic inheritance and interface or semantic inheritance as follows:

[SJE 91] Syntactic inheritance denotes inheritance of structure or method definitions and is therefore related to the reuse of code (and to overriding of code for inherited methods). Semantic inheritance denotes inheritance of object semantics, i.e. of objects themselves. This kind of inheritance is known from semantic data models, where it is used to model one object that appears in several roles in an application.

Saake et al. concentrate on the semantic form of inheritance. Behavioral or semantic inheritance expresses the role of an object within a system.

[Wegner 91] (p. 43) Wegner believes code inheritance to be of more practical value. He classifies the difference between implementation and type inheritance as code and behavior hierarchies. Wegner suggests these are rarely compatible with each other and are often negatively correlated. Wegner also poses the question "How should modification of inherited attributes be constrained?" Code inheritance provides a basis for modularization. Behavioral inheritance provides modeling by the *is-a* relationship. Both are useful in their place. Both require consistency checks that combinations due to inheritance actually make sense.

Both forms of inheritance can be used effectively together. The semantic kind can be used to identify classification hierarchies. Such classification gives us hierarchies based on commonalities, and this gives us a basis for reuse. However, when we build the code, we often begin to find that classes that were not related by the classification hierarchy have very similar code. Instead of duplicating the code in different places, we want to take advantage of the reuse that implementation inheritance enables; thus we build new classes where the common code resides and inherit from them.

The new classes introduced might seem artificial, since they might not correspond to objects in the real world, but this is not much different from abstract classes. Some classes might merely be code respositories, with no real-world or domain equivalents. Such classes can be mixed in with inheritance where other classes need their code facilities. Such inheritance is known as *mix-in* inheritance. Because of this, true multiple inheritance, as we discuss later, is important.

So the design approach that I suggest is to use classification initially to identify a class hierarchy, but do not feel that this hierarchy is fixed during development; it should be changeable to suit practical needs of reuse. If we deny reuse because we are stuck to some rigid hierarchy suggested by some analyst, then inheritance achieves very little in practice. To be able to reuse code, small classes would be best and can be mixed together with multiple inheritance.

So, what is the design of the entire system—the analyst's design hierarchy or the actual code hierarchy? The answer is simple—it is the code hierarchy, because this is what must be maintained. This is why integrated tools that can produce class hierarchy diagrams from program source are important.

Meyer has also produced a classification of inheritance techniques. In his *taxonomy* he identifies 12 uses of inheritance, all of which he finds useful. The 12 inheritance types Meyer divides into three broad categories: model inheritance, software inheritance, and variation inheritance. Model and software correspond to the two main categories of behavioral and code inheritance, and variation can apply to both. This analysis also gives a good idea of when inheritance can be used and when it should not. In fact the concept of the library preceded Eiffel as a project to reclassify and produce a taxonomy of all common structures used in computer science.

[Meyer 96, 97 (Chapter 24)]

[Meyer 94]

Software components are like jigsaw puzzle pieces. When assembling a jigsaw puzzle, the shape of the pieces must fit, but, more important, the resulting picture must make sense. Assembling software components is more difficult. A jigsaw puzzle is reassembling a picture that was complete before. Assembling software components is building a picture that has never been seen before. What is worse is that often the software jigsaw puzzle pieces are made by different programmers, so, when the whole system is assembled, the pictures must fit.

Some examples will help clarify this section. First, when types and classes correspond, we have great opportunities for reuse. An example is *HEIGHT*s and *WEIGHT*s. Since they are different types of measurement they cannot be assigned to each other. *HEIGHT*s and *WEIGHT*s have many common properties and we would waste opportunities for reuse if we implemented these two types entirely separately—after all, *HEIGHT*s and *WEIGHT*s are both examples of *REAL* numbers. We can thus reuse the properties of the *REAL* type for both *HEIGHT*s and *WEIGHT*s. We can also assign *HEIGHT*s and *WEIGHT*s to elements of type *REAL*, but we cannot assign *HEIGHT*s to *WEIGHT*s and vice versa and therefore, not *REAL*s to *HEIGHT*s or *WEIGHT*s. In such simple examples, type and implementation inheritance conveniently correspond.

A more complex example comes from the Eiffel Container library. In this example one particular *STACK* implementation is based on an *ARRAY* as shown in figure 5-1.

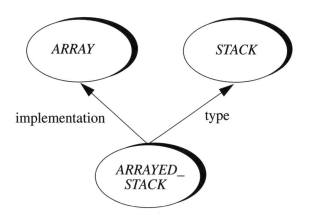

Figure 5-1. *STACK* **implementation**

In the design of the Eiffel library, the class *ARRAYED_STACK* makes heavy use of the implementation of an *ARRAY*. (This is a slight simplification in this presentation because *ARRAYED_STACK* inherits *ARRAYED_LIST* which inherits *ARRAY*.) However, *ARRAYED_STACK* also hides the details of an *ARRAY* that are irrelevant for *STACK*s. This means that we should not assign *ARRAYED_STACK* objects to *ARRAY*s by subsumption because some of the *ARRAY* operations are no longer appropriate for *STACK*s. The problem is that with Eiffel's type system, we can assign by subsumption *ARRAYED_STACK* objects to *ARRAY* references. We can thus treat *ARRAYED_STACK* objects like *ARRAY*s and this is wrong. This problem has come about because some of the features of *ARRAY* have been hidden—hiding features means we have used implementation inheritance since we have broken the subtype relationship.

In Eiffel, programmers can use a convention to sidestep this issue. This is to declare references only to abstract types and not to implementation types. You can use a special form of the creation instruction to attach an actual object to an abstract reference:

s: *STACK* *Eiffel*

! *ARRAYED_STACK* ! *s.make*

With this code, you cannot inadvertently assign a stack object to an array (except by willfully doing so with an assignment attempt). Unfortunately, the compiler will not force you to use this scheme. This is also flexible design because, if you find that the *ARRAYED_STACK* implementation is not appropriate for any reason, you can change the implementation by changing the creation instruction and that is the only change that is needed.

C++ does distinguish type and implementation inheritance. To create a subtype hierarchy you use `public` inheritance. To use implementation inheritance you use `protected` or `private` inheritance. `private` inheritance is the default, since if you do not specify `public`, `protected`, or `private`, you get `private` inheritance. A C++ compiler will not allow you to assign an object of a subclass to a reference of a base class and so avoids the typing problems we have in Eiffel. You should note that C++ makes you decide whether you want to treat the entire base class as implementation or type inheritance. Eiffel allows you to do this on a feature-by-feature basis so some aspects of inheritance from a parent may be type inheritance, whereas some features may be inherited for their implementation. (I love you for your body, not your mind.) This means that if you do assign a subclass to a reference of a parent type, you really want to prevent usage of those implementation features. This is the basis for the catcall proposal to solve these problems in Eiffel.

As we shall see in chapter 7 on interfaces and access control, Eiffel provides a very fine grained means of specifying feature export to other classes. This is based on the fact that what should be hidden from some classes as implementation detail may be accessible to others as interface. In C++ you have an all or none situation, except for the case of *friends*.

Java precludes the hiding in descendants problem because you cannot make members more private than in their parent classes. Java distinguishes between type inheritance and implementation inheritance by using interfaces for types and classes for implementation, although since you can neither redefine arguments covariantly nor hide parent features, the subtype relationship of a subclass to its parent is preserved. You can use multiple inheritance with interfaces but not with classes. Java's distinction between interfaces as types and classes could prove to be artificial and too restrictive. In practice it would probably be better to be able to multiply inherit code than be able to use subsumption up multiple branches of a type hierarchy. Since Java does not have genericity, this is not that useful anyway. If we ignore the multiple inheritance issue, Java's type system proves inflexible for applications of reasonable sophistication. We look at these issues further in signature variance in chapter 9.

From the point of view of type vs. implementation inheritance, Java takes the opposite path to Eiffel and C++. Eiffel and C++ allow multiple paths for code inheritance. Eiffel uses one mechanism for both and therefore you cannot distinguish when a subclass is not a subtype. In C++, you can distinguish between implementation and type inheritance. Java separates the two kinds of inheritance, but this prevents you introducing code at appropriate places in the type hierarchy—even where the subtype relationship would be preserved—because interfaces cannot have any implementation. Eiffel is too flexible and Java is too restrictive, and in this regard, C++ seems to have taken the correct middle ground, although the concepts are obscured by the nature of C++. Java's restrictions coupled with lack of multiple inheritance, genericity, and covariance makes Java very difficult to use to design clean class hierarchies with maximum code reuse. You will find the particular symptoms of this are tending to use `Object` where a more specific type is preferable, particularly in containers, and then plenty of casts to restore the type.

5.3 Multiple Inheritance

Both Eiffel and C++ provide multiple inheritance. Sun claims it results in many problems so, Java provides it in a restricted form. Instead Java provides *interfaces*, which are similar to Objective C's protocols. Sun claims interfaces provide all the desirable features of multiple inheritance. Java interfaces provide semantic multiple inheritance, or types, but not multiple inheritance of code, which as Wegner points out is of more practical value. We should note here that the problems described in the previous section about implementation inheritance do not require multiple inheritance, but will occur in single inheritance.

Sun's claim that multiple inheritance results in problems is true. What seems like a simple generalization of inheriting from multiple classes instead of just one, turns out to be nontrivial. For example, what should the policy be if you inherit items of the same name from two or more classes? Are they compatible? If so should they be merged into a single entity? If not, how do you disambiguate them? And so the list goes on.

Java Interfaces

Java's interface mechanism implements multiple inheritance, with one important difference: the inherited interfaces must be abstract. This does obviate the need to choose between different implementations, because with interfaces there are no implementations. Java allows the declaration of constant fields in an interface. Where these are multiply inherited, they merge to form one entity so that no ambiguity arises, but what happens if the constants have different values?

Mixins

Since Java does not have multiple inheritance, you cannot do *mixins* as you can in C++ and Eiffel. Mixin is the ability to inherit sets of nonabstract routines from different classes to build a new complex class. That is, mixin allows you to inherit useful features, such as utility routines, from different source classes. The concept of mixin comes from a coding technique used in CLOS.

Mixins actually have no formal definition in CLOS; they are just a coding convention, an idiom, or a pattern. Using mixins in CLOS, certain properties of entities can be extracted from subclasses.

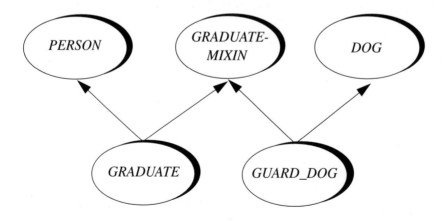

Figure 5-2. Mixin example hierarchy

[Bracha and Cook 90]

The original paper on *Mixin-based Inheritance* gives the definition: "A mixin is an abstract subclass that may be used to specialize the behavior of a variety of parent classes." The example is when the concept of graduate is removed from a class. It can then be applied to several classes as in the class hierarchy shown in figure 5-2.

Here the graduate properties have been extracted out of the *GRADUATE* class itself, and the attributes and routines to do with this property entered into its own class. This class can then be used in different ways and mixed into the *GUARD_DOG* class.

A special case of the mixin concept that has been adopted in widespread practice is to mixin utility routines. When used in the sense of mixing in utility routines, mixin classes are the exact opposite of Java interfaces: mixins provide code, but add nothing to the interface of the inheriting class since the routines inherited are not exported and are for use only in the inheriting class. In most cases, you don't need to be as pure as this; therefore, a mixin class could have some interface. On the other hand, forcing interfaces to provide no code at all is similarly restrictive. The extremes between pure mixins and interfaces are shown in figure 5-3.

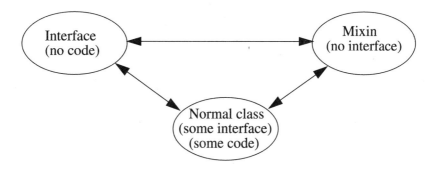

Figure 5-3. Interfaces vs. mixins

In Eiffel all routines must be encapsulated in objects, so the mixin facility is more important than in C++, where functions may be stand alone. Thus, as a pure OO language like Eiffel, Java would do well with mixins. However, Smalltalk is also a pure OO language that has only single inheritance. Here common methods are put in supplier classes, so as with many things mixins are a matter of convenience, not necessity.

Java's interface inheritance is just that—interfaces only, not implementation. For example, you might want to import utility routines from a number of different sources. However, you can achieve the same effect using composition instead of inheritance, so this is probably not a great minus against Java.

Abstract vs. Default

A common consideration in designing an abstract interface is whether you want a routine to be deferred and, therefore, forced to be provided by all inheriting concrete classes, or whether you want to provide some default behavior—typically *do nothing*—and therefore not have to reimplement in descendants unless really necessary. Java's interfaces preclude this. However, Java does have a way of doing this, albeit a bit messy, with inner classes, which we shall examine in section 5.5.

Single vs. Multiple Inheritance

Some feel that single inheritance is elegant by itself, but that multiple inheritance is not.

BETA falls into the "multiple inheritance is inelegant" category: "BETA does not have multiple inheritance, due to the lack of a profound theoretical understanding, and also because the current proposals seem technically very complicated." They cite Flavors as a language that mixes classes together, where, according to Madsen, the order of inheritance matters; that is, inheriting (A, B) is different from inheriting (B, A). The order of inheritance is also important when using mixins with CLOS, as the inheritance order defines the order that mixin routines will be called. [Madsen 93]

Ada 95 is also a language that avoids multiple inheritance. Ada 95 supports single inheritance as the *tagged type extension*.

Others feel that multiple inheritance can provide elegant solutions to particular modeling problems and so is worth the effort. In fact, any design technique can be misused and result in horrendous designs, even single inheritance, but that is no reason to prohibit use, particularly as multiple inheritance can be very useful in software development. Although the above list of questions arising from multiple inheritance is not complete, it shows that the problems with multiple inheritance can be systematically identified. Once the problems are recognized, they can be solved elegantly. While Sakkinen goes into the problems of multiple inheritance in great depth, he defends it. [Sakkinen 92]

Cardelli is also an advocate of multiple inheritance. He writes:

> A class can sometimes be considered a subclass of two incompatible superclasses; then an arbitrary decision has to be made to determine which superclass to use. This problem leads naturally to the idea of multiple inheritance. [Cardelli 88]

Multiple Inheritance

Multiple inheritance occurs when an object can belong to several incomparable superclasses: the subclass relation is no longer constrained to form a tree, but can form a dag. Multiple inheritance is more elegant than simple inheritance in describing class hierarchies, but it is more difficult to implement.

As Cardelli points out, if you come across a case where multiple inheritance is natural, but you have to model it with single inheritance, you must make an arbitrary choice as to which class is used for inheritance and which class or classes get used in other ways. The alternatives are in fact more ugly than multiple inheritance.

Cardelli gives a simple example of where multiple inheritance is natural:

ANY: { }
OBJECT: {*age*: *int*}
VEHICLE: {*age*: *int*, *speed*: *int*}
MACHINE: {*age*: *int*, *fuel*: *string*}
CAR: {*age*: *int*, *speed*: *int*, *fuel*: *string*}

Put another way:

    CAR: *VEHICLE* **and** *MACHINE*

Yet another way:

    MACHINE: *CAR* **ignoring** *SPEED*
    VEHICLE: *CAR* **ignoring** *FUEL*

Here car is naturally a descendant of both machine and vehicle. Cardelli shows that multiple inheritance can be given an elegant mathematical treatment, so those who claim that multiple inheritance lacks a theoretical and mathematical foundation are themselves unfounded.

Resolving Ambiguities

Eiffel has taken the approach that multiple inheritance poses some interesting and challenging problems, but that it rises to the challenge and solves them elegantly. Nor does the order of inheritance matter. All resolutions that the programmer must specify are given in the inheritance clause of a class. This includes *renaming* to ensure that multiple features inherited with the same name end up as multiple features with unambiguous names, *redefining*, new *export* policies for inherited features, *undefining*, and disambiguating with *select*. In all cases, the action taken by the compiler, whether using fork or join semantics, is made clear, and the programmer has complete control.

C++ has a different disambiguation mechanism from Eiffel. In Eiffel, one or both of the features must be given a different name in the renames clause. In C++ the members must be disambiguated using the *scope resolution operator* "::". The advantage of the Eiffel approach is that the ambiguity is dealt with declaratively in one place. Eiffel's inheritance clause is considerably more complex than C++'s, but the code is considerably simpler, more robust, and flexible, which is the advantage of the declarative approach over the operator approach. In C++, you must use the scope resolution operator in the code every time you run into an ambiguity problem between two or more members. This clutters the code and makes it less malleable, as when anything is modified that affects the ambiguity, you potentially have to change the code everywhere the ambiguity occurs.

A further problem with the scope resolution operator is that it overrides `virtual`. When you use the scope resolution operator, it calls exactly the function from the class nominated. If this function is virtual and you have an object of a derived class where the function has been redefined, scope resolution means that this function will not be called. For example:

[CD2 96]
10.3 (12)

C++

```
class B
{
public:
    virtual void f();
};

class C
{
public:
    virtual void f();
};

class D:
    public B,
    public C
{
    ...
};
```

Multiple Inheritance

```
class E:
    public D
{
public:
    E () {};
    virtual void f();
};

E *e = new E ();
e->f();        // calls E::f
e->B::f();     // calls B::f
e->C::f();     // calls C::f
```

[CD2 96]
(section 10)

If you want to redefine both versions of f in E that you have inherited from B and C, you can't. This reduces the flexibility of C++, but it could easily be fixed if renaming was adopted. CD2 covers the many and complex combinations of function calls. It shows that all the complexities of access mechanisms are put to the programmer to sort out. Java avoids this complexity by not having the virtual/nonvirtual distinction and not having expanded types. Eiffel also does not have the virtual/nonvirtual distinction, but, in Eiffel's case, the access mechanisms are only of interest to a compiler writer, and the complexity is masked from the programmer.

[Stroustrup 94]
(12.8)

The ANSI committee considered renaming, but the suggestion was blocked by one member who insisted that the rest of the committee go away and think about it for two weeks. Stroustrup's example shows how the effect of renaming is achieved, without explicit renaming. The problem is, since it took this group of experts two weeks to work this out, what chance is there for the rest of us? The above example can be fixed with the introduction of some extra classes.

C++

```
class BB:
    public B
{
public:
    virtual void B_f() = 0;
    virtual void f() { B_f; }
};

class CC:
    public C
```

```
{
public:
    virtual void C_f() = 0;
    virtual void f() { C_f; }
};

class D:
    public BB,
    public CC
{
public:
    virtual void B_f();
    virtual void C_f();
};
```

This has now introduced a couple of artificial implementation classes just to take care of the simple renaming case. As can be seen, once examples get beyond the basics, C++ becomes considerably more verbose and difficult to understand than Eiffel. The scope resolution operator also adds to C++'s verbosity, but in a way that is at the same time both verbose and cryptic.

The scope resolution operator is used for more than just multiple inheritance disambiguation. Since ambiguities could be avoided by cleaner language design, the scope resolution operator is an ugly complication. Meyers gives more examples of the ambiguity mess in C++ and the problems caused by combinations of libraries that are not really solved by the scope resolution operator. The simple ability to rename removes all this complexity. [Meyers 92] (item 26)

The question of whether the order of declaration of multiple parents matters in C++ is complex. It does affect the order in which constructors are called.

Direct Repeated Inheritance

Another difference between C++ and Eiffel is direct repeated inheritance. Eiffel allows

    class *B* inherit *A*, *A* end *Eiffel*

but

```
    class B : public A, public A {  };
```
not C++

is disallowed in C++.

Further Reflections

Some further reflections can be made on this topic. Multiple inheritance raises some very complex issues. Eiffel handles these issues well, and, while the form of the inheritance clause is complex, this is necessary due to the complexities of multiple inheritance. C++ does not handle these complexities nearly so cleanly.

Some people prefer to avoid the complexity of multiple inheritance by admitting only single inheritance. There is some truth in this position, and it is generally a good thing to restrict design and classification hierarchies to single inheritance, although good examples exist of semantic multiple inheritance. Single inheritance is just a special case of multiple inheritance. Thus a language with multiple inheritance can be used very effectively to implement single inheritance classification hierarchies, and some of the multiple inheritance features, such as renaming, will be of great benefit. The rule should be to keep inheritance hierarchies as simple as possible and to use multiple inheritance only where there is good cause.

Java uses an in-between scheme of single inheritance for classes and multiple inheritance for interfaces and types. Like single inheritance, this is a special case of multiple inheritance. If you believe this is the solution to your inheritance structuring problems, you can do this in C++ and Eiffel by restricting interface classes to have only pure virtual or deferred routines. However, you will probably find this too great a restriction; once you relate interfaces to classes in this way, you will probably find that the natural place to put common implementations of routines is in the interfaces themselves to avoid duplicating implementations in subclasses. In this case we are back to general multiple inheritance, and probably no one will seriously suggest that you adopt such a convention.

5.4 Virtual Classes (C++)

Used in the context of a class, the keyword `virtual` has a different meaning than it does when used in the context of a function. With a class it means that multiply inherited features are merged; with a function it means polymorphism. Virtual class does not mean that members in the class are all polymorphic. In fact, the two uses of virtual really mean the opposite of each other: virtual functions mean that there could be more than one function; virtual classes mean that, if the class is multiply inherited, you get only a single copy.

C++ saves on keywords by overloading one keyword in several contexts, even though the uses have different or even opposite meanings. Static is another case that is used in three different contexts. Measuring language complexity by counting keywords does not prove that C++ is a small noncomplex language; fewer keywords have made C++ more complex and confusing.

So what do virtual classes do? If class D multiply inherits class A via classes B and C, then if D wants to inherit only a single shared copy of A, the inheritance of A must be specified as `virtual` in both B and C. The need for virtual base classes arises because a common ancestor has been inherited via two or more paths in the inheritance graph. A term coined for this is *diamond inheritance*, and because of the complications in C++ that result from diamond inheritance it is the advice of several C++ authors to avoid it. For example Meyers warns "it is certainly true that a diamond-shaped inheritance hierarchy such as this is *not* very friendly." And "[in the example] it's no accident that the dreaded diamond-shaped inheritance graph is conspicuously absent." [Meyers 92] (item 43)

Diamond inheritance is, however, a natural design for many applications, so C++ programmers could very well be avoiding something that is natural in the modeling domain because it is badly handled in the language domain. Eiffel shows that diamond inheritance can be provided elegantly, with none of the self-inflicted problems of C++. In Eiffel terminology, diamond inheritance is called *repeated inheritance*. Where diamond inheritance is discouraged in C++, repeated inheritance is encouraged in Eiffel.

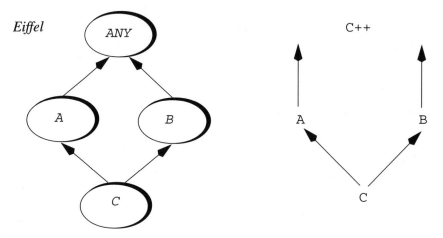

Figure 5-4. A multiple inheritance graph (Eiffel and C++)

Also, in Eiffel, diamond inheritance always results from multiple inheritance, since every class inherits from *ANY*. C++, however, has no root object, so diamond inheritance does not always result from multiple inheritance. Java has the class `Object` at the root of its single code inheritance tree, but not at the root of the interface tree. Figure 5-4 shows a multiple inheritance graph with a class *C* inheriting from *A* and *B* in Eiffel and C++.

C++ virtual classes raise two questions. First, what happens if A is declared `virtual` in only one of B or C? The answer is that any inheritance path where `virtual` is not specified results in a duplicate copy. Second, what if another class E wants to inherit multiple copies of A via B and C? In C++, the virtual class decision must be made early, reducing the flexibility that might be required in the assembly of derived classes. In a shared software environment different vendors might supply classes B and C. Even if a single programmer produces B and C, he or she might not guess that another programmer will in the future merge them together again in class D. Thus the programmer of B and C has to be clairvoyant in order to predict that class D will later be invented. It should be left to the implementer of class D or E exactly how to resolve this problem. And this is the simplest case: what if A is inherited via more than two paths, with more than two levels of inheritance? Flexibility is key to reusable software. You cannot envisage when designing a base class all the possible uses in derived classes, and attempting to do so considerably complicates design.

Another complication arises with virtual base classes: that is, if A has a function `f`, and `f` is redefined in B, but not in C, then, if A is a nonvirtual base, an ambiguity arises if you try to call `f` in D. However, if A is a virtual base class, then when you call `f` in D, `B::f` is called. In this case `B::f` *dominates* the definition in A.

Since Java has no multiple inheritance, there is no problem to be solved here.

The Eiffel mechanism allows two classes *D* and *E* inheriting multiple copies of *A* to inherit *A* in the appropriate way independently. You do not have to choose in intermediate classes whether *A* is virtual, i.e., inherited as a single copy, or not. The inheritance is more flexible and done on a feature-by-feature basis, and each feature from *A* will either fork, in which case it becomes two new features, or join, in which case there is only one resultant feature. The programmer of each descendant class can decide whether it is appropriate to fork or join each feature independent of the other descendants or any policy in *A*.

The fine-grained approach of Eiffel is a significant benefit over C++. While the Eiffel approach is more sophisticated and flexible, the syntax is simpler and the concepts easier to understand.

[Meyers 92] (item 43)   Meyers also explains many of the complications of multiple inheritance and virtual base classes. He suggests, "Perhaps you are convinced that no one in their right mind would ever use it [multiple inheritance]." And "Bear in mind that the designer of C++ didn't set out to make multiple inheritance hard to use, it just turned out that making all the pieces work together in a more or less reasonable fashion inherently entailed the introduction of certain complexities." The implementations of multiple inheritance are perhaps the largest difference between Eiffel and C++ (and Java, which doesn't have multiple inheritance). C++ added multiple inheritance into the language at a late stage. However, multiple inheritance was designed into Eiffel at the beginning. While multiple inheritance is a concept with many complexities, Eiffel's implementation is reasonably straightforward in handling the complexities, while C++ results in many tricky problems.

5.5 Nested Classes (Java and C++)

Simula provided textually nested classes similar to nested procedures in ALGOL. Textual (syntactic) nesting should not be confused with semantic nesting, nor should static modeling be confused with dynamic run-time nesting—do not confuse nested objects with nested classes. The classic example of this confusion is saying that a car contains an engine and four wheels, so you need nested classes to model this. Conceptually, wheels, engines, and cars are separate. You will find that car designers can design engines and wheels independent from the car itself. Thus the *definition* of these entities can be separate, even though, when the real object is assembled, they are part of the one unit. Modeling concerns certainly do not justify nested classes.

As we have already noted, complex systems can be built mathematically by defining the entities we are working with and specifying the operations that compose these entities into more complex entities. The very power of the technique derives from having a few simple kinds of entity and powerful composition operations. Nested classes result in complex entities where it is impossible to further compose the subclasses, so they are not in keeping with simple and powerful mathematical systems. Eiffel derives its power from considering only classes as entities and by using inheritance (*is-a*) and composition (*has-a*, *related-to*, *part-of*) as the composition operations.

This is rather like relational databases where the only entity is the relation, and the relational calculus provides operations to combine entities and relations in powerful ways, without nesting. Although other database paradigms exist, the added complexity does not result in enhanced power to combine existing objects into other objects; in fact, the nesting introduced in other database paradigms reduces this power and flexibility. Nested classes do the same in OO languages.

Modeling is done in the semantic domain, and should be divorced from syntax; you do not need textually nested classes to have nested objects. Nested classes are contrary to good OO design and to the free spirit of OO decomposition, where classes should be loosely coupled to support software reusability.

Instead of tightly coupled environments (shown in figure 5-5),

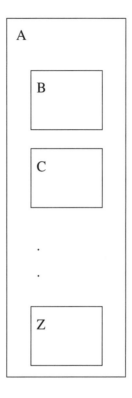

Figure 5-5. Tightly coupled environment

you should decouple depending on the modeling requirements. The decoupled environments shown in figure 5-6 are a more flexible arrangement, both in terms of modeling and program maintenance.

There are two problems with nested classes. First, the inner class is dependent on the outer class, so is not reusable, which is not good OO design, where classes are independent. Second, the inner class has access to the implementation of the outer class, so implementation hiding is violated. Where access to a class implementation is needed, you should use inheritance, but note that this models the *is-a* relationship, not the component-of relationship of nested classes. In fact, nested classes reintroduce a global variable mechanism back into the language: you can structure a whole program with one global object within which nested classes have access to all its internals. We discuss in this book why this is not a good structure and why readmitting such global-like variables into a language with nested classes seems a backward step.

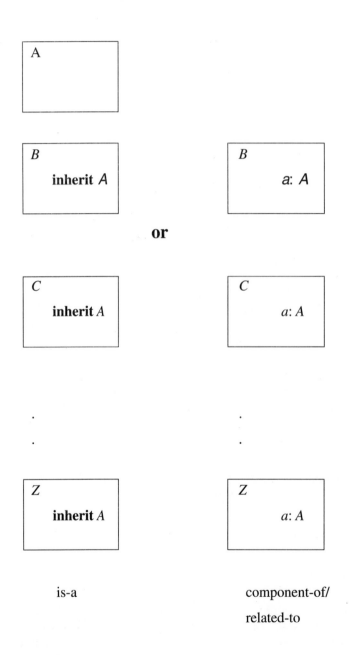

Figure 5-6. Decoupled environment

Semantic nesting is achieved independent of textual nesting. In OO design all objects should interact only via well-defined interfaces, but objects of a class that is textually nested in another class have access to the outer object without the benefit of a clean interface. C avoided the complexity of nested functions, but C++ has chosen to implement this complexity for classes, which is of less use than nested functions.

Pascal and ALGOL programmers sometimes use nested procedures in order to group things together, but this is not necessary. If you want to use a nested procedure in another environment, you have to dig it out of where it is and make it global, which is a maintenance problem. If the procedure uses locals from the outer environment, you have more problems. You will have to change these to parameters, which is a cleaner approach anyway, and you will probably have to unindent all the text by one or more levels. Textually nested classes have worse problems.

Semantically, OOP achieves nesting in two ways—by inheritance and OO composition. Modeling nesting is achieved without tight textual coupling. Thinking about our car example again, in the real world the engine is embedded in the car, but in OO modeling embedding is modeled without textual nesting. Both car and engine are separate classes; the car contains a reference to an engine object. This allows the vehicle and engine hierarchy to be independently defined. Engine is derived independently into gasoline, diesel, and electric engines. This is simpler, cleaner, and more flexible than having to define a gasoline-engine car, a diesel-engine car, etc., which you have to do if you textually nest the engine class in the car. In the real world you can change the car's engine, so it does not make sense to tightly couple the car and the engine. You can find further insights into how to achieve semantic nesting in the work of Clarke, Potter, and Noble.

[CPN 98]

In C++, classes can be nested not only within other classes, but also within functions, thereby tightly coupling a class to a function. This confuses class definition with object declaration. The class is the fundamental structure in OO programming, and nothing has existence separate from a class (including globals).

[Madsen 93] (chapter 18)

Object-Oriented Programming in the BETA Programming Language provides very good insights into modeling; classification and composition are the means to organize complexity in terms of hierarchies. This enumerates four kinds of composition—whole-part composition, reference composition, localization, and concept composition. Madsen says these are not altogether independent since one composition relationship could fall into two or more categories. Whole-part composition models our car example, where the engine is part of the car. Reference composition is illustrated by a person making a hotel reservation—the person is not a part of the reservation, but the reservation references the person. You can consult [Madsen 93] for definitions of localization and concept composition.

Because examples can be given of composition that can be modeled in terms of more than one of the categories of composition, it is better not to provide direct modeling of this in the programming language; your opinion might change later. BETA does have mechanisms for modeling the whole-part composition as embedded objects and reference as references. However, this is quite different from textual nesting. There is no real need to support these different categories in your programming language. It is more important for the analyst to be cognizant of these different flavors so that he or she can recognize different kinds of composition in the problem domain.

We will visit this topic again in chapter 7.

Nested and Inner Classes in Java

First, we should introduce some Java terminology. Java defines a nested class as a class that is a member of another class. Java has two kinds of nested class: the static nested class and the nonstatic nested class. A nonstatic nested class is also known as an *inner* class.

As we saw when we considered Java interfaces, you cannot provide default methods with interfaces; all methods are abstract and must be implemented by any class that implements the interface. An example is the `MouseListener` interface. `MouseListener` provides five abstract method definitions as follows: `mouseClicked`, `mousePressed`, `mouseReleased`, `mouseEntered`, and `mouseExited`. Every class that implements `MouseListener` will have to provide its own implementations of these, even though they will usually be *do nothings*.

Java's solution to this is to use *adapter* classes with inner classes. Do nothing defaults for `MouseListener` are implemented in the class `MouseAdapter`

```
public abstract class MouseAdapter                           Java
    implements MouseListener
{
    public void mouseClicked (MouseEvent e) {}
    public void mousePressed (MouseEvent e) {}
    public void mouseReleased (MouseEvent e) {}
    public void mouseEntered (MouseEvent e) {}
    public void mouseExited (MouseEvent e) {}
}
```

To use this, you generally can't inherit it, because your single opportunity to use the `extends` clause will be needed for inheritance from some other class. You instead use an inner class

Java
```
public class MyApplet extends Applet
{
    class MyMouseAdapter extends MouseAdapter
    {
        public void mousePressed (MouseEvent e)
        {
            clickPoint = e.getPoint ();
            repaint ();
        }
    }
}
```

You can also use an *anonymous* method

Java
```
public class MyApplet extends Applet
{
    class void init ()
    {
        addMouseListener
        (
            new MouseAdapter ()
            {
                public void mousePressed (MouseEvent e)
                {
                    clickPoint = e.getPoint ();
                    repaint ();
                }
            }
        );
    }
}
```

You might observe that this is syntactically a very messy way to achieve default behaviors via an adapter class, which is very simply and elegantly provided by multiple inheritance.

For this purpose, inner and adapter classes have nothing to offer over a language with fully-fledged multiple inheritance. Indeed, Java might have chosen to avoid the complication of multiple inheritance, but the mechanism to replace it is even more complicated.

5.6 Polymorphism and Inheritance

Inheritance provides a textually decoupled form of subblock. The scope of a name is the class in which it occurs. If a name occurs twice in a class, it should be a syntax error. Inheritance introduces some questions over and above this simple consideration of scope. Should a name declared in a base class be in scope in a derived class? There are three choices.

1. Names are in scope only in the immediate class, not in subclasses. Subclasses can freely reuse names because there is no potential for a clash. This precludes software reusability. Since subclasses will not inherit definitions of implementation, this case is not worth considering.

2. The name is in scope in a subclass, but the name can be overloaded without restriction. This is closest to the overloading of names in nested blocks. This is C++'s approach. Two problems arise: first, the name can be reused so the inherited entity is unintentionally hidden; second, because the new entity is not assumed to have any relationship to the original, its signature cannot be type checked with the original entity. Since consistency checks between the superclass and subclass are not possible, the tight relationship that inheritance implies, which is fundamental to OO design, is not enforced. This can lead to inconsistencies between the abstract definition of a base class and the implementation of a derived class. If the derived class does not conform to the base class in this way, it should be questioned why the derived class is inheriting from the base class in the first place. (See the nature of inheritance discussion earlier in this chapter.)

3. The name is in scope in the subclass, but can be overridden only in a disciplined way to provide a specialization of the original. Other uses of the name are reported as duplicate name errors. This form of overriding in a subclass ensures that the entity referred to in the subclass is closely related to the entity in the ancestor class. This helps ensure design consistency. The relationship of name scope is not symmetric. Names in a subclass are not in scope in a superclass (although this is not the case in dynamically typed languages such as Smalltalk). In order to provide consistent customization of reusable software components, the same name should be used only when explicitly redefining the original entity. The programmer of the descendant class should indicate that this is not a syntax error due to a duplicate name, but that redefinition is intended

(we suggest the keyword `override` in the section on virtuals). This choice ensures that the resultant class is constructed logically. This might seem restrictive, but is analogous to strong typing, and it makes inheritance a much more powerful concept.

5.7 Union

At last we come to union, which we postponed from chapter 2 on basic entities. C++ treats union as a basic concept along with classes and structs, even though the use of union is discouraged. We take the view that union is actually a type extension mechanism, closely related to inheritance. Union is an important concept in type theory, but, given a good inheritance scheme, union is not needed in OOP. In this section, we will first take a look at the C/C++ union construct. While union is a useful low-level C construct, its power is limited compared to a conceptual type union.

C-style Union

Similar constructs in other languages are recognized as problematic—for example, FORTRAN's equivalences, COBOL's REDEFINES, and Pascal's variant records. Unions can be used in two ways. The first is simply to reuse the same memory for different data items at different times. The second is to view the same data with different interpretations or types, rather like a type cast. This use of C unions can be very useful in low-level routines, for example, when reading data from a stream file. Several bytes can be read into a `char` field and retrieved from a union type as a different type. For example:

C++
```
union
{
    char [8] c;
    double d;
}
```

When used to overload memory space, unions force the programmer to think about memory allocation. Recursive languages use a stack mechanism that makes overloading memory space unnecessary because it is allocated and deallocated automatically for locals when procedures are entered and exited. The compiler and run-time system automatically allocate and deallocate storage as required, ensuring that two pieces of data never clash for the same memory space at one time. The identifiers that the programmer users are automatically bound to those physical memory locations at run time. This is essential so that the programmer can concentrate on the problem domain, rather than on machine-oriented details.

In OO systems, garbage collection is used to automatically deallocate objects, so the same physical memory can be reused. In fact, if machines had an infinite amount of memory (which actually would consume every atom in the universe and more!), the computing problem would be very different. Structures such as stacks would be almost unnecessary when used for storage recycling; in fact, this is why the Turing machine model of a processor with infinite memory is interesting. Garbage collection, as we shall see, is a mechanism that makes memory seem infinite because you don't ever have to worry about explicitly deallocating things—you just keep allocating them.

When union is used in a way similar to FORTRAN equivalences, it is not needed. Union is also not needed to provide the equivalent to COBOL REDEFINEs or Pascal variant types. Inheritance and polymorphism provide this in OOP. A reference to a superclass can also be used to refer to any subclass, thus providing the same semantics as union, only in a type-safe manner since the alternatives can never be confused. An object reference is implicitly a union of all subclasses.

Union can also be used to suppress type checking. Stroustrup says that "programmers should know that unions and unchecked function arguments are inherently dangerous, should be avoided whenever possible, and should be handled with special care when actually needed." [Stroustrup 9 (14.3.4.1)]

Sun recognizes that the union construct is unnecessary and has removed it from Java. No equivalent exists in Eiffel.

Union in Type Theory

The concept of union also exists in type theory, but this is different from the C union. In type theory, you can declare one container or reference that can take several different types. The type checker in a compiler can check that only objects of the declared types are assigned to the reference. It is more difficult to ensure that any operations applied to the reference are valid for the particular object attached at the time.

An example of a union type is given as follows where we declare a single entity to possibly take several types

    multi_type: {*I, J, K*} -- Hypothetical construct

This says that the element *multi_type* may be any of the types *I*, *J*, or *K*. However, in OO programming, these types as shown in figure 5-7 would be more closely related.

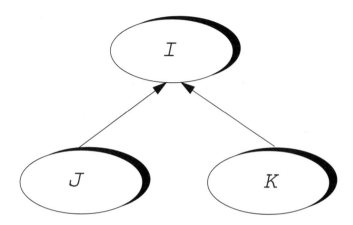

Figure 5-7. Union of *J* and *K*

multi_type: *I*

Here *multi_type* can take an element of any type descended from *I*, including *I* itself. Of course *I* might be an abstract type, in which case there will be no objects created of type *I*.

Unions can have another important property in type theory in that they can be related by the subtype relationship

$$\{J, K\} \leq \{J, K, L\}$$

Since *J* and *K* are also contained in the set *J*, *K*, and $\overline{L}$, {*J*, *K*} is a subtype of {*J*, *K*, *L*}. It is very important for flexible typing systems that types can be related according to the subtype relationship. We see in this chapter that structures such as the C union and enumerations do not behave well when it comes to subtyping. Unions are not necessary to achieve subtyping as we see in the following examples. Enumerations still need to have these problems solved. If constructs do not work well under these considerations, they should not be included in a language—if they are included, problems for the programmer are bound to result, and these result in programs that exhibit more defects.

We can now extend our example in figure 5-7 to show this (see figure 5-8).

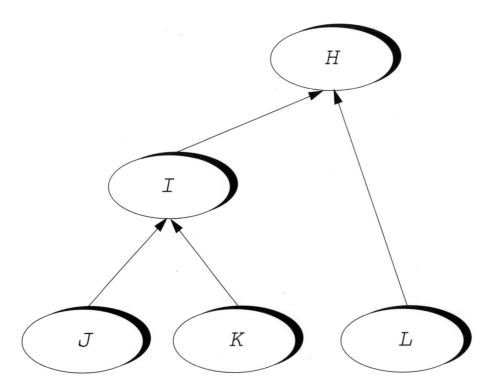

Figure 5-8. Union of *J*, *K*, and *L*

We can see that

$$\{J, K\} \leq \{J, K, L\}$$

and

$$I \leq H$$

If you are familiar with Pascal, you will observe that these concepts are very close to the Pascal variant record, and you should understand that variant records are replaced by subclassing in OO languages. An important consideration with any data structure is, how do you process it? In Pascal variant records are mostly processed in conjunction with **case** statements. OO does not need case statements for this use because the type information automatically determines any dynamic dispatch needed due to polymorphism. The kind of polymorphism introduced by variant types is undesirable in OOP.

5.8 Enumeration Types

Enumerations are a special case of union. The concept of enumeration types seems straightforward enough, but in practice these types have proven to be problematic enough for three languages—Eiffel, Oberon, and Java—to independently discard them. Oberon, which Wirth developed after Modula, discarded enumerations after he found many problems associated with them in Modula. Wirth states [Wirth 90] that enumerations must be made extensible, but he observed that "in a growing number of programs the indiscriminate use of enumerations (and subranges) had led to a type explosion that contributed not to program clarity but rather to verbosity." The explosion of types due to subranges has also been noted in programs written in Ada.

In some ways, this seems unfortunate, as enumerations can very conveniently and succinctly express some types. An enumeration type is a type where the allowable values of the type are explicitly stated, as opposed to types where the number of values is so large that it is not convenient, or even possible, to state them. An example is the type *REAL*.

Some common examples of enumeration types are

> *MONTHS* **is** *January, February, March, April, May, June, July, August,*
> *September, October, November, December*
> *COLORS* **is** *red, yellow, green, purple, orange, blue*
> *FRUIT* **is** *apple, pear, banana, tomato, orange, melon*

Here is our first problem: the label *orange* applies to both a *FRUIT* and a *COLOR*. As they are usually implemented, enumeration types provide no means of being able to qualify which is meant.

Enumerations and Subtypes

The next problem is type extension. What we might want to do is to define another enumerated type *PRIMARY_COLORS*, which obviously has some things in common with *COLORS*

> *PRIMARY_COLORS* **is** *red, green, blue*

The obvious thing to think here is that extending the type means adding more colors, but in fact the opposite is true! *PRIMARY_COLORS* is a subtype of *COLORS*, and therefore a subset of its elements. Consider the following assignments:

c: *COLOR*
pc: *PRIMARY_COLOR*

c := *pc*
pc := *c*

Now it is fine to assign a primary color to a color because a variable of type color can accept any primary color, since a primary color is a color. However, assigning a color to a primary color might not work, because it is possible that the color assigned is not a primary color.

Eiffel's suggestion (I would not call it a solution) is to use a class for your enumeration and to declare the values as constants or, as a convenience, **unique** values, which means the compiler automatically assigns values for you. The problem with **unique** is that, if you want to inherit the original class, the values of your constants will most likely not stay the same. The color example would look like

    class *COLORS*   *Eiffel*
    feature
        red, *yellow*, *green*, *purple*, *orange*, *blue*: *INTEGER* **is unique**
    end

Now we want to extend this to *PRIMARY_COLORS*:

    class *PRIMARY_COLORS*   *Eiffel*
    inherit
        COLORS
    feature
        red, *green*, *blue*: *INTEGER* **is unique**   -- this won't work!
    end

but we have problems in restricting our constants to just the three primary colors. In fact the compiler will probably reassign constants to the unique values so that *PRIMARY_COLORS red* will not be the same as *COLORS red*.

Enumeration Types

Furthermore, the suggestion is that every variable that takes on the values of such an enumeration is declared as *INTEGER*

color: *INTEGER*
month: *INTEGER*

color := *month*
month := *color*

So we have lost the advantage of static type checking! We could also restrict *PRIMARY_COLORS* to just the three required values by introducing an invariant. However, this will also not give us compile-time checking. Neither is the Eiffel syntax as convenient to use as original enumerations.

[Cardelli 88]

While it is a good thing to remove enumerations because of their problems, some type of convenient replacement is desirable. Such a replacement is obviously not simple, as no language has thought of it yet. An enumeration mechanism must express subtype relationships. Cardelli gives a good example of the mathematics and practicality in modeling

PRECIOUS_METAL: [*gold*, *silver*]
METAL: [*gold*, *silver*, *steel*]

Put another way

METAL: *PRECIOUS_METAL* **or** [*steel*]

and another way

PRECIOUS _METAL: *METAL* **dropping** [*steel*]

and subtyping

PRECIOUS _METAL < *METAL*

Here *PRECIOUS _METAL* is a subtype of *METAL*. I believe that, once a language can introduce enumerations and provide the needed concepts, we will have a very powerful and convenient mechanism. However, none of our languages provide this correctly.

C++ Enumeration Problems

Even if you accept enumerations as a good idea, C++'s enumerations have some problems, due to being able to cast integer values to an enumerated type. The rule is that the integer must be within the minimum and maximum bounds of the enumeration, but you can have holes within the enumeration

```
enum e {one = 1, three = 3, four = 4, nine = 9};       C++

e e1 = 6;        // error 6 is not of type e.
e e2 = e(6);     // OK, even though 6 is not in e.
e e3 = e(66);    // error 66 is not in the range of e.
```

We will see later that C++ has introduced a boolean type. Boolean can be viewed as an inbuilt enumerated type with the values true and false. However, the C++ definition of boolean does not follow even the weak rules for C++ enumerations, as any nonzero value can be implicitly cast to true

```
bool b = 66;    // OK, set to true.                    C++
```

In the earlier section on unions, we saw that the union concept is useful within the study of type theory, although inheritance gives us a more restricted form. Unions might also prove to solve the problems with enumerations, as an enumeration can be thought of as a union where all elements have the same type

$$PRIMARY\_COLOR: \{red: COLOR \cup green: COLOR \cup blue: COLOR\}$$

5.9 Name Overloading

Clear names are fundamental in producing self-documenting software and in helping to produce maintainable and reusable software components. Names are fundamental in freeing programmers from low-level manipulation of addresses. Naming is the basis for differentiating between different entities in a software module. In programming, when we use the term *name*, we usually mean identifier. To be precise, a name is a label that can refer to more than one entity, in which case the name is ambiguous. An identifier is a name that unambiguously identifies an entity. (To be mathematical, a name is a relation; an identifier is a function.) Where a name is ambiguous, it needs qualification to form an identifier to the entity. For example, there could be two people named John Doe; to disambiguate the reference, you would qualify each as John Doe *of Washington* or John Doe *of New York*.

Name overloading allows the same name to refer to two or more different entities. The problem with an ambiguous name is whether the resultant ambiguity is useful and how to resolve it, since ambiguity weakens the usefulness of names to distinguish entities.

Name overloading is useful for two purposes. First, it allows programmers to work on two or more modules without concern about name clashes. The ambiguity can be tolerated because within the context of each module the name unambiguously refers to a unique entity; the name is qualified by its surrounding environment. Second, name overloading provides polymorphism, where the same name applied to different types refers to different implementations for those types. Polymorphism allows one word to describe what is computed. Different classes might have different implementations of how a computation is done. For example, *draw* is an operation that is applicable to all different shapes, even though circles, squares, etc., are drawn differently.

These two uses of name overloading provide a powerful concept. The use of the same name in the same context must be resolved. Errors can result from ambiguity, in which case the programmer must differentiate between entities with some form of qualification of the name. A common way to do this is to introduce extra distinguishing names. For example, where two or more people in a group share the same first name, they can be distinguished by their surnames. Similarly a unique first name will distinguish the members of a family with a common surname.

This is analogous to classes, where each class in a system is given a unique name. Each member within a class is also given a unique name. Where two objects with members of the same name are used within the same context, the object name can qualify the members. In this case the dot operator acts as a qualifier; for example, *a.mem* and *b.mem*.

Locals in a recursive environment are an example of ambiguity that is resolved at run time. A single local identifier in the static text of a function can refer to many entities. When the function is called recursively, the name is qualified by the call history of the function to give the exact memory cell where it resides.

Names and Scope

Many block-structured languages provide overloading by scoping. Scoping allows the same name to be used in different contexts without clash or confusion, but nested blocks have a subtle problem. Names in an outer block are in scope in inner blocks, but many languages allow a name to be overloaded in an inner block, creating a scope hole hiding the outer entity and preventing it from being accessed. The name in the inner block has no relationship with the entity of the same name in the outer block. Textually blocks inherit named entities from outer blocks. Inheritance accomplishes this in OO languages, eliminates the need to textually nest entities, and accomplishes textual loose coupling. Nesting results in tightly coupled text.

Contrary to most languages, a name should not be overloaded while it is in scope. The following example illustrates why

```
{                                                                        C++
    int i;
    {
        int i;  // hide the outer i.
        i = 13; // assign to the inner i.
        // Can't get to the outer i here;
        // it is in scope, but hidden.
    }
}
```

Now delete the inner declaration

```
{                                                                        C++
    int i;
    {
        i = 13; // Syntactically valid, but not
                // the intention.
    }
}
```

The inner overloaded declaration is removed, and references to that name do not result in syntax errors due to the same name being in the outer environment. The inner instruction now mistakenly changes the value of the outer entity. A compiler cannot detect this situation unless the language definition forbids nested

[Dijkstra 76] redeclarations. Dijkstra uses similar reasoning in "An Essay on the Notion: The Scope of Variables" in *A Discipline of Programming*.

The above example demonstrates how nesting results in less maintainable programs due to tight coupling between the inner and outer blocks, making each sensitive to changes in the other. The advantage of keeping components decoupled and separate is that a programmer can confidently make modifications to one component without affecting other components. Testing can be limited to the changed component rather than to a combination of components, which quickly leads to an exponentiation in the number of tests required.

Eiffel has recognized overloading as problematic, so even this form is disallowed. Routine arguments and local variables cannot overload names of class features.

[CD2 96] (3.3.1) A further problem is that this kind of name overloading occurs when the names occur in close proximity. Such situations make the language definition more complex and the development of compilers more complicated. It also makes life more difficult for programmers—it's harder to remember what will happen. Of course, sensible programmers will probably avoid such pathological cases.

C++
```
int x = 12;
{ int x = x; }
```

Here the second x is initialized to its own (indeterminate) value.

C++
```
const int i = 2;
{ int i[i]; }
```

declares a local array of two integers.

C++
```
const int x = 12;
{ enum {x = x}; }
```

Here the enumerator x is initialized with the value of the constant x, namely 12.

This complexity of language definition would be much better handled by simply disallowing the redefinition of the name already in scope.

[C++ ARM] (13.1) C++ has another analogous form of hiding a nonvirtual function in a derived class which hides a function with the same signature in an ancestor class. This hiding is explained in the C++ ARM. This is confusing and error prone. Learning all these ins and outs of the language is extremely burdensome to the programmer, who often learns them only after falling into a trap. Java does not have this problem since everything is virtual, so a function with the same signature will override rather than hide the ancestor function.

In order to overcome the effects of hiding, you can use `::`—the scope resolution operator. The scope resolution operator of C++ provides an interesting twist to the above argument. Consider the following example from the C++ ARM:

[C++ ARM (3.2)]

```
int g = 99;

int f(int g)   // hide the outer g.
{
    return g ? g : ::g;
        // return argument if it is nonzero
        // otherwise return global g.
}
```
C++

What you are now doing is having to refer to the outer entity `g` by the ugly name `::g`. This would be simpler and tidier if the compiler reported an error on the redefinition of `g` in the parameter list. The programmer would simply change the name of one of the entities with no need for the scope resolution operator

```
int g = 99;

int f(int h)
{
    return h ? h : g;
}
```
C++

In fact the `::` operator is not very general or powerful; you cannot resolve a hidden local name.

On the topic of hiding, Stroustrup says, "Hiding names is unavoidable when writing large programs. However, a human reader can easily fail to notice that a name has been hidden. Because such errors are relatively rare, they can be very difficult to find. Consequently, name hiding should be minimized." It is not unavoidable to hide names in large programs per se, just difficult not to in C++ because of the way modules must be mixed together.

[Stroustrup (4.9.2)]

With the introduction of namespaces in 1993, the `::` operator now resolves names in namespaces. For example, `A::x` means the entity `x` in namespace `A`.

Name Overloading

Above ::g means the entity g in the global namespace. Since declarations in a namespace are really just members of a fixed structure, it would have been cleaner to use the access operator "." and avoid the ugly scope resolution operator.

Lambda Calculus: Free and Bound Variables

Another form of the argument comes from lambda calculus where variables such as the outer g are free variables in contrast to where the inner g is a bound variable (see section 1.7):

$$x \bullet x + y$$

In this case x is bound and y is free. So if y has the value 5 and we invoke the function as

$$\{x \bullet x + y\}(2)$$

then we have the reduction 2 + 5, which reduces to 7. If, however, we rename the bound variable as y, then we have

$$\{y \bullet y + y\}(2)$$

which instead reduced to 2 + 2 or 4, so we have radically changed the computation in a dangerous way, ignoring that the second y is intended to refer to the free y. Of course trivial examples like this are so trivial as to seem unimportant. However, when you consider hundreds of thousands of lines of code, changes like this become nontrivial, and the danger is more apparent.

Java and Eiffel

Java does not provide a scope resolution operator. However, there are no globals, so the only case where the above is a problem is between class members and method parameters or locals.

Java does have a similar problem, though. The problem is with *shadowed variables*. With shadowed variables, a variable named x in a superclass can be hidden from the current class by another variable named x. You can still access both variables by the use of *this.x* and *super.x*, which are the equivalents of scope resolution. The ambiguity problem would have been better avoided altogether by reporting a duplicate identifier.

Eiffel also has no globals, so a construct such as namespaces is not needed. Eiffel does not allow name clashes—you must either change the name of one of the entities or, when combining classes with inheritance, use a **rename** clause. With this scheme there is no need for scope resolution or super operators. Using declarative techniques makes the imperative part of the language simpler.

5.10 Virtual Functions (C++)

This is a complicated section, due to C++'s complex mechanisms. Although this issue is central because polymorphism is a key concept of OOP, feel free to skim if you want an overview without the details.

In C++ the keyword `virtual` is used in a base class to enable the possibility for a function to be polymorphic when it might be overridden (redefined) in one or more derived classes. However, the `virtual` keyword is unnecessary, because any function that is redefined in a descendant class is polymorphic. A compiler needs to generate only dynamic dispatch for truly polymorphic routines.

The problem in C++ is that, if a base class designer does not foresee that a derived class might want to redefine a function, then the derived class cannot make the function polymorphic. This is a serious flaw in C++ because it reduces the flexibility of software components and therefore the ability to write reusable and extensible libraries.

C++ also allows functions to be overloaded, in which case the correct function to call depends on the arguments. The actual arguments in a function call must match the formal arguments of one of the overloaded functions. The difference between overloaded functions and polymorphic (overridden) functions is that, with overloaded functions, the correct function to call is determined at compile time; with polymorphic functions the correct function to call is determined at run time.

When a base class is designed the programmer can only guess that derived classes might override or overload a function. A derived class can overload a function at any time, but this is not the case for the more important mechanism of polymorphism, where the base class programmer must specify that the routine is `virtual` in order for the compiler to set up a dispatch entry for the function in the class jump table. So the burden is on the programmer for something that a compiler can do automatically and compilers do in other languages. However, this is a relic from how C++ was originally implemented with UNIX tools rather than specialized compiler and linker support.

There are three options for overriding—*must not*, *can*, and *must be* overridden.

1. Overriding a routine is prohibited; descendant classes must use the routine as is.
2. A routine may be overridden. Descendant classes can use the routine as provided, or provide their own implementation as long as it conforms to the original interface definition and accomplishes at least as much.
3. A routine is abstract. The parent class provides no implementation and each non-abstract descendant class must provide its own implementation.

The parent class designer must decide options 1 and 3. Descendant class designers must decide option 2. A language should provide direct syntax for these options.

Option 1 — Overriding Prohibited

C++ does not provide for the prohibition of overriding a `virtual` function in a descendant class; even `private virtual` functions can be overridden. Sakkinen points out that a descendant class can override a `private virtual` function even though it cannot access the function in other ways.

[Sakkinen 92]

Nonvirtual functions are the closest, but in that case the function can be completely replaced. This causes two problems. First, a routine can be unintentionally replaced in a descendant. The redeclaration of a name within the same scope should cause a name clash; the compiler should report a duplicate declaration syntax error as the entities inherited from the parent are included in the descendant's namespace. Allowing two entities to have the same name within one scope causes ambiguity and other problems. (See the section on name overloading earlier in the chapter.)

The following example illustrates the second problem

C++

```
class A
{
    public:
    void nonvirt ();
    virtual void virt ();
};

class B : public A
{
```

```
    public:
    void nonvirt ();
    void virt ();
};

A a;
B b;
A *ap = &b;
B *bp = &b;

bp->nonvirt ();    // calls B::nonvirt as you
                   // would expect.
ap->nonvirt ();    // calls A::nonvirt, even
                   // though this
                   // object is of type B.
ap->virt ();       // calls B::virt, the  correct
                   // version of
                   // the routine for B objects.
```

In this example, class B has extended or replaced routines in class A. B::nonvirt is the routine that should be called for objects of type B. It could be pointed out that C++ gives the client programmer flexibility to call either A::nonvirt or B::nonvirt, but this can be provided in a simpler, more direct way: A::nonvirt and B::nonvirt should be given different names. That way the programmer calls the correct routine explicitly, not by an obscure and error-prone trick of the language. The different name approach is as follows:

```
class B : public A                                              C++
{
    public:
    void b_nonvirt ();
    void virt ();
};

B b;
B *bp = &b;
bp->nonvirt ();     // calls A::nonvirt
bp->b_nonvirt ();   // calls B::b_nonvirt
```

Now the designer of class B has direct control over B's interface. The application requires that clients of B can call both A::nonvirt and B::b_nonvirt, which B's designer has explicitly provided for. This is good OO design that provides strongly defined interfaces. C++ allows client programmers to play tricks with the class interfaces external to the class, and B's designer cannot prevent A::nonvirt from being called. Objects of class B have their own specialized nonvirt, but B's designer does not have control over B's interface to ensure that the correct version of nonvirt is called.

C++ also does not protect class B from other changes in the system. Suppose we need to write a class C that needs nonvirt to be virtual. Then nonvirt in A will be changed to virtual. But this breaks the B::nonvirt trick. The requirement of class C to have a virtual function forces a change in the base class, which affects all other descendants of the base class, instead of the specific new requirement being localized to the new class. This goes against the reason for OOP having loosely coupled classes, so that new requirements and modifications will have localized effects and not require changes elsewhere that can potentially break other existing parts of the system.

Another problem is that statements should consistently have the same semantics. The polymorphic interpretation of a statement like a->f() is that the most suitable implementation of f() is invoked for the object referred to by a whether the object is of type A, or a descendant of A. In C++, however, the programmer must know whether the function f() is defined as virtual or nonvirtual in order to interpret exactly what a->f() means. Therefore, the statement a->f() is not implementation independent and the principle of implementation hiding is broken. A change in the declaration of f() changes the semantics of the invocation. Implementation independence means that a change in the implementation *does not* change the semantics of executable statements.

If a change in the declaration changes the semantics, this should generate a compiler-detected error. The programmer should make the statement semantically consistent with the changed declaration. This reflects the dynamic nature of software development, where you'll see perpetual change in program text.

C++'s virtual is also an example of where the important concept of *separation of concerns* breaks down. There is a conflict between the meanings of *virtual* and *optimization*. The meaning of nonvirtual is that a function cannot be redefined, although the meaning is weak, as it can be replaced completely and this decision must be made in the class where the function is first introduced. Semantically it is best by default to declare functions virtual.

However, this laudable aim is in conflict with the desire to optimize away the dynamic calls and replace them with more efficient nonvirtual static calls. Hence, the concerns are not separate, but in direct conflict. As we will see in the section on global analysis in chapter 10, languages like Eiffel, Object Pascal, and Java handle the static call optimization automatically, so you are not faced with this conflict of interests. In fact, you do not even need to be concerned with the meaning, since routines that are redefined are automatically polymorphic, and only calls where the target routine is polymorphic use dynamic binding. This shows that, where separation of concerns is designed into a language, interests do not come into conflict, and you do not need the engineering compromises and trade-offs that C and C++ programmers must spend their time mastering.

The ARM covers another case of the inconsistent semantics of the statement a->f() vs. constructors. Neither Eiffel nor Java has these problems. Their mechanisms are clearer and simpler and don't lead to the surprises of C++. In Java, everything is `virtual`; to gain the effect where a method must not be overridden, the method may be defined with the qualifier `final`. [C++ ARM] (10.9c)

Eiffel allows the programmer to specify a routine as **frozen**, in which case the routine cannot be redefined in descendants. The benefit of Java's `final` and Eiffel's **frozen** specifications is that, from a base class, a routine can go through several redefinitions, but, from the point that `final`/**frozen** is specified, redefinition is prohibited. In C++, once a function is `virtual`, this is not possible.

Option 2 — May Override

Using the function as is or overriding it should be left open for the programmers of descendant classes. In C++, the possibility must be enabled in the base class by specifying `virtual`. In OO design, the decisions you decide *not* to make are as important as the decisions you *do* make. Decisions should be made as late as possible to prevent mistakes being built into the system in an early stage. When you make early decisions, you are often stuck with assumptions that later prove to be incorrect, or the assumptions could be correct in one environment but false in another, making software brittle and nonreusable.

C++ requires a base class to specify potential polymorphism of a member by `virtual` (although an intermediate class in the inheritance chain can introduce `virtual`). This prejudges that a routine might be redefined in descendants and can be a problem because routines that are not actually polymorphic are accessed via the slightly less efficient virtual table technique instead of a straight procedure call. (This is never a large overhead, but OO programs tend to use more and smaller routines making routine invocation a more significant overhead.) The policy in C++ should be that routines that might be redefined should be declared virtual. Even worse, nonvirtual routines cannot be redefined, so the descendant class programmer has no control.

Rumbaugh et al. further criticize C++'s virtual.

[RBPEL 91]
(15.8.2)

C++ contains facilities for inheritance and run-time method resolution, but a C++ data structure is not automatically object-oriented. Method resolution and the ability to override an operation in a subclass are only available if the operation is declared *virtual* in the superclass. Thus, the need to override a method must be anticipated and written into the origin class definition. Unfortunately, the writer of a class may not expect the need to define specialized subclasses or may not know what operations will have to be redefined by a subclass. This means that the superclass often must be modified when a subclass is defined and places a serious restriction on the ability to reuse library classes by creating subclasses, especially if the source code library is not available. (Of course, you could declare *all* operations as *virtual*, at a slight cost in memory and function-calling overhead.)

Virtual, however, is the wrong mechanism for the programmer to deal with. A compiler can detect polymorphism and generate the underlying virtual code where and only where necessary. Having to specify virtual burdens the programmer with another bookkeeping task. This is the main reason why C++ is a weak OO language—the programmer must constantly be concerned with low-level details that a compiler should handle automatically.

Another problem in C++ is mistaken overriding. A base class function can be overridden unwittingly. The compiler should report an erroneous name redefinition within the same namespace unless the descendant class programmer specifies that the routine redefinition is really intended. The same name can be used, but the programmer must be conscious of this and state it explicitly, especially in environments where systems are assembled out of preexisting components. Unless the programmer explicitly overrides the original name, a syntax error should report that the name is a duplicate declaration. C++, however, adopted the original approach of Simula. This approach has been improved upon, and other languages have adopted better, more explicit approaches that avoid the error of mistaken redefinition.

The solution is that `virtual` should not be specified in the parent. Where run-time polymorphic dynamic binding is required, the child class should specify `override` on the function. When compile-time static binding is required, the child class should specify `overload` on the function. This has advantages. In the case of polymorphic functions, the compiler can check that the function signatures conform; in the case of overloaded functions, the compiler can check that the function signatures are different in some respect. Furthermore, during the maintenance phases of a program, the original programmer's intention is clear. As it is, future programmers must guess whether the original programmer made some kind of error in choosing a duplicate name or whether overloading was intended.

In Java, there is no `virtual` keyword; all methods are potentially polymorphic. Java uses direct call instead of dynamic method lookup when the method is `static`, `private`, or `final`. This means that there will be nonpolymorphic routines that must be called dynamically, but the dynamic nature of Java means further optimization is not possible.

Eiffel and Object Pascal provide for this option since the descendant class programmer must specify that redefinition is intended. This has the extra benefit that a later reader or maintainer of the class can easily identify the routines that have been redefined and that this definition is related to a definition in an ancestor class without having to refer to ancestor class definitions. Thus option 2 is exactly where it should be, in descendant classes.

Both Eiffel and Object Pascal optimize calls. They generate dispatch table entries for dynamic binding only where a routine is truly polymorphic. How this is possible is covered in the section on global analysis in chapter 10.

Option 3 — Must Define

The `pure virtual` function (which we examine in more detail in the next section) provides for leaving a function abstract; that is, a descendant class must provide its implementation if it is to be instantiated. Any descendants that do not define the routine are also abstract classes. This concept is correct, but see the section on `pure virtual` functions coming up for criticism of the terminology and syntax.

Java also has abstract methods. In Eiffel, the implementation is marked as **deferred**.

Summary

The main problem with `virtual` is that it forces a base class designer to guess that a function might be polymorphic in one or more derived classes. If this requirement is not foreseen or not included as an optimization to avoid dynamically dispatched calls, the possibility is effectively closed rather than being left open. As implemented in C++, virtual coupled with the independent notion of overloading make an error-prone combination. Unfortunately, this is one of the key features in OO programming and polymorphism, and C++ gets it wrong.

`Virtual` is a difficult notion to grasp. The related concepts of polymorphism and dynamic binding, redefinition, and overriding are easier to grasp, being oriented toward the problem domain. Virtual routines are an implementation mechanism that instruct the compiler to set up entries in the class virtual table; where global analysis is not done by the compiler, this burden is left to the programmer. Polymorphism is the what, and virtual is the how. Smalltalk, Objective-C, Java, and Eiffel all use a different mechanism to implement polymorphism.

[Meyers 92] (item 37)

Simply stated, the problem with the virtual mechanism of C++ is that function redefinition and virtual are separate concepts. Meyers advises against redefining nonvirtual routines. Virtual functions, however, are not necessarily redefined, resulting in unnecessary, less efficient dynamic calls where not needed. In Java everything is virtual, so you do not have the problem of redefining nonvirtual functions. In Eiffel, only redefined routines become virtual, requiring dynamic calls; routines that are not redefined remain nonvirtual, resulting in more efficient static calls. In fact, in Eiffel a call to a redefined routine results in a dynamic call only when the routine is called via a parent reference; any call to the routine directly through a reference to the class where the last redefinition took place, or through any descendant class, can be a static call.

Virtual is an example of where C++ obscures the concepts of OOP. The programmer has to come to terms with low-level concepts, rather than the higher-level OO concepts. Virtual leaves optimization to the programmer. Other approaches leave the optimization of dynamic dispatch to the compiler, which can remove 100 percent of cases where dynamic dispatch is not required. Interesting as underlying mechanisms might be for the theoretician or compiler implementer, the practitioner should not be required to understand or use them to make sense of the higher-level concepts. Having to use them in practice is tedious and error prone and can prevent the adaptation of software to further advances in the underlying technology and execution mechanisms (see concurrent programming), thereby reducing the flexibility and reusability of the software.

5.11 Pure Virtual Functions (C++)

Pure virtual functions provide a means of leaving a function undefined and abstract. While the concept is necessary, this section shows that both the syntax and the terminology of pure virtual leave something to be desired. A class that has such an abstract function cannot be directly instantiated. A nonabstract descendant class must define the function. The C++ pure virtual syntax is

C++

```
virtual void fn () = 0;
```

This leaves the reader new to C++ to guess its meaning, even those well versed in OO concepts. =0 might make sense for the compiler writer, as the implementation is to put a zero entry in the virtual table. This shows how implementation details that should not concern the programmer are visible in C++.

A better choice would have been a keyword such as *abstract*. Abstract should have syntactic significance since abstract functions are an important concept in OO design. The C++ decision in keeping with the C philosophy of avoiding keywords is at the expense of clarity. A keyword would implement this concept more clearly. For example

```
pure virtual void fn ();
```

or

```
abstract void fn ();
```

The mathematical notation used in C++ suggests that values other than zero could be used. What if the function is equated (or is that assigned?) to 13?

```
virtual void fn () = 13;
```

A function is either implemented or undefined. To any analyst this suggests a boolean state, which a single keyword conveys. A simple suggestion to fix this is to define = 0 as abstract

```
#define abstract = 0
```
C++

then

```
virtual void fn () abstract;
```
C++

Let's look at =0 a slightly different way, as a key phrase or a keyword that is spelled with the characters =0. Looking at it this way, the objection to keywords becomes a nonissue.

As for the terminology, *pure virtual* is a contortion of natural language. It combines words that are somewhat opposite in meaning. *Pure* means something that really is what it appears to be, as in *pure gold*. *Virtual* means something that appears to be what it actually is not, as in *virtual memory*. Perhaps `pure virtual` gold is fool's gold. As mentioned before, virtual is a difficult concept to grasp. When it is combined with a word such as pure, the meaning becomes more obscure.

[Stroustrup 94] (13.2.3) Stroustrup recounts the tale about the "curious =0" syntax. "The curious =0 syntax was chosen over the obvious alternative of introducing a keyword pure or `abstract` because at the time I saw no chance of getting a new keyword accepted. Had I suggested `pure`, Release 2.0 would have shipped without abstract classes. Rather than risking delay and incurring the certain fights over `pure`, I used the traditional C and C++ convention of using 0 to represent 'not there.'"

Mathematically, 0 does not normally represent "not there." Usually, 0 is just another number. Using 0 to represent "not there" leads to semantic problems that result in many interesting discussions on topics such as 3-value and 4-value logic, etc. In the C world, there are constant arguments over whether NULL is 0 or something else. In the database world, a value is needed for "not known." If 0 is used for "not known," then there is a problem if the value is known, but happens to be 0. The =0 syntax is an aggregation of errors. Not only are keywords such as `virtual` and `static` overloaded; worse, a number such as zero is used to mean things that it does not mathematically represent.

Java and Eiffel use much clearer syntax. Java simply uses

Java

```
abstract void fn ();
```

In Eiffel you specify the routine as **deferred**, meaning the details of implementation are deferred to a descendant class.

Eiffel

  r **is deferred end**

The **end** might look like syntactic baggage, but you can specify other abstract properties of a deferred routine in the form of *pre* and *post* conditions, thus you can specify contract conditions in a deferred routine that all implementations must fulfil.

If any feature in an Eiffel class is **deferred**, then the class itself must also be marked as **deferred**. Furthermore, the class can be marked as **deferred** only if it has **deferred** features. You might want to mark a class as **deferred** if there are no **deferred** features, particularly for mixin classes. Java allows a class to be marked as `abstract`, even if it has no abstract members, even though this would be of more use in multiple inheritance.

A significant point about Eiffel's **deferred** features is that, if a feature has a type but no parameters, it can be effected by a function, a variable, or, if it is a basic type, a constant. In this case it is best to use the term *deferred feature*, rather than *deferred routine*. This flexibility in Eiffel is a direct consequence of the *Principle of Uniform Access*. This is illustrated in figure 5-9.

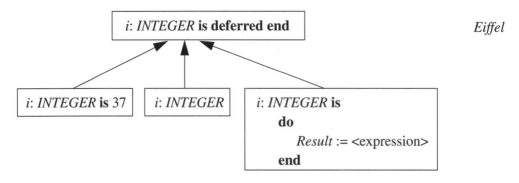

Figure 5-9. Eiffel's Principle of Uniform Access

Eiffel has the most precise terminology, since **deferred** means that the implementation is deferred. A routine that has an implementation still has an abstract form. The abstract definition of the routine is obtained by the *short* tool, which extracts the routine signature—that is, name, parameters, type, and pre and post conditions—from the implementation details. The term abstract does not necessarily mean not implemented, but rather that the interface is separated from the implementation details.

5.12 Function Overloading (C++ and Java)

C++ allows functions to be overloaded if the arguments in the signature are different types. Overloaded functions are different from polymorphic functions—for each invocation the correct function is selected at compile time; with polymorphic functions, the correct function is bound dynamically at run time. Polymorphism is achieved by redefining or overriding routines. Be careful not to confuse overriding and overloading. Overloading arises when two or more functions share a name. These are disambiguated by the number and types of the arguments. Overloading is different from multiple dispatching in CLOS, where multiple dispatching on argument types is done dynamically at run time.

Reade points out the difference between overloading and polymorphism. Overloading means the use of the same name in the same context for different entities with completely different definitions and types. Polymorphism, on the other hand, has one definition, and all types are subtypes of a principal type. Strachey referred to polymorphism as parametric polymorphism and overloading as ad hoc polymorphism. Cardelli refines the definition further. [Reade 89] (2.1.3)

Function Overloading (C++ and Java)

[Cardelli 93]   Polymorphism is the ability of a function to handle objects of many types [Strachey 67]. In ad hoc polymorphism a function can behave in arbitrarily different ways on objects of different types. We shall ignore this view here, and consider only *generic* polymorphism where a function behaves in some uniform way over all the relevant types. The two forms of generic polymorphism are *parametric* polymorphism, where uniform behavior is embodied by a type parameter, and *subtype* polymorphism, where uniform behavior is embodied by a subtype hierarchy.

The qualification mechanism for overloaded functions is the function signature. Overloading can be useful, as these examples show:

C++
```
int max (int, int);
real max (real, real);
```

This will ensure that the best max routine for the types `int` and `real` will be invoked. OO programming, however, provides a variant on this. Since the object is passed to the routine as a hidden parameter (this in C++), an equivalent but more restricted form is already implicitly included in OO concepts. Our simple example would be expressed as

C++
```
int i, j;
real r, s;
i.max (j);
r.max (s);
```

but `i.max (r)` and `r.max (j)` result in compilation errors because the types of the arguments do not agree. By operator overloading, of course, these can be better expressed by `i max j` and `r max s`, but min and max are peculiar functions that could accept two or more parameters of the same type so they can be applied to an arbitrarily sized list. So the most general code in Eiffel-style syntax will be something like:

Eiffel
   il: COMPARABLE_LIST [INTEGER]
   rl: COMPARABLE_LIST [REAL]
   i := il.max
   r := rl.max

Eiffel now has a language extension proposal to introduce *TUPLE* types for lists of arbitrary size.

These examples show that the OO paradigm, particularly with genericity, can achieve function overloading without the need for the function overloading of C++. C++, however, does make the notion more general. The advantage is that more than one parameter can overload a function, not just the implicit current object parameter.

Another factor to consider is that overloading is resolved at compile time, but overriding at run time, so it looks as if overloading has a performance advantage. However, global analysis can determine whether the *min* and *max* functions are at the end of the inheritance line and, therefore, can call them directly. That is, the compiler examines the objects *i* and *r*, looks at their corresponding *max* function, sees that no polymorphism is involved, and so generates a direct call to *max*. By contrast, if the object *n* were defined to be a *NUMBER* that provided the abstract *max* function from which *REAL.max* and *INTEGER.max* were derived, then the compiler would need to generate a dynamically bound call, as *n* could refer to either an *INTEGER* or a *REAL*.

If you feel that C++'s scheme of having parameters of different types is useful, you should realize that OO programming provides this in a more restricted and disciplined form. It does this by specifying that the parameter needs to conform to a base class. Any parameter passed to the routine can be only a type of the base class or a subclass of the base class. For example:

```
A.f (B someB) {...};                                            C++
class B ...;
class D : public B ...
A a;
D d;
a.f (d);
```

In this example, the entity d must conform to the class B, and the compiler checks this.

The alternative to function overloading by signature is to require functions with different signatures to have different names. Names should be the basis of distinction of entities. The compiler can cross-check that the parameters supplied are correct for the given routine name. This also results in better self-documented software. It is often difficult to choose appropriate names for entities, but it is well worth the effort.

Wiener contributes a nice example on the hazards of virtual functions with overloading. [Wiener 95] (7.7)

Function Overloading (C++ and Java)

C++

```cpp
class Parent
{
  public:
     virtual int doIt (int v)
     {
        return v * v;
     }
};

class Child : public Parent
{
  public:
     int doIt (int v,
               int av = 20)
     {
        return v * av;
     }
};

void main()
{
   int i;
   Parent *p = new Child();
   i = p->doIt(3);
}
```

What is the value in `i` after execution? One might expect 60, but it is 9—the signature of `doIt` in `Child` does not match the signature in `Parent`. It does not override the `Parent` `doIt`; merely overloads it, so the default is unusable.

Another question that arises is what happens if a function in a nested scope overloads a function in an outer scope do overloading or hiding semantics apply? C++'s answer is that hiding applies. Our *max* example would thus be:

C++

```cpp
int max (int, int);

void inner()
{
   real max (real, real);
   max (1, 2);      // calls max (real, real)
                    // not max (int, int)
}
```

Java also provides *method overloading*, where several methods can have the same name but different signatures.

The Eiffel philosophy is not to introduce a new technique, but to use genericity, inheritance, and redefinition. Eiffel provides covariant signatures, which means the signatures of descendant routines do not have to match exactly, but they do have to conform according to Eiffel's strong typing scheme.

Eiffel uses covariance with anchored types to implement examples such as *max*. The *Vintage 95 Kernel Library* specifies *max* as

    max (*other*: **like** *Current*): **like** *Current*   *Eiffel*

This says that the type of the argument to *max* must conform to the type of the current class, and so must the return result. Therefore you get the same effect by redefinition without the overloading concept. You also get type checking to see that the parameter conforms to the current object. Genericity is also a mechanism that overcomes most of the need for overloading.

We shall see more on covariance and what it means in the section on signature variance in section 9.6. However, we can learn more by considering any binary operator like *max* in a more conventional way

    max (*a*: **T**; *b*: like *a*): **like** *a*   *Eiffel*

If we had just declared the argument types *a*, *b* and the return value all to be *T*, then we have the possibility that all may be varied covariantly independently in redefined versions of *max*. That is, each could assume an unrelated type as their types diverge down different paths of the type tree. *max* ceases to make sense as a binary operator if this happens. So the types are anchored to each other with the **like** type definition, so that they can vary only in parallel with each other.

Anchored declarations are an important semantic part of the Eiffel type system. Not only do anchored types make software more flexible by being able to specify a type in one location, but anchored types solve some type problems. You should not think that anchored types are for esoteric cases—it is a good idea to use them wherever the types of entities are related.

Diagrammatically we have the types from the *max* example varying as shown in figure 5-10. In this diagram, we can see that it would be wrong for the types to diverge—they are tied to each other.

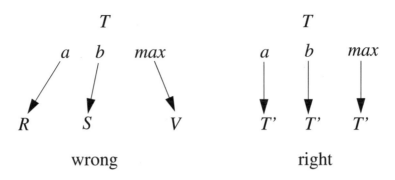

Figure 5-10. Type correctness with like

Another example of where an anchored type is essential is if we consider an identity function (or any function that returns an entity of the same type). The idea of an identity function is that it returns an object of the same type as the object it is invoked on. However, without anchored types, this proves to be not so simple. For example

Eiffel

    class *A*
    feature
        id: *A* **is**
            do
                Result := *Current*
            end
    end

    class *B*
    inherit *A*
    end

    ...

    b1, *b2*: *B*
    b2 := *b1.id* -- error

This last assignment cannot work because the type of the right-hand expression is *A*, which cannot be assigned to an entity of type *B*. The answer is to rewrite *A* as follows:

```
class A                                              Eiffel
feature
    id: like Current is
        do
            Result := Current
        end
end
```

Then the assignment will work. The `clone` function in Java has exactly this problem, since Java has no anchored types.

5.13 Virtuals and Inlining

An interesting question is: can you optimize a polymorphic function using inlining? The answer is that you can. Consider the class hierarchy

```
class A                                              Eiffel
feature
    f is deferred end
end

class B inherit A redefine f end
feature
    f is do ... end
end

class C inherit A redefine f end
feature
    f is do ... end
end
```

Can a compiler inline the following code?

```
a: A                                                 Eiffel
b: B
c: C

b.f
c.f
a.f
```

The answer is yes in every case. Only the call *a.f* must dynamically determine whether to call *B.f* or *C.f* at run time. The calls *b.f* and *c.f* can be optimized to a straight procedure call and therefore inlined if the routines meet other criteria for inlining. The compiler may also optimize the *a.f* call as follows:

-- a.f
IF TYPE (*a*) = *A* **THEN** CODE (*A.f*) **ELSE** CODE (*B.f*)

The programmer cannot inline virtual functions in C++, but, as you can see, such optimization is not done at the site of the function declaration, but rather at the site of the invocation.

6

Type Extension: Generics and Templates
(C++ and Eiffel)

In the last chapter, we saw one form of type extension: inheritance or *subtype polymorphism*. This chapter examines how our three languages implement the orthogonal notion of parameterized types, also known as generics or templates, *or parametric polymorphism*. Some see genericity as a more fundamental software assembly mechanism than inheritance and certainly less problematic. Ada is an example where genericity is more fundamental than inheritance.

Templates are C++'s mechanism to implement the concept of *genericity*. Templates are much the same as *parameterized classes*, which is the mechanism Eiffel uses for genericity. Genericity is a major feature of Ada and ALGOL 68 and is a valuable addition to C++. In C++'s Standard Template Library (STL), genericity is used almost exclusively instead of inheritance. Meyer states that genericity is an essential part of an OO language. Palsberg and Schwartzbach see genericity as a mechanism that achieves type substitution, something you cannot do with inheritance. Thus genericity is essential as a complementary concept to inheritance.

[Meyer 97]

[Palsberg and Schwartzbach 94]

Genericity allows you to build collections of items, where the type of items is known and items can be retrieved from the collection as that type without type casting. In a language without genericity, you code a *LIST* class, and objects of any type can be added to lists. If the list is only for shopping items, it makes semantic nonsense to add a person to the list. Without genericity you have no static type check to ensure you can't add people to your shopping list. You might be able to catch this occurrence at run time, but the advantage of static typing is lost.

Without genericity you could code specific lists for shopping items, people, and every other item you can put in lists. The basic functionality of all lists is the same, but you must duplicate effort and manually replicate code; that is, you must duplicate effort if you are going to preserve semantics and be type safe. Genericity means you don't have to replicate code, but type safety is also not sacrificed. In languages like Smalltalk, you don't have static type safety and therefore do not need the mechanism of generics.

Languages such as Eiffel and C++ allow you to declare a *LIST* of *shopping items* so that the compiler can ensure that you cannot add people to such a list. You can also easily add lists that contain any other type of entity, just by a simple declaration. So, you could make a *LIST* of *people*, reusing the code of the list concept without having to recode for a different element type. You do not have to manually replicate the basic functionality of the list for every type of element you are going to put in it.

You might be wondering, what is the difference between inheritance and genericity? You use inheritance where you have the same interface to different types, but the algorithms are different; that is, the types behind the interface are polymorphic. Genericity is where you have different types, but the algorithm for certain operations is the same. Note that we distinguish between algorithms or behavior that belongs to the problem domain and implementation. You can have many possible implementations of the algorithms and behaviors of the problem domain. As we have seen, inheritance can be used for both abstract behavior and implementation.

For example, inheritance is used for shapes, where operations such as *draw* have different algorithms for different shapes, such as circle, triangle, and square. The shape entity itself has no real *draw* operation; *draw* can be specified only for actual shape types. The operation *draw* on shapes has the more abstract property that it is common to all shapes even though the implementation is different for each shape.

Genericity is typically used for containers such as *LIST*. Lists can contain many elements such as integers, shapes, debts, and other lists. The algorithms for manipulating the list remain unchanged, no matter what element type is stored in the list.

So, to put this another way, inheritance is useful where different types have the same operations but the algorithms for the operations are different; genericity is useful where the algorithms are the same for different types.

6.1 Basic Structures

With generics you can extend classes in ways not possible with and complementary to inheritance. If you are familiar with the basic constructs of generics and templates you could skim or skip the next few sections.

Eiffel

In Eiffel, you define a generic class as follows:

```
EIFFEL
    Formal_generics      ≜   "[" Formal_generic_list "]"
    Formal_generic_list  ≜   { Formal_generics "," ... }
    Formal_generic       ≜   Formal_generic_name [Constraint]
    Formal_generic_name  ≜   Identifier
    Constraint           ≜   "->" Class_type
```

A generic class in Eiffel is a class where the header contains one or more formal generics. Each generic in the list can be unconstrained or constrained. Including a constraint is frequently important, as often you want to make certain assumptions about the type of the generic in order to be able to apply certain operations without the need for a type cast. This is an important difference between Eiffel and C++ that we will explore in more depth later.

An example is

Eiffel

```
class SHELF [I -> SHELF_ITEM]
feature
    put (item: I) is
        ...

    remove: I is
        ...
end
```

The syntax for instantiating a class type with actual generics is

---
EIFFEL

        Class_type   ≜   Class_name [Actual_generics]
        Actual_generics ≜   "[" Type_list "]"
        Type_list   ≜   { Type "," ... }

And an example looks like

    book_shelf: *SHELF* [*BOOK*]   *Eiffel*
    CD_shelf: *SHELF* [*CD*]

Both the types *BOOK* and *CD* here must conform to *SHELF_ITEM*; that is, *SHELF_ITEM* must be an ancestor of *BOOK* and *CD*.

C++

C++ allows both types and functions to be generic with its `template` construct. Since C++ is not as pure in its object orientation as Eiffel, it is probably a good thing for a C extension to have the template facility also available on functions. The syntax is defined as follows:

C++

template-declaration:
    export$_{opt}$ `template` < *template-parameter-list* > *declaration*

template-parameter-list:
    template-parameter
    template-parameter-list , *template-parameter*

The *declaration* that you can apply `template` to may be a declaration or definition of a function or a class; a definition of a static data member of a class template; a definition of a member function or a member class of a class template; or a definition of a member template of a class.

The template parameters are themselves defined as

C++

template-parameter:
    type-parameter
    parameter-declaration

type-parameter:
    `class` *identifier$_{opt}$*
    `class` *identifier$_{opt}$* = *type-id*
    `typename` *identifier$_{opt}$*
    `typename` *identifier$_{opt}$* = *type-id*
    `template` < *template-parameter-list* > `class` *identifier$_{opt}$*
    `template` < *template-parameter-list* > `class` *identifier$_{opt}$*
                                                         = *template-name*

An example is

C++

```
template<class T> class Shelf
{
public:
    void put (T& item);
    T& remove ();
};

template<class T> void Shelf<T>::put (T& item)
{...}
template<class T> T& Shelf<T>::remove () {...}
```

Java

Java has no generic facility, so we have no syntax or examples to look at here. The Java recommendation is to use type casts whenever retrieving an object from a container class. Extensions to Java such as Pizza, GJ, and NextGen have been developed, but have not become widely available. The majority of Java programmers will probably have to wait for generics to be implemented in the Java base.

[Flanagan 96]

6.2 C++ Syntax

While the concept of genericity and templates is correct, there are several problems with templates in C++. The syntax leaves a lot to be desired. Of course you can form your own opinion of that. However, again C++ masks what is a simple and powerful mechanism with complicated syntax, so people will baulk at using it. There are examples of where the quirky syntax is a trap for young players. For example, declaring a list of a list of integers could easily be written

[Stroustrup 9 (15.7)]

```
    List<List<int>> a;
```
not C++

However, this results in a syntax error as >> is the right shift or output operator. You must write this as > >.

```
    List<List<int> > a;
```
C++

Further, *template* is confusing terminology, as the conceptual view is that a class is a template for a set of objects. "Object-oriented languages allow one to describe a template, if you will, for an entire set of objects. Such a template is called a class." This is not the meaning of the C++ term `template`, which refers to genericity. The problem in C++ is that it uses implementation-oriented terminology for the concept of genericity.

[Ege 96]

6.3 Constrained Genericity

The major difference between C++ and Eiffel is that C++ has no constraint on the types that can be used as the parameters to the templates. As the ARM says on this topic, "Specifying no restrictions on what types can match a type argument gives the programmer the maximum flexibility. The cost is that errors – such as attempt-

[C++ ARM] (14.2)

ing to sort objects of a type that does not have comparison operators – will not in general be detected until link time."

This shows the need for at least an optional type constraint on the actual types passed to the template. Eiffel has such optional constraints in the form of *constrained genericity*. For example

Eiffel

    class *SORTED_LIST* [*T -> COMPARABLE*]
        ...
    feature
        insert (*item*: *T*) **is** ... **end**
    end

ensures that the type of the item to insert has appropriate comparison operators from type *COMPARABLE* in order to insert *item* in the right place in the *SORTED_LIST*. Note that multiple inheritance is important, so any type eligible for insertion in the *SORTED_LIST* includes the comparison operators.

6.4 Genericity and Code Bloat

A common criticism of the C++ template mechanism is that you get *code bloat*; that is, for every type based on a template definition, the compiler might replicate the code. Seeing that the purpose of templates is to save the programmer from manual replication, this does not seem like a bad thing. A good implementation of C++ will avoid code bloat where possible. In fact it is allowed for in the C++ ARM. "This can cause the generation of unnecessarily many function definitions. A good implementation might take advantage of the similarity of such functions to suppress spurious replications." Even so, most C++ implementations of templates suffer from code bloat because they use simple text substitution as the mechanism to expand the templates. As we have seen, template is implementation-oriented terminology, suggestive of one copy per parameter.

[C++ ARM]
(14.4)

[Meyer 97]
(10.5)

Meyer also points out that the fears should be baseless.

> Genericity should not imply code duplication: it is possible with appropriate language design and a good compiler, to generate a single target code for any generic class, so that all of the following will be small or zero:
>
> • Effect on compilation time.
>
> • Effect on size of generated code.

- Effect on execution time.
- Effect on execution space.

When working in such an environment, you can use the full power of genericity without any fear of unpleasant effects on either compile-time or run-time performance.

Thus I am more forgiving than some of C++ on the basis of code bloat, although most C++ implementations could be criticized for code bloat. The whole concept of generics and templates is simple and yet powerful, and it allows the generation of quite sophisticated programs from simple specifications. If you are overly worried about code bloat, simply do not use genericity. As Stroustrup points out, "What you don't use, you don't pay for." This is a good principle for compiler implementers, but often simple principles of optimization prove not so easy to implement. Many people will use genericity, however, since few will find it practical to code a different kind of *LIST* for every possible list element.

[Stroustrup 9

6.5 An Alternative Form of Genericity

Palsberg and Schwartzbach have a good chapter on genericity. Genericity is the ability to build a derived class from a base class by type substitution. Compare this with inheritance, where you can add class members and redefine inherited routines. They criticize the parameterized class/template mechanisms of Eiffel and C++ for three reasons: first, there are two kinds of class—generic and nongeneric; second, you can apply generic instantiation only once; and third, a generic instance is not a subclass.

[Palsberg and Schwartzbach 9

BETA uses a different mechanism—*virtual binding* or *virtual classes*—that is more flexible than the Eiffel/C++ parameterized classes, but Palsberg and Schwartzbach show that you can produce derived classes that are not statically type correct.

[Palsberg and Schwartzbach 9

A problem with the parameterized class mechanism is that the base class designer must think about it in advance, and then only the types nominated in the parameter list can be substituted. This reduces flexibility. Palsberg and Schwartzbach suggest a genericity mechanism known as *class substitution*, which makes inheritance and genericity orthogonal rather than independent concepts. Class substitution has the advantage that a base class designer does not need to design genericity into the base class; any subclass can perform class substitution. Furthermore, any type in the base class may be substituted, not only those given in

[Palsberg and Schwartzbach 9

the parameter list. And class substitution can be applied repeatedly, whereas instantiation of a parameterized class can be done only once.

An example of class substitution in Eiffel-like syntax is

class *A*
feature
    x, y: *T*

    assign **is**
      do
        x := *y*
      end
end

This can be modified using class substitution

A [*T* <- *INTEGER*]
A [*T* <- *ANIMAL*]

You can also use constrained genericity with exactly the same syntax that Eiffel now has, as in the *SORTED_LIST* example, except that semantically the [*T* -> *COMPARABLE*] specifies only that any class substituting *T* must be a subclass of *COMPARABLE*, it is not a parameter list, as in Eiffel. You can build new types out of sorted list.

SORTED_LIST [*T* <- *INTEGER*]
SORTED_LIST [*T* <- *STRING*]

Java might be in the best position to implement this flexible class substitution mechanism for genericity because it has not yet implemented genericity (which is nonetheless a serious omission at this stage, more serious than the omission of multiple inheritance). Eiffel and C++ could extend their mechanisms, but then there would be two ways of doing the same thing, except the class substitution mechanism is more flexible than parameterized classes. I do not know of any languages that implement class substitution as yet, and other consequences must be thought through before adding it to languages, so don't dispose of your Eiffel and C++ compilers just yet!

Virtual Types

As mentioned earlier, BETA introduced the notion of virtual classes. The problem with BETA's virtual classes is that they are not statically type safe, but need some run-time checks to guarantee safety. This is much the same type of problem that Eiffel has with its argument covariant types. The BETA people claim that you can have two but not all three of static typing, subtype substitutability, and covariance.

[Madsen 95]

Much recent work has been done on this, and one paper claims you can actually have all three. The example is taken from David Shang's *Are Cows Animals*, which looks like this.

[Torgersen 9]
[Shang 95]

```
class ANIMAL
type
    FOOD_TYPE -> FOOD
feature
    eat (f: FOOD_TYPE) is ...
end


class HERBIVORE
inherit
    ANIMAL
type
    FOOD_TYPE -> PLANTS
end


class COW
inherit
    HERBIVORE
type
    FOOD_TYPE = GRASS
end
```

This is in Eiffel-like syntax for clarity, but we have introduced the **type** clause. Note that the virtual type *FOOD_TYPE* is not unlike a formal generic parameter. It is covariantly constrained as the type hierarchy descends (the syntax used here being the Eiffel -> to suggest the arrows in inheritance diagrams, whereas <= is used in Torgersen's paper to suggest subtype or same type). The claimed benefit of virtual types is that it gives you both generics and covariance in one concept. We discuss covariance and Shang's work further in section 9.6.

Note that the problem we are trying to solve both here and in covariance is where we have two or more related types that separately vary as the type hierarchy descends. Here it is *ANIMAL* and *FOOD_TYPE*. Other examples are commonly found in *COLLECTION* and *ITERATOR* or *VIEW* and *MODEL*.

The problem in the animal example comes with collections. Suppose we have a farmer who feeds his collection of animals.

```
class FARMER
feature
    feed_animal (a: ANIMAL; f: FOOD) is
        do
            a.eat (f)
        end
end
```

But here, if *a* is bound to an object of *COW* type, we have no check to guarantee that the food is *GRASS*. The idea with virtual types is to use the type information for *FOOD_TYPE* in the *ANIMAL* object

```
class FARMER
feature
    feed_animal (a: ANIMAL) is
        do
            a.eat (create a.FOOD_TYPE.make)
        end
end
```

In this example, the correct kind of food is derived from the type of animal at run time. Hence no type error can occur. This is rather like the *clone* operator, which will create a new object of the same type as the object being cloned. As we shall see, Eiffel declares *clone* to return an object of **like** *Current* type. The virtual type idea is similar because the actual type of another entity that is tied to the current entity is derived at run time.

In Eiffel, we could probably extend the concept of anchored types so that an anchored type could be tied to a virtual type

```
class FARMER
feature
    feed_animal (a: ANIMAL; f: like a.FOOD_TYPE) is
        do
```

         a.eat (f)
      end
   end

This section has explained virtual types with some hypothetical extensions to Eiffel. The concept of virtual types is very new and is still being researched. A good deal more thought and consideration of alternatives needs to be given before adding this facility to a language such as Eiffel. Rémy and Vouillon to the contrary claim that parametric polymorphism is in all cases preferable to virtual types. [Rémy and Vouillon 98]

6.6 Java and Genericity

Lack of genericity is admitted to be Java's greatest shortcoming. "The most serious impediment to writing substantial programs in the Java programming language is the lack of a *genericity* mechanism." Also: "Nevertheless, Java has some significant limitations from the perspective of software engineering that could be eliminated by judicious language extensions." However, it is also admitted that extending Java is not such an easy task. "Ironically, Java's portable programming model makes refining the language more difficult because it imposes severe constraints on the implementation of language extensions." [Cartwright and Steele 98]

[Cartwright and Steele 98]

While the concept of genericity seems deceptively simple, when you take into account all the subtleties of the concept and the variants of implementation, there is room for plenty of controversy about what exactly should be done. A number of proposals to retrofit genericity into Java already exist, notably among these, Pizza, GJ, NextGen, and Solorzano and Alagić have a counterproposal. Other extensions have been proposed, but examining these proposals will bring out the main problems.

Time will tell if these problems make Meyer's words prophetic. As he says, we have certainly seen all this before with C++, but people have short memories.

> Java is one of the most innovative developments in the software field, and there are many reasons to be excited about it. Java's language is not the main one. As an O-O extension of C, it has missed some of the main lessons learned since 1985 by the C++ community; as in the very first version of C++, there is no genericity and only single inheritance is supported. Correcting these early oversights in C++ was a long and painful process, creating years of havoc as compilers never quite supported the same language, books never quite gave accurate information, trainers never quite taught the right stuff, and programmers never quite knew what to think.

[Meyer 97] (35.5)

Of course, it can be said that Meyer has Eiffel to promote in opposition; however, Meyer has frequently admitted the technical obstacles that many of these concepts provided in the construction of Eiffel compilers and run-time environments, so the comments are made from painful experience, even from a language where these concepts were designed in from the start.

As Meyer says, implementation of these facilities in C++ meant that each C++ compiler provided somewhat different features. Java has an extra problem, that of the Java Virtual Machine (JVM). In order to implement genericity correctly, the JVM should also be modified. However, this would mean that several versions of the JVM would exist at one time, some of which could not run newer programs that were written with genericity. The problem of coordinating updates of JVMs has led to proposals that do not require updates to the JVM, but that also do not support genericity fully.

Pizza and GJ

The first of these proposals and trial implementations was Pizza, by Martin Odersky and Philip Wadler. Pizza is backward compatible with Java since all Java programs are also legal Pizza programs. However, this is not quite true for the libraries—the types `Collection` and `Collection<A>` are incompatible, which meant all legacy code needed rewriting. This led them to develop a new proposal in conjunction with Sun: GJ, for "Generic Java."

[BOSW 98] GJ introduces the concept of *raw types*. In this case, `Collection` is the raw type of `Collection<A>`, and an argument of `Collection<A>` can be passed wherever a formal argument of `Collection` is expected. A problem with this is that a reference to `Collection` may be used to place any arbitrary object into a structure that has been given a specific generic entity type, which breaks the purpose of genericity in the first place. If this is done, a run-time error could occur when retrieving the object from the collection. In this case the compiler generates an *unchecked warning* on assignments to raw types.

GJ translates the generic enabled code into standard Java. It does this by removing the generic types. Normally, the types corresponding to the generic parameter will be converted to Object. However, as in Eiffel, the genericity may be constrained by a *bounding* type.

```
class OrderedCollection<A implements Comparable<A>>
```

In this case, any actual generic parameter is constrained to implement the `Comparable` interface, and the types corresponding to A will be replaced by `Com-`

parable. Note that the bound Comparable<A> is stated in terms of the generic parameter A. This is known as *F-bounded polymorphism*.

The other notable part of the GJ translation is that the translator must insert casts to the actual generic type when retrieving the generic elements from the structure. For example

```
LinkedList<String> lls;
...
String s = lls.first();
```

does not require a cast because it is known that elements retrieved from lls are of type String, and hence the assignment works. GJ translates this to

```
LinkedList lls;
...
String s = (String)lls.first();
```

where an explicit cast is needed and will be needed on every access to the structure. This shows that a single specification of the type in the generic version can replace a plethora of casts and hence save the programmer a significant bookkeeping task, especially if the type is later changed, which in the nongeneric case will require every cast to be changed.

You can find a comprehensive description of GJ in [GJ 98]. [BOSW 98]

NextGen

NextGen is a more general parametric extension to Java than GJ. NextGen is in fact a superset of GJ, as GJ is a superset of Java. With NextGen, type parameters may be used in places where they cannot be used in GJ.

[Cartwright & Steele 98]

Like GJ, NextGen requires no extensions to the JVM. Hence true run-time types of parameterized classes are not available. To overcome this to some extent, NextGen introduces mangled class names to represent the parameterized classes. The NextGen compiler also generates lightweight wrapper classes for each instantiation of a parameterized class.

For each instantiation of a parametric class C<A, ...>, the NextGen compiler generates an empty wrapper interface $C<A, ...> and a wrapper class $$C<A, ...>. Figure 6-1 shows how a simple parametric type hierarchy expands.

Java and Genericity

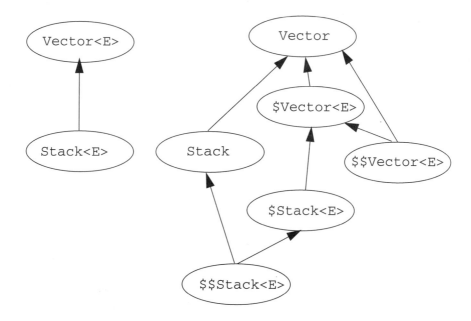

Figure 6-1. A NextGen-generated type hierarchy

While NextGen is an improvement on GJ, it does not support reflection, that is, run-time determination of actual types, nor can you use primitive types as actual type parameters.

Another thing that you cannot do in GJ, but you can in NextGen is create generic types.

```
public class GenCreate<T>
{
    public meth()
    {
        T t = new T;
        T [] ta = new T [n];
    }
}
```

Creation on generic parameters was not allowed in Eiffel until recently.

Another drawback of the definitions of GJ and NextGen is that primitive types cannot be used to parameterize generic classes. In other words, the following is not allowed.

```
public Vector <int> vi;  // Not legal
```

Such generics with primitive built-in type parameters are allowed in Eiffel.

You can find a comprehensive description of NextGen in [C&S 98].

6.7 Some Theory on Genericity

[Solorzano and Alagić 98] evaluates many different schemes of genericity, explaining the many concepts behind genericity and revealing why the GJ and NextGen schemes are not enough because they do not support full run-time types for generics for reflection. The unfortunate thing is that, in order to implement genericity properly in Java, extensions to the JVM are necessary; if this were done, many millions of JVMs would not be able to run newer Java programs using genericity. Hence the GJ and NextGen proposals, even if adopted, will not implement genericity fully.

[Solorzano a Alagić 98]

Reflection and Introspection

A *reflective system* is one that can see information about itself at run time. With a reflective system you will be able to find out the class and type of an object as well as the attributes of an object. Java provides this with the class `Class` and other classes in the package `java.lang.reflect`, and Eiffel has a similar set of classes to determine such information at run time. Reflection is also sometimes called introspection.

Homogeneous and Heterogeneous Instantiation

The important distinction in supporting true reflection with genericity is how generic classes are instantiated. The two methods are homogeneous and heterogeneous instantiation. With the homogeneous method, generic code is generated for all instantiated classes; the classes therefore share this code. With the heterogeneous method, specific code is generated for all instantiated classes. The major drawback with the heterogeneous method is clear: much more code is generated, and this leads to the code bloat that C++ is often criticized for.

While this is not a problem with the homogeneous approach, that approach has a problem that is less obvious. It does not support reflection—the generic code must strip the type information for each instantiated class. In other words, the true type of a feature in an instantiated generic class cannot be determined at run time. For example, you will not be able to determine whether a `List` is a `List<Document>` or a `List<Integer>` using reflection; this information is lost.

The problem with the homogeneous solution in GJ and NextGen means that you can't have instantiations on generic classes with primitive types; that is, you can't have a `List` of `int`, but you can have a `List` of `Integer`.

The probable solution is to have heterogeneous class records that record the reflective type information for each instantiated class, but to still generate generic code, which can look up the type information in the class record of the current object. This way the generated routines are homogeneous and shared among class instantiations where possible. Unfortunately, it is not always possible for the code to be generic; specific code must be generated for primitive and expanded types. However, for every generic reference type in a routine, generic code can be generated and shared between every actual generic that is a reference type. Thus different instantiated generic types share routines where possible, which avoids most of the code bloat.

Textual Substitution

Textual substitution is one of the possible compilation methods for heterogeneous translation. In textual substitution, each actual generic type parameter is substituted wherever the formal generic parameter occurs, so that an instantiated generic class is created. Most C++ implementations use this method. Not only does this produce the problem of code bloat, but it means that the source of the template class must be available for the compiler to perform substitution.

Polymorphism, Bounded Polymorphism, F-Bounded Polymorphism

Genericity is also known as parametric polymorphism. Simple parametric polymorphism is also known as universal type quantification. In this scheme, no limit is placed on what an actual generic parameter may be. C++ supports only parametric polymorphism. An example is

```
public class List<T>
{
    public T first ();
    public addElement (T el);
}
```

Note that the examples in this section are not real Java, but reflect the proposed genericity extensions to Java. If we want a sorted list, then we must at least be able to order the elements. Thus we can add a static indication to tell the compiler that this is a type requirement on the actual generic parameters. This is known as *bounded polymorphism* or *bounded type quantification*.

```
public interface Ordered
{
    public boolean lessThan (Object o);
}

public class OrderedList<T implements Ordered>
{
    public T first ();
    public addElement (T el);
}
```

In this example, we require that any instantiation guarantees that the elements are ordered; thus we have the test `lessThan` in them so that we can compare one to the other. Eiffel implements this with constrained genericity.

The problem with bounded polymorphism is that the method `lessThan` takes an `Object` parameter, which is not necessarily ordered itself. Unfortunately, what we would really like is to constrain the genericity further, so that we can guarantee not only that the parameter itself is ordered, but that the type of the parameter is the same as the actual class of the `Ordered` object itself. This is a form of recursive bounding called *F-bounded polymorphism*.

```
public interface Ordered <T>
{
    public boolean lessThan (T o);
}

public class OrderedList<T implements Ordered<T>>
{
    public T first ();
    public addElement (T el);
}
```

The parameter `T` is recursively used as a parameter to the now-generic class `Ordered`. The proposals for genericity in Java include F-bounded polymorphism, as does Eiffel. C++ does not support bounded or F-bounded polymorphism.

6.8 Genericity and Covariance

One of Eiffel's type conformance rules can result in type problems. The rule is the VNCC validity rule (VNCC is a systematic validity reference to the Eiffel language definition in [Meyer 92]), which allows the following example. Suppose we have a generic class B $[T]$. If Y1, Y2, etc., are subclasses of X, then the rule says that B $[Y1]$ can be assigned to B $[X]$ as follows:

a: B $[Y1]$
b: B $[X]$

$b := a$ -- OK

This assignment is legal because the rule says that, as long as the actual generic of the entity on the right conforms to the actual generic of the class on the left, then the assignment is allowable. Consider the case where B is a *LIST*; then we can do the following:

a: *LIST* $[Y1]$
b: *LIST* $[X]$
y2: *Y2*

$b := a$ -- OK
b.put (*y2*)

This adds an element of type *Y2* to a *LIST* that was originally declared to take elements of type *Y1*, a clear type error. The language could have avoided this unfortunate type consequence by not allowing covariant generic parameters. However, to preclude this situation would make the language inflexible. Conformance rules govern not only valid assignments, but valid parameter passing (which really is a kind of assignment).

Consider a case in which you want to write a utility routine that ranges over all the elements of a *LIST* $[X]$. This routine calls only routines on the list elements that apply to all *X*s. These routines can of course be redefined for *Y1*, *Y2*, etc., so that the specific routines are dynamically selected for the correct type. Without the VNCC rule, writing such a routine would not be possible, and hence opportunities for reuse would be lost. However, the routine must guarantee not to replace or add elements to the list, as it does not know what the correct type for the list is.

It is also difficult to preclude such a routine that accepts *LIST* $[X]$ as a parameter from adding elements to the list. If the actual type of the list really is *LIST*

[*X*], then elements of types *Y1*, *Y2*, etc., can legitimately be added to this list, but if the list is *LIST* [*Y1*], which conforms to LIST [*X*], it is actually wrong to add elements of type *Y2* to the list, but the VNCC rule allows this.

7

Interfaces and Access Control

Access control is defined by interfaces. Interfaces define which external classes can access features in a given class, and how they may access them. This access control is class based and is enforced at compile time, which restricts what other programmers may access in a class.

This chapter looks at the different mechanisms used in our three languages and finds, in looking at the differences between Eiffel and C++, that these languages have very different views of the role of subclasses with respect to the concepts of reusability and extendability. We will see that access control is actually a complex topic that aids in defining well-structured software and therefore in reasoning about correct software.

7.1 Basic Structures

We have already seen the grammar specification for C++ and Java for access control. It very simply specified `public`, `protected`, and `private`. We have seen most of the grammar structures before, but we shall repeat them here to refresh our memory.

If you are familiar with these languages, you can skim or skip to the next section.

Eiffel

The Eiffel syntax for export controls looks like

```
┌─EIFFEL─────────────────────────────────────────────────────────┐
│                                                                │
│        New_exports         ≜   export New_export_list          │
│        New_export_list     ≜   { New_export_item ";" ... }     │
│        New_export_item     ≜   Clients Feature_set             │
│                                                                │
│        Creators            ≜   creation                        │
│                                { Creation_clause creation ... }⁺│
│        Creation_clause     ≜   [Clients] [Header_comment]      │
│                                Feature_list                    │
│                                                                │
│        Features            ≜   feature { Feature_clause feature ... }⁺│
│        Feature_clause      ≜   [Clients]                       │
│                                [Header_comment]                │
│                                Feature_declaration_list        │
│                                                                │
│        Clients             ≜   "{" { Class_name ";" ... } "}"  │
│                                                                │
└────────────────────────────────────────────────────────────────┘
```

Here we see three places where export access (Clients) occurs. First, we have the ability to change access policies on any or all features inherited from a parent. Second, each creation routine can be independently exported to different classes. Third, each feature group can be exported to the given list of clients.

C++

The C++ *access-specifier* looks like

```
┌─C++────────────────────────────────────────────────────────────┐
│                                                                │
│    access-specifier:                                           │
│        private                                                 │
│        protected                                               │
│        public                                                  │
│                                                                │
└────────────────────────────────────────────────────────────────┘
```

This can be used on a group of members in the class or when inheriting a base class to give the allowed access for members of that class. As we have seen, in the base class case, `public` means subtype inheritance and `protected` or `private` means implementation inheritance. We take a closer look at this in this chapter.

Java

In Java the access is specified on each member individually, not on a group of members as in C++ and Eiffel. The grammar productions are

---
Java

FieldModifier: *one of*
    `public    protected    private`
    `final     static       transient    volatile`

MethodModifier: *one of*
    `public    protected    private`
    `abstract  static       final        synchronized    native`

For access control the only modifiers of interest are `public`, `protected`, and `private`.

As you can see from the grammars, Eiffel's export mechanism has much more to it than the C++ and Java mechanisms. This is because Eiffel's mechanism is much more fine grained and, in fact, is much more flexible than C++ and Java. This has the effect that Eiffel has one consistent way to achieve many effects, whereas C++ and Java must push this complexity elsewhere. We shall see more on this in the following sections of this chapter.

7.2 Friends (C++)

Friends are a mechanism to override data hiding. Friends of a class have access to its private data. Friend is a limited export mechanism. Friends have three problems.

1. They can change the internal state of objects from outside the definition of the class.
2. They introduce extra coupling between components and therefore should be used sparingly.

3. They have access to everything, rather than being restricted to the members of interest to them.

Friends are useful, and a case can be made for shades of gray between public, protected, and private members. An alternative to friends is multiple interfaces which provide the functionality of friends and avoid the above problems. Each interface to a class can be exported to everything, or to selected classes only. A selective export mechanism is more general than public, private, protected, and friend, and it explicitly documents the couplings between entities in the system. Selective export specifies not only that a member is exported but to which classes it is exported. Some people feel that using friend is bad practice, but in fact this is not so, as friend gives control similar to Eiffel's selective export. Possibly the closest match to Eiffel would be to make everything private (or protected) where any kind of access control is needed, and to use friends only to explicitly state the dependencies between classes.

One reason given for friends is they allow more efficient access to data members than a member function call. The way C++ is often used is that data members are not put in the public section because this breaks the data hiding principle. (See the section on encapsulation and implementation hiding in chapter 1 for this book's position on data hiding.)

As mentioned in the section on inlines in chapter 4, implementation hiding is different from data hiding. As long as you access your data functionally, you do not have to hide your data, only the access mechanism.

Another question is, since there are inlines, is there a need for the similar mechanism of friends? If you mark a function inline, it is going to expand inline and avoid the function call overhead. So in this case, friend is a superfluous mechanism.

In Java, classes in the same package can access instance variables from other classes in a *friendly* fashion. This is contrary to good OO design, as it means you can access things without going through the published interface of a class. Thus all classes in a single package are really friends. This might be all right, since you expect a package to be developed by a single vendor, but this is by no means guaranteed in Java, and therefore an "unfriendly" class could be introduced into a package.

Eiffel offers the pure OO approach, where everything must go through publicized interfaces. It is easy to get the same effect as friend classes with access to all or some private data; Eiffel's export mechanism allows all this, but it is the one simple scheme. Note in Eiffel that data attributes in a class may be exported in the published interface, since access is uniform. In that case, external entities can read the data, as if it were invoking a function, but you cannot write to a data item in an external class.

To update a data item in Eiffel, you must call an update procedure. This is also Eiffel's data validity mechanism, because the caller must satisfy preconditions built into the owning class in order to update data. Eiffel's assertion mechanism ensures that an object's data is always in a consistent state. Part of the purpose of friend is to update an item directly, without the overhead of a procedure call. In Eiffel the compiler will automatically inline procedures where possible, so the efficiency concern is addressed.

To summarize: Eiffel does not need the friend mechanism for two reasons. For one thing, external classes can access data attributes for reading; for another, for update, a procedure is expanded inline where practical. Accessing a data item does not contravene encapsulation or implementation hiding. Data hiding is not encapsulation, although with encapsulation *implementation* data is hidden, the operative word being implementation, not data.

7.3 Controlled Exports vs. Friends

As noted in the previous section on friends, there is a case for finer-grained control of exports than `public`, `private`, and `protected`. Except for friends, Java uses the same mechanism as C++, but adds *default* access, where access is only permitted from within the package. Eiffel does not have friends—it allows classes to be related by a finer-grained export mechanism; for any set of features, you can specify exactly to which classes they are exported. Classes that are closely related export to each other interfaces that are not available to other classes outside of that group.

Also in Eiffel, you can export a routine to a different set of classes based on whether the routine is called as a creation routine (constructor) or normal routine call.

In Eiffel all features are public by default. Public access can also be explicitly stated by exporting to class *ANY*, that is, the universal set. If a set of features is to be protected, i.e., internal and not visible to clients, it is exported to class *NONE*. Such a set of features is *secret*. *NONE* is the equivalent of the empty set in set theory, which is notionally a subset of all sets; *NONE* is a subclass of all other classes and has only one possible value—*Void*.

In Eiffel there is no equivalent of `private`, where features can be hidden from subclasses. Eiffel views `private` as not only unnecessary, but undesirable—private features would be locked away from reuse in subclasses. This differs greatly from the C++ view, where `private` is the default. C++ considers that the concept of `private` would be meaningless if programmers of subclasses could access `private` members. This difference between Eiffel and C++ shows that these two languages have very different views on the role of subclasses. When writing a class that you suspect could be subclassed, it is often best to make members `protected` rather than `private` in order to allow the subclasses some flexibility.

[Stroustrup 9 (15.3.1.1)]

The Eiffel philosophy is that with inheritance you get unrestricted access to the implementation as this is key to the flexibility of reuse and extension. As a subclass, you can redefine any routine inherited from a parent. When you redefine a routine, you are changing the implementation. Since you are changing the implementation, the private restriction could be a nuisance to some subclass that hasn't been written yet. If you need to access a variable and the parent class designer has made it `private`, you are out of luck. At best you could go to the programmer who owns that class and try to convince him or her to make the variable `protected`. Good luck—that kind of request often generates a lot of heat. At worst you can do nothing about it because the class might be from outside and closed to you. Again in C++, the parent class designer is forced to make decisions that should be left open. This is why it is better to make members `protected` rather than `private` to allow some flexibility.

In C++ and Java, private precludes undisciplined changes to a superclass's part of the state of an object. In Eiffel, such undisciplined changes are less likely because a superclasses invariant that controls its state must also be enforced in all subclasses.

In C++, `private` restricts only access; it does not restrict visibility in a subclass. With `private`, it is still possible to redefine a `private virtual` function from a base class in a subclass. This is not a problem, but you cannot prevent redefinition in a subclass the way you can with the Eiffel **frozen** mechanism.

In Java you cannot override a private method, but you can overload it.

> Note that a private method is never accessible to subclasses and so cannot be hidden or overridden in the technical sense of those terms. This means that a subclass can declare a method with the same signature as a private method in one of its superclasses, and there is no requirement that the return type or throws clause of such a method bear any relationship to those of the private method in the superclass.

[Sun 96]

Another feature of `private` in C++ and Java is that it is on a class basis, not an object basis; that is, any objects in the same class can access private features of other objects. You cannot be more restrictive. Thus the following examples are legal

Controlled Exports vs. Friends

C++

```
class access_test
{
public:
    access_test *at;

    void access_fn ();

private:
    int priv_int;
};

void access_test::access_fn ()
{
    int i;

    i = priv_int;    // own copy
    i = at->priv_int;
}
```

and in Java:

Java

```
public class AccessTest
{
    void access_fn ()
    {
        int i;

        i = priv_int;    // own copy
        i = at.priv_int;
    }

    private AccessTest at;
    private int priv_int;
}
```

In Eiffel, however, you can get exactly the export mechanism you want, either restricting to the current object or to objects of the same or descendant classes

Eiffel

class *ACCESS_TEST*
feature
    access_proc **is**

```
        local
            i: INTEGER
        do
            i := at.priv_to_class   -- OK
            i := at.priv_to_object  -- error can't access
        end

    at: ACCESS_TEST

feature {ACCESS_TEST}
    -- Any features here will be available to objects of type ACCESS_TEST
    -- and no others.
    priv_to_class: INTEGER

feature {NONE}
    -- Any features here are restricted to the current object only.
    priv_to_object: INTEGER
end -- class ACCESS_TEST
```

With Eiffel's *NONE*, subclasses can access a feature controlled by *NONE*, but this is the same object, not external objects. Cardelli defines private this way: "Objects often have *private* variables, which are useful to maintain and update the local state of an object while preventing arbitrary external interference." Eiffel's *NONE* achieves this, whereas C++ and Java's `private` do allow outside interference from other objects of the same class. [Cardelli 88]

Another problem specific to C++ is that, if you can get a reference or a pointer to a `protected` or `private` member, then you can subvert the protection mechanism and access the member anyway. C++, `private` does not offer absolute protection against outside interference. "The protection of private data relies on restriction of the use of the class member names. It can therefore be circumvented by address manipulation and explicit type conversion. But this, of course, is cheating. C++ protects against accident rather than deliberate circumvention (fraud). Only hardware can protect against malicious use of a general-purpose language, and even that is hard to do in realistic systems." Hackers must love this reasoning. (A realistic system where such hardware protection is built in is Unisys A Series, but, unfortunately, these machines are overlooked by the industry.) [Stroustrup 97 (10.2.2)]

Pointers are like giving an "access-all-areas" pass to someone you don't necessarily trust. You need another style rule that functions should not return references or pointers to `private` or `protected` members. Such restrictions, however, make software less malleable—what if you want to change the access on a member from `public` to `private` or `protected`? Then you might have to change functions that return pointers or references. Not that this is a good idea even on `public` members, as it means that you can access or update the member without even having a reference to the object. This aliasing in C++ makes it difficult to reason about C++ programs—that is to have any certainty that they are correct. Add to this the fact that you have more dependencies between modules and that software becomes more brittle.

`public`, `private`, and `protected` Inheritance

A further complication in C++ is that `public`, `private`, or `protected` can be specified when inheriting a base class. This gives one policy for how every inherited member from the base class is to be treated in the new class. `Public` inheritance implements type or interface inheritance, or the *is-a* relationship. `Private` inheritance is implementation inheritance because none of the inherited members is accessible in the interface of the derived class. Meyers says, "no one seems to know what protected inheritance (a latecomer on the scene) is supposed to mean."

[Meyers 92] (item 35)

`Public` inheritance is a bit more complicated because you get interface inheritance only in the case of pure virtual functions; otherwise you inherit interface and implementation. A problem with this is that, once a member is `private` or `protected`, it cannot be reexported, i.e., `protected` cannot be made `public`, and `private` cannot be made `protected` or `public`. Thus the temptation for a C++ programmer is to keep things `public`, as a derived class might want something to be `public`, even though it does not make sense to be `public` in the base class. The section on signature variance in chapter 9 points out that you have problems of covariance with this scheme. Again design decisions must be made early on issues you don't know about, but, as usual in C++, if you get it wrong, you can code to subvert the original design. For example:

C++

```
class A
{
public:
    int mine;
};

class B : private A
{};

B *b1;
```

```
    b1->mine;      // Error

    A *a1 = b1;       // Error
    A *a2 = (A*)b1;   // Okay
    a2->mine = 666;   // Undermine private:
                      //       a covariant catcall!
```

Eiffel again has a more fine-grained approach but shares some of C++'s problems. The export policy for each feature inherited from a parent class can be reviewed on a case-by-case basis. The export status of each feature can be changed and made more or less restrictive. If there is no new export policy, the default is the same as the parent class. Eiffel has much more flexibility than private and public inheritance for implementation and interface inheritance—you can decide for each inherited feature whether it should be part of the class interface, generally exported, or perhaps exported only to specific classes, or if the feature is implementation and only accessible within the class. The designer of a parent class does not have to consider what descendant classes need or worry about the case where their needs will be in conflict with each other because the designer of the descendant class has complete flexibility, which enhances reuse and extensibility.

Covariant exports can be a problem in Eiffel, though. The definition of the reexport clause should be changed so that the feature being reexported is allowed to be accessed by the union of the set of classes exported to in the parent, and the new set introduced in the subclass. This makes good modeling sense, because the designer of the parent class will decide which classes can access a feature based on the classes that the parent designer knows about. The subclass designer will be introducing a new set of classes that the parent designer will not know about. The subclass designer will want to add some of these classes to the export list. Therefore, export should become less restrictive down the inheritance hierarchy.

Java has no equivalent of public, protected, and private inheritance; each member is inherited with the same public, private, or protected attribute as the base class. In Java, a member can be made only more public than it was in a parent class—so Java avoids the problems of C++ and Eiffel.

7.4 Multiple Interfaces

A common requirement is to provide different clients with different interfaces. We have seen how this is straightforward in Eiffel since you can decide for each feature exactly which other classes the feature is exported to. Java uses a completely different approach of using multiple inheritance for interfaces. For any class, you can define as many interfaces as you require. However, you can still only make your interfaces `public` or not—you cannot explicitly state the relationship of these interfaces to other classes. The use of any particular public interface is therefore by convention only and the compiler cannot check for improper accesses. In Eiffel, the compiler does enforce that a class cannot use an interface that has not been exported to it. This is *role-based security*, and in fact is a very important form of security in Java's environment—the Internet.

Role-based security is becoming a very important area of research because it enables optimization since the system does not have to check that every invoked operation is valid. This is because an object is validated for a set of operations only when it is instantiated. For example, when super users log on they are validated for a set of privileged operations and the validation does not need to be repeated for each operation. This also contributes to safety since a security system can check up front that an object can indeed invoke all the operations that it requires—you won't suddenly get a security violation after running a job for several days. For an Internet language, Java is curiously lacking in this area.

In Java, you must define a type hierarchy in order to provide multiple interfaces. You can also do this in Eiffel, if it suits the design, but you are not forced to do so to provide multiple interfaces to one class.

[Stroustrup 97] (8.2.4)

[Stroustrup 97] (9.3.2)

In C++, the situation is more complicated—in order to provide multiple interfaces, you should use namespaces. You can define one namespace definition for clients and one for the environment related to the implementation. In order to make use of these different namespace definitions, you put the client interface in the usual `.h` file and the implementation interface in a special `.h` file. For every separate interface you need, you will have to provide another `.h` file. All these files can become unmanageable. In C++, as in Java, you have no compiler enforcement that an external class only accesses an object via the correct interface.

7.5 External Assignment (C++ and Java)

A fundamental access control is to forbid external entities to update an object. However, both C++ and Java allow class members to be assigned externally to the class

```
x.m = exp;
```

as long as the member m in the object x is `public`. This completely breaks the principle of encapsulation, since state changes should be allowed only from within a class itself; this way the class can enforce contracts and dynamic schemas built into preconditions. But of course C++ and Java are weak in their support for this.

In order to restore encapsulation, you should make m `private` and update it only via a function or method:

```
x.set_m (exp);
```

which now looks like Eiffel where external assignment is not allowed. You must call a *set* operation in the class to perform state updates. Because any single assignment might leave an object in an invalid state that violates the class invariant, it is best to perform all updates within a single routine so that the invariant is checked when the routine finishes. In Eiffel, if a field is exported to an accessing class, then you can read the field directly as a function. However, in C++ and Java, because the field is now `private` for encapsulation, you must provide an accessor function get_m, which adds to the clutter of a class.

You might be concerned that setting any field in an object requires the overhead of a routine call. However, the automatic inlining feature of Eiffel again comes to the rescue so that encapsulation is preserved without sacrificing efficiency (see section 4.6).

7.6 Export Controls and Nesting

The export controls of Eiffel allow you to relate classes in a far more precise manner than the `public`, `protected`, and `private` mechanisms of C++ and Java. Nesting classes is a way to get an intimate relationship in C++ and Java. Nesting means that the nested class can be accessed only via objects of the outer class. In Eiffel, without nesting, you can achieve a similar effect using the clients part of the creators and features clauses.

A usual example is a *LIST* with *LINK*s.

```
template<class T> class List                                   C++
{
    class Link
    {
        Link* next;
        Link* previous;
```

Export Controls and Nesting

```
            T item;
            ...
        };

        Link* head;

    public:
        ...
    };
```

This scheme is desirable because it ensures that `Links` cannot be aliased from outside the `List` structure and this makes the software easier to reason about. (You can consult the work of Potter, Noble, and Clarke on aliasing since aliasing is a very important topic in well-structured software.)

[CPN 98]

In Eiffel, the desirable effects of hiding objects within a surrounding structure, that is logical nesting, is obtained without the undesirable effects of textual nesting—you simply write this as two separate classes with appropriate access controls.

Eiffel

class *LINK* [*T*]
creation {*LIST*}
    make
feature {*LIST*}
    next, *previous*: *LINK* [*T*]
    item: *T*
end -- class *LINK*

class *LIST* [*T*]
feature {*NONE*}
    head: *LINK* [*T*]

feature {*ANY*}
    ...
end -- class *LIST*

In practice you might not want to make *LINK* so restrictive. For example, you might also want to define some form of *CURSOR* class that can iterate through the links independent of *LIST*. This mechanism allows you to have different parts of your program iterating through the same list independently. If the iteration itself is built into the *LIST*, this is not possible, so you then have to invent independent *CURSOR*s.

Note that in Eiffel and C++ we have no mechanism for saying whether a whole class definition is usable by another class. Java has an approximation to this facility in that a class itself can be marked `public`. If a class (or an interface) is marked `public`, then any class that has access to the package in which the class is defined can access that class; otherwise the class can be accessed only from other classes within the package.

7.7 Mutable Const (C++)

As we shall see, this section relates to the previous section on exports. `Const` has a very good purpose—it helps in reasoning about software correctness. It is easier to reason about the changes a software element makes if you know by some guarantee those things that it cannot change. In purpose, this relates C++ `const` to invariants in Eiffel.

An object declared with the `const` qualifier cannot be modified, or can it? In fact the `constness` of an object can be overcome. The most disciplined way to do this is to use the storage class specifier `mutable` on members of the class. This says that, even though an object of the class might be declared `const`, members specified as `mutable` can be modified. Note that, except for mutable members, any attempt to modify a `const` object "results in undefined behavior." [CD2 96]

If you are faced with the situation where a member you want to modify is not mutable, you can use the `const_cast<T>` form to cast this care away. If your compiler does not support `const_cast`, you can use an old C-style cast to cast away the `constness` of *this. Remember that you can modify members in an object from outside of the object, although this is very bad style.

As mentioned previously for the access protection mechanism, if you can get a pointer or reference to data within a `const` object, you may use this path to subvert `constness`. The writer of a class that could be used for `const` objects should be careful not to return pointers or references from functions.

So what has this to do with export? `Const` has to do with who may modify which objects and members. In Eiffel, remember, modifications may be done only in routines encapsulated in the class. This is also good style in C++, but it is not enforced. In Eiffel you can specify exactly who can access your update procedures and who can access functions, so you have explicit control over who may modify certain features and who has a functional view of features. Eiffel has no way to subvert this because if you have the need to modify a feature to which you don't have modification access, then the design is wrong, and you should correct the design rather than enter into subversion. This also shows the elegance of the Eiffel export mechanism, as opposed to C++'s access control, which, combined with several qualifiers and specifiers, makes it difficult to work out the semantics of the combinations.

In C++, a constant must be initialized at the time of declaration. In a class, certain functions can be marked as `const`, guaranteeing not to change state. In Eiffel, you can get similar (although not identical) effects by initializing an object when it is created through its creation routine and writing all other routines so that they don't change state. If you want to hedge your bets a bit more, you can export to *ANY* all state-preserving routines and selectively export state-changing routines, which will get a similar effect to C++'s mutable `const`.

A C++ example, where we have no direct equivalent in Eiffel, involves passing two arguments of the same type with one `const` and one not `const`.

C++
```
f (C& c, const C& cc) {}
```

Thus C++'s `const` applies on a per object basis, whereas restricting exports to nonstate-changing routines is class based.

Java is simple but weak in this case, only providing the specifier `final` to specify a constant value when an entity is declared. This will satisfy the majority of cases, but you don't have the ability to add more access control restrictions in order to provide better structure to large software projects. Of course, for small projects in Eiffel and C++, you need not be concerned with their more advanced features, but, as software grows and becomes more complex, these features become more useful.

7.8 Generalization

Access control is a good case study of generalization and how a single mechanism or at least small number of mechanisms can replace multiple mechanisms. Computing has been good at generalizing: programming would not be very powerful if we were limited to a number of given functions. Rather, we can build our own functions. Similarly, modern languages have realized that providing only a few built-in types is limiting, and therefore programmers can build their own powerful types.

With access control, instead of providing a limited number of access modifiers, such as `public`, `protected`, and `private`, Eiffel effectively allows the programmer to specify an unlimited number of access kinds that reflect the relationships between classes. C++ provides this kind of control with friends and Java with multiple interfaces, but now we have several mechanisms instead of one.

Besides, with Java interfaces, we cannot restrict the use of those interfaces to particular other interfaces or classes.

Hence the advantages of Eiffel's generalization of access control include: you have only one mechanism; this mechanism is more directly related to the problem of access control and hence it is easier for programmers to understand and then use; it is more powerful, as programmers can invent their own access control kinds between classes.

8

Constructors, Destructors, and Other Operators

This chapter looks at several operators, most notably, constructors and destructors, which initialize and clean up objects. These are used on classes and in C++ structs. (The relationship is apparent from the words `constructor`, `destructor`. The English word *destruct* also means to destroy, which has connotations of a disorderly end of existence. However, the very point of destructors in programming is to bring about orderly termination.)

8.1 Nameless Constructors (C++)

Multiple constructors must have different signatures, similar to overloaded functions. This precludes two or more constructors having the same signature. Constructors are also not named (apart from having the same name as the class), which makes it difficult to tell from the class header the purpose of the different constructors. Constructors suffer from the same problems we described in our discussion of overloaded functions in chapter 5. First, it would be easy to mark routines as constructors; for example

```
constructor make (...)...
constructor clone (...)...
constructor initialize (...)...
```

where each constructor leaves the object in valid, but potentially different, states. Named constructors would aid comprehension as to what the constructor is used for in the same way as function names document the purpose of a function. Second, named constructors would allow us to have multiple constructors with the same signature. Third, it is easier to match an object creation with the constructor actually called. Fourth, the compiler could check the arguments given in the invocation to the constructor signature.

Java's constructor scheme is the same as C++'s. Eiffel allows a series of *creation* routines. These are indeed independently named as suggested above.

Eiffel has another advantage in that creation routines can also be exported as normal routines that can be called to reinitialize an object. In C++ you cannot call a constructor after the object is created.

8.2 Default Constructors (C++ and Java)

In C++ a default constructor is a constructor that can be called without supplying an argument. If the programmer does not supply such a constructor, the compiler will try to generate one if needed. A constructor may have default arguments, and, if this means it can be called without arguments, it can become a default constructor. For example

```
class A                                                         C++
{
    A (int i = 13) {...}
}
```

This can make good sense when initializing bounded data structures, where the bound can take a default size. However, as described above, it can cause problems with more possible matches between overloaded constructors.

In Java, you cannot provide a default constructor; rather, the default constructor is defined to simply invoke a constructor with no arguments from the superclass. For the root class `Object`, this is simply a null method.

8.3 Constructor Inheritance

In C++ and Java, constructors are not inherited, so you can provide constructors with the same arguments in a subclass. If you want to use constructors from a parent class, because the code is the same, you can't. To allow for this case, Eiffel enables **creation** clauses to name routines from parent classes as well as the current class; you never need to duplicate code.

8.4 Expanded Initialization (Eiffel)

Eiffel expanded types are created at the same time as their enclosing environment, either as a local in a routine on the stack or as a field of an enclosing object. This is the same as declaring a nonreference object in C++. C++ allows nonreference objects to be initialized with general constructors; any constructor can be used to initialize such an object.

Eiffel does not have the syntax to initialize an object at the point of declaration, which is also the point of creation for an expanded type. Thus the potential for creation routines on expanded types is restricted to a single routine with no arguments. As far as initializing such objects, C++ constructors have a distinct advantage.

Java does not have a facility for nonreference objects, so the question of initialization of such objects does not arise.

8.5 Constructor Initialization (C++)

It is recommended that you use initialization in constructors rather than assignment. For example, consider a class C with int members a and b. The constructor for this class should be written

C++
```
C::C (const int i,j)
  a(i), b(j)
{ ... }
```

rather than

C++
```
C::C (const int i,j)
{
    a = i;
    b = j;
}
```

The initialization is a static schema. A static schema asserts that, after a certain occurrence in a system, the system is in a state that obeys the rules in the static schema. Other kinds of schemata are dynamic schema and invariant schema. A dynamic schema asserts that, if a system obeys certain conditions before a sequence of code is executed (preconditions), then it will obey certain conditions after the execution (postconditions). An invariant schema gives conditions over the state of an object that must always be met, both before and after any operations.

We can make a few comments about constructor initialization in C++. First, the syntax is somewhat strange. Since initialization is akin to a set of assertions, a more natural syntax would be

```
C::C (const int i,j)                                            C++
  a = i, b = j
  { ... }
```

You should note that = here is the logical equals operator, not assignment. For a criticism on that see the section on the assignment operator (so the syntax should probably be ==).

A more interesting situation arises from the order in which members are initialized. No matter how you order them in the list, the members are initialized in the order in which they appear in the class, not the order in the list. A typical example is

```
class Buffer {                                                  C++
private:
    int *buf;
    unsigned size;
public:
    Buffer (int initSize);
};

Buffer::Buffer (int initSize)
    size(initSize),
    buf(new int [size])
{...}
```

Unfortunately, what happens here is `buf` is initialized first with size of 0.

8.6 Destructors (C++)

If you do not specify a destructor in a class, a nonvirtual destructor is automatically generated. The problem with this is that, if you then include a destructor in a derived class, it is possible that this destructor will not be called when the object is deleted. This happens if an object of the derived class gets attached to a reference of the base class and is then deleted via the base class reference. This is a specific case of the problems discussed in the section on virtual functions in chapter 5.

Neither Java nor Eiffel has destructors, but Eiffel does provide a library-based mechanism for cleaning up an object before it is collected.

8.7 Dispose (Eiffel)

Many people worry that Eiffel has no equivalent of destructors in the language. We must consider what destructors are for, and that is orderly termination and freeing of resources that the object might have used. Destructors per se would be against automatic garbage collection, but, in some cases, you do want to close files and release other resources. For this purpose, Eiffel provides a routine *dispose* in the class *MEMORY*. In order to get the *dispose* routine called before the memory manager reclaims an object, you simply inherit from *MEMORY*.

You should take care that neither this routine nor destructors themselves link the current object back into the valid objects of a running system. Thus, what you do in destructors should be very limited.

8.8 Operator = (C++)

[Meyers 92] (item 11) Meyers recommends that you always define an assignment operator for classes with dynamically allocated memory. This is because, if you allow the C++ default assignment to be generated, it will copy all fields into the object, but it will not deallocate memory that the object previously held. In the assignment operator that you write for a class, therefore, you should determine if it is appropriate to deallocate members (a nontrivial task in itself), and if so deallocate them. This is not necessary in systems with garbage collection, so you will not have to write your own assignment operators.

[Meyers 92] (item 16) Meyers also advises that all members should be assigned to only in your assignment operator function. This creates a maintenance problem. If you delete members, then the compiler will give you an error, and you will then remove the member assignments in the function. However, if you add members, you must remember to add code to the assignment function. You will have to add code to constructor functions anyway. Similarly in Eiffel, you will need to add initialization of features in a creation routine, but this will be so that after creation the object state does not violate the class invariant. The bad news about this is that you will find out your omission only when you run the program and the invariant is violated.

And if you didn't think this was enough, a further problem arises if you use an `operator =` function to assign an object to itself. It is unlikely that you will do this explicitly, as in

```
o = o;
```
C++

but this is definitely a possibility when two distinct references refer to the same object. In this case, your `operator =` will deallocate members that are referenced from the object before assignment, so you do not end up with a copy of the same object. (This is part of the problem of reasoning about software with aliases.) Thus you must check that the right-hand side of the assignment is not equal to the current object `this`.

```
if (*this == rhs) return *this;
```
C++

It gets even more complicated. Suppose the objects are not the same, but that some members refer to the same objects. In this case you must make sure that you don't deallocate the member. As I said, determining whether you can deallocate a member is a nontrivial task.

8.9 . and -> (C++)

The `.` and `->` member access syntax came from C structures and illustrates where the C base adversely affects flexibility. Semantically, both access a member of an object. They are, however, operationally defined in terms of how they work. The dot (`.`) syntax accesses a member in an object directly—`x.y` means access the member `y` in the object `x`.

```
OBJ x;   // declare object x of class OBJ
         // with a member y.
x.y;     // access y in object x directly
x->y;    // syntax error ". expected"
```
C++

The specific error is

```
error: type 'OBJ' does not have an
    overloaded member 'operator ->'
error: left of '->y' must point
    to class/struct/union
```

The -> syntax means access a member in an object referenced by a pointer x->y (or the equivalent *(x).y) means access the member y in the object pointed to by x.

C++

```
OBJ *x;  // declare a pointer x to an
         // object of class obj.
x->y;    // access y via pointer x
x.y;     // syntax error "-> expected"
```

The specific error is

```
error:'.OBJ::y' : left operand points
    to 'class', use '->'
```

In these examples, *what* we are computing is "access the element y of object x." In C++, however, the programmer must specify for every access the detail of *how* this is done; that is, the access *mechanism* to the member is made visible to the programmer, which is an implementation detail. Thus the distinction between . and -> compromises implementation hiding and very seriously compromises the benefit of encapsulation. We saw in the section on inlines in chapter 4 how the visible difference of access mechanisms between constants, variables, and functions also breaks the implementation-hiding principle, and how the burden is on the programmer to restore hiding rather than fix the language.

The compiler could easily restore implementation hiding by providing uniform access and remove this burden from the programmer, as in fact most languages do. The key to this is abundant in OO languages, that is, polymorphic operators—the access operator . can access any member dependent on whether its left-hand side is a pointer or not. This difference is statically determined by the compiler, so no run-time overhead is incurred in dynamically determining the access mode. The major benefit of implementation hiding is that, if the implementation changes, the effect is contained within the class itself and not manifest beyond the interface. Where implementation hiding is broken, the effects of implementation change become visible, and this reduces flexibility.

For example, if the `OBJ x` declaration is changed to `OBJ *x`, the effect is widespread because all occurrences of `x.y` must be changed to `x->y`. Since the compiler gives a syntax error if the wrong access mechanism is used, this shows that the compiler already knows what access code is required and that it can generate it automatically. Good programming centralizes decisions: the decision to access the object directly or via a pointer should be centralized in the declaration. So again, C++ uses low-level operators rather than the high-level declarative approach of letting the compiler hide the implementation and take care of the detail for us.

Java supports only the dot form of access. The `->` form is superfluous as Java objects are accessed only by reference; there are no embedded objects.

Eiffel provides a more interesting case. In Eiffel an optimization is provided since an object can be expanded inline in another object in order to save a reference. Eiffel calls such objects **expanded** objects. There is still no need for explicit dereferencing. The compiler knows whether the object is expanded or referenced, and thus the dot accessor is used for both, providing uniform access with a hidden access mechanism. This makes the program more malleable, because the programmer can later change an object to expanded and not have to worry about changing every `->` to a dot. Conversely, if **expanded** turns out to be inappropriate, as in the case of a circular reference, then the **expanded** status of the object can be removed from the declaration without having to change another line of code. Thus Eiffel preserves the implementation-hiding principle, which results in convenience for the programmer.

There is even more to Eiffel's scheme that is particularly relevant to concurrent and distributed processing. In Eiffel the form *x.f* means passing the message *f* to the object *x*. *x* may be anywhere on the network. In other words, *x* might not be a reference that is implemented by an underlying C pointer, but it may be a network address, for example, a WEB *uniform reference locator* (URL).

Now, if we think enough is enough—Java and Eiffel have got it right, Java with only one kind of access for `.`, and Eiffel selecting the correct kind of access polymorphically—C++ has even more variations. We in fact have four operators for the single conceptual operator of "member selection."

```
object . member
pointer -> member
```

```
object  .* pointer-to-member
pointer ->* pointer-to-member
```

8.10   Delete and Delete [] (C++)

C++ has two forms of delete: `delete` and `delete []`. If you used `new []` to create an array, you must use `delete []`, and if you used `new` without `[]` you must use `delete` without `[]`. In either case, if you mix them up, the results are undefined. The problem arises because, as in C, C++ pointers do not distinguish between whether they point at an individual object or to an array. You can't find this out at compile time, or at run time.

It sounds trivial to avoid this problem, but that is not always the case, since you might be passed the target you are deleting from another module, and it is difficult to tell whether it is an array or not. In some cases, the compiler can report an error if the wrong construct is used, but not always. If the compiler could always tell, then there would be no point in burdening the programmer with having to use the correct form of delete, as the compiler could automatically generate the correct form. Stroustrup gives the following example.

C++

[Stroustrup 94]
(10.5.1)

```
void f(X* p1) // p1 may point to an individual
              // object or to an array
    X* p2 = new X[10]; // p2 points to the array
    delete p2;    // error p2 points to an array
    delete[] p2;  // ok
    delete p1;    // maybe ok, trust the programmer
    delete[] p1;  // maybe ok, trust the programmer
}
```

The curious phrase "trust the programmer" indicates the common attitude in the C world that C is for advanced programmers who know what they are doing as opposed to those other "teaching" languages for those who are not "real" programmers. However, the above example shows that it is not so much trusting the programmer; the compiler writer has no choice but to hope the programmer has it right. If you really trusted the programmer, then you might as well not bother to report that `delete p2` is wrong!

However, error reporting has nothing to do with not trusting the programmer. You trust the programmer to get it right, but there is no harm in checking—if the programmer really got it right, then no error will be reported, so the "trust the programmer" argument is spurious. In the above case, it might be quicker to guess at the correct construct and have the compiler report an error so that you can fix it rather than looking up the details in an external module. As already mentioned, however, if the compiler did detect this error for you, there would be no need for two separate constructs, as the compiler could generate the correct code for the programmer automatically, saving either compiling to detect the error or having to look up the external module.

Java and Eiffel have no such problems since they have garbage collection built in. Further, Eiffel does not have the problem that the compiler cannot determine the exact kind of entities from other modules (classes). We will see the advantages of closed-world, systemwide analysis in the global analysis section in chapter 10.

8.11 Prefix and Postfix Operators (C++)

C++ allows you to overload the ++ increment and -- decrement operators. The problem is distinguishing the prefix from the postfix form. In order to declare the prefix operator, this is, as you would expect, a function with no arguments. However, to distinguish the postfix form, you must declare the function with an `int` parameter, which is not used but which the compiler will pass as 0. Hence the following

```
++a;      // a.operator++();                                   C++
a++;      // a.operator++(0);
```

This is not the only strange attribute of these operators. From the prefix form, you should return a reference to the variable, but, in order to make postfix work, you want to return the value of the variable before it is incremented or decremented. Hence, prefix returns a reference, but postfix returns a value.

With the built-in operators, you cannot apply them twice, as in

```
int i;                                                         C++
i++++;           // error
```

so it is good style to prevent this for user-defined types. You should do this by declaring the postfix operator to return a `const` value.

Further problems arise from the increment and decrement operators as inherited from C, and you can find these problems in chapter 14. Eiffel provides no increment or decrement operators; they are only a small syntactical convenience, and the problems with them outweigh any convenience. Java has no operator overloading.

8.12 || and && (C++)

In C++, || is the "logical or" operator and && the "logical and" operator. In both C and C++, these are defined to be shortcut operators. For example, in the expression a && b, b is evaluated only if a is true; in the expression a || b, b is evaluated only if a is false. This makes for both safe and efficient code. For example, in the expression

C++
```
if ((p) && (p.cond)) ...
```

we check that p is not null before we check whatever condition is associated with p.

This feature by itself is very good, but as is the case so often in C++, we must be careful of its combined effect with other features. The problem here comes with overloading. If we overload the && or || operators, the shortcut evaluation is not effective, and each expression is evaluated in an undefined order as function arguments.

The Java || and && operators work the same as in C++ as shortcut operators. However, Java ensures that the operands are of boolean type, whereas C++ does not, even though the result is boolean in both cases. C++ also has operators | and & which provide bitwise or and ands. Java has the same operators for primitive integral types that perform bitwise operations. However, in Java, if the operands are boolean, then these operators are logical. Thus the semantics of these operators in Java is cleaner than C++, which retains the deficiencies of C. Java also does not have operator overloading, so the problem with overloading these operators does not exist.

Eiffel represents the logical operators with the keywords **and**, **or**, **and then**, and **or else**. These cannot be overloaded. **And** and **or** are regular logical operators where both operands are evaluated, and **and then** and **or else** represent the shortcut operators.

8.13 Operator Overloading (C++ and Eiffel)

The term *overloading* is somewhat overloaded here. It is not so much overloading in the exact form that we have seen in C++ and Java, where any function can be overloaded at compile time on the exact arguments passed to it. Rather, we are talking about the ability to be able to identify functions with common operator names such as +, -, *, /, and others. Eiffel is careful to make this distinction and calls such functions *operator features*. Thus, no form of overloading is implied, this is just a mechanism to give functions fancy names. (We intentionally use the term function here, as operator names cannot be applied to nonvalue-returning routines, i.e., procedures.)

Java does not offer the ability to use operators as function names at the moment, but in actual fact this is only a bit of syntactic sugar, so Java's omission is not serious, though not everyone would agree with this assessment. A recent article in a sidebar entitled "Java's approach – forget it!" sees lack of operator overloading as a serious flaw:

> Java in most respects an object-oriented language, doesn't support overloaded operators at all. That choice we're told, was made, not in order to keep the language small, but in order to "protect" programmers from misusing the facility!
>
> " ... the language designers decided (after much debate) that overloaded operators were a neat idea, but that code that relied on them became hard to read and understand."
>
> David Flanagan, *Java in a Nutshell*, O'Reilly Associates, 1996, p. 35.)

[Weisert 97]

So instead of this (C++):

```
total = unitPrice*quantity + shipChg;
```
C++

we have to code something like this (Java):

```
total.setValue (shipChg.add(unitPrice.mpy(quantity)));
```
Java

You may wonder about people who think the second is easier to read and understand than the first, but it's unlikely anyone really does. More likely, Java just wasn't designed for non-trivial type-safe computation. If you're going to do much with elementary numeric classes, Java isn't a suitable language.

By the way, Java's own library Date class doesn't support any date arithmetic, not even with the clumsy function-call syntax.

In fact, this overstates the case. The quote from Flanagan is contained in a small footnote about using the + operator for string concatenation. While you might

[Weisert 97] have the problem of verbose dot function syntax with the class types, this will not be the case for primitive numeric types as given in the example. Weisert also uses the tired old C argument against language designers trying to protect programmers from themselves. It is time that argument was laid to rest once and for all. Language designers are trying to help programmers not to fall into common traps; if this were not the case, there would be little point in designing new high-level languages at all. The argument tries to paint all language designers of languages other than C and C++ as being patronizing old bores. Instead it is this argument itself that has become patronizing, old, and boring.

8.14   Implicit Conversions and Overloading (C++)

Part of C++'s C heritage means that silent conversions from `char` to `int` and `short` to `double` can take place. Such conversions are not so bad, except that conversions from `int` to `short` and `double` to `char` cause loss of information.

Implicit conversion also happens when passing parameters to functions. This becomes even trickier when overloading is involved. When a call is made to an overloaded function, the compiler will first choose the *viable functions*. These are the functions where the number of arguments in the call matches the number of parameters declared in the function. Functions with fewer parameters may also be viable where an ellipsis occurs in the parameter list. Functions with more parameters can be counted viable where there are default arguments.

The compiler will attempt the find the *best viable function*. This involves perhaps implicitly converting arguments to match parameters. If exactly one viable function is found that is better than all the other viable functions, the compiler chooses that function. Otherwise we have an ill-formed call.

This sequence in C++ means it can be difficult for programmers to tell exactly which function will be called. Eiffel does not have overloading, but also implicit conversions are used only for standard mathematical promotions of *INTEGER* to *REAL* and *REAL* to *DOUBLE*. Java does have overloading, but reduces the number of potential conversions by disallowing implicit narrowing conversions—for example, `double` to `int`.

Another complication is that parameters passed to functions can cause implicit conversions and temporaries to be created. You should note that in C++ a temporary is an entity that is created without any programmer declaration. Temporaries are created invisibly, and it is the diligent C++ programmer's duty to recognize potential spots where a temporary might be created and to avoid them. An example of where such a temporary will be created is

```
f (const string& s);
```
C++

```
char ca [N];
f (ca);
```

In this case, there is a mismatch between the type of `ca` and the type of `s`, but the compiler will happily arrange for a temporary to be created to plug into `s`. Fortunately, this temporary will be automatically deallocated when `f` returns, but the problem here is that the very expensive operations of allocating and destroying an object have happened in a way that is hidden from the programmer.

Another complication in the example is that, if we remove the `const` on the declaration of `s`, this whole situation changes.

```
f (string& s);
```
C++

```
char ca [N];
f (ca);          // Error!
```

Now `f` is expecting a parameter it can change, but of course, if it makes changes to a temporary string, it does not make changes to the original `ca`, so the changes would be lost when the temporary is destroyed, an effect you might not have guessed.

In C++ you can also create user-defined implicit conversions. Meyers warns against using these and gives some interesting examples of why you should avoid them. [Meyers 96] (item 5)

8.15 Calling Parent Features

It often happens that a child routine is just an extension in some way of a parent routine; you do not want to completely replace the parent routine because its code is mainly what you want. An important part of making this work is to keep routines small; if they get large, it is more likely that they do something you don't want, so large routines become less reusable.

The problem with calling a routine's parent with the normal call mechanism is that, if you invoke the name of the routine, you are effectively doing a recursive call on the current routine.

Eiffel
>   f **is**
>   **do**
>   f   -- recursive call
>   **end**

What we need here is a way to make the call to the predecessor routine. For this Eiffel introduces the *Precursor* keyword:

Eiffel
>   f **is**
>   **do**
>   *Precursor*
>   **end**

Eiffel has no need to use the routine name, as that is implicit, and it might also have been renamed, so the name of the precursor routine might be different.

Precursor is a new feature to Eiffel, being one of the few extensions to the language since *Eiffel: The Language* was published in 1992. The previous way to do this in Eiffel was effective, but rather tedious: that was to inherit the parent class twice and ensure that the routine became two separate routines by renaming it in one parent and redefining it in the other.

Eiffel
>   **class** *C*
>   **inherit**
>   *B*
>   **redefine**
>   *f*
>   **end**
>   *B*
>   **rename**
>   *f* **as** *g*
>   **end**
>   **feature**
>   *f* **is**
>   **do**
>   *g*

>   **end** -- *f*
> **end** -- **class** *C*

Java has a very simple way of accessing any parent class member with the `super.name` construct.

>   `super.f ();`   *Java*

Notice that the major difference between Eiffel and Java is that in Java you must specify the name of the parent member, whereas in Eiffel the precursor must be the parent of the current routine. Why does Java have this extra complication? The reason is that in Java you can hide parent members by declaring a member of the same name in the current class. In Eiffel, such hiding is never sanctioned and is treated as an error; you can only redefine a feature or rename it to remove a clash. Remember that the section on name overloading in chapter 5 gives reasons why such clashes should be avoided and why they need complex mechanisms to disambiguate them.

In C++, you use the scope resolution operator

>   `A::f ();`   *C++*

Note that in C++ and Java you could call any parent method, thus circumventing a method in the subclass or any further subclasses that have code specific to the subclass. This can break down the semantics of a class.

C++ and Eiffel have another complication with multiple inheritance. Because multiple inheritance is of great benefit, the complication is necessary; that is, if the precursor of a routine does not come from a unique parent, but is the join of several precursors, you have to specify exactly which parent you want to call. C++ in fact needs no extra construct here, so the complication works out to be a nonissue; the scope resolution operator is sufficient since any parent can be specified. In Eiffel, the parent must be specified: in single inheritance, the parent is implicit. The Eiffel syntax is thus

>   *f* **is**
>   **do**
>   {A} *Precursor*   *Eiffel*

end

8.16 Calling Descendant Features

Simula worked in a slightly different way. In Simula the construct was to call from the parent routine to the specific subclass routine when the parent routine wanted to defer some processing to the subclass. Simula used the *inner* keyword to effect such a call. The scheme looked like this.

Simula
```
Procedure inner_example;
Begin
    % do some generic processing
    inner;   % call down to subclass 'inner_example'
             % for specific processing
    % do some more generic processing
end of inner_example;
```

The clue to the solution to this in the previous description is the word *defer*. In Eiffel, we know that we can easily defer decisions to a descendant class. An example of this is

Eiffel

class *WINDOW*
   ...
   nw := *new_window* (*window_kind*)

   window_kind: *INTEGER* **is deferred end**
end

class *DIALOG_WINDOW*
   ...
   window_kind: *INTEGER* **is** *3*
end

class *ROUND_WINDOW*
   ...
   window_kind: *INTEGER* **is** *5*
end

This can be similarly achieved in Java and C++.

8.17 Conditional Expressions

ALGOL 60 introduced a very convenient form of expression called the *conditional expression*. The form of the conditional expression is

    if <boolean expression> **then**   *ALGOL*
        <expression> **else** <expression>

You could use this in any form of expression; for example

    x := **if** perfect **then** 777 **else** 666;   *ALGOL*

This kind of expression is essential in functional programming languages, and C/C++ also has a form.

    x = perfect? 777 : 666;   *ALGOL*

Java also has this form. Eiffel does not have the conditional expression. ALGOL also has a form of case expression:

    x := **case** y **of** (13, 17, 19, 666);   *ALGOL*

where x would receive the values 13, 17, 19, or 666 if y had the value 0, 1, 2, or 3. This form was not very widely used in ALGOL, but is useful in functional languages.

9

Casts

In this chapter we examine the subject of type casts and how, if we treat them functionally, casts are not needed in a well-typed language. Statically untyped languages such as Smalltalk have no need for such mechanisms as casts and so, on the surface, seem simple and elegant; this simplicity and elegance comes at the cost of lack of static type safety. However, we do not want to throw away static type safety in order to abolish casts. This chapter shows that a language can be statically safe, and yet be flexible enough not to require casts.

9.1 Type Casts (C++)

[Stroustrup 94] "Syntactically and semantically, casts are one of the ugliest features of C and
(14.3)   C++."

Mathematical functions map values from one type to values of another type. For example, arithmetic multiplication maps the type pair of integers to an integer.

Mult: *INTEGER* x *INTEGER* -> *INTEGER*

A language type system enables a programmer to specify which mappings make sense. Like functions, type casts map values of one type onto values of another type, but this *forces* one type to another against the defined mappings, undermining the value of the type system. A strongly typed language with a well-defined type system does not need casts; all type-to-type mapping is achieved with functions that are defined within the type system, and no casts outside the type system are needed.

Type casts have been useful in computer systems. Sometimes it is required to map one type onto another, where the bit representation of the value remains the same. Type casts are a trick to optimize certain operations, but provide no useful concept that general functions don't provide. In many languages, the type system is not consistently defined, so programmers feel that type casts are necessary, otherwise the language would be restrictive.

An example often used in programming is to cast between characters and integers. Type casts between integers and characters are easily expressed as functions using abstract data types (ADTs):

TYPE
    CHARACTER

FUNCTIONS
    ord: *CHARACTER -> INTEGER*
    // convert input character to integer.
    char: *INTEGER /-> CHARACTER*
    // convert input integer to character.

PRECONDITION
    // check *i* is in range.
        pre char (*i*: *INTEGER*) =
            $0 <= i$ **and** $i <=$ **ord** (*last character*)

The notation -> means every character will map to an integer. The partial function notation /-> means that not every integer will map to a character; a precondition, given in the **pre char** statement, specifies the subset of integers that maps to characters. OO languages provide this consistently with member functions on a class:

    i: *INTEGER*
    ch: *CHARACTER*
    $i := ch.ord$
    // *i* becomes the integer value of the character.

ch := i.char
// ch becomes the character corresponding to i.

but a routine *char* would probably not be defined on the integer type so this would more likely be

ch.char (i)
// set ch to the character corresponding to i.

The hardware of many machines provides for such basic data types as character and integer, and it is probable that a compiler will generate code that is optimal for any target hardware architecture. Thus many languages have characters and integers as built-in types. An OO language can treat such basic data types consistently and elegantly by the implicit definition of their own classes.

Another example of type conversion is from double or real to integer, but there are several options: do you truncate, round, or return the next-highest integer?

TYPE
    REAL

FUNCTIONS
    truncate: *REAL -> INTEGER*
    round: *REAL -> INTEGER*

    r: REAL
    i: INTEGER
    i := r.truncate
    // *i* becomes the closest integer <= *r*
    i := r.round
    // *i* becomes the closest integer to *r*

Again many hardware platforms provide specific instructions to achieve this, and an efficient OO language compiler will generate code best optimized for the target machine. Such in-built class definitions might be a part of the standard language definition.

Another way to think of casts to show they should be functional is to write only one set of casts in a program and call them only through functions. This gives the advantage of keeping the low-level mechanism of casting centralized. Consider casting doubles to integers—this can be centralized in one function:

```
int double_to_int (double d)
{
    return (int) d;
}
```

You can do likewise with casting reals to integers. If you feel this is too heavy and results in too many `<x>_to_int` functions, using OO, you only need a single polymorphic function—`to_int`—called as `r.to_int` for a real or `d.to_int` for a double. Such conversions can be defined in the language libraries, but handled specially by the compiler to generate inline code.

9.2 RTTI and Type Casts (C++)

C++ added run-time type information (RTTI) in March 1993. This is a good and necessary feature, and a discussion of it helps clarify the notion of casts.

Palsberg and Schwartzbach make a case against rejecting all programs that are not statically type correct. If a program is shown to be statically type correct, its type correctness is *guaranteed*, but static type checks can reject a class of programs that are otherwise type valid. [Palsberg and Schwartzbach 9

List classes are an example of where static type checking can reject a valid program. A list class can contain objects of many different types. Genericity and templates allow constructions such as *list of objects*, *list of animals*, etc. These are types built from the generic *list* class.

In the list of animals, you might know that squirrels occur in even-numbered slots in the list. You could then assign an even-numbered list element to a variable of type squirrel. Dynamically, this is correct, but statically the compiler must reject it because it does not know that squirrels only occur in even locations in the list.

Things are not always this simple. The programmer probably won't know the pattern of how particular animals are stored in the list. Consider a vet's waiting room. The vet might view his waiting room as being the type *list of animals*. Calling in the first animal from the waiting room, it is important to know whether the animal is a cat or a hamster if the vet is to perform an operation on the animal. For many such cases OO dynamic binding and polymorphism will suffice, so that the programmer does not have to know the exact type of the object, as long as the objects are sufficiently the same so that the same operations can be applied, even though the implementations might be different.

However, this is not always sufficient, and sometimes it is important to know that you have retrieved a hamster from a list of animals. For example, once our vet has performed the operation on the hamster or cat, he must know enough about its type to decide whether to put the animal in the hamster cage or the cat basket. Casting can solve this problem, but it is like using a sledgehammer approach where much more elegant and precise solutions exist. As Stroustrup notes: "The C and C++ cast is a sledgehammer."

[Stroustrup 94]
(14.3.1)

Assignment Attempt

Eiffel has an elegant and precise solution called the *assignment attempt* (previously known as *reverse assignment* or *reverse assignment attempt*, but the reverse terminology was confusing and has now been dropped), notated as ?= instead of := —a simple example is:

Eiffel

    waiting_room: *LIST* [*ANIMAL*]
    fluffy: *HAMSTER*
    h_cage: *HAMSTER_CAGE*

    fluffy := *waiting_room.first*   -- error.

    -- The above assignment will be rejected by the compiler as
    -- **type** (*fluffy*) = *HAMSTER and*
    -- *ANIMAL* is not a subtype of *HAMSTER. Even* though we
    -- know that the animal will be a *HAMSTER*, and the
    -- program is valid, static type checking considers it invalid.

    fluffy ?= *waiting_room.first*

    -- If the first animal in the waiting room is indeed a *HAMSTER*, then *fluffy*
    -- will refer to that animal, else *fluffy* will be *Void*.

    if *fluffy* /= *Void* **then**
        h_cage.put (*fluffy*)
    end

The Eiffel assignment attempt provides a precise and elegant solution to the dynamic type problem where static typing is too restrictive. Since the assignment attempt has the desired effect of bypassing static type checking and leaving it to run time, type casting is not needed.

If you want to be as flexible as Smalltalk, you could use the assignment attempt instead of straight assignment everywhere. However, since this invokes run-time type checks and because you must check for *Void* references, there is a large overhead to assignment attempt over straight assignment. This shows that static typing is important not only for proving compile-time correctness, but also for run-time efficiency. The only real effect of ?= as far as the programmer is concerned is that it suppresses the compiler's static type checking and puts in a run-time check.

`dynamic_cast`

As I said, C++ introduced RTTI in March 1993. RTTI has the operator `dynamic_cast`, which achieves the same effect as the Eiffel assignment attempt. `dynamic_cast` returns a pointer to a derived class from a pointer to a base class if the object is an object of the derived class; otherwise it returns 0 (or should that be null? But 0 isn't really zero; it's any bit pattern representing null).

In C++, the above assignment attempt would be coded

```
    fluffy =                                               C++
        dynamic_cast<hamster*>
            (waiting_room.first());
```

A few observations. Wow! Eiffel uses an operator and C++ uses a keyword. This is of course contrary to belief that C++ uses operators where Eiffel uses keywords. It should be noted, however, that, in correctly designed programs, neither assignment attempt nor `dynamic_cast` is used very often. So this is a relatively unimportant point.

The second observation is that in C++ you must specify the type. In this example it is superfluous since the compiler can determine **type** (*fluffy*) = HAMSTER, as the compiler does in Eiffel.

In C++ you can dynamically cast to any derived class from `hamster*`, but that does not seem to gain anything. Also, you don't need to use `dynamic_cast` directly in an assignment, but you can use it in a general expression. However, again it is stressed that run-time casting should be used so little that this is of minimal advantage. Perhaps the only small advantage is the ability to be able to pass a dynamically cast pointer.

C++

```
h_cage.put
    (dynamic_cast<hamster*>
        (waiting_room.first()));
```

Looks good, right? But remember, if the first animal out of the waiting room is not a hamster, but a rat, you get 0 (well, null...etc.) returned, which will cause h_cage.put() to fail.

This shows that the use of dynamic_cast in an expression is not such a good idea, possibly causing the whole expression to fail.

Thus Eiffel's assignment attempt is safer and syntactically cleaner. And there is another reason for this remark: if you don't put the **if** *fluffy* /= *Void* **then** test in—either deliberately or because you forgot—then the precondition that is most likely included in the Eiffel version of *h_cage.put* tests that the argument is not *Void*. If you deliberately left out the *Void* test, you will have included a **rescue** clause to handle this exception. (However, using **rescue** clauses in such a fashion is not recommended because you will probably disable preconditions in production code.)

[Stroustrup 94] (14.2.8.6) Although the Eiffel syntax ?= for assignment attempt is cleaner, Stroustrup points out that such clean syntax would be inappropriate for C++. This is because the ?= would be "difficult to spot" in C++'s otherwise clumsy syntax. Eiffel's syntax is much clearer making it possible to use this neat notation. Since Eiffel programmers will code small routines, the ?= is not so difficult to spot. The reasoning against using ?= in C++ is strange since C already provides assignment operators like += and -=, which are just a small syntactic convenience.

typeid

[Stroustrup 94] (14.2.5) Another RTTI feature is the typeid operator. Stroustrup warns against using this to determine program flow control based on type information. Instead of using switch statements, you should use dynamic binding on polymorphic (virtual) functions. This will need to be built into your style rules that programmers will hate, or you will end up having to fix the dirty deed after the fact, which adds to the expense of your software developments.

Eiffel has no built-in operator to achieve the same effect as typeid, so the OO principle of using dynamic binding instead of switch statements is better enforced. Eiffel removes type identification from the language, but places it in the libraries in some routines built into the *GENERAL* class. So, in Eiffel, it is harder

[Stroustrup 94] to commit the bad programming practices that Stroustrup warns about.

9.3 New Type Casts (C++)

Not only did C++ introduce RTTI and `dynamic_cast` in March 1993, but it also introduced three more cast operators in November 1993. These operators are

```
static_cast<T>(e),
reinterpret_cast<T>(e), and
const_cast<T>(e).
```
C++

Again, for all these the specification of the <type> seems superfluous, as the compiler can derive it from the context. (This is known as type inference, see below.) These casts just about cover all the cases where you would need to use C-style casts.

Stroustrup indicates a desire to discard the C casts.

> I intended the new-style casts as a complete replacement for the `(T)e` notation. I proposed to deprecate `(T)e`; that is, for the committee to give users warning that the `(T)e` notation would most likely not be part of a future revision of the C++ standard. ... However, that idea didn't gain a majority, so that cleanup of C++ will probably never happen.

[Stroustrup 9 (14.3.5.1)]

It is also interesting that these constructs are deliberately ugly in order that casts are noticeable and also that they can be detected by automatic tools. Old-style casts are difficult to detect.

The bottom line to these sections on type casts: "In all cases, it would be better if the cast – new or old – could be eliminated." It can! The cleaner type system of Eiffel shows that it is true that casts can be eliminated.

[Stroustrup 9 (14.3.5.4)]

9.4 Type Inference

As mentioned in the previous section, compiler techniques exist that can infer the type of an element or expression without a programmer having to explicitly declare the type. This technique is mainly found in functional programming languages such as ML, where you see very few type definitions. Techniques such as type inference are another reason why casts should be relegated to the past. However, type inference is still an active area of research—one of the main problems is how to make it easy enough for the programmer to understand how a compiler derives the types.

9.5 Java and Casts

Unfortunately, Java needs casts in our veterinary examples, but has improved the situation because certain casts can be shown to be illegal at compile time. Not all casts can be proven correct at compile time, though, and must be allowed to compile with a run-time check. If the run-time check detects an illegal cast, a `ClassCastException` is thrown.

The original on-line Java Language Specification said,

[Java 96]
> Not all casts are permitted by the Java language. Some casts result in an error at compile time. For example, a primitive value may not be cast to a reference type. Some casts can be proven, at compile time, always to be correct at run time. For example, it is always correct to convert a value of a class type to the type of its superclass; such a cast should require no special action at run time. Finally, some casts cannot be proven to be either always correct or always incorrect at compile time. Such casts require a test at run time. A ClassCastException is thrown if a cast is found at run time to be impermissible.

As we saw in the chapter on genericity, you can build generic classes that take any type, but, in order to retrieve those entities without specifying the actual type statically with an actual generic type, you must restore the object's type with a cast. Without genericity in Java, this is exactly what you must do. Thus the topics of generics and casts are related since with genericity, you would need no casts at all.

9.6 Signature Variance (Eiffel)

When redefining a routine, there is an opportunity to redefine the signature as well. A signature can be varied in three ways—*no variance*, *contravariance*, and *covariance*. The first and most obvious part of a signature that can vary is the return type. In this case both functions and variables may vary (variables being a special case of functions with no arguments). Such types can vary covariantly without problem. The problems (and arguments—as in debates, not parameters) arise when we consider how arguments can vary, and this section looks at some of the background issues.

Signature variance is an issue of type safety in a language. Signature variance is related to casts because, without signature variance, you will have to resort to type casts. This section might seem complicated, but you should realize that it is to solve a type system problem and remove the need for type casts. The result is intuitive and natural. As long as C++ and Java have type casts, they cannot be considered strongly typed languages.

No variance means that the language does not permit the signature to change—neither the argument types nor the variable or function types change. The signature must match the signature inherited from the parent exactly. In Java, if the argument types vary, even if they are a subclass or superclass of the original, the method is overloaded. You cannot change the return type.

Contravariance means that the signature in a subclass can modify each argument so that it is a superclass of the matching parent argument. For example, if you have classes A and B and B inherits from A, then, given a argument of type B in your parent, you can keep it as B or modify it to A. That is, you have extended the arguments that you accept from just B to B and all other descendants of A. This does seem counterintuitive, but there are some good examples of where it works.

Covariance is the opposite of contravariance. In our example, if your parent has a argument of type A, you can keep it as A, or redefine it to any descendant of A. This is more intuitive than contravariance. Return types can be covariant, but covariant arguments result in type problems.

An example of contravariance is this. Consider you provide an Internet service to print files that clients send you. You might start out with a service that accepts text and PostScript files. However, some customers complain that they would also like to be able to send you pdf files. Being customer driven, you decide to improve the service and also accept pdf files. This is contravariant modification. Your service object has improved the service and therefore subclassed the original service.

The contravariant scheme works because a service can accept data in at least the format that the customer expects to send, but possibly other formats as well. In the Internet service, if you start out by advertising that you process files of types H, I, and J, then customers will expect you to add types to that service. If you remove processing for type I and a customer sends you a file of type I, problems will occur and the customer will be dissatisfied because you have broken your agreement, that is, contract with the customer. If you add processing for files of types K and L, though, you will probably attract new customers.

When you subclass you are doing a similar process. If a parent class A advertises that a routine takes a argument of type I, it takes objects of exactly type I or any of I's descendants—a subclass of A should guarantee that the routine takes at least arguments of type I and its descendants, and possibly others.

Signature Variance (Eiffel)

What happens if we try to be more restrictive with the data types that you can pass to a routine? Consider the hierarchy in figure 9-1.

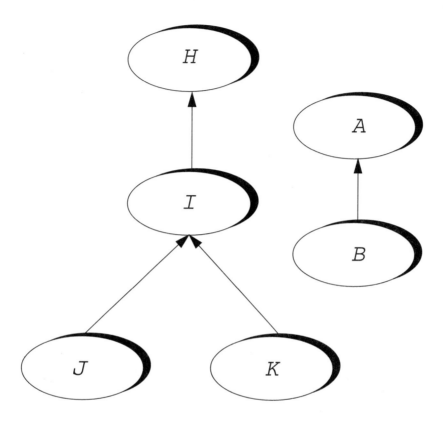

Figure 9-1. Example hierarchy

In class A, we have a routine r that accepts a argument of type I.

Eiffel

    class A
    feature
        $r\ (p: I)$ **is ... end**
    end

    class B
    inherit A **redefine** r **end**
    feature
        $r\ (p: J)$ **is ... end**

```
end

class C
inherit A redefine r end
feature
    r (p: K) is ... end
end
```

If class *B* covariantly modifies *r* to take arguments of type *J*, then *B.r* cannot take arguments of type *K*. This is a problem if you have a *B* object attached to an *A* reference because you cannot ensure that the following calls are correct.

Eiffel

```
a: A
i: I
j: J
k: K
a.r (k)  -- no good: a might refer to a B object.
a.r (j)  -- no good: a might refer to a C object.
a.r (i)  -- no good: neither objects of type B nor C can take an I.
```

Unfortunately, current Eiffel compilers accept these calls because *A.r* advertises that it can take arguments of type *I*, and *j* and *k* are of type *I* by inheritance. However, the object attached to the reference *a* could be a *B* object, which cannot handle objects of type *K*. To be safe, the compiler must disallow the above call. Meyer provides an analysis of this problem and gives it a name—*catcall*. This name comes from the acronym *CAT* for *changing availability or type*.

[Meyer 97] (17.7)

C++ and Java offer novariance on arguments of polymorphic methods; although the C++ standard now allows the return type of an overriding function to be covariant. "The return type of an overriding function shall be either identical to the return type of the overridden function or *covariant* with the classes of the function."

[CD2 96]

The reason for C++ having novariant arguments is the same as Java—if you have a routine with a different signature, even if the arguments of the parent and child are type conformant, the method overloads rather than overrides the original method.

As stated before, a simple solution to the overloading problem would be to require that programmers mark the methods `override` or `overload`. The compiler could then check for consistency, that the arguments for an overriding method are an exact or co/contravariant match, and that, for an overloaded method, the arguments are different. Making overriding and overloading explicit is also good documentation, as it is a double check of what the original programmer really intended. Remember that overriding chooses between the alternative methods at run time, based on the type of the owning object; overloading chooses between the alternative methods at compile time based on the argument types.

Despite the above arguments in favor of contravariance, covariance also has some compelling arguments in its favor, but these are practical reasons rather than theoretical in nature—hence the basis for the controversy. For these reasons, Eiffel uses covariance and will have to include checks in compilers to disallow catcalls. The choice of covariant arguments in Eiffel is based on the argument that covariance is better for real-world modeling. One observation is that contravariance works in client/server relationships, which are familiar to networking and distributed processing people, while covariance models better peer-to-peer relationships, such as in the following example. This example is an animal hierarchy, where birds and elephants are specific types of animal. Each animal can take a mate, but the partner must be the same type as the animal.

Eiffel

```
class ANIMAL
feature
    mate: ANIMAL

    take_mate (other: ANIMAL) is
        do ...
            mate := other
        end
end

class ELEPHANT
inherit
    ANIMAL
        redefine mate, take_mate
    end

feature
    mate: ELEPHANT

    take_mate (other: ELEPHANT) is
        do ...
            mate := other
        end
end
```

```
class BIRD
inherit
    ANIMAL
        redefine mate, take_mate
    end

feature
    mate: BIRD

    take_mate (other: BIRD) is
        do ...
            mate := other
        end
end
```

This is illustrated diagrammatically in figure 9-2.

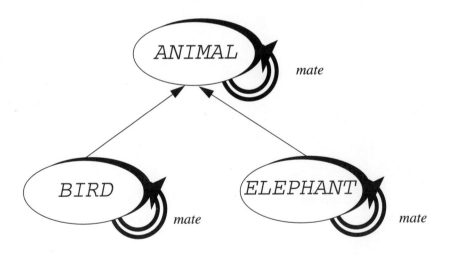

Figure 9-2. Animal hierarchy

The observation to be made here is that the *mate* attribute is indeed covariant, and that satisfies the theoretical considerations. The problem is that, when you call a set routine passing in a value to set that attribute to, you want the argument to vary covariantly as well.

In the animal example, we now have three versions of *take_mate,* and each does the same thing. You might justifiably be thinking "so much for reuse!" It is for this reason that Eiffel introduces the **like** *Current* type. The following example shows this in class *ANIMAL* so that the redefinition in subclasses is implicit.

Eiffel

    class *ANIMAL*
    feature
        mate: *ANIMAL*

        take_mate (*other*: **like** *Current*) **is**
            do ...
                mate := *other*
            end
    end

[Shang 95]   David Shang gives another valid example of covariance in his short paper, "Are Cows Animals?" Shang's example considers what kinds of food animals eat, and I adapt the bird/elephant example.

Eiffel

    class *ANIMAL*
    feature
        eat (*food*: *ANY_FOOD*) **is do ... end**
    end

    class *ELEPHANT*
    inherit
        ANIMAL
            redefine *mate*, *take_mate*
        end
    feature
        eat (*food*: *LEAVES*) **is do ... end**
    end

    class *BIRD*
    inherit
        ANIMAL
            redefine *mate*, *take_mate*
        end
    feature

>   *eat* (*food*: *SEED*) **is do ... end**
> **end**

The problem is that the type predicate of *ANIMAL.eat* promises that any creature of the set *ANIMAL* will gladly eat any food. While it is true that animals eat food, specific animals eat specific kinds of food. What is really needed is a type predicate that specifies that the argument is some kind of food, but the exact type of food cannot be specified at this point. This means that you cannot guarantee that the call

> *a*: *ANIMAL* *Eiffel*
> *birdy_num_num*: *SEED*
> *a.eat* (*birdy_num_num*)

is type safe, since *a* could be an *ELEPHANT*. We have here an example of the children's game 20 questions, where you try to work out what the thing is from its characteristics. "Does *a* eat seed?" "No!" "Does *a* eat leaves?" "Yes!" "Then it's an elephant."

Again, the routine *eat* could be unnecessarily repetitive, with the only change being the type accepted. The **like** type specification can also be very useful here to avoid repetitive and wasteful coding.

> **class** *ANIMAL* *Eiffel*
> **feature**
>   *last_meal*: *ANY_FOOD*
>   *eat* (*food*: **like** *last_meal*) **is do ... end**
> **end**

Now the *eat* routine will be reused and not repeated in each subclass. This example also makes it clear that the types of arguments can be tied to the type of some variable in the class. As we have noted, function and variable types are covariant, and, since many input arguments to routines are tied to variables, this is a good reason for such arguments to also be covariant. We still must be careful in calling the *eat* routine via a reference of type *ANIMAL* since this could still allow us to feed bird seed to an elephant.

You might think that, since both covariance and contravariance have problems, we should just accept C++ and Java's novariant scheme. However, that

Signature Variance (Eiffel)

gains us nothing because we then have a type casting problem. The following example shows what must be done in C++.

C++

```
class ANIMAL
{
public:
    ANY_FOOD food;
    eat (ANY_FOOD food) {...};
};

class BIRD : public ANIMAL
{
public:
    SEED bird_food;
    eat (ANY_FOOD food)
    {
        bird_food = static_cast<SEED>(food);
    }
};
```

You could use genericity and templates in these examples, but C++ does not have constrained genericity, so you cannot guarantee that the generic type will be some kind of food. Thus you will eventually have the need for a type cast in C++.

Since argument passing is really a form of assignment, perhaps a solution is to have a *pass attempt*, which passes the argument as *Void* if the type does not match at run time

   a.*eat* (?*birdy_num_num*)

This could tell the compiler to accept the call and generate a run-time check even though it looks dubious; from analysis of all the descendant *eat* routines, the compiler can tell that the argument varies. Such an argument-passing attempt is not necessary, though—you can simply use an assignment attempt to assign the suspected *BIRD* object to a *BIRD* reference.

Eiffel

   a: *ANIMAL*
   b: *BIRD*
   birdy_num_num: *SEED*

```
    b ?= a
    if b /= Void then
        b.eat (birdy_num_num)
    end
```

Eiffel has recently introduced the rule that catcalls are invalid; that is, you cannot pass a argument of a subtype to an argument that is known to be modified covariantly when an object is polymorphic. This is not yet implemented in all compilers however.

Another point to consider is that preconditions are contravariant. Preconditions and argument types are related, as both are predicates on the conditions that must be satisfied for a routine to succeed. For example

Eiffel

```
class A
feature
    r (p: I) is
        require <precondA>
        do ...
        ensure <postcondA>
        end
end

class B
inherit A redefine r end

feature
    r (p: J) is
        require else <precondB>
        do ...
        ensure then <postcondB>
        end
end
```

In the example the precondition for *B.r* is precondA **or** precondB, but its postcondition is postcondA **and** postcondB. Thus preconditions are contravariant because they are the union of the conditions, and postconditions are covariant because they are the intersection of the conditions. Function covariance is in fact the correct way to go (function meaning value-returning routine or attribute). C++ has recently adopted covariance for function return types.

Signature Variance (Eiffel)

Eiffel

```
class A
feature
    f: I
end

class B
inherit A redefine f end

feature
    f: J       -- Covariant redefinition
end

class C
inherit A redefine f end

feature
    f: H       -- Contravariant redefinition not valid.
end

a: A   -- Can refer to A, B, or C objects.
i: I

i := a.f
```

The last assignment will be fine if *a* refers to an *A* or a *B* object, as *f* returns an *I* or a *J*. However, if *a* is attached to a *C* object, an *H* object will be returned, which *i* cannot accommodate. Now perhaps we can see that the rationale behind covariance and contravariance is based upon which direction the data is flowing. The rule should be that the receiver should always be able to accept at least as many types as the sender can send.

We can also consider that calling a routine in an object is actually passing the object to the routine, and, expanding on that, it is every feature in the object that we are actually passing. Since feature types themselves must be covariant, we are in fact implicitly passing covariant arguments. Consider an object *a* with the features *i*, *j*, and *k* of arbitrary types and a routine *r* in *a*.

$$a: \{i, j, k\}$$

$$a.r$$
$$\rightarrow r\,(a)$$

--> r (i, j, k)

Another case where we can be bitten by covariance in inheritance is with export status. For example, if a function in a C++ parent class is public, and if in a descendant class it is private, then we have the same problem with catcalls—that a client can call the private function of an object via a parent reference. To avoid this problem, you should be able to make members of a class more available only as you descend the inheritance chain, which is exactly the opposite of what C++ and Eiffel do. Java does not let you make members more private than they are in parent classes, so has no catcall problem for changing availability.

Thus to avoid catcalls with export problems, you should adopt a once-public, always-public policy. It does not make sense to hide what was public in a parent, because this is fundamentally changing the interface, removing facilities rather than adding them; this indicates some sort of mismatch of design between the parent class and the descendant. In such a case, it is doubtful that inheritance is the appropriate relationship. Such a strict dogma might not suit all situations, but you should be suspicious and very careful about modifying an interface in a child class in this way.

Contravariance has a problem in the case where a routine can call its predecessor routine in a parent. In this case, the child routine will pass on its arguments to the parent. If the arguments have varied contravariantly, then the child will have types passed to it that the predecessor routine has not been designed to handle. Thus contravariance and the ability to call a routine's predecessor do not always go together.

As you can see, arguments for both contravariance and covariance are compelling, but complex, and neither can be seen as 100 percent right or wrong. The existence of this conflict shows that more work must be done in order to clean up this aspect of inheritance in object models.

Such work has already been done by Castagna. He points out that arguments used in determining the routine dispatch should be covariant; others should be contravariant.

> Given a method *m* selected by a message with parameters, when m is overridden, the parameters that determine the (dynamic) selection must be covariantly overridden (i.e., the corresponding parameters in the overriding method must have a lesser type). Those parameters that are not taken into account in the selection must be contravariantly overridden (i.e., the corresponding parameters in the overriding method must have a greater type).

[Castagna 97]

Castagna's conclusion is that the covariance vs. contravariance problem was based on a misunderstanding. "Our formalization shows that the issue of 'contravariance versus covariance' was a false problem caused by the confusion of two mechanisms that have very little in common: substitutivity and overriding."

10

Compile Time

This chapter examines a few issues that can be treated at compile time and examines the different focus of our languages from the viewpoint of these issues. These are very important issues, as they show some great differences between the languages.

10.1 Global Analysis

[Palsberg and Schwartzbach 94] (2.1.3)

Palsberg and Schwartzbach note that there are two *world assumptions* about type safety. The first is the *closed-world* assumption, where all parts of the program are known at compilation time and type checking is done for the entire program. The second is the *open-world* assumption, where type checking is done independently for each module. The open-world assumption is useful when developing and prototyping. However, "when a finished product has matured, it makes sense to adopt the closed-world assumption, since it enables more advanced compilation techniques. Only when the entire program is known, is it possible to perform global register allocation, flow analysis, or dead code detection."

One of the major problems with C++ is the way analysis is divided between the compiler, which works under the open-world assumption, and the linker, which is depended on to do very limited closed-world analysis. Closed-world or *global* analysis is essential for two reasons: first, to ensure that the assembled system is consistent; second, to remove burden from the programmer by providing automatic optimizations.

The main burden that can be removed from the programmer is that of a base class designer having to help the compiler build class virtual tables with the virtual function modifier. As explained in the section on virtual functions in chapter 5, this adversely affects software flexibility. Virtual tables should not be built when a class is compiled; rather virtual tables should be built only when the entire system is assembled. As we have seen, a programmer must be somewhat clairvoyant to determine where and how best to use `virtual`. However, during the system assembly (linker) phase, the compiler and linker can determine which functions need virtual table entries. Since virtualness can be determined automatically, there is no need for a programmer to be clairvoyant. Other burdens on the programmer include that operators must be used to provide the compiler with information it cannot see in other modules, and that other information must be maintained in header files.

In Eiffel and Object Pascal, global analysis of the entire system is done to determine the truly polymorphic calls and to accordingly construct the virtual tables. In Eiffel this is done by the compiler. In Object Pascal, Apple extended the linker to perform global analysis. Such global analysis is difficult in a C/UNIX-style environment, so in C++ it was not included, leaving this burden to the programmer.

To remove this burden from the programmer, global analysis should have been put in the linker. However, since C++ was originally implemented as the Cfront preprocessor, necessary changes to the linker weren't undertaken. The early implementations of C++ were a patchwork, and this has resulted in many holes. The design of C++ was severely limited by its implementation technology, rather than being guided by the principles of better language design, which would require dedicated compilers and linkers. In other words, C++ has been severely limited by its original experimental implementation.

Such technology dependence has seriously damaged C++ as an OO language and more particularly as a high-level language. A high-level language removes the bookkeeping burden from the programmer and places it in the compiler, which is the primary aim of high-level languages. Lack of global or closed-world analysis is a major deficiency of C++ and leaves it substantially lacking when compared to languages such as Eiffel. Since Eiffel insists on *system-level validity* and therefore global analysis, Eiffel implementations are more ambitious than C++ implementations; Eiffel compilers must have access to the information in other modules in order to remove the burdens from the programmer and to check consistency between modules. This is a major reason why Eiffel implementations have been slower to appear.

Java dynamically loads pieces of software and links them into a running system as required. Thus static compile-time global analysis is not possible, because Java is designed to be dynamic. This is one reason why Java and Eiffel are substantially different tools, although Eiffel has recently introduced *dynamic linking in Eiffel* (DLE). For its dynamic environment, Java has made the valid assumption that all methods are virtual.

10.2 Type-Safe Linkage (C++)

[C++ ARM] (7.3c)

The C++ ARM explains that type-safe linkage is not completely type safe. If it is not 100 percent type safe, then it is unsafe. Statistical analysis showed that, in the Challenger disaster, the probability against an individual O-ring failure was 0.997. But when six O-rings were used in combination, this small margin for failure became significant, meaning the combination was very likely to fail. In software, we often find that strange combinations cause failure. It is the primary objective of OO to reduce these strange combinations.

It is the subtle errors that cause the most problems, not the simple or obvious ones. Often such errors remain undetected in the system until critical moments. The seriousness of this situation cannot be underestimated. Many forms of transport, such as planes, and space programs depend on software to provide safety in their operation. The financial survival of organizations can also depend on software. To accept such unsafe situations is at best irresponsible.

C++ type-safe linkage is a huge improvement over C, where the linker will link a function f (p1, ...) with parameters to any function f (), or maybe one with no or different parameters. This results in failure at run time. However, since C++ type-safe linkage is a linker trick, it does not deal with all inconsistencies like this.

[C++ ARM] (7.3c)

The C++ ARM summarizes the situation: "Handling all inconsistencies – thus making a C++ implementation 100% type-safe – would require either linker support or a mechanism (an environment) allowing the compiler access to information from separate compilations."

So why do C++ compilers (at least AT&T's) not provide for accessing information from separate compilations? Why is there not a specialized linker for C++ that actually provides 100 percent type safety? C++ lacks the global analysis of the previous section. Building systems out of preexisting elements is the common UNIX style of software production. This implements a form of reusability, but not in the truly flexible and consistent manner of OO reusability.

In the future, UNIX might be replaced by OO, or more likely *component-oriented* operating systems that are indeed open to be tailored to best suit the purpose at hand. By the use of pipes and flags, UNIX software elements can be reused to provide functionality that approximates what is desired. This approach is valid and works with efficacy in some instances, like small in-house applications or perhaps for research prototyping, but is unacceptable for widespread and expensive software, or safety-critical applications. In the last 10 years the advantages of integrated software have been acknowledged. Classic UNIX systems don't provide those advantages. Integrated systems are more ambitious and place more demands on their developers, but this is the sort of software now being demanded by end users. Systems that are cobbled together are unacceptable. Today the emphasis is on *software component technologies* such as the public domain *OpenDoc* or Microsoft's *OLE*. The Unisys A Series operating system, the Master Control Program (MCP), is already considerably component based with the A Series libraries.

A further problem with linking is that different compilation and linking systems should use different name encoding schemes. This problem is related to type-safe linkage, but is covered in the section on reusability and compatibility in chapter 13.

Java uses a different dynamic linking mechanism, which is well defined and does not use the UNIX linker. Java allows implementation flexibility as to when linking takes place as long as the language semantics are preserved. Java thus has good separation of concerns between language specification and linking details, unlike C++ where the language definition has been influenced by linker considerations. Since the Java linkage mechanism is dynamic, this is further considered in the chapter on run time. Eiffel does not depend on the UNIX or other platform linkers to detect such problems—the compiler must detect these problems.

Eiffel defines **system-level validity**. An Eiffel compiler is required to perform closed-world analysis and not rely on linker tricks. A disadvantage of Eiffel is that compilers have a lot of work to do. (The common terminology is slow, but that is inaccurate.) This is overcome to some extent for example by ISE Eiffel's melting-ice technology, where changes can be made to a system and tested without the need to recompile every time.

Java and Eiffel do have type weaknesses though. Java's problem is that class definitions can get out of synch; the compiler in some circumstances is not sufficient to catch errors that will occur at run time. We look at this problem in more detail in the next chapter. Eiffel's problem is with its covariant arguments; these allow you to pass an argument of a type that the routine cannot handle. We looked at this issue in great detail in the previous chapter.

To summarize the last two sections, global or closed-world analysis is needed for two reasons—consistency checks and optimizations. This removes many burdens from the programmer, and its lack in C++ is a great shortcoming.

10.3 Class Interfaces

[C++ ARM]
(9.1c)

The C++ ARM points out that C++ has no direct support for "interface definition" and "implementation module." In a C++ class definition, all `private` and `protected` members must be included in the public text of the class. The ARM points out that, whenever the `private` or `protected` parts are changed, the whole program must be recompiled. In addition to what the ARM says, all modules that are dependent on the header file must be recompiled, even though the private and protected members do not affect other modules. `Private` members should not be in the abstract class interface, as this exposes implementation details to programmers of client modules. This means that splitting classes into .h and .c files is only a poor approximation of interface/implementation separation.

Java does not have the .h and .c separation mechanism, but you get the effect by splitting your classes into an interface and a class. Each class can have multiple interfaces.

Eiffel provides the tools *short* and *flat* to extract interface definitions from class texts. In ISE's EiffelBench development environment, these tools are built in, so the programmer can quickly navigate around classes. The text for the short flat (it's not only Java that uses coffee terminology) forms can be generated as a disk file so that libraries can be distributed to third parties.

11

Run Time

This chapter examines a few issues that can be treated at run time, as well as the different focus of our languages from the viewpoint of these issues. In this respect Java and Eiffel are probably the most similar languages, providing garbage collection and concurrency mechanisms defined in the language.

11.1 Concurrency — It's about Time!

We have two basic needs for concurrency. First, to satisfy our impatience, we want to reduce the elapsed time for a computation, and an obvious way to do this is to increase the compute time within a real time period. In some ways the need to do this has been reduced, as the power of single processors has increased by so much over a not-very-long period (Moore's Law). However, the high end will always need more power than a single processor can offer. Even on a single processor, it is desirable to make sure other activities can progress if the one currently using the processor becomes blocked.

The second reason for concurrency is modeling: some problems are naturally concurrent in the real world, and, to model these effectively, it is better to have concurrency support in the underlying language rather than to always develop your own.

The object of concurrent programming is that computing resources can be harnessed to compute efficiently problems that would otherwise be inefficient to compute using a single processor. In the next 10 years multiple processor arrays that execute programs concurrently will likely become common, although this prediction has been around for at least the last 10 years. Concurrency requires much cleaner languages than the single processor languages of today.

Simula, the first OO language, had such concurrency built in, so this is not a new feature; however, it is new to so-called *modern* OO languages. Simula introduced coroutines and process classes. Coroutines explicitly specify where control should be given to another process, and to which process. Process classes are built on top of coroutines, but higher-level calls, such as wait, just suspend the processes, which then have no control over which process is executed next. When using process classes, the coroutine calls should not be used explicitly, as this will interfere with the process scheduling.

The desirable features of concurrency do not come without the obligatory price tag. The first problem is increased complexity. You cannot just take a sequential program and carve it up; the pieces can interact in undesirable ways.

The second problem is that concurrency can cost a significant amount of processor overhead. One effect of this was that the first Macintoshes and personal computers concentrated on running a single program only (although 8086-based Burroughs B20s available at the same time were multiprocessing machines). If you are familiar with multiprocessor machines, you will know that adding processors does not give you proportionately more computing power. Two processors does not double your capacity, and four processors are more likely to yield only three times as much power. In fact, as you add more processors, you are more likely to get degraded performance.

The problem of overhead with concurrency is an implementation concern, and we should not worry about it here. However, the first problem of undesirable interactions between processes must be handled in our programs. In order to avoid the undesirable interactions, we must synchronize our processes. Synchronization acts like a traffic cop in multiprocessing, ensuring that two processes do not occupy the same "compute space" at the same time. The traffic cop must ensure that two vehicles do not occupy an intersection at one time or damage results. But this is not all the traffic cop must do—he must maximize the traffic flow through the intersection, minimize wait time, make sure his decisions are fair, and make sure that no vehicles are forgotten. By compute space, I mean access to some resource. Such a resource is usually a set of data, which must only be updated by one process at a time. It's easy to imagine hardware resources also suffering from multiprocessing conflict—for example, if one process moves a disk head to where it wants to write data, but another process then writes its data there, we have a corrupted system. This contravenes our first essential property of concurrent systems, that is, the *safety* property.

In order to maximize the benefits of concurrency, we must carefully choose where we place synchronization constraints. If we place them incorrectly, we could get undesired interactions, often called *race conditions*, and so we have not ensured that the safety property holds. However, if we place too many synchronization constraints, potential for concurrency is lost, and we might not keep our processor as busy as it could be. In the worst case, we place synchronization constraints in such a way that two or more processes lock each other out of access to a common resource permanently. In this case one or more processes must be terminated, which represents wasted work that must be redone.

In this last case, we want to ensure that processes are not irrevocably blocked and are able to make progress. This second property is called the *liveness* property (remember our traffic cop must not forget any vehicles). Processes that become irrevocably blocked waiting for common resources are said to be *deadlocked*. It is often difficult to tell whether a process is deadlocked or not, making it difficult to prove the liveness property. A process might temporarily be suspended waiting for something to happen, not consuming any processor time while it waits. If this is the case, the process is alive, but not active, and you don't want to terminate such a process.

Some Definitions

We should give a few more definitions before progressing. A *process* is a unit of work to be accomplished. A *processor* is a resource that performs work. The problem is assigning processes to processors to perform some or all of their work in order to attain effective *load balancing*.

Multiprocessing is where more than one processor is involved in the processing. Multiple processors can be *tightly coupled*, which means they share memory and other resources. Processors can also be *loosely coupled*, in which case they can be part of the same system, sharing some resources, but not memory. Or we can have *distributed systems*, where distinct systems do not share resources, but are coordinated by messages flowing over a network. Distributed processing comes in several flavors: first there is the *client-server* model in which processing is shared between a presentation client and a server. Then we have *three-tier* processing, in which we have so-called *thin clients* handling user presentation and interactions, a middle-layer application processor, and a back-end resource, usually a database. In *peer-to-peer* processing, all processors assume equivalent responsibilities in processing some problem.

In *multiprogramming* several processes share a single processor. When one or more processes become blocked waiting for resources, other processes can use the processor to do useful work. Processes may be allocated processor time, even when a running process has not become blocked. This is known as *preemptive multitasking*. Processes can be assigned priorities, so that those of a higher priority obtain proportionately more processing time. In such an environment it is essential to make sure that all processes make some progress; this property is called *fairness*.

In concurrent processing we find another reason to distinguish procedures from functions. When we call a procedure in another process, we can happily continue, but, if we call a function, we must wait for the result. (We could also notify the other process to begin processing the result and poll for the result later.) For example

>   a.p (...) -- We can continue asynchronously.
>   i := a.f (...) -- We must wait for the result.

We should also consider what the difference between a *process* and a *thread* is, although such definitions will not be exactly correct for all operating systems. As always, we should keep an open mind. Because some system does not implement our definitions exactly does not mean that system is wrong. In fact, some of the best systems have been those that have defied the traditional definitions. You can consult Tanenbaum if you want a fuller explanation of much of the definitional material in this section. [Tanenbaum 9

A process has its own address space and its own thread of control; other processes do not have access to this address space. Most processes are single threaded; however a process can be multithreaded, in which case separate threads execute independently, except that they run in the single address space of the process and therefore can interact with each other.

Interaction is a desirable property of threads, but it can result in interference, which is undesirable. The threads run in quasiparallel within the process, using a lightweight scheduling mechanism which should be cheaper in terms of swapping than the underlying operating systems process swapping. Thus threads are often known as *lightweight processes*.

A thread has its own program counter, stack, child threads, and state. The items in a process that threads share are address space, global variables, files, semaphores, and others depending on the implementation.

Of course some operating systems do not share the definition of processes having separate address spaces. For example, Unisys A Series MCP is a stack-based operating system that allows a "cactus tree" of subprocesses to be built, where the subprocesses can access variables in the parent process that are more global in scope.

This scheme has one problem—global variables—which we discussed in chapter 2. Many processes access the same global space, making coordination mechanisms necessary, even more so since accesses are now asynchronous. The solution in this operating system is to invert the whole structure and define libraries that control access to the shared resources, in much the same way that objects control access to their internals—access to shared entities can be through only the exported interface.

Such libraries are indeed *components*, which have been the subject of much research and even more hype in the last few years. The idea is not new, though, but up until recently it's been mostly ignored. Thus languages that support the absence of global variables are better placed to support this more modern form of software structuring. For more on components, see the section on components in chapter 2.

Concurrency in Simula

Concurrency can be built into a language in several ways. It is interesting to see how Simula, the first OO language, provided concurrency. The first mechanism is **coroutines**. The features for coroutines are inherited by all classes. The first feature is *detach*. Detach creates a coroutine and the object becomes *detached* and is now waiting to be resumed. Detach works like a return in that the calling routine now resumes processing from the point where it called the detaching routine. Unlike return, when the object is resumed, it picks up from the point of the detach.

The second feature is *resume*. This is used to resume a coroutine from where it relinquished control, either by a detach or another resume.

Call is used to reattach a coroutine. A coroutine terminates when it falls through the final **end** of the routine where it was detached.

The second form of concurrency in Simula is the **process class**. This is done by a class modifier rather than inheritance. It is actually built on top of the coroutine mechanism, but process classes should not use detach or resume of coroutines explicitly or undesirable results will occur. When a process object is created it becomes detached and enters the passive state. The process is then woken up using activate.

Activate causes the given process to run. *Hold* tells a process to wait for a given simulation time. If all processes are waiting, the scheduler picks up the first process and advances the simulation time to that of the first process. *Cancel* removes the given process from the waiting list. *Passivate* cancels the current process. A process becomes terminated when it falls through the final **end**.

Threads in Java

Threads in Java are implemented in a class `Thread` and an interface `Runnable`. `Thread` implements the interface `Runnable`. You can instantiate a thread directly.

```
Thread t = new Thread ();
t.start ();
```
Java

However, this will not do much. The effect of `start ()` is to call the thread's `run` method. Run calls the `run` method of the `Runnable` object associated with the thread; otherwise it does nothing. Since no `Runnable` object has been associated with the thread in our example, this does nothing.

In order to actually do something with threads, you should either define a class that extends `Thread` or a class that implements `Runnable`. This `Runnable` class is then passed to the `Thread` as an argument to its constructor, and, as we have seen, `run ()` in `Thread` calls `run ()` in its `Runnable` object. To actually do something, you have to put code in your `run` method.

Why should we want to use this more complicated way of implementing `Runnable` and passing it to another `Thread`? The answer is that often we want the class we are defining to extend some other class. Without multiple inheritance we cannot extend with `Thread` as well, making things more complicated.

Most features needed for threads are in the `Thread` class.

```
public
class Thread implements Runnable {
    public static native void yield();
    public static native void sleep()
            throws InterruptedException;
    public synchronized native void start();
    public void run();
    public final void stop();
    public final void suspend();
```
Java

```
            public final void resume();
            public final void join()
                    throws InterruptedException;
    }
```

This is an abstract version. Other thread features are inherited by all objects from `Object`.

Java

```
    public class Object {
        public final native void notify();
        public final native void notifyAll();
        public final void wait()
                throws InterruptedException;
    }
```

Now we need to know how to prevent undesirable interactions. Java achieves this by having a single lock per object. This lock is locked by the `synchronized` keyword. Methods and blocks of statements can be `synchronized`. `Synchronized` methods implicitly lock the current object; with `synchronized` statements, you specify which object to lock, so this provides a fully general locking mechanism. `Synchronized` methods are really a notational convenience over `synchronized` statements.

When the `synchronized` method or statement ends, the locked object is implicitly unlocked, relieving the programmer of this error-prone burden.

Synchronization is not inherited in Java; if a method overrides a parent method, none of the parent's method is inherited. You can override a `synchronized` method as non-`synchronized` method and vice versa.

Concurrency in Eiffel

Eiffel has two concurrency mechanisms. The first is a *THREAD* class, rather like the mechanism in Java. The second is a more radical extension to the language itself (although the extension of a single keyword is not too large, the idea is somewhat radical). This language extension is called SCOOP for *simple concurrent object-oriented programming*. Note this is simple concurrency and should satisfy the marjority of applications. However, for full generality you can use Eiffel threads.

Eiffel Threads

Let us first look at the thread model, which, if you have a compiler with SCOOP support, is not recommended for use in most applications. The Eiffel thread mechanism is mostly based on providing access to underlying C thread support. The thread support is rather like Java threads. We have a *THREAD* class.

Eiffel Interface

    class interface
        THREAD
    feature
        launch
        launch_with_attributes (*attr*: *THREAD_ATTRIBUTES*)
        execute
        exit
    end

Note that any thread can be mixed with any other class with multiple inheritance; we do not have the complication of a `Runnable` interface or class as in Java.

Another note: the keyword **interface** indicates that this representation has been extracted from the class text by some tool such as *short*. Programmers do not actually write separate interfaces in Eiffel. Included in the interface are entry points, routine arguments, header comments, pre- and postconditions, and class invariants.

The Eiffel *THREAD* class is much the same as Java's `Thread`. In a *THREAD* class, you can call a creation routine when creating the *THREAD* object. Like Java, this does not actually set a thread running; to do this you must call *launch*. *Launch* calls *execute*, which you should provide in your class with some sort of processing loop, which will keep running until *execute* exits.

Then we have the *THREAD_CONTROL* class.

Eiffel Interface

    class interface
        THREAD_CONTROL
    feature
        yield
        join_all
        join
    end

THREAD_CONTROL is inherited by THREAD. *Yield* causes the thread to yield execution in favor of another thread. *Join* waits for a child thread to complete, and *join_all* waits for all child threads to complete.

Synchronization in Eiffel *THREAD*s is more conventional than Java's `synchronized` methods and statements. Java adds language support, whereas Eiffel provides the support in the threads library. The Eiffel solution is more general, but you have to do more work, manipulating *SEMAPHORE*s, *MUTEX*s, and *CONDITION_VARIABLE*s. Depending on your application, you will use only one of these mechanisms.

You can get this generality in Java, but the code required to do this with `synchronized` statements is tricky. Fortunately, Doug Lea has provided an excellent library of concurrent objects to provide general synchronization. You can find these at his WEB site.

*SEMAPHORE*s are a low-level exclusion mechanism. Semaphores were used on early railways to make sure that only one train occupied a single two-directional track at a time. When entering the *critical region*, the train driver would be handed a token, which he would hand back when the train exited the region at the other end. The rule was simple: no token, no entry. This is an example of a *binary semaphore*, in which case there is only one token.

We can also have *general semaphores*. Consider a 2,000-seat movie theater. As long as you have less than 2,000 people in the audience, another ticket can be sold. Once all 2,000 tickets have been sold, no more people can enter the theater; they must wait for more tickets to become available, probably for the next performance. However, imagine a continuous newsreel, with no start or end time, where people come and leave at any time. Another example is a parking garage, although the semaphores in this case are more imaginary than tickets and tokens, but the effect of a full parking garage is no less real.

[Ben-Ari 90]

Dijkstra's original description of semaphores had two operations on a semaphore: $P(S)$ and $V(S)$. These are really *wait*(S) and *signal*(S), P and V coming from the corresponding words in Dutch. The *wait* and *signal* operations must be *atomic*—that is, uninterruptable by other processes.

S is initialized to the number of tickets we have; if it is a binary semaphore, S is initialized to 1. On a *wait*, if S is greater than 0, S is decremented, and the process can enter the critical region. If S is negative then the process must wait for another process to exit the region, sending a *signal* as it does so, which increments S and wakes up one of the waiting processes. A negative S represents the number of processes waiting on the semaphore. You can see that this works rather like our parking garage example, as a car leaving a full parking garage means that a waiting car is permitted to enter.

The operations on an Eiffel *SEMAPHORE* are *wait*, *post* (for *signal*), and *try_wait*. *try_wait* is used in a case where you just want to test the *SEMAPHORE* and then have the option of going and finding another parking garage, or something else to do.

Semaphores, as we have seen, require a fair degree of responsibility on the part of the user. If our movie patron forgets to hand back the ticket when leaving, one seat will be permanently left unoccupied. The same is true with our parking garage—a situation that would result in many irate drivers. To ensure this does not happen, we shift the responsibility from the user to the provider.

Of course, we know this is not the way a real parking garage works; patrons have no responsibility to hand back a token when they leave, just to pay the bill. It is really up to the gatehouse attendant to let the departing car out and a new car in. In this case the attendant acts as a *monitor*, which is a higher-level control than semaphores, as the responsibility is centralized with one authority. Now, isn't that just OO programming?! Note that you can emulate semaphores by monitors and vice versa.

[Ben-Ari 90]

While monitors are no more powerful than semaphores, since the compiler automatically provides the locking instead of the programmer needing to do things explicitly, they are more convenient and lead to less programming errors—the very essence of better higher-level languages. It is of course important when considering concurrent programming structures whether a structure is necessary to perform a particular computation or whether it makes it easier for programmers to write. In fact this is an important consideration in evaluating any language feature.

MUTEX and *CONDITION_VARIABLE* are other classes that the Eiffel threads library provides. *MUTEX* is a simple kind of semaphore—in fact it's a binary semaphore restricting the state, being allowed to be locked or unlocked, corresponding to the values 0 and 1 in a semaphore. *MUTEX* has the operations *lock*, *unlock*, and *try_lock*. The difference between a mutex and a binary semaphore is really only a matter of interpretation, mutex meaning, more specifically, a lock.

CONDITION_VARIABLE has a *wait* operation. This waits for some condition to become true. Processes become queued on the condition variable. You must lock a *MUTEX* object first and pass this object to the *wait* operation of the condition variable. If the condition is not true, then the mutex is unlocked so that some other process can change the condition. After the process is awakened, the mutex is again locked and the *wait* returns. The process should then unlock the mutex and continue.

You use a mutex for short-term locking around a critical region. Conditional variables are used for long-term waiting on a condition such as availability of a resource.

An interesting property of Eiffel threads is that both **once** routines and garbage collection are on a per-thread basis. We shall look at garbage collection more closely in the next section. In the Eiffel *THREAD* mechanism, threads are very independent. Objects belong to only one thread. A thread cannot (or should not) refer to an object belonging to another thread, except via a *PROXY* object. If an object becomes orphaned in a thread, it will be garbage collected, even if another thread has access to it. You must use *PROXY* to prevent this from happening.

Eiffel SCOOP

[Meyer 97] chapter 30)

The SCOOP mechanism is a novel approach to concurrency. With the introduction of a single keyword and a small extension to the semantics of preconditions the power of concurrency and safety of synchronization have been added to Eiffel. To extend preconditions from the single threaded case—which fails on a false condition that can never change—to a multithreaded case where another thread can change and satisfy the condition, preconditions wait for conditions to become true instead of failing. Thus in a concurrent environment, preconditions are used for sychronization.

The single keyword extension is **separate**, which can be applied to a class, a single object, or an argument to a routine. It means that the entity marked with **separate** is assigned to a different processor or thread of control. Eiffel has rules that you can assign a separate object only to a separate target.

Unlike threads, which are active processes, **separate** objects are mainly passive. This seems a little confusing at first, because a **separate** object is assigned its own logical processor. However, a thread is independent and usually has a process loop in its run method; a thread just keeps on running, sometimes blocking on a resource with an operation such as a file read.

In contrast, a **separate** object is passive until it has one of its routines invoked. It then processes until the routine exits. You can look at this as every routine in a separate object is a special case of run or execute. With the **separate** mechanism, threads can be easily emulated—you simply write a single *run* routine. Normally, you won't use a single *run* routine, the main paradigm is to execute only when a message is passed to a **separate** object from a client.

To turn **separate** objects into really active objects, you should inherit from class *PROCESS*. After creating the object and possibly calling a creation routine, you call the routine *live,* which runs the process from a loop.

Now we have the question as to how we obtain objects for exclusive use and how we lock things. The answer is that, to perform a separate call—that is, a call whose target is a separate object—the target must be passed as an argument to the calling routine. You cannot perform a separate call on an object feature, at least directly. This rule is known as the *separate call rule*.

The simple reason for this restriction is that the mechanism obtains every separate argument for exclusive use on entry to a routine. Thus, at the point of a separate call, you know the target object will be exclusively yours. The scheme is rather like database transaction processing systems, where all resources needed for the transaction should be locked during the first phase of the transaction, and then, once all resources are locked, updates may occur in the second phase. During the second phase, resources may only be released—no more resources may be locked. This is a major technique to avoid deadlock.

In Eiffel, the separate arguments passed to a routine are the resources that will be used during the routine.

One of the seemingly worst things about mixing concurrency into Eiffel is that it seems to invalidate one of the central techniques of Eiffel: design by contract with assertions, mainly preconditions. Why is this? It is because the client must satisfy the precondition—that is, must test and satisfy any conditions—before calling the routine. In a sequential situation this is fine, because nothing will change between the test and the call; if it does, we have a programming error, or perhaps the client programmer has not understood the calling convention.

Concurrent execution introduces the problem that another process can take over in between the test and the routine invocation, and could invalidate the condition, without any programming error on the part of the calling client. Meyer calls this the *precondition paradox* which he sees as a central issue of concurrent OO programming.

[Meyer 97] (30.7)

To solve this, we must change the semantics of preconditions. An example will help. If we are adding an element to a bounded buffer b, we should first ensure that the buffer is not full: **not** *b.full*. The precondition of the *put* routine will reflect the fact that this is required. However, once we, as the client, have done the test, we might be suspended, and another process might get there first.

What we really want is to wait for the condition **not** *b.full* before *b.put* is invoked. This is exactly the change of semantics to preconditions that has been put into Eiffel—instead of preconditions being a *correctness condition*, preconditions become a *wait condition*. Remember that any separate argument passed to a routine will automatically be locked for exclusive use of the routine before the body of the routine is entered. Any conditions stated in the preconditions clause must also be satisfied before the routine body is entered. Obviously, if a condition on a separate argument cannot be satisfied, the object must remain free for others to use so that the condition can be changed.

You might note that this mechanism is rather like the condition variables we met in the section on Eiffel threads. Precondition clauses that do not involve separate argument objects have the normal sequential semantics; that is, raise an exception in the caller.

As you can see, the only way to satisfy a condition in the sequential case is to notify the client that something must be changed in order for the routine to be called. In the concurrent case, the condition is expected to be satisfied beyond the control of the client, by another process.

A last detail in this scheme is that finer-grained control is provided by the class *CONCURRENCY*. This should be inherited by any **separate** class needing to have more explicit control over concurrency, in much the same way as *EXCEPTIONS* provides finer control over exceptions and *MEMORY* provides finer control over memory management. *CONCURRENCY* allows more urgent tasks to preempt a separate object that is already executing another task.

Concurrency in C++

Concurrency in C++ is mainly in the realm of research projects. Such a project is Synchronous C++ (sC++), which defines active objects that contain their own execution threads. C++ itself defines nothing to do with concurrency; however, the many familiar mechanisms of `fork ()`, etc., are available from C. You might also note that Eiffel's threads library is built on top of C threads. These same libraries are certainly available for the use of the C++ programmer. Of course, the fact that C++ builds on top of C is an advantage, making much of the functionality available in C also available in C++. Of course this does not mean that, because Java and Eiffel are different languages, they are excluded from using C features; they can do so with Java's native interface and Eiffel's externals.

[Petitpierre 98]

The Inheritance Anomaly

The term *inheritance anomaly* is a misnomer. It suggests that inheritance has some fault that is impossible or at least difficult to overcome. In fact the anomaly is really with the statement of the problem and the particular way that inheritance and synchronization constraints have been married. The problem is therefore somewhat artificial, but it is always popular to ask a question on the inheritance anomaly whenever OO is presented along with concurrency.

A language exhibits the inheritance anomaly if, with synchronization constructs, you either have to redefine functional code or restate synchronization constraints in a subclass. Thus the inheritance anomaly really comes down to a lack of reuse. As we have seen, with Java, synchronization is not inherited. Eiffel needs no restatement of code or synchronization constraints, as these constraints are inherited in routine redefinitions, just as preconditions and postconditions are.

In Eiffel there are two reasons why the inheritance anomaly does not occur. The first is that Eiffel does not enumerate valid states in which a list of routines may operate; rather the valid states in which a routine can be called are listed within the routine as preconditions. Second, you do not have to restate these conditions in child routines in subclasses, since preconditions from parent routines are inherited. Eiffel, therefore, avoids the so-called inheritance anomaly.

11.2 Garbage Collection

One of the hallmarks of high-level languages is that programmers declare data without regard to how the data is allocated in memory. Programmers concentrate on the logical data structures of the problem domain rather than the physical machine-based memory structures. In block-structured languages, local variables are automatically allocated on the stack and automatically deallocated when the block exits. This relieves the programmer of the burden of allocating and deallocating memory. Garbage collection provides equivalent relief in languages with dynamic entity allocation.

We have also seen that making the programmer consider how to map a program into a finite memory considerably changes the computing problem. If we assume an infinite memory, the programming problem becomes much simpler because the need for any data structure that recycles memory disappears. As there is not really such a thing as infinite memory, we do want to ensure that, when objects are no longer required, they are discarded before the program aborts with a no-more-memory condition. We should therefore be clear on whether we are using a particular structure because it naturally fits the problem or whether we are using it because it is a part of our memory allocation scheme. For example, very often stacks fall into this latter category. Of course, ideally, an application should be well designed enough to minimize the objects that are created in the first place; in this case the garbage collector will not even have to reclaim them. (The best optimization is to not perform work that does not need to be performed. So much process improvement is to improve processes in activities that should be abolished entirely.)

If we remove much of the need to design our data structures around memory allocation schemes, then we use the correct data structures that best match the problem. As with everything, this is a trade-off. Any structures used in the implementation detail of memory allocation should be ideally hidden behind an OO interface. Garbage collection is an essential mechanism that provides the view that memory is an infinite resource, since memory is reclaimed only when the physical resource is almost exhausted and an object is no longer needed in the program.

[Reade 89]
(1.1)

Recall that Reade points out that we should separate the concerns of describing what is to be computed from administrative tasks such as memory management. Reade furthermore suggests that these tasks should be automated in the language system.

For these reasons many OO languages have seen garbage collection as important enough to the OO paradigm to include it; for example, Smalltalk, Java, and Eiffel.

C++ does not have garbage collection in its current form, and the programmer must manually manage storage. This is the most difficult bookkeeping task C++ programmers face and can lead to two opposite problems: first, an object can be deallocated prematurely, while valid references still exist (dangling pointers); second, dead objects might not be deallocated leading to memory filling up with dead objects (memory leaks). Attempts to correct either problem can lead to overcompensation and the opposite problem occurring. A correct system is a fine balance that is difficult to obtain and in most cases cannot be provably correct. Figure 11-1 illustrates this.

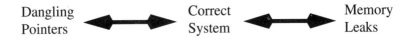

Figure 11-1. Problems without garbage collection

These problems contribute to the fragility of C++ programs and usually result in system failure. Garbage collection solves both problems, but has an undeserved bad reputation due to some early garbage collectors having noticeable performance problems instead of working transparently in the background as they can and should. These problems are often overemphasized as a justification for C++ ignoring garbage collection. A possible solution is to build garbage collection into the run-time architecture, but to allow the programmer to activate and deactivate it manually. Garbage collection can be disabled in systems where it is inappropriate.

Temporaries

Garbage collection is now a well-researched topic, and efficient solutions are available. If you need a more detailed knowledge of garbage collection, Jones and

Lins have written an excellent book. You should also note that garbage collection is a complex topic. That is why many people feel they don't want the added overhead of automatic garbage collection. However, without automatic garbage collection, the application itself must handle this complexity. Meyers gives an example.

[Jones and Lins 96]

[Meyers 92] (item 23)

```
Complex w, x, y, z;

w = x + y + z;
```
C++

looks innocent enough but results in a memory leak if the + operator of `Complex` is as follows:

```
// Wrong way to write this function.
inline
Complex& operator+(const Complex& lhs,
                   const Complex& rhs)
{
    Complex *result =
        new Complex (lhs.r + rhs.r,
            lhs.i + rhs.i);
    return *result;
}
```
C++

This results in unnamed temporaries being constructed that the programmer can't subsequently reference in order to destruct. It turns out that you must return the new `Complex` by value, but also construct and delete the temporary constants in the + function. Meyers says, "as in life itself, there is no free lunch." However, garbage collection does give the programmer a somewhat free lunch.

[Meyers 92]

Of course, this lunch is not entirely free, since garbage collection has an overhead. However, as this example shows, in a non-garbage-collected system, the programmer must code this overhead into the application, so a program loses its logical integrity under unnecessary implementation details. If you measure the overhead of garbage collection in a garbage-collected system, you must remember that a proportion of this overhead will be built into a non-garbage-collected application, and therefore the processor cost of garbage collection is offset. However, with garbage collection, the complexity to the programmer is completely eliminated; hence this part of the lunch is free.

Garbage Collection and Nesting

The example in the previous section shows the problem with temporary variables, but we should consider how garbage collection affects the way we model things. In the section on nested classes in chapter 5, we saw the example of a car being an aggregate of an engine and wheels. However, this kind of real-world aggregation does not mean that nested classes are needed at design time or run time. For a start we need to discard the idea of aggregation being a special relationship distinct from associations and other forms of relationship. However, in the real world, the difference between an aggregation and association is that, when the aggregate object is destroyed, so are the subparts, but an association does not destroy other parties involved in the association.

Why is it then that the systems designer can ignore the aggregation/association distinction? Garbage collection is part of the answer. Although the wheels of a car might be created as separate entities, garbage collection means that, when all references to a car are lost, the car object will be garbage collected. At the same time all subparts will also become unconnected to the system, so they will also be garbage collected. Thus the programmer is relieved of the burden of destroying manual subpart objects. In the database world, this is known as *cascaded deletes*.

In an association, you don't want such cascaded deletes. In a garbage-collected system, as long as the object has associations still accessible in the system, the object will not be deleted. We can now see why the aggregation/association distinction is not needed, and in fact this distinction in a programming language results in brittle software. Suppose we do not want to destroy the wheels, but that we want to assign them to a spare-parts depot. The fact that we built aggregation knowledge into the system and destroy wheel objects at the same time as the car object means we have to undo this code in order to assign the wheels to spare parts. If we give up the aggregation/association distinction in conjunction with a garbage collector, we indeed get this lunch for free.

[CPN 98]

We can also use such knowledge to optimize garbage collection. If we know that wheel objects are entirely private to the owning car objects and are not referenced from outside, a garbage collector can reclaim the wheel objects when the car object is disposed without having to do the usual garbage collection processing needed to prove that the wheels are also unreachable. Thus some garbage collection decisions can be made statically, saving time proving the nonreachability of objects at run time. This is an active area of research.

While the export restriction {*NONE*} suggests that a reference field might only be used within a current object, it cannot guarantee that the referenced object is not attached to anything else. That is, we know that the reference cannot be passed out from this object, but we can't tell that the reference has not been passed in, and therefore is referenced from other objects in the system. To do this, some extra restrictions are needed. Perhaps a small extension to Eiffel introducing the export restriction {*Current*} could be introduced to make such a guarantee:

    class *NO_ALIAS_CAR*   *not Eiffel*
        feature {*Current*}
            -- Features guanranteed to be accessed only from the
            -- current object.

            driver_front, *driver_rear*,
            passenger_front, *passenger_rear*: *WHEEL*
    end

Note that this scheme would completely remove the need for textual nesting to represent nested objects.

Meyer lists garbage collection as an essential element in OO. This is not surprising in a language that has exception handling—keeping track of live and dead objects without garbage collection in the presence of exceptions is extremely difficult. Without garbage collection you must carefully write your code to dispose of temporarily allocated objects. Determining where an object should be deleted within the normal flow of control is a difficult enough task. With exceptions this is much more difficult because exceptions break the normal flow of control; hence code carefully written to delete objects could be bypassed. This also means that it is difficult to add exceptions to existing C++ code to improve programs because you really need to have designed your program with exceptions from scratch to have a good chance of deleting objects correctly without leaks. A suggestion in C++ to alleviate this difficulty is to use smart pointers such as the template class `auto_ptr`. Thus exception handling without garbage collection makes your programs much more difficult to write, follow, and then change. Garbage collection removes all this complexity. [Meyer 97] (2.2)

Adding Garbage Collection to C++

In C++ the lack of garbage collection might seem like an engineering compromise. Its inclusion is nearly an engineering impossibility, since a programmer can undermine the structures required for implementing correctly working garbage collection. While garbage collection might not actually be an impossibility in C++, it is difficult, and programmers would have to settle for a more restricted way of programming. This could be a good thing. But then the compromise to remain compatible with C becomes difficult if the compiler is to detect practices inconsistent with the operation of garbage collection.

[Sun 95]	Sun states that "explicit memory management has proved to be a fruitful source of bugs, crashes, memory leaks and poor performance." Sun has built garbage collection into Java.
[Stroustrup 94] (10.7.1)	Stroustrup is also an advocate of optional garbage collection. "When (not if) garbage collection becomes available, we will have two ways of writing C++ programs." My question is not if or when, but how? Unless you restrict pointers and pointer operations, garbage collection will be very difficult and probably inefficient. By inefficient, I mean either it will be slow or it won't clean up very well, or even both.

Stroustrup adds,

[Stroustrup 97] (C.9.1)	The standard does not require that an implementation supply a garbage collector, but garbage collectors are increasingly used for C++ in areas where their costs compare favorably to those of manual management of free store. When comparing costs, consider the run time, memory usage, reliability, portability, monetary cost of programming, monetary cost of a garbage collector, and predictability of performance.

We should also remember that C++ was originally developed in the early 1980s, and it was not widely recognized how essential garbage collection would be until people were personally burned by the problems. Also, for low-level systems programming, it is not clear that garbage collection is necessarily beneficial, without unwanted overhead. For example, can you write a garbage collector in a language designed for garbage collection itself? Stroustrup recognized these considerations.

[Stroustrup 94] (10.7)	Also, garbage collection would make C++ unsuitable for many of the low-level tasks for which it was intended. I like the idea of garbage collection as a mechanism that simplifies design and eliminates a source of errors. However, I am fully convinced that had garbage collection been an integral part of C++ originally, C++ would have been stillborn.

Many other problems of C++ just disappear if you have garbage collection. One such example is the problem of temporaries.

A lot has changed in the 1990s, and the percentage of low-level systems programming has become insignificant as compared to applications programming and higher-level systems programming. Into higher levels of systems programming, you can include upper levels of operating systems, compilers, and system utilities that will benefit from garbage collection. Since the vast majority of programmers are doing applications programming now, even if it is in C++ using

MFC and Visual C++, or something similar, most projects will benefit from a garbage-collected language.

Controlling Garbage Collection

Garbage collection can be made optional in Eiffel. The garbage collector can be disabled during critical real-time phases of program execution. It cannot be completely disabled because, if a program runs out of memory in this state, the garbage collector will be invoked, which is preferable to the application crashing with a *no memory* error. You can toggle the state of garbage collection by calling *MEMORY.collection_off* and *MEMORY.collection_on*. Also, you can force a collection at any time simply by calling *MEMORY.collect_now*.

In Java, you can disable the garbage collector when you run the program; the details of this will be environment dependent. In order to force a collection in this situation, your program should call `System.gc ()`.

You should note that, because of garbage collection, neither Java nor Eiffel has destructors. However, you might still want to release some underlying system resource when the object is disposed—for example, closing a file. For this case, Eiffel introduces the routine *MEMORY.dispose*, and Java introduces a `finalize` method. If you define these in your class, then they will be called before the object is discarded. You should not relink the object into the system in any way. If the program finishes running before the `finalize` method or dispose routine is called, the operating system must release the resource. Thus providing this destructor-like mechanism does not guarantee that your program will get to release the resource, but this is also true of C++.

Garbage Collection and Multithreading

Garbage collection also becomes interesting in a multithreaded environment. In Eiffel, you get a separate garbage collector per thread. This is because, if one thread needs garbage collection, other threads do not need to suspend.

While Java does not specify how its garbage collection should work with regard to threads, the implementations at the moment do not have per-thread garbage collection. Thus, if the garbage collector is initiated, all threads must be suspended. Java is not so separatist about objects as Eiffel, since it is possible to refer to a single object directly from several threads. While this makes things simpler, part of the concurrency power of threads is lost. Eiffel's garbage-collection strategies are more sophisticated (and, at the time of writing, Eiffel's implementations are also more sophisticated).

11.3 Constructors and Temporaries (C++)

[C++ ARM]
(6.6.3)

A return <expression> can result in a different value than the result of <expression>. The C++ ARM says, "If required, the expression is converted, as in an initialization, to the return type of the function in which it appears. This may involve the construction and copy of a temporary object (S12.2)."

[C++ ARM]
(12.2)

The ARM further explains, "In some circumstances it may be necessary or convenient for the compiler to generate a temporary object. Such introduction of temporaries is implementation dependent. When a compiler introduces a temporary object of a class that has a constructor it must ensure that a constructor is called for the temporary object."

The following note says: "The implementation's use of temporaries can be observed, therefore, through the side effects produced by constructors and destructors."

Putting this together, creation of a temporary is implementation dependent. If a temporary is created, a constructor is called as a side effect, which can change the state of the object. Different C++ implementations could therefore return different results for the same code.

[Stroustrup 94]
(6.3.2)

Temporaries present further problems, with some very innocent-looking code. Exactly when a temporary should be destroyed was debated in the C++ committee for several years until it was finally resolved in 1993. However, the resolution was not to come up with the perfect solution, but to choose one of several flawed alternatives. Stroustrup gives the details of what happened. He gives the example:

C++

```
p = s1 + s2;
printf ("%s", p);
```

Unfortunately the temporary object representing the concatenated string s1 + s2 has disappeared. The committee decided that temporaries should be destroyed at the end of a statement. However, they then had the problem with the meaning of end of statement. The committee felt that

C++

```
if (p = s1 + s2) printf ("%s", p);
```

should be equivalent to the first example, so a more restrictive form was chosen—temporaries would be destroyed after a full expression. This solution reaches a balance between two extremes, but satisfies neither. At worst it leads to bad coding errors, and at best it leaves the programmer with the headache of having to code around such problems. At one extreme temporaries are not left around for long enough, and at the other temporaries are left around for too long, causing memory problems or virtual memory thrashing, thereby seriously degrading performance.

Destroying a temporary at the end of an expression leads to obvious examples, such as the one above, where the temporary is destroyed too soon. Alternatives would be to destroy temporaries at the end of block or function, but this could lead to the opposite extreme, and it still does not guarantee that a more global pointer hasn't been assigned to the temporary, which means the temporary is required beyond the scope of the block or function.

The solution sounds rather trite—destroy the temporary after it is no longer useful—but that is precisely the policy of a garbage-collected system! Thus garbage collection is the solution to our problems, and it means that programmers do not have to treat temporaries differently from any other object. If temporaries are left around without an invocation of the garbage collector for long enough, then memory problems will automatically trigger the garbage collector (even if it has been disabled). As Stroustrup says of the problem of prematurely destroying a temporary object, "its general solution is the use of garbage collection." [Stroustrup 9 (6.3.2)]

Any garbage-collected languages, such as Java and Eiffel, will not have these problems, and that makes life considerably simpler and more productive for the programmer and hence significantly reduces the overall cost of software development.

11.4 Bad Deletions (C++)

The following example is given in the C++ ARM as a warning about bad deletions that cannot be caught at compile time and probably not immediately at run time either. [C++ ARM] (p. 63)

```
p = new int[10];
p++;
delete p;   // error
p = 0;
delete p;   // ok
```
C++

Deleting an object twice will also result in some sort of undefined disaster.

C++

```
Thing* p = new Thing;
delete p;
delete p;    // disaster
```

Of course it is most unlikely that you would delete the same object two lines in a row, but the likelihood of such a mistake is greater when the deletes are separated by just a few lines, or even worse in different modules or referenced by several different pointers.

One of the restrictions of the design of C++ is that it must remain compatible with C. This results in examples like this one, that are ill-defined language constructs and that can be covered only by warnings of potential disaster. Removal of such language deficiencies would result in loss of compatibility with C. This might be a good thing if problems such as these disappear. But then the resultant language might be so far removed from C that C might be best abandoned altogether.

Bad deletions are the kind of problem the Java designers set out to avoid. You do not get bad deletions in either Java or Eiffel for two reasons: first, they do not have pointers; second, they provide garbage collection and so programmers don't need to delete objects.

11.5 Slicing (C++)

If an object is assigned to another object causing a copy, either by direct assignment or by passing an object as a value parameter, and the target object is of a parent class to the source object, the subclass part of the object will not be copied. This is known as *slicing*. Obviously, since subclasses may have more fields, their objects will be bigger, so when assigning to a smaller object data must be lost. Slicing occurs when the copy constructor of the new target object is called. A constructor is not virtual, but is called according to the declared type of the new object, not based on the dynamic type of the source object. For example, if b refers to an object of type B which is a subclass of type A

C++

```
B b;
A a = b;
```

Java does not have this problem because objects are always accessed via a reference, and, in parameter passing, it is this reference that is passed. So in object assignments and parameter passing, no object copying is done.

Eiffel provides a more complex case. In order to allow certain optimizations, such as having objects on the stack or objects embedded within other objects, Eiffel has **expanded** types. This is only an optimization, as it offers no extra power over Java, particularly with garbage collection. However, the semantics of creation is slightly different, as an embedded object is automatically created with the embedding object, and the longevity of an embedded object is tied to the longevity of the embedding object. References cannot be assigned to embedded objects, and thus assignments of embedded objects cause copy operations and possibly creations.

Although Eiffel has expanded objects, it does not have the slicing problem because it has a conformance requirement that, if the target of an assignment is expanded, then the source must be the same type (expanded or not). This disallows objects of a subclass being assigned to an expanded object.

Another interesting possibility that neither C++ nor Eiffel implements is that inline objects could be created of such a size that the object could receive the largest object of any of its subclasses. The compiler would need to analyze this case, which would be possible in Eiffel, but probably difficult in C++ with its lack of global analysis. If you were able to do this, you would have a restricted kind of C *union*. However, to avoid the problems with C union, the compiler would need to keep the object type in the object, resulting in a discriminated union. The object type information is extra space overhead, and one of the advantages of the Eiffel approach is that, since the compiler knows exactly what type an expanded object must be, the extra run-time information is not required. Hence, the Eiffel built-in types are memory efficient.

11.6 Program Execution

The details of how a program is initiated are different for each of our languages. C++ has the simplest mechanism, based on C. When a program is started, its `main()` function is executed. In an OO context, this is a very non-OO start to a program. Java does a little better: it moves `main()` into a class and it executes the `main()` function in a nominated class. The Java language and virtual machine specifications do not define how the initial class is specified; one suggestion is it is entered in the command that executes the program. Java is therefore more flexible than C++, since several classes can have functions named main, but the programmer does not need to rename any of these if classes are mixed and matched in a different way. In C++, the programmer must ensure that in any link only one main function is defined in the modules linked. This of course is not often a big problem in practice.

Eiffel's strategy is similar to Java, but it goes a step further. You specify separately the initial class and routine names, which you put in the *Ace* specification (or equivalent) for an Eiffel system:

Eiffel
LACE

    root
        BIG_BANG: *begin_time*

where the class *BIG_BANG* is first instantiated when the system starts up, and then the creation routine *begin_time* is called to get the system going. For UNIX and C programmers, it might be quite a surprise to see that no `main` function is needed. Depending on the implementation, the Eiffel compiler will have created an implicit `main` function that instantiates a *BIG_BANG* object and then enters *begin_time*.

11.7 Dynamic Linking

Dynamic linking allows the linking step to be deferred until run time. The advantage of this is that, when testing, all a programmer needs do is compile a new module and then run the system. If the system is large, a long link step is avoided, and testing can take place immediately. It has been reported that this greatly expedites Java development over C++, where a programmer must wait for potentially long link times after trivial changes. Another advantage is that dynamic linking can simplify the distribution means. If part of a production program is updated, then only this part needs to be updated in the code repository. Clients will then automatically pick up this new version. This is one of the strengths that Java brings to the Internet environment.

ISE Eiffel has recently announced its own dynamic linking mechanism, DLE. This allows ISE Eiffel systems to rely on one or more classes that were not known when the system was assembled and which will be dynamically linked at run time. In order to prepare a system for dynamic classes, ISE LACE has added the following option:

    extendible (*yes*)
    extending (*<directory name>*)

Some extra classes are defined to be used as ancestors for your own dynamic classes:

DYNAMIC
DYNAMIC_CLASS

The flexibility of dynamic linking does come with a cost since certain errors will be deferred until run time that would otherwise be detected at link time. Java defines several loader and linker errors. The loader errors include errors such as `NoClassDefFoundError`, which means a class referenced at run time cannot be found, and `ClassCircularityError`, which means that a circularity has been detected in inheritance, where a class would be its own ancestor. [JVM 97]

Linker errors include `AbstractMethodError` and `NoSuchMethodError`. These errors show that run-time safety has been sacrificed for flexibility, so, if you have discarded Smalltalk in favor of Java, you should probably think again. Java does not mandate that linkage be dynamic or *lazy*, as it could be done earlier, as long as the language semantics are preserved. Since the Java loader and linker errors cause exceptions, this can greatly complicate a programmer's task in including exception-handling code for errors that would otherwise not occur.

Exception handling is a topic that greatly increases the complexity of an applications code. Indeed if two different Java Virtual Machines implement different linking schemes, then this could change the way that programmers must write code. In the static case, of course, you can ignore that such errors will occur, but, in the dynamic case, you will probably need to include exception handling or get the default behavior, which is probably to terminate the application. Thus we have the potential that what you get working on one implementation of the JVM might not work on another.

It will be interesting to see what the Eiffel implementations that target the JVM do—whether they statically link into one application that is loaded into the JVM or provide equivalent safety checking, or whether they use dynamic linking. The first approach is preferable for final production systems in order to ensure that dynamic link errors cannot occur. During testing, however, you will probably appreciate the faster turnaround time and will tolerate the occasional dynamic link error. Such errors in production systems could be dangerous, causing lost business time or even catastrophic failure for real-time device controllers. Thus before a system is put into production it would be a good idea to perform a complete compile in order for such errors to be detected.

11.8 Exception Handling

The previous section touched on the topic of complexity in exception handling. Many applications become much more complicated when exception handling is added. With dynamic binding, I suggested that having to handle exceptions such as "class not found" will greatly complicate code. The need to handle many such exceptions can be avoided by static analysis at compile and link time.

Some errors will need to be handled at run time. Suppose an application reads a file, but the read detects that the file is not present, or perhaps not available to be read because it might have been opened by another application. The most primitive solution to this problem is to terminate the application. In many cases, this won't suffice, so an application programmer might choose to either check if the file is available for reading before the read code, perform the read in such a way to get error values returned, or code an exception handler to catch the error. In an asynchronous environment, checking for the file's presence might not work because another process might remove the file between the check and the read, so you end up having to code for errors anyway.

However, do we really need to code for errors at all? In asynchronous processing, a file is a resource, and, if you open it for reading, it is a resource produced by some other process. When we issue a read, the read call itself can be used for process synchronization. Thus, the program should be suspended waiting on the resource, not terminated, which is what many commonly used operating systems do. In this case most of the need for exception handling disappears, and application coding becomes far simpler. We have already seen this idea in the section on Eiffel SCOOP earlier in this chapter, where preconditions no longer raise an exception if a temporal condition does not hold but waits for the condition to be fulfilled.

Another scenario might be that a file will be produced occasionally to communicate with our process, and we must check it periodically. In this case we need a "read no wait" call, but again no exception handling is needed.

Many errors like this example are so common that it is amazing that many applications currently reinvent this exception handling code all the time. For many applications it would suffice to have better operating system or file manager support, where these would take care of the common cases of most exceptions that would otherwise need to be recoded in each application. Design by contract needs to be in more widespread use in the design of operating system interfaces, and this would show that operating systems could do a better job of resource management and save many applications from having to reinvent the exception-handling wheel all the time. It would also mean that users and operators would be presented with a consistent interface in any environment, rather than something different for each different application. This suggestion does not stop some time-critical applications from continuing to handle exceptions, but it does make coding much simpler for the vast majority of applications.

Exception Handling and C++

For exception handling C++ has the reasonable mechanism of `try`, `catch`, and `throw`. Try arms a block and, if exceptions occur in the block from a `throw` statement, the exception is caught by the corresponding `catch` clauses. This is fine, but we now have many ways of doing very similar things in C++, as we still have the `raise` and `signal` and the `setjmp` and `longjmp` mechanisms, which you should avoid.

A problem with exception throwing is that a `throw` is based on the static declared type of an entity, not on the actual dynamic type of the object. For example

```
B b;
A& a = b;

throw a;
```
C++

throws an exception of type A, not according to the actual type of the object B. Furthermore, the object is passed to the exception `catch` statement by value, which causes slicing to take place.

`Catch` clauses have another catch if they are coded in the following order:

```
try
{ ... }
catch (A& e)
{ ... }
catch (B& e)
{ ... }
```
C++

then a throw on an object of type B will result in the `catch (A& e)` clause being called because the exceptions are handled in order, and this is the first catch clause that the object matches as B is a subclass of A. You must be careful in which order you code catch clauses.

**Meyers 96]
(item 13)**

A further complication arises because you can pass the object to the `catch` clause by value, pointer, or reference. Meyers recommends that only the reference form be used, which begs the question as to why C++ exceptions were made so complicated in the first place by having the other forms?

In C++, function definitions can have an *exception specification*. The following examples illustrate this.

C++

```
f();     // Any exception can occur
f() throw (int, char*);  // Only int and char*
                         // exceptions can be
                         // thrown in this function
f() throw ();            // No exceptions will
                         // occur in this function
```

If an exception is thrown that is not listed in the exception specification, a special function `unexpected()` is called. Although you can write your own `unexpected`, the default version terminates the program. Unfortunately, it is not so easy to tell exactly which exceptions might occur in a function when other functions that might cause other exceptions are called. This is particularly the case for template functions, where a single operator on the template type might represent many possible functions. Meyers writes about this problem

**[Meyers 96]
(item 14)**

We can almost never provide a meaningful exception specification for a template, because templates almost invariably use their type parameter in some way. The conclusion? Templates and exception specifications don't mix.

Exception Handling and Java

Java exceptions look very similar, but they add an extra clause to the `try` statement, `finally`. The block in the `finally` clause is always executed whether or not an exception was caught in a `catch` clause. This means that, if an exception occurs that is not handled in a `catch` clause, some code still gets executed to clean up. In this case, the `try` statement terminates abnormally, as the exception was not handled.

Another Java difference is that the exception objects used in `throw` statements and caught by `catch` statements must be subclasses of the `Throwable` class.

Perhaps the most significant difference in Java is that, if there is no `throws` clause attached to a method definition, this means the method throws no exceptions, whereas, in the C++ case, this means any exception can occur, with the resulting confusion and `unexpected` function. The Java compiler can also check that `throw` statements occurring in the method throw only declared exceptions and that other methods called will also result only in exceptions declared in the calling method.

Exception Handling and Eiffel

Eiffel's exception mechanism is better integrated with the language, as it is a fundamental part of design by contract. An exception may be triggered by an assertion violation (precondition, postcondition, or other assertion), a called routine failing, use of a Void reference, or a failed operation such as divide by zero, out of memory, etc. When an exception is raised, the run-time stack is cut back until an exception handler is found, much as in the C++ and Java case. However, exception handlers in Eiffel come in the form of **rescue** clauses. Each routine can have one rescue clause.

If an exception occurs in a routine without a rescue clause, the routine fails and raises an exception in the calling routine. This continues until a rescue clause is encountered (although this is only conceptual, as in fact the implementation will cut the stack straight back to the rescue clause). When a rescue clause is entered, you have the opportunity to do some cleaning up, and then either **retry** the operation, or fail, which raises an exception in the calling routine, in which case the next rescue clause entered on the stack will be executed. An Eiffel routine with exception handling looks like this.

exception_example **is** *Eiffel*
    require
        -- If any assertions in here fail, this routine will fail, and an
        -- exception will be raised in the calling routine. This is
        -- sensible because the fault is in the calling routine.
    do
        check
            -- If an assertion in here fails an exception is raised and the
            -- most recent rescue clause is entered.
        end
    ensure
        -- If an assertion in here fails, the most recent rescue
        -- clause (including the rescue clause in this routine) is entered.
    rescue
        -- Code in the rescue clause cleans up to try to restore some
        -- sense of normality in the containing object. The rescue clause

```
            -- will be entered if an assertion in the check or ensure clause
            -- failed, or if a called routine failed. The rescue clause is also
            -- entered if the class invariant is violated when the routine
            -- exits.
    retry -- If a retry instruction is executed in a rescue clause,
            -- the routine will be restarted from the beginning.
    end
```

The rescue clause does not allow for very fine control of exceptions. If finer control is needed in the rescue clause, you can inherit the *EXCEPTIONS* class. This class enables you to detect exactly which exception occurred and whether it was from a precondition, postcondition, invariant, etc. You can also enable and disable particular exceptions using the *catch* and *ignore* routine, respectively.

As mentioned, Eiffel also has class invariants that can trigger exceptions. Invariants are an important design technique that helps to capture the valid behavior of a class. C++ and Java have no equivalent of class invariants.

11.9 LinkageError (Java)

We have already seen how dynamic linking can cause some run-time problems that would otherwise be detected by static analysis done by the compiler. We now have a look at some of these specific errors.

While it is true that Java as a language is specified to detect many errors statically, unfortunately in Java's environment, it is possible for a significant class of errors not to be detected statically which otherwise should be. These are the errors in the general classification of `LinkageError`. `LinkageError` is an exception that is thrown at run time if any of these conditions are detected. These exceptions include `NoClassDefFoundError`, `NoSuchFieldError`, and `NoSuchMethodError`.

When compiled normally, a Java compiler will detect these errors. However, in Java's dynamic environment, not all classes might be compiled at the same time and this leaves the potential for these type holes. You don't need a dynamic environment to get these errors though—Java compilers are notoriously bad at dependency analysis, and often won't recompile classes that have had changes made to them, so again these errors can go undetected into a running system.

Another bad aspect of this is that the exceptions are only thrown when the offending statement is executed, not when the class is dynamically linked in. This means that a system could do significant amounts of processing before the error is encountered. It would be better to check for such potential errors when the class is first linked.

12

Other Details

This chapter looks at a few details that are either topics in themselves, or don't relate to the topics of the other chapters.

12.1 Comments

Some might consider comments to be a trivial topic. After all—from the point of view of the language definition—comments simply indicate to a compiler to ignore text that is meant only for a human reader. To do this, we must delimit the compiler-ignored text at the start and at the end. However, when considering comments, we should consider the whole topic of project documentation, and how to make comments helpful so that humans don't ignore them. I say more about this in the section on reusability and communication in chapter 13, so this section concentrates mainly on the language definition and implementation aspects of comments.

Comment delimiters, like any other programming language construct, can be seen as just an instruction telling a compiler what to do. In fact, we really need to step back a little from this description and say that any language construct is actually an instruction to an abstract machine that is able to interpret programs in the language directly. Then compilers just become machines themselves that translate from onc machine's language into another's, which could be the native code for a real processor, an intermediate code, or another language.

Since we are dealing with high-level languages, though, programs have another purpose, and that is to communicate with other human beings. When we think of programs in this way, comment delimiters become more than just an abstract machine instruction to ignore what follows; they are vital visual clues for the reader that what follows might be an informal explanation for their benefit.

An alternative way to define comments is to treat the whole program text as a document; instead of explicitly flagging the comments, flag the translatable or executable parts of the program. No commercial languages seem to do this, but it is the basis of Don Knuth's *Literate Programming*.

Comments can be used for several purposes. At the highest level, they can document the overall design of a module or the system. At lower levels, they can explain individual instructions or perhaps document how previous flaws were corrected. Comments, therefore, act at several levels of abstraction, and it is a good idea to have different visual clues as to their purpose. Many projects adopt conventions to visually emphasize the different purposes of comments. In some cases such distinctions are included in the language.

Most languages are textual in nature and use textual clues in the text to delimit comments. More visual languages might be integrated with an editor that emphasizes comments in another way, without the visual distraction of text delimiters. These editors could also be built over text-based languages to do such processing. But let's dream for a while that a program is not just text, but that, like a word processor, has invisible characters that instruct the editor how to display certain constructs, including comments. An example of an appropriate highlight might be to put a graphical box around comments of a certain purpose.

Language Constructs

C++ has two forms of comment, the /* ... */ form and the // ... end of line form (the // form for short). These are merely textual delimiters and represent no difference in the semantics of the comments. C++ has reintroduced the // form from BCPL because the /* ... */ form has a few problems. The first problem is that the comments do not nest, so the form

```
/* outer comment /* inner comment */ more comment */   C++
```

will be terminated at the first */. This is a nuisance during bug finding because, if you want to comment out a group of lines and those lines contain their own comments, the outer comment will lose its effect. A second problem arises if you somehow forget the terminating */. Often this will result in some kind of syntax error, but other times it might result in essential code not going into a production version of a program. Hence C++ has very wisely added the // form, and its use is recommended.

Java has these same comment structures but adds a third kind—the /** ... */ form. This is the *documentation comment*, and it is semantically different from the other forms. The documentation comment may be processed by some other tool to prepare specific documentation from the program source itself. For other comments, the // form should be used, reserving the /* ... */ form for temporarily commenting out sections of code during debugging.

Eiffel has only one textual form of delimiter, the --. This form is reminiscent of the em-dash, —, that you see in this and other publications, signifying supplementary information. Perhaps visual presenters of Eiffel could change the double hyphen into the more typographic em-dash.

[Meyer 92] (25.4)

In Eiffel, comments are given special semantic significance depending on where they occur in the program. Eiffel defines two types of comment—the **expected** comment and the **free** comment. Expected comments are mostly **header** comments. The position of expected comments is defined in the language grammar and they occur where an entity of significance is being documented—for example, in a routine header. Free comments can occur anywhere and have no extra significance. Expected comments, like the documentation comments in Java, can be processed by language processors other than the compiler to produce separate documentation. For example, these comments will be retained in the output of the *short* documentation tool.

Eiffel has no equivalent of the /* ... */ explicitly terminated comment, so it does not have the problems associated with these comments. However, Eiffel does not have the convenience of being able to temporarily comment out blocks of code with nested comments, but this convenience is not so important since Eiffel routines will usually be quite small, and this kind of debugging to track down obscure bugs will be needed much less in Eiffel than in C++.

12.2 Hexadecimal Literals (Eiffel)

Eiffel has no way of writing hexadecimal constants. These are often important for interfacing to data produced by other programs, where bit fields might have to be masked in order to retrieve the meaning. In such cases, hexadecimal literals are easier to interpret than equivalent decimal numbers.

12.3 Double, double toil and trouble [Wilson 21]

The class hierarchy of numeric values is also interesting and provides some unexpected surprises in OO languages. The complication arises because we want the efficiency of built-in types for numbers, but, we also want some consistency due to OO design. In Java, you might be surprised to find that, for every number class, Java has two types that are nonconformant. For example, Java has the types `double` and `Double`. Type `double` represents the built-in numbers, whereas type `Double` is the class of objects of double numbers. The two do not freely intermix, and relying on case sensitivity is confusing. However, the distinction between the two is necessary.

Eiffel's numeric hierarchy is similar to Java's, with the *DOUBLE_REF* type, being similar to Java's Double, representing double objects and the *DOUBLE* type representing built-in double numbers. Apart from the obvious difference that Eiffel uses different words rather than relying on case distinction to distinguish between the two, the important difference is that Eiffel makes *DOUBLE* a subclass of *DOUBLE_REF*. Thus *DOUBLE* is type conformant to *DOUBLE_REF*, and the operations that apply to *DOUBLE_REF* also apply to *DOUBLE*, so you do not have to worry about the difference between the two from this aspect.

That said, there is something aesthetically unsatisfying about having classes like *INTEGER* and *INTEGER_REF*. A recent suggestion is to abolish the two classes and have only *INTEGER*, but when an *INTEGER* object is required, its declaration is given as

   iref: **reference** *INTEGER*

This proposal is still under consideration, and is being analyzed for any hidden flaws.

An advantage in Eiffel is that conversions to other numeric types are completely functional. For example, converting a *DOUBLE* to an *INTEGER* is handled by a number of functions depending on whether you want to raise to the next whole integer, truncate, or round. Java `Double` also provides such facilities, but `double` does not, so you must rely on casts.

Another advantage in Eiffel is that the built-in types such as *INTEGER* are integrated into the class type hierarchy; no entity exists outside of this. The primitive types of `int`, `float`, etc., are not integrated into the type hierarchy in C++ or Java, and constant conversion between `int` and `Integer` is particularly needed in Java. Note also that Java has not been able to break from C naming tradition—while `double` is the type equivalent of the `Double` class, as is `float` of `Float`, `int` is the primitive of `Integer` and `char` of `Character`—so the nomenclature is inconsistent. Not only do we have this inconsistency, but the integral types include the following: `byte`, `char`, `int`, `long`, and `short`.

One advantage of the Java scheme is that the exact value ranges of these primitive types are defined, so Java arithmetic will be portable—particularly numeric overflows will occur in the same places on all platforms. The disadvantage is that, on platforms where the ranges are different, performance penalties will be incurred. Eiffel and C++ use whatever ranges the underlying platform provides, so performance will not be degraded. However, you will have to pay careful attention to the portability of arithmetic.

`Float` is another area where Java has not been able to break C conventions. The type *REAL* is the abstract mathematical type, whereas `float` is a particular implementation of *REAL*. More precisely, floating point numbers are an approximate representation of *REAL* since a very small subset of *REAL*s can be represented and floating point arithmetic is an approximation of *REAL* arithmetic. This might sound like a compelling argument to call the programming type `float`, except there are other possible representations of *REAL*. Furthermore, the computer types *INTEGER* and *STRING* can also represent only a very small subset of all the possible values of these types. We should note that *DOUBLE* is a concession to performance considerations on computers, because in mathematics both *REAL* and *DOUBLE* are covered by the single *REAL* type.

The foregoing argument is from the point of view of the OO abstractionist. As such, it will satisfy the large majority of program development. However, it might not satisfy those doing numerical computation in many scientific fields. To them, it is important to know the exact precision of numbers and, because their computations are very processor intensive, the speed that computations can be done on these types. This group of people may feel more comfortable with a *FLOAT* type and the exact restrictions that make it different from *REAL*. For such numerical computations, a particular processor (often a supercomputer) will be chosen for its exact floating point handling characteristics. IEEE also has a floating point standard to help make floating point calculations portable.

Now we can observe that *FLOAT* is a subset of *REAL* and also an implementation of *REAL*. If particular characteristics are needed in an implementation of *REAL*, we can arrange this easily within an OO type hierarchy—*FLOAT* and other implementations can inherit from *REAL*. The same can be done for *INTEGER* types; we can have an abstract type *INTEGER*. *LONG_INTEGER* should inherit *INTEGER*, *FAST_INTEGER* should inherit *LONG_INTEGER* and *SHORT_INTEGER* should inherit *FAST_INTEGER*. These types will probably be platform dependent but we could also define a platform independent hierarchy for programs where portability is more important than speed.

All our languages fall short in providing facilities that will satisfy all sets of needs on numeric processing, although the definition of such types does not belong in the languages, but in the libraries. Eiffel does have a *Math* library. As we should know by now, types should not be designed into the language because an OO language is used to design types. Basic types can be given special treatment by the compiler though.

`Array` is also a problem in Java since it is not a class. However, `Array` is the closest thing to a generic type that Java offers. It seems that Java's designers could not design arrays in keeping with their own language definition of classes. Any other containment structure in Java suffers from not being generic.

Neither Java nor Eiffel has a type or class for complex numbers. C++ has the template class `complex`. Java is not built for speed, and probably never will be satisfactory for heavy-duty numeric computations. Eiffel will require some special treatment for vector and matrix operations. At the moment, FORTRAN is still the language preferred by numerical scientists.

12.4 Class Header Declarations (C++)

C's syntax for function declarations is [<type>] <identifier> (<parameters>). For a very simple example

```
class C                                                          C++
{
    a ();
    b ();
    int c ();
    d ();
    char e ();
    virtual void f ();
};
```

To find an identifier in this layout, the eye must trace a course around the type specifications and modifiers, which is a tiring activity. There is a greater chance of missing the sought identifier, and the programmer must resort to using the search function of a text editor to help out.

Other languages place the entity names first. For example

```
class C                                                      not C++
```

```
        {
            a ();
            b ();
            c () int;
            d ();
            e () char;
            f () virtual void;
        };
```

For those who are used to the ALGOL and FORTRAN style of type first, this seems backwards. But name first is logical as a real-world example illustrates—imagine if we published a dictionary that didn't have the keywords placed first, but rather the following entry order

```
        noun /obvrzen/ obversion, the act or
            result of obverting
```

Such a dictionary would not sell many copies unless the marketeers managed to fool many people that the explanation of the meaning was better because the order of layout had properties mysteriously superior to a more straightforward layout (but this has often been the case in the computer industry). This example illustrates how important subtle syntax decisions are and why Pascal-style languages have ordered things contrary to FORTRAN, ALGOL, and others. The language designer must consider these trivial but important alternatives. The layout of programming entities is essential for effective communication. The dual roles of language syntax and programming style affect comprehension. A dictionary- or index-style layout suggests placing entity names first, followed by their definitions.

Java obviously has to retain this layout since it is C based. In fact the *hello world* program in Java shows how putting an entity name after modifiers can obscure the program

Java
```
        public static void main(...)
```

For the most part, Eiffel puts the feature name first, making features easier to find. An exception is the **frozen** case, but the **frozen** modifier is not used very often. One language design philosophy in Eiffel is to avoid such modifiers where possible, whereas Java and C++ use many modifiers, which clutter the appearance.

13

Projects, Design, and Other Factors

The development of software entails many different aspects, not just writing instructions for a computer. These aspects include design, project organization, communication, and simply getting teams to work together. In this chapter we examine some of these topics and what features our languages provide to support these activities. Not only are these aspects subtle, but language support is also subtle, but nonetheless must be intentionally designed into a language. When language design considers these aspects, we have an environment that supports seamless software engineering.

Those who have worked on large-scale projects will identify with the topics in this chapter. However, if you are just starting out in programming and intend to follow it as a career, it is best to be forewarned about many of these aspects. It is important for students and practitioners to do small exercises to master the fundamentals of programming. These are like the finger exercises a pianist does (Hanon, Czerny, Brahms, and Liszt), to gain a solid technique in order to be able to accomplish the major works.

13.1 Design by Contract

A common problem programmers face is that implementation hiding is very nice in theory, but you are often forced to look at the internals of a class and its routines to determine what the class does and how to use it. Before you call a routine, instead of finding out all the information you need to know from a routine's signature, you must examine the internals of a routine so that it works correctly, and so you can determine its exact effect on system state after the routine has executed. The signature specification of a routine is not enough; routines can have side effects. In order to hide implementation effectively, we need a formal means of describing which data items are affected and in which ways.

One of the important benefits of design by contract is that enough information is included in the signature so you no longer need to examine the internals of a routine to call it. Routine signatures are an abstract definition of the routine itself. This is good abstraction, because the right detail is included in the abstract form without needing to futher examine the internals.

Eiffel extends the concept of routine signature—the conditions you must set up prior to calling a routine are documented in the **requires** clause as preconditions, and the exact effects (or the changed conditions) of a routine are documented in the **ensures** clause as postconditions. The *short* tool extracts the preconditions and postconditions with the abstract part of a routine signature, as documentation for clients of a class. Preconditions document the obligations of the caller and the benefits to the called routine, and postconditions document the obligations of the called routine and the benefits to the caller—hence the term *design by contract*. [Meyer 97] (chapter 11)

Design by contract is a major technique in saving programmers from having to look at implementation code and is most important to library vendors who don't want to give away the internals of their implementation, but who do want people to buy and use their library.

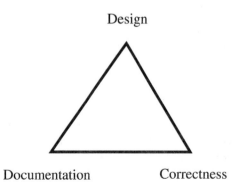

Figure 13-1. Aspects of design by contract

Design by contract is not merely a fancy documentation scheme—the preconditions and postconditions provide run-time checks to ensure that all units of the program are behaving correctly and thus fulfilling their contracts. This is the mechanism that detects the run-time inconsistencies discussed in the section on correctness in chapter 1. In Eiffel, this mechanism is integrated with the exception handling mechanism. In C++ and Java you can use assertions for run-time checks, but these are not integrated into the programmer's mindset as they are in Eiffel. Eiffel's strength in design and specification comes from its Z heritage.

To summarize the foregoing discussion, design by contract addresses three aspects: design, documentation, and correctness (see figure 13-1).

Design by contract is the equivalent of integrated circuit specifications in the electronic component world and tolerances in physical engineering disciplines. In Eiffel, the combination of static type checking with preconditions and postconditions, integrated with exception handling, forms a significant way to test that the software jigsaw puzzle fits together and that the resulting picture makes sense. These techniques significantly reduce dependence on after-the-fact manual testing.

Neither Java nor C++ have design by contract integrated in class interface descriptions. Another interesting case lacking design by contract is CORBA IDL—since this is an interface language for distributed objects, contract information describing the interaction between components at interfaces is vital. Design by contract is a glaring omission from CORBA IDL, which has glaring *inclusions* of struct, typedef, union, etc., which aren't particularly helpful in a distributed object environment. This is the kind of environment where the concept of design by contract is even more important in considering how to connect all the system components together and where you want more confidence that the distributed jigsaw fits together. In fact this biases CORBA to C implementations. The industry should take time to stop and think and start to design things carefully and correctly, rather than designing everything to look like C. Many C constructs are low level and inappropriate and make it difficult to adopt high level and necessary concepts.

The latest buzzword in the industry is *components*. Components are similar to high-level objects like an application or a run-time library, providing external interfaces to which other programs and libraries can link. The concept is not new and has been around on some mainframes for years—for example, Unisys A series libraries, which underpin much of the working of transaction processing on these machines. Components will mean almost nothing unless their interface descriptions express what you can also expect the component to do. Thus design by contract should be an important part of the components business. For more on components, see chapter 2.

13.2 Preconditions, Types, and Invariants

Preconditions and types serve very similar roles; they are predicates on the validity of calls to a routine. The difference between preconditions and types is that types are checked at compile time and preconditions at run time. Because of this, it is preferable to design your software to use types as predicates for valid calls rather than preconditions. That is where class invariants come in. An invariant is a predicate that characterizes a type. In order to redesign preconditions into types so that potential errors can be caught at compile time, make a new type and move the precondition into the type as an invariant. For example

```
class A                                                      Eiffel
feature
    sqrt (p: REAL): REAL is
        require
            p >= 0
        do ...
        end
end
```

Instead you could make this

```
class A                                                      Eiffel
feature
    sqrt (p: POSITIVE_REAL): REAL  is
        do ...
        end
end

class POSITIVE_REAL
feature
    item: REAL

    set (p: REAL) is
        do
            value := p
        end
invariant
    item >= 0
end
```

Better still, we could use the fact that *POSITIVE_REAL* is a subset of *REAL*

Eiffel

    class *POSITIVE_REAL* **inherit** *REAL*
    invariant
        item >= 0
    end

Here we can see that, because *POSITIVE_REAL* is a subset of *REAL*, the invariant introduces an extra constraint that characterizes the subset of *REAL*s that are considered *POSITIVE_REAL*s. Invariants are covariant; that is, they must preserve invariants of all ancestor classes, as well as adding their own more restrictive conditions.

A problem with this scheme in Eiffel is that, in a practical system, for production code you will probably disable invariants but keep preconditions enabled. However, this example does show the relationship between design, types, assertions, and predicates.

13.3 The Software Life Cycle

The software life cycle has attracted a great deal of attention, particularly from those who must manage ongoing projects; it is not of great interest to those who write one-off programs. It is generally accepted that the activities in the life cycle are analysis of requirements, design, implementation, testing and error correction, and extension. Unfortunately, identifying these activities has resulted in a school of thought that the boundaries between these activities are fixed and that they should be systematically separate, each being completed before the next is commenced. It is often argued that, if they are not cleanly separated, then you are not practicing disciplined system development.

This view is simplistic and incorrect. Someone who writes a program straight-away is actually doing all the steps in parallel. It might not be the best way to do things in many circumstances and may or may not suit the style and thinking of different people, but this works in some scenarios and can be the methodology of choice of disciplined thinkers. While that is an extreme example, the ideal way to work probably lies somewhere between that and a strictly regimented environment that assigns different people or teams to the life-cycle phases.

Some people can hold a whole problem and solution in their head and work in a disciplined fashion until the solution is complete. Mozart is said to have composed this way, producing his last three symphonies in as many months in 1788.

Beethoven toiled far more over the production of his works, taking years to complete one symphony. Both composers produced masterpieces. Mozart wrote music directly, whereas Beethoven wrote themes and ideas in his famous sketchbooks. While Beethoven and Mozart had their own methods, the production of masterpieces depends on skill, not on external methodologies. Even if we could work out exactly how these composers wrote their music, we could not be reproduce the masterpieces. In fact, Beethoven produced most of his last works while he was deaf—what employer would have given him a job as a composer following employment guidelines (ie., processes) under those circumstances!

A view that is gaining acceptance is that the software life cycle should be an integrated process. Analysis, design, and implementation should be a seamless continuum. The activities of the life cycle should progress in parallel to expedite software development. Facts found out only as late as the implementation stage can be fed back into the analysis and design stages. The OO approach supports this process. Artificial separation of the steps leads to a large semantic gap between the steps. The transformations required to bridge such semantic gaps are prone to misinterpretation and are time consuming and costly.

We should cease dependence on testing. This is not to say that systematic or even random testing by an independent test group is not important, but we should rely more on better techniques in the preceding phases. Software testing can never prove the absence of errors; it can only be used to detect errors if they are there.

The same people should be responsible for all life-cycle stages, so that they take responsibility for the system as a whole, rather than passing the buck and blame, which occurs when analysts, designers, and implementers are different groups. This is not a popular view in traditional hierarchical management structures where organizational structure is prized over quality and programmers get promoted to designers, who get promoted to analysts, and managers stay aloof from the technical process, just making sure the old structure is maintained. Or even worse, those who become analysts, designers, and managers have little knowledge of or experience with programming and large-scale software engineering. Scott Adams' Dilbert comics have become widely known as accurate comments on such organizational problems. Hierarchical management discourages people from feeling responsible for a product. This culture must radically change if we are to produce quality systems.

We should beware of the *methodology gap*, which Bach points out leads to the disconnected worlds of methodology and practice. "The wider the gap, the less relevant software engineering ideas are to practice." Bach also astutely points out the myth of management power. [Bach 97]

> It's a fantasy to think that top management has the power by simple force of will, to assure good methods are followed. Using direct

authority to force or intimidate intellectual workers only creates the kind of resistance that absolutely guarantees a methodology gap. Management is powerful, but it takes more talent and training than most managers have to coax an organization to improve quickly.

[Peter 69] This was certainly my experience at a recent employer, where the quality officer could not relate at all with the technical people and continually forced processes that were 20 years out of date down people's throat by making them "management policy." In order for such management policy to be mandated, a strict hierarchy was maintained with a class barrier between technical people and management. Most of those at the management level knew little technically and had positions in which they were incompetent. This was rather like the Peter Principle, except that these people had never *been* competent technically and had actually been rewarded for their incompetence by rising to positions in which they became dangerous. Peter might still be correct because it can also be observed that often such people are appointed from outside the organization directly into a high-level job of incompetence, so they never really have to perform at a lower level where they are incompetent.

Such people realize they can't perform technically, so they leave one organization where they are known to be incompetent and aim for easier, higher-level jobs in other organizations where they can perform *nontechnical* tasks such as "strategy," "quality," and "gannt chart maintainer." These terms are in quotes because this is not really what these people are doing at all, and properly done they are important *technical* tasks. In reality these positions should be filled by the most technically competent people—organizations where this happens excel. Both Adams and Peter point out that such incompetent people will fill their lives doing things that are not directly related to production. They substitute these other activities, which in fact prevent the right technical people from being able to do these jobs, keep them in their right perspective, and do them effectively. The resume system is also a problem, since incompetents can list any project they have participated in on their resume, even though they have made no meaningful contribution.

This system feeds itself. When incompetent people work in technical jobs, they observe other technical incompetents performing such managerial roles and notice that these people are rewarded with higher salaries and better working conditions—they are given offices instead of cubicles and such trappings to impress other people. Then young people joining such organizations observe how disempowered the technical people are and decide, maybe subconsciously, that developing their technical skills is not worth the effort. Meanwhile the senior technical people become more and more dissatisfied, and, if they point out the injustice of this situation, the incompetents in higher-level positions will have to devise ways to rid themselves of the complainers or risk losing their own jobs. This is not difficult as they are management and control the processes like employee reviews, which can be used to discredit those senior technical people who can see through them. You might also think that such managers would end up fighting amongst themselves, but these people are very much into the hierarchies of the Peter Principle, so they close ranks in defense of each other. Taken alone, incompetent people aren't so bad, but when they progress to the higher levels which they must defend, they become the nasty people in an organization. The result is that morale and quality in such organizations become nonexistent many times resulting in failed organizations.

The methodology gap has also manifested itself in several forms of thinking. Some believe that methodology is all-important, while programming and programming languages are unimportant. Arcane and machine-oriented programming languages strengthen this attitude, concentrating on the *how* of computation, whereas the modelers correctly demand notations that express the *what* in order to be implementation independent. A modern software language supports the integration of the activities of design and implementation by being readable and problem oriented. A language should be as close to design as possible. The needs and requirements of an enterprise can change much more rapidly than programmers can keep up, especially in a highly competitive and commercial world.

Where does C++ fit into this picture? Well, it is based on C, which was designed mainly as an implementation and machine-oriented language. It is an old language that did not need to consider the integrated life-cycle approach. C++ might have added most OO concepts, but it is an uncomfortable marriage of a problem-oriented technique with a machine-oriented language. It addresses implementation, but does not address other aspects of the software life cycle so well. Since C++ is not so integrated with analysis and design, the transformation required to go from analysis and design to implementation is difficult and costly. There is a semantic gap between design languages and the implementation language.

We should have learned from the structured world that this is the incorrect approach to the software life cycle. But in the OO world we are again falling into the trap of dividing the life cycle into artificially distinct activities of OOA, OOD, and OOP instead of adopting an integrated approach. Modern languages provide a much more integrated approach to the complete software development process than C++ does. C++ supports classes and inheritance and other concepts of OO, but still does not address the entire software life cycle.

Eiffel is specifically designed around the clusterfall model of the project life cycle. In this model, several subparts of a project may be in different phases at any instant. It also recognizes that feedback occurs from later phases to earlier phases.

Eiffel itself is quite a good specification language. Its assertions and invariants are something like you would see in a formal specification language like Z. While not as comprehensive as Z, Eiffel's specification mechanisms suffice in most cases. (Bertrand Meyer was involved in the early work on Z.) Thus you can use Eiffel as a documentation language in phases as early as analysis. The problem of different notations in different phases and error-prone translation between them is removed.

The mechanism that Eiffel includes to eliminate dependence on testing is the assertion mechanism, integrated with exception handling. Organizations will find it difficult to make significant progress toward the higher levels of the Software Engineering Institute capability maturity model (SEI CMM) until techniques such as the assertion mechanism in Eiffel are in widespread use. In fact the CMM model is wrong because it is meant to be applied to organizations. It should really be applied on a project-by-project basis; each organization will have projects at different levels. This does not mean that one project's organization is inferior to another's, but they might be at different stages. Obviously, a long-standing piece of software that customers are already using must have a disciplined approach to updating and regression testing, and therefore it will achieve a high CMM level. However, projects that are in early stages will naturally be at lower levels of maturity. Does this mean that organizations will discourage start-up projects in order to achieve higher CMM levels?

Eiffel is also integrated with a graphical computer aided software engineering (CASE) tool called BON (business object notation) for those who feel more comfortable with classification and component relationship diagrams. Most important, Eiffel and BON are based on the same underlying abstract concepts. Eiffel can be generated from BON and vice versa. This means you can easily reverse engineer your text, but the major advantage is that your diagrams and your text are always synchronized. There is no costly maintenance when your program changes. Thus Eiffel is a step toward seamless software engineering.

13.4 CASE Tools

[Madsen 93] (18.8)

The previous section raises the topic of CASE tools. Madsen has a good discussion on graphical notation and, although his presentation of the BETA language is textual, he points out that BETA can be used for analysis, modeling, and design. To a certain extent, this comes with any language that supports classes, since these are the elements of OO analysis and design, but it is important to develop the language with analysis and design specifically in mind.

If you are using both graphics and textual notations, it is important that both are based on the same underlying abstract language—text and graphics should represent the same concepts. A major problem with SA/SD was that the graphical notations and the programming notations were so far apart that costly and error-prone manual translation was required between the two. Unfortunately, this has set up the precedent in people's minds that graphical and textual notations are necessarily far apart, and they are surprised to see how close they can be in good OO systems.

Do not think that graphics are high level and text is low level; that is the nature of abstractions, not the tools or notations. In fact, text is a highly evolved form of graphics; both forms of information enter our brains through our eyes. Because of the nature of graphical notations, less detail can be shown. With an integrated editor, detail in text can be suppressed. In identifying classes during analysis, it makes no difference whether you document them as a series of graphical boxes with class names in the middle or as a textual list of class names. In fact many people will find the list easier to work with and later read. At any stage the notations should be interchangeable. In some cases the graphical notation will abstract away details, which is an advantage when you don't want to see the details. As you add details, though, graphical forms become unwieldy and text is easier to manage. Unfortunately, many sectors of the industry have become convinced that graphical forms are more formal and result in magically better designs than text equivalents.

Graphics and text are best in an integrated environment. A programmer may have a class diagram as a starting point, like GUI file icons. Selecting a class will expand the class so that the interface of the class can be seen. At a different level, internal features of the class might be seen. Eventually, a level is reached where text is seen. The major failing of most CASE tools is they do not support this level of seamless integration. For the most benefit graphics should flow into the programming language. So-called visual environments do little better than putting program text in a GUI window.

Why bother with graphics then? For the simple reason that looking at the same problem in different ways aids understanding. It is also a matter of taste. Some people will find they understand graphics better, and some text. It is a good idea to provide for personal tastes as long as there are not too many options. If there are too many options, everyone will end up speaking their own language, and there will be no effective communication—a Tower of Babel. This has already been the case in the industry—design methodology notations are far apart, and the analysts/designers do not want to read programs, and programmers do not want to read structure charts and data flow diagrams. This should not be a problem—computers are very good at translation. They are also good at formatting and so different preferences for style can be accommodated easily, making the notation and style rule wars obsolete. Some aspects of the Tower of Babel are solved.

A common design method with C++ is to use the object modeling technique (OMT) of Rumbaugh et al. (now UML) or some equivalent methodology. This seems like a good marriage because UML addresses the design and modeling aspects and C++ the implementation aspects. Both are over complicated in their own domain, being collections of disparate techniques. Unfortunately, using these two together does not help bring about seamless software engineering, where design naturally flows on to implementation. The object models are different since the graphical and textual languages are not based on the same underlying abstract language. Thus there is a semantic gap between the text and graphics. This results in more costly and error-prone development. But then as the OMT people have said, "Eiffel is arguably the best commercial OO language in terms of its technical capabilities." The object model of Eiffel is certainly closer to OMT than C++.

[RBPEL 91]
(p. 327)

In conclusion, if CASE tools and graphical notations are to be of use, they and the programming language must be based on the same abstract concepts.

13.5 Reusability and Communication

Reusability is a matter of communication.

Clear communication is a courtesy concern. In order to use a software component, you must be able to understand it. The writer must communicate the purpose, intent, and correct usage of the component to the client. In the OO world, clear and concise definition of software modules is not a mere nicety, but essential for reusability. Arising out of the issue of reusability is extendability. In order to maximize the reuse of software, it must often be tailored for new applications, while factoring out and sharing the commonalities. The client programmer must decide whether a software component is suitable for a new task and, if so, what is the best way to extend it.

Communication is aided by having integrated text and graphics environments, where the concrete languages of both are based on the same underlying abstract languages or object models. Communication is also dependent on clear and clean syntax.

Because C/C++ suffers from arcane and cryptic syntax, it does not support the goal of clear communication. A common misconception is that conciseness is the main measure of clarity. Often the two go together: the clearest form might be concise, but it may not be the *most* concise. Often a slightly more verbose form will be clearer, where a concise form might leave the reader guessing. In many ways, conciseness does mean clarity—many find their most productive days occur when a program becomes shorter in lines, improving functionality, readability, and reusability. The goal, however, is clarity and communication, not conciseness for its own sake.

Java cleans up a fair bit of C/C++. The mess that is caused by the preprocessor is removed. However, Java still suffers from some of the deficiencies of C syntax.

Eiffel has been designed with communication in mind and is not bound by the shackles of C syntax. It borrowed from the clean syntax of Ada. Along with the Eiffel syntax, style guidelines were designed, so the Eiffel syntax lends itself to a clear style.

[Meyer 92]
(appendix A)

Eiffel also has utilities such as *short*, where the abstract interface of classes can be extracted from the full details.

Eiffel provides an extra significant mechanism—integrated assertions. The short tool will extract the assertions with the interface descriptions. I described this in the section on design by contract early in this chapter. Design by contract helps decide whether a class is usable in a new situation and then shows how to use it, so this is an important tool for communicating the purpose, intent, and correct usage of a software module. Thus assertions are very much a courtesy concern.

Reusability is well supported with clear communication in Eiffel.

Brooks sees communication as a crucial element in successful projects. He analyzed why the Tower of Babel project failed. The Tower of Babel, if you recall, was a project described in the Bible about building a tower to reach the heavens. Brooks analyzes that all other conditions for the project's success were in place. The element that led to the failure of the project was breakdown of communication. We should not underestimate the value of communication in program development, from the standpoint of communication between team members as well as the communication that comes with a clean language syntax used purposefully by a good programmer with clean layout and readable identifiers.

[Brooks 95]
(chapter 7)

13.6 Reusability and Trust

Reusability is a matter of trust.

Building trustworthy components is a safety concern. Trust results from confidence that safety concerns have been met. If you do not have confidence in a software component, then you won't want to reuse it. You might doubt that the software component provides enough functionality or whether it provides the correct functionality. You might doubt that the component is efficient enough or, worse, that it might fail. Because so many traps in C++ result in bugs, it is difficult to trust a software module, so it is less reusable.

In chapter 1, we took a look at correctness from the viewpoint of what a language should provide. The other side to this coin is that it is ultimately the programmer's responsibility to produce correct software. Correctness is the number one goal, not cleverness. Correct code often looks obvious and too simple, but obvious code is trustworthy, reusable, and maintainable.

In the real world of reusability, the ideal of trusting programmers is inappropriate and results in less trustworthy software; in reality, customers doubt the claims of suppliers. The onus is on the suppliers to prove their claims and thus trustworthiness of the software. The client is not required to trust the supplier's programmers. Potential clients of a software component require assurance that the component is trustworthy.

Trusting programmers is against the commercial interest of both parties. This is not to cast aspersion on programmers, but merely recognizes that computers are good at performing mundane tasks and checks, but people are not. If people were good at such things, we would not need computers in the first place.

Even though you might not trust your programmers, this is not an excuse to employ anyone but the best skilled programmers. Furthermore, programmers should be given the best training. Consider a Stradivarius violin—it will sound bad in the hands of an incompetent violinist. But a talented violinist will insist on a Stradivarius rather than a cheap brand knowing that the Stradivarius will make the best use of those talents. In computing, we frequently argue whether it is the tools or the programmers that lead to success. It is a combination of the two; if either is lacking, trustworthy software will not result.

[Sun 95] Java "eliminates entire classes of programming errors that bedevil C and C++ programmers." This means that externally developed Java packages are more trustworthy.

Likewise Eiffel is not bedeviled by the same classes of errors as C and C++. Thus you are more likely to produce software that can be used in other contexts, and you will be able to find software that can be reused in your context.

Eiffel assertions are also important here. As assertions are checked at run time, they ensure that the software is working correctly, so the level of trust in external components is higher, and you reuse them with more confidence.

13.7 Reusability and Compatibility

Compatibility is essential for reusability.

In order to use different components together they must be compatible. This usually means compatibility of interfaces and therefore the messages that are passed between the components. It can also mean that the object models must be compatible. Compatibility does not mean standardization on a single technology—the technologies can be different as long as they can talk to each other. Standardization efforts do not reduce the number of disparate technologies, but standardize the links between the technologies.

Noncompatibility can be used in a manner to exclude competitors from markets. If one company controls one segment of two technologies, it can exclude a competitor from another segment by making nonconforming interfaces. For example, if you control telephone exchanges, you could exclude competitors from providing telephones that connect to your exchanges. Fortunately, the telecommunications industry is well standardized. If you control operating systems, you can exclude third party applications developers from competing with your applications. This isn't necessarily done by preventing a competitor from developing an application on the operating system, but can be done by giving your own applications a value added interface to the operating system that you don't publish for competitors.

In the rest of this section, we consider some technical aspects of compatibility and reuse in our languages. Different compiler implementations need to be compatible in order to realize reusability between libraries and components. Different C++ compilers generate different class layouts, virtual function calling techniques, etc. The name encoding schemes used for type-safe linkage can also be different. If two different compilers generate different run-time organizations, then different name encodings are desirable to prevent two incompatible libraries from being linked. The C++ ARM states, "If two C++ implementations for the same system use different calling sequences or in other ways are not link compatible it would be unwise to use identical encodings of type signatures." [C++ ARM] (p. 122)

This can be solved in two ways. First, a library vendor could provide the entire source of a library so it can be compiled with the customer's compiler. Otherwise, if the sources are proprietary, the vendor will need a separate release for every environment and every compiler in that environment.

Because of this problem a strong case exists for a universal intermediate machine-readable representation of programs. Interestingly, some systems are already using C as a universal assembler, notably AT&T C++ and Eiffel. But this cannot solve the above problems of compatibility between components without a standardization effort on run-time layouts and name encoding schemes.

An important feature of Java is that it is architecture neutral because Java compilers produce byte code instructions for a virtual machine. Java provides a universal intermediate machine-readable representation of programs, a goal I have supported in the papers that preceded this book. Also, as long as different Java compilers conform to the Java class file specification, then classes compiled with different Java compilers can be used together.

Eiffel implementations provide a high level of source code compatibility. However, the generated C from different implementations can have different object layouts. Thus a class library will have to be recompiled if it is to be used in a system compiled with a different vendor's implementation.

Another form of incompatibility between libraries is incompatibility of type definitions. An example in C++ is the number of ways the simple type *boolean* can be defined. For more on this, see the section on booleans in chapter 14.

13.8 Reusability and Portability

Since true OOP ensures that objects are loosely coupled to the external environment, portability to diverse environments is possible. C is highly coupled to UNIX-style environments and as such is not particularly portable to diverse environments.

Java is the winner in this category, due to its virtual machine and removal of pointers. Java is in fact more than portable. Classifying a system as portable suggests that you must still do some work in porting from one system to another, at least recompiling. With Java, you don't need to do even this—Java's philosophy is "write once, run anywhere." At least this is currently the theory. In practice Java virtual machines have differences that need to be ironed out and standardized. In particular, differences in the GUI interfaces are apparent; this is not necessarily a bad thing, but it can be somewhat annoying for the developer.

Eiffel code is also highly portable, but it is compatible only with systems where Eiffel compilers exist, of which there are many. Since most Eiffel compilers generate C, you can port the generated C to platforms where there is no Eiffel compiler. With Java, only a virtual machine interpreter needs to be available on the platform in order to run Java programs.

Because the Java virtual machine seems to be sufficiently semantically rich, it could be that other languages target the Java virtual machine and that it becomes a universal machine code. Such a marriage might not be as easy as it appears if the object models of different languages are sufficiently different from the Java model. Sun does seem to have kept the virtual machine independent of physical object layout and any assumptions that would make this too hard.

The Java virtual machine also brings up another important example of portability. If the Java language could operate only within the JVM, it would be limited. Since Java can also be compiled with a just-in-time (JIT) compiler to native machine code, it extends into C++'s domain. So you can consider Java for applications where previously C++ would have been the choice. C++, however, does not generate code for the JVM and probably never will because the mechanisms in C++ that Java has abandoned are inherently unsafe in this environment.

Languages such as Ada 95 and Eiffel cover more of the C++ domain than Java, as this is their native domain. However, since some Ada 95 and Eiffel compilers can also generate Java byte codes, they cover the Java domain as well as a larger part of the C++ domain than Java. Hence, for broad applicability and portability, languages that have the attributes of having native-code-generating compilers (via C in many cases) and that are sufficiently high level to target new high-level environments such as JVM are in a very strong position to be considered for implementing a broad range of applications.

13.9 Reusability and Size

The relationship between reusability and size is very simple. The larger a programming structure, the less reusable it is likely to be. Take for example a large routine of, say, 100 lines. The routine might be segmented into 20 logical sections, each of which performs one action on the state of the surrounding system. You might find that this routine does almost what you want, except for one of these logical steps, which you want to change.

Since the routine is a large block, you cannot reuse it, so are forced to rewrite, just to change a small piece. It would be better if the original routine were coded as 20 small routines, with one controlling routine that calls the 20 routines in order. Thus you have to rewrite only the one routine that you want to change and perhaps provide a new controlling routine that calls the same routines in the same order, except that a call to the new routine is substituted for the old call. In a language with dynamic binding, even this will not be necessary, because the original controlling routine will automatically call the new version of your specific routine.

Good design will also result in small routines; so good design and reusability are two sides of the same coin.

13.10 Idiomatic Programming

Some argue that a strength of C++ is the ability to program in different idioms. Idiomatic programming, however, is a weak form of paradigmatic programming; it is programming in a paradigm without necessarily having compiler support for that paradigm. The compiler cannot check for inconsistencies with the idiom, or paradigm. Defines can often be used to invent idioms. Anyone who has attempted to do OO programming in a conventional language using defines will find out that it is impossible to realize the benefits easily, if at all, without compiler support. It is of course possible because both C++ and Eiffel have compilers that generate C code.

[Meyers 92] (item 44)

Meyers says, "I emphasized the importance of understanding what different object-oriented constructs in C++ *mean*. This is quite different from just knowing the rules of the language." This is indeed a problem that many programmers face in many languages. The constructs of the language do not fit the meanings of the problem domain that the programmer must express very well. The programmer is often left wondering about where and when it is appropriate to use certain constructs. Since in many cases C++ constructs do not match the meaning, C++ becomes a cryptic language in which to work. Eiffel, on the other hand, has been carefully designed to match the constructs of the language with the intended meaning.

Both Java and Eiffel are strongly object-oriented: the idiom is OO. You don't have to bring together various subprojects, each of which might have used its own favorite idiom.

13.11 Low-Level Coding

One of the stated advantages of C++ is that you can get free and easy access to machine-level details. This comes with a downside: if you make a great deal of use of low-level coding, your programs will not be economically portable.

Java has removed the capability from C to access machine-oriented details, and one of Java's great strengths at least in theory is its portability between systems, even without recompilation.

Again, the Eiffel solution is somewhat different. In Eiffel you have no access to machine- and environment-level details in the language itself. You can use libraries that provide access to routines written in external languages like C. You can still write your low-level C routines and easily access this level from Eiffel. The major advantage of this approach is that all system-level code is centralized in a few places, and this provides good *separation of concerns*. If you have to port your system, you know exactly which parts of code will need attention. System interfaces are thus provided in a set of well-designed classes and routines. The concept of *hardware abstraction layer* is now becoming widely used. In C++ you can only enforce this as a matter of discipline over your programmers.

13.12 Knowing the Correct Construct

Meyers points out that C++ provides both a C way to do things and a C++ way. You should, he advises, forget the C way and use only the C++ way, except of course for exceptions where the C way is better. For example, you should use `const` and `inline` instead of `#define`, `iostream` instead of `stdio`, `new` and `delete` instead of `malloc` and `free`, and `//` instead of `/* .. */` for comments. Knowing the history of which C constructs have been replaced by C++ constructs adds to the programmer's burden to keep up with what is going on in the C++ world, as well as to the learning curve of new C++ programmers, whether coming from a C background or not. All the other languages in this book fare well against C++ regarding this factor, including Java, which also has a C base, but which discards C constructs that you should not use.

[Meyers 92] (items 1-4)

13.13 Efficiency and Optimization

A well-designed language will automatically encourage the efficient use of resources, and efficiency is a prime characteristic of any well-engineered artifact. Optimization is a process that produces efficient programs, but it is a process that is neither necessary nor sufficient. A program might never have undergone an optimization process, but could satisfy efficiency considerations. Furthermore, optimization does not guarantee that a program will satisfy efficiency constraints.

Optimization is also a different process from debugging. When removing a software defect, the efficiency profile of a program can radically change both for the better or worse. Of course, if it is for the worse, we have already seen that a program that is very efficient at producing the wrong results is worthless, so correctness is the overriding concern.

We can use some computer science theory at this point to distinguish what is meant by optimizing and what is meant by debugging. Computer science theory tells us that you cannot prove that a program terminates, nor can you prove that two programs are equivalent. When you optimize a program P to P' you must ensure that the property $P = P'$ holds—that is, the two programs are equivalent. You do not want to change the functionality of the program, only improve its performance. Optimization is therefore a *nonfunctional* activity. When debugging, however, you want to end up with a program that is not equivalent to the original—the behavior of the new program must differ in exactly how the defect affected the program, but in no other way. Thus when debugging it would be important to prove that $P \neq P'$, and that P' differs from P in exactly the desired way; i.e., $P - \text{bug} = P'$.

Now that we understand that optimization and debugging are fundamentally different in theory, it needs to be said that in practice they are often achieved by the same process: cleaning up the code, or *code refactoring*. This is because poorly performing programs and software defects often have the same root cause, and that is that the programmer did not clearly understand the problem in the first place. This is not necessarily a bad thing, as the act of writing the program might be the path to understanding the problem, so one should be careful about being critical of what seem obvious problems in other people's code.

Now how do efficiency concerns affect our languages in a practical sense? C++ is promoted as being a language that is extremely efficient—but this claim is questionable. Perhaps if you are working on your own projects, or you have a project with very generous funding, you might have the luxury of being able to optimize. This means that many projects in fact never get time to optimize, and most of C++'s optimizations are manual and depend on the programmer to do them.

Thus automatic optimizations that can be built into a compiler are preferable over manual programming optimizations, even if they don't quite squeeze every last ounce of performance out of a system. However, compiler optimizations can often do much better than programmer optimizations. Optimizations are being built into C++ compilers, but this is much more difficult to do, as C's philosophy has always been that the programmers know what they are doing, so they might be doing something obscure for some good reason. This makes optimizers for C and C++ much more difficult to develop.

We should consider various optimization techniques and see how Eiffel and C++ compare for compiler vs. compiler optimizations, compiler vs. manual optimizations, and manual vs. manual optimizations. Eiffel is a much more regular language than C++ which means the compiler can optimize a lot more in Eiffel, while a C++ compiler will often have to give up and assume that the programmer must have done this for a good reason, so don't touch it.

As has also been seen in this book, many optimizations are automatically done in an Eiffel compiler that must be done manually by a C++ programmer, such as virtuals and inlines. With manual vs. manual optimizations, Eiffel obviously needs less manual attention, and this leaves the programmer free to optimize where it counts, in the algorithms themselves. In C++, a single manual optimization means the programmer might have to do a lot of work. For example, if you want to avoid a pointer dereference to an object and reduce the number of object creations and deletions, all you have to do in Eiffel is change the object declaration to **expanded** and recompile. In C++, you must remove the * in the declaration, but change all the -> accesses to . also. Other examples are that the C++ programmer must specify `virtual`, but must manually remove `virtual` if it is not needed, and must manually add inlines if needed. When you compare Eiffel to C++ for optimization capabilities, this shows that high-level languages can also attain efficiency without the low-level facilities of C++.

13.14 Standardization, Stability, and Maturity

OO is now over 30 years old, beginning with Simula 67. Smalltalk is about 20 years old, and Ada 95 is only a few years old, but it is based on Ada 83, which is about 16 years old. C++ is over 15 years old, Eiffel is not far behind, and Java is still relatively new.

The age of a language does not relate to its stability and maturity. Java is the youngest language, but Java appears to have a well-thought-out and stable language base, also having a comprehensive set of OO libraries. Thus Java is off to a good start, but only time will tell, especially because issues such as adding genericity after the fact look likely to destabilize the language (see the Java and genericity section in chapter 6). Java has already had quite a number of books written about it. Its implementations are not renowned for their stability. The libraries in particular have drawn a lot of criticism.

Ada 95 is three years old. But that is three years since the standard was ratified, so it is a good deal older than that. Ada 95 is the product of an ISO/ANSI/DoD standard. Thus, Ada 95 vendors have a very stable base from which to implement. This gives Ada 95 a good start over other languages, where there might be implementations, but they are shooting at a moving target.

Eiffel is not subject to the formal ISO/ANSI standards; it has its own non-aligned standards body Non-profit International Consortium for Eiffel (NICE). Eiffel is now in its third incarnation, Eiffel 3 which is fully described in *Eiffel: The Language*, the Eiffel equivalent of the C++ ARM. However, the definition of Eiffel 3 has been very stable since 1992, requiring only a few extra validity rules and small clarifications. Eiffel is probably the best-designed language ever intended for commercial use. The largest change to the language is now under consideration—to add the **separate** keyword to allow support for concurrent and distributed processing. This will not affect existing programs, and early releases of implementations are now available with this mechanism. Eiffel also has a standard library. The standard library is more changeable than the base language, but it is also under the control of NICE. Thus Eiffel has attained a great deal of maturity over 10 years, and the standards are very stable. This gives Eiffel a considerable advantage in that libraries are much easier to update to address new and changed requirements than are compilers. Therefore, Eiffel should evolve more quickly into new problem domains without the traditional resistance from compiler vendors.

[Meyer 92]

The most serious problem that Eiffel has faced in the past was stability of implementations. Because Eiffel is an ambitious language and environment, many new and difficult concepts have been pioneered and made into industrial-strength packages. Eiffel is very demanding on compilers and the environments in which compilers run—compilers need to do things like global analysis, which is an issue that C++ conveniently avoids. Eiffel does not concede to compromises that place burdens on the programmer in the same way that C++ does.

However, stable forms of Eiffel environments have been available for several years. ISE announced version 4 of its environment in 1996, which addresses many issues that users did not like previously and now includes menus and other facilities, giving it a more Macintosh/Windows look and feel. Version 4.3 released in 1999 is another significant advance. Object Tools (formerly SIG Computer) released its compiler and programming environment *Visual Eiffel* in 1996 as well. Object Tools is also the vendor of EiffelS for UNIX and now for Macintosh. There is also an independent experimental version known as SmallEiffel, which has become the GNU version that can be downloaded for free.

[Meyer 88]

[Meyer 92]

[Meyer 97]

Another problem that Eiffel has had is the lack of titles. *Object-Oriented Software Construction* was the classic book on OO; however, it was based on Eiffel 2.0, not version 3. Meyer's next book on Eiffel, *Eiffel: The Language*, is the language lawyer's reference, but it is possible to navigate for an overview. Now, with the publication of the completely revised second edition of *Object-oriented Software Construction* and over 10 other titles on programming in Eiffel, quite a few of which are used to teach university courses on OO, we have a very adequate library for Eiffel.

Out of the languages here, C++, although 12 years old, has provided the fastest-moving target for vendors. The standard was finally completed in 1997. (You can check the status of the standard on the X3J16 WEB page in the WEBliography.) C++ was submitted to the standardization process too early, and the committee has had to do too much design work that should have been done before the standardization process.

[Stroustrup 94]
(Preface)

In the preface to *The Design and Evolution of C++*, Stroustrup writes, "C++ is still a young language. Some of the issues discussed here are yet unknown to many users. Many implications of decisions described here will not become obvious for years to come."

[Stroustrup 94]
(2.8.2)

Coming to consensus in the C++ world is a difficult task. Stroustrup states this frustration as "dealing with stubborn old-time C users, would-be C experts, and genuine C/C++ compatibility issues has been one of the most difficult and frustrating aspects of developing C++. It still is."

Many comments in *The Design and Evolution of C++* show that C++ is still a moving target. Garbage collection is mentioned as "when (not if)." Thus when garbage collection is fitted to C++, developers will be faced with quite a transition in paradigm. This uncertainty in C++ might keep the programmers busy—after all, many of them want to code exclusively in C++ while ignoring all else—but it will be very costly for the companies that are locked into C++.

[Stroustrup]

On C compatibility Stroustrup says

> The "compatibility wars" now seem petty and boring, but some of the underlying issues are still unresolved, and we are still struggling with them in the ANSI/ISO standards committee. I strongly suspect that the reason the compatibility wars were drawn out and curiously inconclusive was that we never quite faced the deeper issues related to the differing goals of C and C++ and saw compatibility as a set of separate issues to be resolved individually.

[Stroustrup (3.12)]

Since C compatibility results in so many problems, serious consideration should be given to this basic tenet of C++.

The C++ world seems to think that using a flawed tool is acceptable and that the rest of the world must wait for it to straighten these issues out, which in many cases isn't even possible. It is also a hidden cost to companies that their programmers must continually keep up-to-date and abreast of the arguments for and against certain constructs. Many other languages have solved these problems.

As a postscript to this section, I will remark that a lot of argument for or against particular languages seems to come from people who believe that there will be an eventual winner in the evolution of languages, and they want it to be their favorite and so will fight for dominance. I see no evidence that this will happen. I think new languages will continue to be invented—some will be based on continuing mistakes from old languages while adding new features for compatibility; others will avoid previous errors while adopting new paradigms. I can't see that the programming language world will ever become stable. If people in the industry can accept that, then we will have programmers that are more amenable to changing language, being able to use the language that is best suited for the purpose, and the maturity of language criticism will improve as we see each language as a passing phase to which we owe no long-term allegiance.

13.15   Complexity

There are several kinds of complexity. While this book focuses mainly on the complexity of programming languages, when considering complexity, we need to consider the complexity of the development task as a whole. The complexity of the language might only be a small part of that.

Apart from the language, we need to consider the programming environment—for example, editors and tools—the methodologies and tools, and the supporting libraries.

With C++ the conventional wisdom is often to use a methodology such as UML, but the concepts of the methodology do not exactly match the concepts in the programming language. Thus you have a semantic gap where translation must occur. This translation is costly and frequently ends in specifications that do not match what was eventually implemented.

Both Eiffel and BETA see it as important to develop their methodologies and graphical notations based on the same underlying concepts. The importance of this integrated approach should not be underappreciated.

As for environments, Stroustrup says

[Stroustrup 94] (9.2.2.2)
Every language in nontrivial use grows to meet the needs of its user community. This invariably implies an increase of complexity. C++ is part of a trend towards greater language complexity to deal with the even greater complexity of the programming tasks attempted. If the complexity doesn't appear in the language itself, it appears in libraries and tools. Examples of languages/systems that have grown enormously compared to their simpler origins are Ada, Eiffel, Lisp (CLOS), and Smalltalk. Because of C++'s emphasis on static type checking, much of the increase in complexity has appeared in the form of language extensions.

C++ was designed for serious programmers and grew to serve them in the increasing large and complex tasks they face.

[Plauger 93]
Plauger argues that the complexity of C++ has put it on par with PL/I, Ada (83), and ALGOL 68. He does not accept the complexity in C++ as a good thing. Criticizing the complexity of Ada is somewhat unfair. Part of Ada's complexity is due to its support of multitasking and real-time programming. Simula also has facilities for coroutines and processes, and Ada and Simula are reasonably unique for their built-in support of these facilities. In the 1980s, the need for such facilities was not widely recognized. However, the need for concurrency and distribution is now recognized.

Ada has been criticized for being complex, but most of this criticism is due to not understanding essential features such as genericity and concurrency. Again the charge that this makes the language overcomplex is based on not understanding genericity. I have already covered this topic in the section on templates (chapter 6). Many C programmers have been guilty of dismissing features they don't understand as complexity, and Ada has been a favorite target. I am not saying that Plauger is in this category because he makes some valid points about Ada. But the accusation of complexity against Ada should not be overstated as has happened too frequently and too emotionally in the past. In the computing industry, there is a low level of understanding and experience that one must have before becoming an expert or vocal critic, particularly of languages like Pascal and Ada.

C++'s complexity is not solely due to static type checking. Eiffel is more strongly type checked than C++, but it doesn't suffer from the same complexity problems.

As for the environment, the burden of environment is far less for the cases of Eiffel, Java, and Ada 95. In Eiffel, a separate simple language—*LACE*—exists to specify to the compiler how to compile the program. This contains such things as environment variables, debug and other options, etc. It also provides the basis for *separation of concerns* so that environmental details are completely removed from the Eiffel language. Eiffel is also integrated with complete editing and development environments. Java has removed such environmental considerations as `#include` and `make`.

The Eiffel libraries are very large and comprehensive, but this merely reflects the richness of the existing data structures and the number of application domains. Eiffel libraries are available for networking, compiling and parsing, and Macintosh and Windows GUI programming as well as platform-independent user interfaces and many other things. The Eiffel libraries simplify naming complexity by standardizing the vocabulary between classes. For example, *put* is used to enter an item into any collection data structure like *ARRAY, LIST, QUEUE*, and even *STACK* where the routine would normally be named *push*. The libraries enable the complexity of specific domains to be removed from the language, which is simple and yet general purpose.

Java also provides a comprehensive library to deal with many aspects, including java.net, java.awt (abstract windows toolkit), etc. Eiffel, Smalltalk, and Java do not ignore the issue of complexity—they put it where it should be: in the libraries. In terms of complexity, they implement Stroustrup's principle of "what you don't use, you don't pay for." In C++ you pay very heavily for complexity, since it is in the language.

C++ can to some extent be extracted from the complexity of its environment. But as long as the mechanisms of `#include` persist, the environments to which C++ is ported will have to adapt to the C/UNIX style of doing things. Where the environment is separate from the language, there is no environmental adaptation that needs to be done; thus, less retraining of programmers is necessary for each environment they need to program in.

I can accept that C++ was designed for serious programmers. However, both Ada 95 and Eiffel are designed for serious software engineering. (Java remains to prove itself in this arena.) Eiffel in particular shows that complexity can be dealt with in a serious industrial-strength software engineering environment.

Complexity is not the necessary companion of seriousness. This does not ignore the complexity of any application domain; in fact, it enables you to focus on the complexity of the programming task at hand, not on the complexity of the tool.

[Sakkinen 92]
[Wiener 95]
[Ellemtel 92]

Several books have been published on the shortcomings of C++. A paper on the recommended practices for use in C++ from Ellemtel suggests that C++ is a difficult language in which there may be a very fine line between a feature and a bug. This places a large responsibility upon the programmer. Is this a responsibility or a burden? The fine line is a result of an unnecessarily complicated language definition. The C++ standardization committee warns that C++ is already too large and complicated for their taste.

[X3J16 92]

[Sun 95]

Sun's Java white paper says that, in designing Java, the first step was to *eliminate redundancy* from C and C++. In many ways, the C language evolved into a collection of overlapping features, providing too many ways to do the same thing, while in many cases not providing needed features. C++, even in an attempt to add classes to C, merely added more redundancy while retaining the inherent problems of C.

[Meyer 92]
(appendix B)

Meyer, the designer of Eiffel, states in the appendix *On language design and evolution* some guiding principles of language design such as simplicity vs. complexity, uniqueness, and consistency. The Principle of Uniqueness, Meyer says, is easily expressed: "the language design should provide one good way to express every operation of interest; it should avoid providing two."

[Meyer 92]
appendix B.1)

[Meyer 97]

Meyer has produced a seminal work on OO—*Object-Oriented Software Construction*. All software engineers and OO practitioners should read and absorb this work. Another short book, *Object Success*, is directed to managers (probably the reason for the pun in the name), with an overview of OO.

[Meyer 95]

While C programmers can immediately use C++ to write and compile C programs, this does not take advantage of OO. Many see this as a strength, but it is often stated that the C base is C++'s greatest weakness. However, C++ adds its own layers of complexity, like its handling of multiple inheritance, overloading, and others. I am not so sure that C is C++'s greatest weakness. Java has shown that, in removing C constructs that do not fit with OO concepts, C can provide an acceptable, albeit not perfect, base.

Adoption of C++ does not suddenly transform C programmers into OO programmers. A complete change in thinking is required, and C++ actually makes this difficult. A book on C++ cannot be separated from criticism of the C base language, since it is essential for the C++ programmer to be fluent in C. Many of C's problems affect the way that OO is implemented and used in C++. This book does not exhaust the weaknesses of C++, but it illustrates the practical consequences of these weaknesses with respect to the timely and economic production of quality software.

13.16   C++: The Overwhelming OOL of Choice?

This headline comes from Cutter Information Corp's, "Object-oriented Strategies," May 1996 edition. Based on Cutter's findings at that time, C++ accounts for 80 percent of all OOLs, with Smalltalk running a distant second at 11 percent. Cutter claims that in 1995 OO software development products hit $1.3 billion. The years since then have certainly seen some changes, and no report could claim that C++ is that popular anymore, even since the long-awaited standard was finalized. Even if these figures were still correct, let's examine how C++ is used. Many C programmers have not wanted to touch C++, but they do use a C++ compiler to compile their C. This greatly exaggerates the market penetration of C++ and the size of the OO market, so it is impossible to determine the true market penetration of OO—you are not doing OO just because you are compiling with C++.

Microsoft and Borland have put most of their development environment energies into C++, so this makes it attractive to buy a C++ environment even if you are just programming C. Probably the true number of C++ installations being used for OO would be between 10 and 50 percent, which cuts down the size of the OO market by a large amount, meaning the other OOLs in the market have a much higher significance than Cutter indicated. Smalltalk and Eiffel are pure OOLs, so you can count every sale as an OO installation, whereas you cannot do the same for C++. Measured C++ sales are riding on C's success. C++'s success is less than overwhelming. It is a marketing success rather than a technical or programming success. Companies using C++ are paying for it with longer cycle development times and less reliable end product.

One way managers might perceive C++ to be a winner is the sheer number of books on C++ they see in a bookshop. This is matched by a huge number of courses being offered on C++. My observation about the nature of many of the books available is that they are often titled something like *How to Build a Widget in C++*, or *Compiler Construction in C++*. "Books appear like mushrooms after rain."   [Plauger 93]

The mushrooming book market is a great boon for publishers, as it implies that, for every possible software artifact you can build, they can publish a book about it in every possible programming language—all you really need are the books *Programming in C++* and *How to Build Widgets* or *Compiler Principles and Construction*. Then your programmer needs experience and lots of it—don't be fooled by this marketing trick to get a high title count or by inordinately thick books on the shelves.

Many C++ books are on how to avoid the traps and pitfalls and how to develop rigorous coding standards, which might appeal to management as the solution, but they don't solve the root cause of the problem. Making sure everyone is well trained and versed in these style standards is an expensive and usually ineffective Band-Aid measure, especially since different companies have different standards and expectations, so you need to retrain every new recruit. And new employees can decide they don't like your way of doing things anyway and leave after a short period. Of course you can satisfy yourself that their dissatisfaction was due to their inappropriateness for your organization, which is better organized than most. After all, you are ISO 9000 accredited and are turning out a very successful line of concrete life jackets (a Tom Peters quote).

[Sakkinen 92] Sakkinen observes the "Endemic C++ Culture." He notes that too many courses on design have the appended phrase "with C++." This is because C++ has its own curious terminology, which is in many ways different from the rest of the OO world or plain uses of language. He makes a case that concepts and principles should be taught; then teach how to map them onto any particular language.

Of course books are aimed at different audiences—professionals vs. those who just program for a hobby; those who have an academic interest in languages; implementers of compilers and other language processing tools who need formal, nonambiguous statements about how the language works; beginners vs. those for whom this is their fourth or fifth language. C++ should not be for beginners, as it is better to learn the principles from a clearer language than to be confused by what all the syntactic "knobs and dials" and superfluous constructs do in C++. But then you should also not consider that C++ is something you should progress to in order to become an expert programmer, once you progress past the beginner level. Stevens finds it laughable that there are books titled *Teach Yourself C++ in 14 (or 21) Days* as "most people couldn't learn all of C++ in a year, not even with a Vulcan Mind Meld. Most of the experts are still learning."

[Stevens 97]

As for courses, C++ has proven so difficult to learn that you need lots of courses. Not only do you need to learn the language, but the complexities of the environment add an even more substantial overhead. It is probably best to start on C++ with a course. However, with simpler languages such as Java and Eiffel, buying a good book and experimentation will quickly cover every aspect of the language. It is a bonus if you can get a course, but it is not essential to get started.

What application domain is C++ relevant for? The answer to this is that C++ might be used as a better C. But for what applications is C relevant? C is relevant for low-level UNIX-style programming, but it is not an ideal language in view of its low-level nature and flaws. C is not applicable for large project organization, hence C++'s attempt to improve it. C++, however, has not solved C's flaws, as I once hoped it would, but has painfully magnified them.

The Peter Principle also comes into effect. Many people who are less technically competent will follow whichever bandwagon seems to be the biggest to them. It has been my pleasure to also know some very good C++ people, and they are very open-minded about C++'s flaws; it is usually those of less knowledge who vocally defend C++. Managers are also guilty, as they have risen beyond their ability to be able to select an appropriate language, so they are more likely to select the industry default standard in order to protect their jobs. The managers have some economic rationalization for this because they think they will more easily find C++ people whom they don't need to train. But of course they are at risk of picking up those who have ignored other languages, hoping to make an easy living at C++, or of employing those who do not understand OO because it is obscured by C++. Training in languages such as Java and Eiffel will be much more effective, so the economic rationalization of these managers is a false economy.

14

General Issues

Looking over what we have discussed so far in this book, we have covered the main issues of project organization and OO. We have reserved analysis of some specific language issues until this stage. In the last chapter we looked at some wide-scale issues. By contrast, in this chapter, we look at some finer details at the other end of the spectrum and find some differences in our languages at a fine-grained level. As for C++, many of these issues have to do with the C base, rather than C++. As Stroustrup notes, there are no shortage of passionate opinions on some of these matters—you will find no shortage of comment on many of these things on the Internet. We reserve these issues until last because the emphasis of this book has been to examine the higher-level issues, which we consider as more important.

Fixing the problems of C has been no easy task for the designers of C++. Indeed, had they foreseen the problems, one wonders if they would have ever started. It is with these difficulties that C++ has had to contend, being unduly hampered and constrained. It is hardly surprising that the designers of Java chose to discard those constraints even while retaining the slightly cryptic C syntax. Eiffel altogether abandoned anything to do with C, thus being unhampered by C's conceptual constraints and able to adopt a much more readable syntax.

[Mody 91]   Mody gives an excellent general criticism of C. He says that to properly understand C you must understand the insides of the compiler, giving many examples of how C obscures rather than clarifies software engineering. His conclusion is somewhat blunt, but he is

> appalled at the monstrous messes that computer scientists can produce under the name of improvements. It is to efforts such as C++ that I here refer. These artifacts are filled with frills and features but lack coherence, simplicity, understandability and implementability. If computer scientists could see that art is at the root of the best science, such ugly creatures could never take birth.

The passions in defense of C and C++ are just as strong. In this book, I have sought to have some balance and to illustrate the difficulties in the design of programming languages, particularly OO ones. However, after over 30 years of OO languages, it is really time to reassess what we have not accomplished and why, to adopt new technologies and not be constrained by the mistakes of the past—carrying such constraints forward means the problems are never fixed, only rehashed.

14.1 Pointers

C pointers are a low-level mechanism that should not be the concern of programmers. Pointers mean the programmer must manipulate low-level address mechanisms and be concerned with lvalue and rvalue semantics, which are machine oriented and not problem oriented as you would expect of a high-level language. A compiler can easily handle such issues without loss of generality or efficiency. Memory models of different environments often affect the definition of pointers. Memory model details such as near and far pointers should be transparent to the programmer.

The programmer must also be concerned with correct dereferencing of pointers to access referenced entities. Use of pointers to emulate by reference function parameters is an example. The programmer has to worry about the correct use of &s and *s. (See the section on function arguments in this chapter.)

Pointer arithmetic is error prone. Pointers can be incremented past the end of the entities they reference, with subsequent updates possibly corrupting other entities. This is a major source of the undetected inconsistencies that result in obscure failures, discussed in the section on correctness in chapter 1. In the STL library, iterators are provided as the generalization of C pointers for access to elements of structures such as arrays.

Programmers can bypass encapsulation with pointers; C undermines OOP by providing a mechanism where the state outside an object's boundaries can be changed. Since pointers are intrinsic to writing software in C, this exacerbates the problem. Pointers as implemented in C make the introduction of advanced concepts like garbage collection and concurrency difficult.

Another consideration is that dynamic memory implementations vary between platforms. Some environments make memory block relocation easier by having all pointers reference objects via a master pointer that contains the actual address of the block. The location of the master pointer never changes, so relocation of the block is hidden from all pointers that reference it. When the block is relocated, only the master pointer needs to be updated.

On the Macintosh, for example, the double indirection mechanism of handles facilitates relocation of objects. Object Pascal makes handles transparent to the programmer. This is similar to the Unisys A Series approach where object *descriptors* access target objects via master descriptors that store the actual addresses of objects. On the A Series this is transparent to programmers in all languages because this transparency is realized at a level lower than languages. The A Series descriptor mechanism also provides hardware safety checks—this means that pointers cannot overrun and arrays cannot be indexed out of bounds. C cannot be implemented particularly well on such machines, since C's pointer mechanisms are at a lower level than the target environment.

Simpler environments might not provide object relocation, so double indirection would be an unnecessary overhead. In order for programs to be portable and efficient in different target environments, such system details should be the concern of the target compilation system, not of the programmer.

C's pointer declaration syntax causes another small problem.

C
```
int* i, j;
```

This does not mean, as might be easily read

C
```
int *i, *j;
```

but

C
```
int *i, j;
```

and should be written thus to avoid confusion.

You should note that this applies to any declarator operator. For example

```
char u, v[10];                                            C
```

is different from

```
char u[10], v[10];                                        C
```

Java has abolished pointers because "most studies agree that *pointers* are one of the primary features that enable programmers to put bugs into their code. Given that structures are gone, and arrays and strings are objects, the need for pointers to these constructs goes away." [Sun 95]

Eiffel also has no pointers, only object references. In Eiffel, the exact referencing mechanism does not matter. For example, in the expression $x.f$, the reference x might be a pointer to an object in the same address space, or it might be an Internet address of an object. References enable the location and access method of an object to be transparent.

14.2 Booleans

C has no boolean type and this is a serious omission. Booleans are fundamental to programming as conditions in **if**...**then** and loop constructs. C++ also has no built-in boolean. It is interesting to see long Internet discussions on how booleans should be defined and how the values true and false should be represented. Using 0 to mean false and any other value to mean true is unsatisfactory.

Java includes the basic type boolean and so has rectified this situation. To accomplish C-style conversions you can use the expressions

```
b = (i != 0);                                             Java
i = (b)? 1 : 0;
```

Java provides no other conversions to or from boolean. "There is no permitted conversion to the type boolean other than the identity conversion. There is no permitted conversion from the type boolean other than the identity conversion and string conversion." The problem with Java is that it distinguishes between primitive types and object types, and so it has boolean as a primitive type and Boolean as an object type. The primitive types are not related to the object type hierarchy, and this causes conversion problems that must burden the programmer, as operations that apply to the class Boolean are not available for the primitive boolean [Java 96] (5.1.7) type. This is a problem with all Java's primitive types as we have discussed in the section Double, double toil and trouble in chapter 12.

Eiffel takes a slightly different approach. As a language, Eiffel provides the mechanisms for building types. It has no assumptions about particular types built into the language. Types like *BOOLEAN* are defined as classes in the Eiffel Kernel Library, as are other basic types such as *INTEGER*, *REAL*, *STRING*, and *ARRAY*. This view is very similar to Smalltalk. These types are not built into the *language*, but they are usually built into an Eiffel *compiler* so that there is no run-time performance penalty. This illustrates Eiffel's philosophy of keeping the language as small as possible and as open as possible so that programmers can build their own powerful types. Eiffel does have two *BOOLEAN* types, for the built-in **expanded** *BOOLEAN* and *BOOLEAN_REF*. However, unlike Java, these are related as *BOOLEAN* is a subclass of *BOOLEAN_REF*, and therefore all operations can be used in both classes without conversion. Even this can be tidier; and for a recent language extension to improve this also see the section Double, double toil and trouble in chapter 12.

Recently the ANSI/ISO C++ committee has accepted `bool` as a distinct integral type. Prior to this the definition of a boolean type in C/C++ could be any number of definitions with slightly different semantics. If you were combining libraries that used these slightly different definitions, life could be difficult. This is probably a fundamental reason why libraries have not been as successful in C++ as they should be in an OO environment. The simple fact that there is no root type in C++, so that type hierarchies in different libraries have no common ancestors, also makes the combination of libraries difficult. Not all compiler implementations have implemented `bool` yet, so you can expect it to be years before this mess is cleaned up.

[CD2 96]

Even though `bool` is now defined in the standard, several peculiarities exist that you won't find in the *BOOLEAN*s of other languages. First, the postfix operator ++ is defined to set an operand of type `bool` to true (5.2.6), although this use is deprecated in appendix D. In contrast, though, the -- operator is not allowed on `bool` operands at all.

C++'s `bool` also does not ensure type safety. The following examples are all right according to the C++ standard.

C++

```
bool b = 15;
int i = true;
```

You can also implicitly cast pointers to `bool`: zero-valued pointers convert to `false` and nonzero ones to `true`.

An advantage of the `bool` type is that you can overload a function on a `bool` parameter as opposed to an `int` parameter. Meyers points out that expressions with relational operators result in type `int`; therefore, a function call `f (x < y)` will result in a call to `f(int)` not `f(bool)`. In contrast to Meyers, the C++ standard defines that relational operators all yield the values `false` or `true` of type `bool`. Such a definition has the potential to break existing C++ programs when it becomes implemented in C++ compilers. At least this means that the committee is now finally biting the bullet and fixing up the mistakes of the past, even though it could cause some pain. (One could draw comparisons to the widely publicized Y2K problem, which is reportedly costing the industry billions of dollars for a seemingly simple fix.)

[Meyers 96] (Introduction)

[CD2 96] (5.9)

So Eiffel again shows the strongest definition, because *BOOLEAN* is related to the rest of the type hierarchy and the same operations are applicable to both the **expanded** and reference versions. Java comes in between with built-in booleans, but unfortunately these do not relate to the object type hierarchy, making `boolean` and `Boolean` further apart than *BOOLEAN* and *BOOLEAN_REF*. C++ has belatedly introduced a weak form of what is probably the most fundamental type in computing.

14.3 Logical and Bitwise Operators

We have already looked at some aspects of `&&` and `||` in section 8.12. However, if we treat boolean as a proper type, there is another aspect to this. C defines `&&` and `||` to be the *logical and* and *logical or* operators, and `&` and `|` to be the bitwise *and* and *or* operators. A moment's reflection should tell you that, if C had introduced type-safe boolean types, then these extra operators would not be necessary and that a single `&` and `|` operator could be polymorphic – dependent on the type of the operands (just as `.` and `->` are unnecessary, since `.` could be polymorphic – dependent on whether the left-hand side is a pointer or not). Thus a whole class of common error would be avoided.

Java has cleaned this up: `&`, `^`, and `|` are used for both integer bitwise operators and boolean logical operators. Now, to confuse you more, Java uses `&&` to mean conditional-and, and `||` to mean conditional-or; that is, the right-hand boolean expression is only evaluated depending on the value of the left-hand boolean expression.

Eiffel also has polymorphic **and** and **or** operators. On *BOOLEAN* entities, these are logical operators; on *BIT N* types, these are bitwise operators. Eiffel has the equivalent of Java's conditional operators as **and then** and **or else**.

14.4 Arrays

[C++ ARM]
(p. 137)

The C++ ARM notes that C arrays are low level, yet not very general, and unsafe; it admits "the C array concept is weak and beyond repair." Modern software production is less dependent on arrays, especially in the OO environment. The trade-off to be optimal rather than general and safe no longer applies for most applications. C arrays provide no run-time bounds checking, not even in test versions of software. This compromises safety and undermines the semantics of an array declaration, i.e., an array is a particular size and can be indexed only by values within the bounds of the array. The array size might not be determined at compile time, but dynamically at run time. An index to an array is a parameter in the domain of the array function. An index out of bounds is not a member of the domain and should be treated as severely as "divide by zero." But in C this is another significant source of undetected inconsistency that can result in obscure failures.

C has no notion of dynamically allocated arrays, whose bounds are determined at run time, as in ALGOL 60. This limits the flexibility of arrays. You cannot resize C arrays. You cannot even determine the size of an array at run time, which means you can't put in a programmer-defined test for index in bounds, or determine that the array might need resizing (if you could do that). Multidimensional arrays are only really one-dimensional. You cannot individually resize the rows of a multidimensional array. The C definition of arrays compromises both safety and flexibility.

[GWS 94]

There are many ways you can undermine arrays in C and C++, since an array declaration is really equivalent to a pointer. The following example comes from [GWS 94]

C

```
char *str = "bugy";
```

then the following are true

```
0[str]       == 'b';
*(str+1)     == 'u';
*(2+str)     == 'g';
str[3]       == 'y';
```

This is amazingly flexible syntax for something as inflexible as C arrays, providing several ways to do the same thing, but still not doing it particularly well,

[Meyer 92]

which is against Meyer's Principle of Uniqueness that states that you should provide only one good way of doing things.

The unsafeness of C arrays is shown in the next example.

```
#include <stdio.h>
#include <string.h>

main ()
{
    char str[] = "TEST";
    char *p = "TEST2";
    const char str3[] = "TEST3";
    char *p3;

    printf ("str = %s p = %s str3 = %s\n", str,
            p, str3);
    p3 = str;
    strcpy (p3, "some junk");
    printf ("str3 = %s\n", str3);
    str[6] = 'X';

    printf ("str = %s p = %s str3 = %s\n", str,
            p, str3);
}
```

C

The results from one C compiler were

```
str = TEST p = TEST2 str3 = TEST3
str3 = junk
str = some  Xunk p = TEST2 str3 = Xunk
```

and the results from Metrowerks CodeWarrior C are

```
str = TEST p = TEST2 str3 = TEST3
str3 = TEST3
str = some  Xunk p = TEST2 str3 = TEST3
```

One view of arrays is that they are just another OO entity that should be treated in an OO manner as a class of data structure. Arrays should have interface definitions and consistency checks inherent in OO systems. Another view is that an array is an implementation of a function where, rather than computing the result, the values stored in the array are explicit results, so the index/value pairs map the domain uniquely to the range. This suggests that ALGOL was incorrect in syntactically distinguishing arrays by using square brackets. An array simply maps the input argument (the index) to the value stored in that location in the array. Since arrays usually take an *INTEGER* as the index, many libraries provide other types such as *MAP* and *DICTIONARY* that can take any type as the domain.

[Ince 92] Ince considers that arrays and pointers need not be relied upon so heavily in modern software production, because higher-level abstractions such as sets, sequences, etc., are better suited to the problem domain. Arrays and pointers can be provided in an OO framework and used as low-level implementation techniques for the higher-level data abstractions. Ince suggests that arrays and pointers should be regarded in the same way gotos were in the 1970s. He suggests that languages such as Pascal and Modula-2 should be regarded in the same way as assembler languages in the 1970s. This applies even more to C and C++ because pointers and arrays are far more intrinsic in the use of C and C++, with lower-level, less flexible arrays. Although Pascal arrays are weak compared to those of ALGOL, they are still much better than C arrays.

In both Eiffel and Java, arrays are first-class objects. Both languages have no need for the `sizeof` function. In Java to get the size of an array you use *myArray.length*. In Eiffel this is *my_array.count*. Arrays can also be resized.

Both Eiffel and Java provide bounds checking on arrays. Java's checking is built in. Eiffel's checking is conceptually integrated with the assertion mechanism, although the implementation can be built in.

Eiffel goes a step further in array element access. You access an element with the *item* function

Eiffel
```
v := my_array.item (i)
```

This can also be accessed by an infix operator, @

Eiffel
```
v := my_array @ i
```

The item function is defined as

Eiffel
```
item (i: INTEGER) G
    require
        lower <= i;
        i <= upper
```

This shows how Eiffel's assertion mechanism is used to document semantics in the interface; it is also used for a checking mechanism.

C++ introduces another problem with arrays if the array elements are polymorphic. Consider

```
class AA { ... };
class AB : public AA { ... };

void doit (const AA a [], int n)
{
    for (int i = 0; i < n; ++i)
        ... process a[i];
}

AA a[666];
AB b[666];

doit (a, 666);     // this works
doit (b, 666);     // problems!
```

C++

So why does the second call fail? The compiler won't find any error. The problem is in the loop. It will be compiled for objects the size of an `AA` object being placed in the array. Thus when you pass it an array with `AB` objects, even though such an array conforms to an array of `AA`s, you will get undefined results.

We should also note that arrays can be polymorphic; that is, each array element does not have to be the same type. Unfortunately, this does seem to be the C/C++ view. "An array is an aggregate of elements of the same type." If the wording is changed here slightly to "same *static* type," then this is correct. However, dynamically at run time, different array elements can be different types, so long as they *conform* to the static type.

[Stroustrup (5.7)]

It is in fact a powerful paradigm to be able to process the array elements according to their type. As long as the elements have some common routines, with possibly different implementations, then you can process through the array invoking those routines. For instance, an array might represent a list of shapes, each with its own *draw* routine.

This last point will also help you to determine when to use lists and when to use arrays. Arrays are generally more efficient, but the elements in the array are usually in fixed positions. You cannot in general insert elements in the middle of an array as efficiently as you can in a list.

14.5 Function Arguments

Arguments are a fundamental mechanism for reuse in software construction. Without arguments you would be forced to write a different routine for every possible input parameter. Arguments allow one algorithm to be reused on sets of input values.

[Hext 90]

Arguments pass routines simple values (by-value arguments) or references to entities (by-reference arguments). (Actually, there are more possibilities than this. Hext gives an excellent enumeration of the possibilities.) Arguments are inputs to routines and should not be changed. When memory was expensive, reusing parameter space could conserve space. Changing arguments, however, is semantic nonsense, and most languages get this wrong. Arguments are not variables.

By-reference arguments enable a routine to change the value of an entity external to the routine. Such updates beyond the environment of a routine are side effects. This introduces a mechanism of updating the state space, other than straight assignment (although the routine can use assignment to achieve the dirty deed). The problem is that the state of an object can be changed without using the well-defined interface of the object, so encapsulation is compromised. By-reference arguments should not be used to change external entities. Values should be passed to external entities only by the return value of a function. Semantically, this is different from assignment to a reference parameter; data flows through the program in one direction—in via arguments and out via return values. Mathematically this maps a value of an input type to a value of an output type. Both input and output types can be compositions of other types, i.e., $f: I1 \times I2 \times \ldots Im \rightarrow O1 \times O2 \times \ldots On$. Abstract data types can be used to design such systems. This will also help target environments to increase parallelism and concurrency in a way transparent to programmers.

In OO programming, by-reference arguments are used to pass the original object, not a copy. The called routine, however, should not change the state of the referenced object. Only calling a routine in the passed object's interface can change the state, although introducing side effects into arguments like this is dubious and should be avoided. Passing an object using a by-reference argument has the desired effect of the object being given to you without it being yours to change, although you can effect change in the object. C++ does have a nice concept called *const correctness* that provides a modifier on arguments—const—that disallows any changes to that argument.

C shares faulty arguments with many other languages. The interaction of C's pointer mechanism with a faulty parameter mechanism, however, makes C considerably worse than most other languages. In C, pointers are used to simulate by-reference arguments with by-value arguments. The programmer must perform tedious bookkeeping by specifying *s and &s for referencing and dereferencing. Distinguishing between by-value and by-reference arguments is not just a syntactic nicety included in most high-level languages, but a valuable compiler technique, because the compiler can automatically generate the referencing and dereferencing without burdening the programmer. Again C adopts operators to provide the functionality, rather than using a declarative approach that would centralize decisions and let the compiler do the rest.

In Java arguments can be passed by-value (as in C) only for simple types; objects are automatically passed by-reference without the mess of added *s and &s. However, there are no pointers, so passing by-reference cannot be simulated in the C fashion.

Eiffel routine arguments are read-only arguments. This means that they are pass-by-constant which is stronger than pass-by-value, where the arguments are treated as local variables that may be updated; pass-by-constant disallows this.

The restrictions to arguments to data flowing through in one direction—in via arguments and out via return values—might seem overly burdensome. However, it is enabled by good design—your routines should be small.

14.6 void and void*

> Passing paths that climb half way into the void
>
> *Close to the Edge*, Yes

Is `void*` the C equivalent of an oxymoron? A pointer to void suggests some sort of semantic nonsense—a dangling pointer perhaps? Maybe we should tell the astronomers we have found a black hole! While we can have some fun conjecturing what some of the obscure syntax of C suggests, the fact that `void*` declarations are used to compromise the integrity of the type system is a serious problem. A consistent, strongly typed system does not require such facilities. In OO type systems, the root class of the inheritance hierarchy provides the equivalent of void.

When an entity is assigned to a reference of `void*`, it loses its type information. In C++, when it is assigned back to a typed reference, the programmer must explicitly specify the type information with a type cast, but C does not require such a cast. This is error prone and should at least result in a run-time check. Without a run-time type check, the routines of one class can be mistakenly applied to objects of another class, resulting in undetected inconsistencies that lead to obscure failures.

[Stroustrup 94]
(14.3.4.1)

As Stroustrup points out, "having `void*` unsafe can be considered acceptable because everybody knows – or at least ought to know – that casts *from* `void*` are inherently tricky."

Interestingly, `void*` is the exact opposite of `void` so, yes, this is a programming oxymoron. Void means no object of any type—that is, the empty set. Void* on the other hand means any object of any type—that is, all objects of the all encompassing set, or the universal set of all objects that can exist in a system. So `void` and `void*` represent complementary sets.

Eiffel and Java both provide a class that is at the root of the inheritance tree. In Java it is `Object`, and in Eiffel it is *ANY*. Any object can be assigned to a reference of these types. In C++ this is provided by `void*`, but `void*` is not at the root of the inheritance tree, hence its type unsafeness. In Eiffel and Java all classes defined in any libraries are related through their relationship to the root class. This is significant because it means that objects from different classes can be entered together in collections. Remember, in Java collections take objects of type `Object`, but in Eiffel you can use genericity to retain type information in collections. Since classes from different libraries in C++ are not related it is difficult to use different libraries together while keeping type safety in collections without casts.

We have already criticized Java on the fact that the primitive types and arrays are not integrated with the interface type hierarchy (remember that in Java, it is interfaces that define the type hierarchy, not the classes, and types can be related by multiple inheritance). Arrays in Java are outside of the type hierarchy because arrays really need to be generic, and Java provides no genericity. In C++, at least you can define arrays based on templates. However, C++ still has primitive types that are not related to the type hierarchy and the fact that `void` and `void*` do not relate to the type hierarchy—leaving C++ without a top or bottom to the type hierarchy—is even worse.

[Castagna 97]

Only Eiffel provides an entirely consistent type system in which all entities created in a running program belong in the type hierarchy. Unfortunately, because Eiffel uses covariant arguments, subclasses cannot be considered subtypes of parent classes. Using covariant arguments, rather than contravariant arguments, is an entirely pragmatic choice based on modeling requirements. At present there is no good solution to this problem, although, as we have mentioned, Castagna calls it a conflict without a cause.

If you have read through this entire book, then congratulations. The previous three paragraphs present in a nutshell all I have learned about type systems as they apply to our languages from my participation in John Potter's types reading group at Macquarie University and other research over many years. Read and understand these few paragraphs and observe the effects in action as you put our languages into practice and you will have mastered what most of this book is about.

Now as to the bottom of our type hierarchies, Eiffel defines the type *NONE* at the bottom of the inheritance tree, which is a class to which no objects belong. *NONE* is the complement of *ANY* and vice versa. Type *NONE* has the single value *Void*, which signifies no object. *Void* is the equivalent of 0 (meaning NULL) in C++. This means that Eiffel's type system is more consistent, as *ANY* and *NONE* reside within the type hierarchy at the top and bottom, respectively. However, void and void* do not fit into the type hierarchy in C++.

Java defines a *null type,* which is the type of the expression denoted by null. The null type has no name and, to the programmer, null really appears as a special literal, the value of which can be assigned to any variable of a reference type.

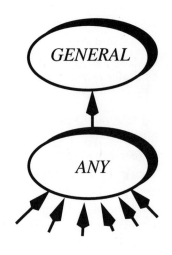

Figure 14-1. Eiffel type hierarchy

Eiffel has class *GENERAL* as the ancestor of *ANY*. Users can add their own all-pervasive features to *ANY*. The Eiffel type hierarchy is shown in figure 14-1.

Eiffel uses the term *routine* for called units of code and distinguishes between two kinds of routine—*procedures* and *functions*. It is recommended practice that only procedures change object state; functions do not. Functions always return a value; that is, they follow the mathematical definition of function that takes a value of one type (the type may be compound, hence multiple arguments) and maps it to a value of another type. The Java hierarchy is shown in figure 14-2.

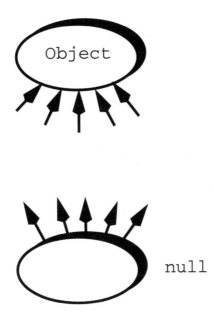

Figure 14-2. Java type hierarchy

The classes `Object` (Java) and *ANY* (Eiffel) define features that are available to all objects. *ANY* is actually an empty class where a project can add global routines, but you cannot do this in Java. *ANY* and `Object` are shown in the next two code listings.

Eiffel
        indexing
             description: "Project-wide universal properties. This class is an ancestor to all developer-written classes. ANY inherits from PLATFORM, itself an heir of GENERAL, and may be customized for individual projects or teams."

class interface
    ANY

feature -- Comparison

    frozen *deep_equal* (*some*: *GENERAL*; *other*: **like** *some*):
                                           BOOLEAN
    frozen *equal* (*some*: *GENERAL*; *other*: **like** *some*): *BOOLEAN*
    is_equal (*other*: **like** *Current*): *BOOLEAN*
    frozen *standard_equal* (*some*: *GENERAL*; *other*: **like** *some*):
                                           BOOLEAN
    frozen *standard_is_equal* (*other*: **like** *Current*): *BOOLEAN*

feature -- Status report

    conforms_to (other: *GENERAL*): *BOOLEAN*
    consistent (*other*: **like** *Current*): *BOOLEAN*
    same_type (*other*: *GENERAL*): *BOOLEAN*

feature -- Duplication

    frozen *clone* (*other*: *GENERAL*): **like** *other*
    copy (*other*: **like** *Current*)
    frozen *deep_clone* (*other*: *GENERAL*): **like** *other*
    frozen *deep_copy* (*other*: **like** *Current*)
    setup (*other*: **like** *Current*)
    frozen *standard_clone* (*other*: *GENERAL*): **like** *other*
    frozen *standard_copy* (*other*: **like** *Current*)

feature -- Basic operations

    frozen *default*: **like** *Current*
    frozen *default_pointer*: *POINTER*
    default_rescue
    frozen *do_nothing*
    frozen *void*: *NONE*

feature -- Output

    io: *STD_FILES*
    out: *STRING*
    print (*some*: *GENERAL*)

frozen *tagged_out*: STRING

invariant

-- from *GENERAL*
reflexive_equality: *standard_is_equal* (*Current*);
reflexive_conformance: *conforms_to* (*Current*);
end -- **class** *ANY*

The Java Object class looks like this.

Java

```
/* * @(#)Object.java 1.40 98/04/22 *
 * Copyright 1994-1997 by Sun Microsystems, Inc.,
 * 901 San Antonio Road, Palo Alto,
 * California,          94303, U.S.A.
 * All rights reserved.
 * * This software is the confidential and
     proprietary information
 * of Sun Microsystems, Inc. ("Confidential
     Information"). You
 * shall not disclose such Confidential Information
     and shall use
 * it only in accordance with the terms of the
     license agreement
 * you entered into with Sun.
 */

package java.lang;
public class Object {
    /**
     * Returns the runtime class of an object.
     *
     * @return   the object of type
       <code>Class</code>
       that represents the
     *           runtime class of the object.
     * @since    JDK1.0
     */

public final native Class getClass();
public native int hashCode();
```

```
    public boolean equals(Object obj);
    protected native Object clone()
                throws CloneNotSupportedException;
    public String toString();
    public final native void notify();
    public final native void notifyAll();
    public final native void wait(long timeout)
                throws InterruptedException;
    public final void wait(long timeout,
                int  nanos) throws InterruptedException;
    public final void wait()
                throws InterruptedException;
    protected void finalize() throws Throwable;
}
```

14.7   NULL vs. 0

Ellemtel recommends that pointers should not be compared to or assigned to NULL, but to 0. Stylistically, NULL would be preferable. It would also allow for environments where null pointers have a value other than 0. [Ellemtel 92]

Stroustrup also comments on the unfortunate properties of NULL.

> Nothing seems to create more heat than a discussion of the proper way to express a pointer that doesn't point to an object, the null pointer. C++ inherited its definition of the null pointer from Classic C [Kernighan, 1978]:
>
>> "A constant expression that evaluates to zero is converted to a pointer, commonly called the null pointer. It is guaranteed that this value will produce a pointer distinguishable from a pointer to any object or function."
>
> The ARM further warns:
>
>> "Note that the null pointer need not be represented by the same bit pattern as the integer 0."
>
> The warning reflects the common misapprehension that if p=0 assigns the null pointer to the pointer p, then the representation of the null pointer must be the same as the integer zero, that is, a bit pattern of all zeros. This is not so. C++ is sufficiently strongly typed that a concept such as the null pointer can be represented in whichever way

[Stroustrup 9 (11.2.3)]

[C++ ARM] (4.6)

the implementation chooses, independently of how that concept is represented in the source text.

No wonder people are confused and there is much heated debate.

[Meyers 92] (Item 25)

Meyers gives us another problem of NULL vs. 0 and overloaded functions

C

```
void f (int x);
void f (char *p);
f (0);    // calls f(int) or f(char)?
```

This calls f(int), but that might not be what you want. Meyers shows that you can play around with different definitions of NULL to get around this, but there is no satisfactory solution. The recommendation in the end is to avoid overloading on numerical and pointer types. This leads to the conclusion that there should be a keyword to denote the pointer value NULL, of pointer type, built into the language and compilers.

In Java, null is a reserved word. Eiffel uses *Void*, the single value of type *NONE*, to indicate no object is referenced.

C++ provides yet another way to write the value zero by using constructors as in this strange example.

C++

```
i = int();  // assign 0 to i
```

14.8 char; signed and unsigned

What is the meaning of +'a', -'b', etc.? There is simply no real-world equivalent. In C char, unsigned char, and signed char yield three distinct types, all occupying 8 bits (although char is not necessarily 8 bits in all implementations). These types are integers rather than characters. The definition is highly platform dependent, and the semantics is nonsensical. Pascal's technique of specifying integer subranges 0..255, -127..+127, -63..+154, and so forth is better.

Java's primitive types are much better specified in order that all implementations will have the same ranges. This does come at the cost of execution efficiency on some platforms, but it ensures portability, an attribute lacking from C's basic types.

14.9 void fn ()

The default return type of a function is `int`. A typeless routine returning nothing should be the default, but this must be specified by `void`. Syntactically no <type> suggests nothing to return. This is an example of where C's syntax is not well matched to the concepts and semantics. What is more, a typed function can be invoked independently of an expression, which is a shorthand way of discarding the returned value, but it compromises type safety. Using a typed function as a void should result in a type error. Indeed in the final C++ standard this was finally changed, and a type specifier is mandatory on functions.

In fact, there should be no such thing as a `void` function. A `void` function is a procedure. Procedures and functions should be distinguished. This distinction belongs to the problem domain. A procedure is a routine that changes the state of its object, but returns no value. A function should, in general, not cause any change to the state of an object, but should merely return some result dependent upon the object's state.

Mathematically, a function is an entity that returns a value of a given type. Procedures are untyped and do not return a value, so it is incorrect to regard procedures as functions. Functions have more in common with variables than procedures. Procedures may have side effects; functions should not cause side effects. These distinctions are useful when considering concurrency.

Stroustrup also voices the opinion that default `int` is bad. He had tried to make the type specifier explicit, but was forced to withdraw by users.

[Stroustrup 9 (2.8.1)]

> I backed out the change. I don't think I had a choice. Allowing that implicit int is the source of many of the annoying problems with C++ grammar today. Note the pressure came from users, not management or arm-chair language experts. Finally, ten years later, the C++ ANSI/ISO standard committee has decided to deprecate implicit int.

[Stroustrup 9 (2.8.1)]

One improvement in Java is that the result type of the method is not optional; that is, you don't get `int` by default. Otherwise, Java does not clean up most of the deficiencies of C. In order to specify a procedure rather than function, Java still requires the `void` specifier. Java does discard the C term function (which was wrongly used anyway), but makes the situation no better by calling both procedures and functions *methods*. Thus there is no clear distinction between procedure and function.

Java also allows you to ignore returned values because a method invocation can be used as an expression statement that discards the value.

[Java 96] (14.7)

14.10 fn ()

We have already seen that C functions are a poor relation of mathematical functions in the section on inlines (chapter 4). C functions expose implementation detail—whether an entity is implemented as a constant, a variable, or a value-returning routine. C functions are different from the mathematical concept of a function. C uses the term *function* to mean parameterized invokable code, which other languages call procedures, subroutines, etc. Java calls them *methods*. Data can be accessed functionally in the mathematical sense, but this differs from insisting that all data be accessed through a C function. Functional access to data really means that data can only be retrieved, not assigned to. Another way to think of functions is as *derived* attributes, that is, attributes that are not stored, but are computed.

Empty parentheses represent the function call operator in C. Even though ( ) looks mathematical, it is semantically equivalent to FORTRAN's CALL, COBOL's PERFORM, and JSR in assembler. The design of these operators was influenced by the underlying machine architectures. The function call operator is low level, machine and execution oriented, and in the how domain. True high-level languages require no such operator; the compiler realizes from the declaration that the entity referenced is a function and automatically generates the machine call operator.

This is the opposite of most UNIX shells, where invocation operators such as run and exec are not needed. One of the nice things about UNIX shells is that the set of in-built commands is extensible. The ability to execute file names as commands extends the command repertoire. This is widely accepted as an elegant and effective convenience. C's ( ) operator introduces the equivalent of a run command into the language.

No invocation operator exists in the problem-oriented domain of high-level languages. This is because the semantics of a function is to return a value of a given type. How this value is computed is unimportant—it could be computed by a routine invocation, by sending a message across a network, by forking an asynchronous process, or by retrieving a precomputed result from a memory location, i.e., a variable.

Languages that have an invocation command or operator have an unnecessary distinction between value-returning routines and constants and variables.

It is trivial for a compiler to provide transparency of view for constant and variable access and function invocation. In ALGOL-style languages, the compiler automatically deduces invocation when it sees a name that was declared as a routine rather than as a variable. The compiler knows that the identifier refers to a routine because the compiler stores much information about an entity. A compiler can check that the programmer uses the entity consistently with the declaration. A compiler can generate correct code, without burdening the programmer with having to use an explicit invocation operator. This enhances flexibility and implementation independence.

Variables and functions should be interchangeable for optimization. ( ) is a good example of how the operator approach of low-level languages, as opposed to the declarative approach of high-level languages, adversely affects flexibility. In C, it is not possible to change a function to a variable without removing all the ( ), or a variable to a function without adding ( ) to all the invocations. This might be spread over many files, and the programmer might not bother with optimization to avoid the tedium of the task. So the ( ) operator reduces flexibility. The ( ) operator is another bookkeeping task imposed on the C programmer. The C++-recommended style is to code superfluous accessor functions to blur the distinction. Pure functional languages such as SML remove the variable/function distinction altogether by not having variables at all.

If you still don't believe me, Meyers is another source for the argument promoting uniform access. He says, first you should be consistent, so that clients of your class don't have to remember whether they are accessing data or a function. Second, he says, you can have more control over the accessibility of data members. [Meyers 92] (item 20)

Third, if you are still not convinced, he brings out the big gun of functional abstraction. That is, if you decide to replace the data member with a computation, you can do that and no clients will have to change. However, you the programmer have to implement this as a matter of coding convention in both Java and C++. Eiffel designs uniform access into the language from the start—a coding convention is not required.

Java has made no improvement here. The visible implementation difference between variables and functions remains.

Eiffel removes this distinction since constants and variables are accessed functionally. A programmer can flexibly change a variable to a function in a class interface and vice versa for optimization or extension without the need for all clients to change their code. Thus, even though changes have been made, the class interface remains unchanged.

Another advantage of Eiffel is that there will be less implementation once you have designed your interface—there is very little to implement, and there is less to go into the equivalent of your `private` or `protected` sections. Consider these examples.

C++
```
class A
{
private:
    int f1;
    char *name;
    ...
public:
    int get_f1();
    void set_f1(int i);
    char *get_name();
    void set_name(char *n);
};
```

In Eiffel no private implementation is needed; you get it for free with the interface definition.

Eiffel

class *A*
feature
    f1: *INTEGER*
    set_f1 (*i*: *INTEGER*)
    name: *STRING*
    set_name (*n*: *STRING*)
end

Such examples explode the myth that Eiffel is more verbose than C and C++. This example shows that Eiffel can be less verbose than C++ where it counts—the programmer has to do less.

C also has pointers to functions. Function pointers are analogous to the call-by-name facility in ALGOL, which was recognized as having pitfalls. Consistent application of the OO paradigm avoids the need for function pointers. Function pointers are commonly used to explicitly set up jump tables. Jump tables are the mechanism behind virtual functions. The design of a program can take advantage of this fact without resorting to explicit jump tables.

Another use is to jump to a function in a table that is indexed by an input character. A `switch` statement that makes what is meant explicit, can provide this mechanism while keeping underlying mechanisms (and possibly optimizations) transparent. C++ allows function pointers to member functions to be stored in tables (via the . * and ->* operators).

14.11 fn (void)

In C f() means the function f can take any number of arguments of any type without type check. ANSI C has adopted f(void) to mean a function that has no arguments. Kernighan and Ritchie say of this: "Some syntactic ugliness was required for the sake of compatibility, namely void as an implicit marker of new-style functions without parameters." C++ sensibly differs from this in that f() now means a function that has no arguments.

[K&R 88]

[Stroustrup 9‹

14.12 return

In C, you can use return without a value in a function that expects a return value.

```
int return_test ()
{
    return;
}
```
C

Java and C++ use the same return mechanism as C, but do not allow the above, insisting that, if the function is typed other than void, the return must be an expression of the same type as the function. There is still a problem in C++ though, as you can exit the function by merely getting to the end without a return. Thus

```
int return_test ()
{
}
```
C

is actually equivalent to the first example. Java does not allow this since it insists on a return on all code paths through a typed method.

ALGOL-style languages commonly have no return statement at all. This is true of ALGOL itself, Pascal, and Eiffel. In order to return a value from typed routines, ALGOL and Pascal assign a value to a variable of the same name as the function. For example, in ALGOL syntax

```
integer procedure twice (n);
    value n; integer n;
```
ALGOL

```
    begin
        twice := n * 2;
    end twice;
```

ALGOL gives variables default values, usually zero. Pascal, however, does not initialize, but rather has an uninitialized flag. Thus, if the function variable is never assigned to, *uninitialized* is returned, which immediately results in an error. The function variable scheme has another problem; you cannot read the value back out of the variable. In fact, if you try, you can accidentally get recursion

ALGOL
```
    integer procedure dont_read;
    begin
        integer x;
        x := dont_read + 2;
    end dont_read;
```

Eiffel solves this problem by clearly separating the name of a function, which you invoke, from its return value, which is like a variable. Each function gets a variable—*Result*—declared, which is the same type as the function.

Eiffel

    twice (*n*: *INTEGER*): *INTEGER* **is**
        do
            Result := *n* * 2;
        end

If *Result* is not assigned in any execution of the function, the default value of zero or *Void* is returned. Thus you must be careful that this is the effect you want

Eiffel

    twice (*n*: *INTEGER*): *INTEGER* **is**
        do
            ...
        end

returns the default of zero.

[Java 96]
(14.15)
    Java shows us that the `return` statement has some problems. Firstly, if you are returning an expression, evaluating the expression may itself cause an exception. If a `return` is executed in a `try` block with a `finally` clause, the

`finally` clause is executed before the `return` completes. If the `finally` clause completes abruptly, then the `return` statement can be disrupted.

Eiffel has no return so does not have these problems.

14.13 Switch Statements

A well-known trap in C is that `case` blocks in `switch` statements fall through unless you explicitly put in a `break` statement. This feature of C is very rarely useful (in terms of doing less work), and, if it is to be used, you must order the case blocks very carefully. If it is necessary that code in a following case block is executed, it is better structuring to put the code in a routine and to execute that routine from each case block where it is needed. In fact, this scheme is much more flexible.

Unfortunately, Java has not made any improvement here. Eiffel's **inspect** instruction avoids the problem since it doesn't fall through. An example of `switch` in C-, C++-, and Java-like syntax is

```
n = 1;                                              C
                                                    C++
switch (n)                                          Java
{
    case 1: printf ("one ");
    case 2: printf ("two ");
    case 3: printf ("three ");
}
```

The result is

```
one two three
```

The equivalent in Eiffel is

$n := 1$ *Eiffel*

inspect
    n

       when 1 **then**
          io.put_string ("one ")
       when 2 **then**
          io.put_string ("two ")
       when 3 **then**
          io.put_string ("three ")
       end

The result is

```
one
```

14.14   Metadata in Strings

The implementation of strings in C mixes metadata with data. Metadata is information about an object, but it is not part of the data itself. Examples of metadata are address, size, and type information. Such metadata is often referred to as data descriptors and can be kept independent of the data, with the advantage that the programmer cannot mistakenly corrupt the metadata.

In C strings, metadata about where strings terminate is stored in the string data as a terminating null byte. This means that the distinction between data and metadata is lost. The value chosen as the terminator cannot occur in the data itself. Since inserting a null is often the responsibility of the programmer and not the run-time environment, there is the potential for more undetected inconsistencies resulting in obscure failures.

A common alternative is to store a length byte in a fixed location preceding the string as Pascal does. The advantage is that the length of a string is easily obtained without having to count the number of elements up to the terminating null, which gives an erroneous result anyway, as `sizeof("trick")` = 6.

Similarly

C
```
char trick [5] = "trick";
```

is an error.

Another advantage of Pascal-style strings is that 0 is a valid value in a string. This implementation is hidden from the programmer, and other methods could be used without the programmer having to change the program. C's null terminator makes the implementation visible to the programmer.

Java's strings are first-class objects. You can't determine the length of a string by scanning for a null, you must use the *string.length* method (function). Eiffel *STRING*s are also first-class objects.

14.15 ++, --

The increment and decrement operators ++ and -- are often used as an example that C was designed as a high-level assembler for Digital Equipment's (DEC) PDP machines. These operators certainly match the auto-increment and auto-decrement addressing modes of the PDP-11. The range of PDP machines had many different architectures. The increment and decrement operators were actually implemented in B, the predecessor to C (as shown in figure 2-1), and B was developed on a PDP-7, which did not have such addressing modes. UNIX itself was developed on this machine, which was a disused machine at AT&T until Dennis Ritchie and Ken Thompson found a use for it.

Increment and decrement provide a shorthand, but are an unnecessary convenience. There are no less than four ways to perform the same thing.

```
a = a + 1                                                    C
a += 1                                                       C++
a++                                                          Java
++a
```

For full generality, only the first form is required. a++ is the postfix form and ++a the prefix form, both of which can be used in the context of another expression. Thus several updates can be performed in one expression. This is a very powerful and convenient feature, but it introduces side effects into an expression that sometimes have surprising effects and can lead to program errors. The shorthand += and -= are more powerful because values other than 1 can increment the variable. For example

```
i = v[i++];  // the value of 'i' is undefined
```
[C++ ARM] (Chapter 5)

The C++ ARM points out that compilers should detect such cases, but the exact interpretation appears to be left to the implementation, which contributes to non- [C++ ARM]

portability. If this can't be defined for a sequential processor, then it is even worse for a concurrent environment.

If it is believed that a multiplicity of operators is required to produce more optimal code, then it should be pointed out that code generators, especially for expressions, can produce the best code for a target architecture. A plethora of operators complicates the task of an optimizer. A compiler can optimize well beyond what a programmer can do. An optimizing compiler will analyze the surrounding code, and, if an entity is used several times in a local scope, it will keep the value of that entity handy locally at the top of a stack or in a register rather than retrieve it from slow main memory several times. The nature of such optimizations depends on the machine's architecture, which a programmer should not need to be aware of. Open systems demand that programs can be ported among diverse architectures and environments, very different from the original machine, and not only run, but run efficiently. Optimizers work best with simple, well-defined languages.

In fact constructs such as

C
```
while (*s1++ = *s2++);
```

might look optimal to C programmers, but they are the antithesis of efficiency. Such constructs preclude compiler optimization for processors with specific string-handling instructions. A simple assignment is better for strings because it will allow the compiler to generate optimal code for different target platforms. In the OO case, a simple assignment will probably assign a reference only to the original string, so the equivalent of our sample loop is *copy*.

Eiffel $s1 := s2.copy$

Copy is completely general and applicable to all entities. Thus the programmer no longer needs to learn such idioms as our sample loop for each different type. Compilers can still optimize for different types—if the target processor does not have string instructions, then the compiler should be responsible for generating our sample loop code, rather than requiring the programmer to write such low-level constructs.

Our loop construct for string copying is also not safe, since there is no check that the destination does not overflow—again an undetected inconsistency that could lead to obscure failures. Our code example also makes explicit the underlying C implementation of strings that are null terminated. Such examples show why C cannot be regarded as a high-level language, but rather as a high-level assembler.

Stroustrup gives a long derivation of why our sample loop construct is good, but also why it might be obscure to non-C programmers. However, he makes no mention of the problem of the destination overflowing. After the long defense of the construct, Stroustrup advises against using it in favor of using `strcpy`, because this will be optimized for your particular machine and will probably even be inlined.

[Stroustrup 9 (6.2.5)]

He probably wanted to advise against such machine-oriented idioms all along, but had to appease the anger of C advocates by patronizing them about how good the idiom was. I agree that it is a very good machine-oriented idiom, but, as a machine-oriented idiom, it has no place in a high-level language except as compiler output, which should also generate a check to make sure the destination won't overflow. A compiler should have machine-oriented idioms built in to its code generator, hiding them from the programmer and generating them where applicable.

Memory update is a problematic, but necessary part of programming. A language should provide it in a consistent and expected way. Many languages recognize that memory update is problematic, and thus typically provide only the assignment operator as a sufficient update mechanism. (Many languages have block memory copies as well, but assignment can also provide block copy.) Furthermore, many languages avoid side effects by limiting updates to only one per statement. C provides too many ways to update memory. These add nothing to the generality of the language, while increasing the opportunity for error and complicating automatic optimization. Restrictive practices are justifiable in order to accomplish correctly functioning and efficient software.

Java retains the ++ and -- operators. However, with the removal of pointers and the addition of a decent string class, they are less necessary for idioms such as string and array manipulation. It is not clear whether they could cause side effects and subsequent problems as in C.

Eiffel has no such operators. They would merely be an unnecessary shorthand in Eiffel.

14.16 Assignment Operator

Using the mathematical equality symbol for the assignment operator is a poor choice of symbols; assignment is not equality (= != =). Designers of ALGOL-style languages realized assignment and equality were semantically different and so took the care to distinguish between them, using = only in the sense of mathematical equality assertion. In C the confusion of notation leads to error, since it is easy to mistakenly use = (assignment) where == (equality) is intended.

The difference in semantics between mathematical equality and assignment can easily be shown because equality allows you to make statements such as

expression = expression

An example of such being

$a + b = c + d$

This form is also familiar to programmers as boolean expressions, but is nonsensical for assignments

$a + b \leftarrow c + d$

(using $\leftarrow$ to mean assignment). Now the difference between mathematical equality and assignment becomes apparent: assignment stores a value into a memory location.

Yet another difference is that

$a = b$

and

$b = a$

are equivalent expressions, whereas

$a \leftarrow b$

and

$b \leftarrow a$

certainly are not.

This leads to a more general criticism of C, in that it has a pseudomathematical appearance. But C is not very mathematical at all, as = does not represent equality, and C functions are not really functions. Few people are proficient at interpreting mathematical theorems, most passing over such sections in text, making the assumption that the mathematics proves the surrounding text. The pseudomathematical appearance of C is difficult to read, while lacking the semantic consistency and precision of mathematical notation. One of the keys of reusability is readability.

Java also uses the = symbol to mean assignment, so Java is not an improvement over C. However, the = vs. == confusion has been improved because in the syntax

```
if ( Expression ) Statement
```
Java

the Expression must have type boolean, or a compile-time error occurs.

Eiffel makes the clear distinction between the assignment operator and mathematical equality, choosing the := symbol for assignment and = for mathematical equality.

14.17 Assignment Expressions

Aside from the plain vanilla assignment, C, C++, and Java have a family of assignment operators

```
=    *=    /=    %=    +=    -=    <<=    >>=    &=    ^=    |=
```

These are merely a shorthand expression meaning "left-hand side becomes itself <operator> <expression>"; for example, "itself plus <expression>," etc. Eiffel has only the := assignment, which is sufficient. In good programming, assignment should be used sparingly; functional programming has no assignment at all. The "left-hand side becomes itself <op> <exp>" form is useful only in a small percentage of actual assignments. Thus having so many assignment operators seems like overkill, even when one admits that they are an occasional handy notation convenience. Then when you consider that the major use for these is to increment or decrement a loop control variable

Assignment Expressions

C
C++
Java

```
i = i + 1;
i += 1;
```

but in C will normally be

C
C++
Java

```
i++;
```

It has been suggested that there should also be &&= and ||= operators. These assignment operators certainly provide a good shorthand in C, where the left hand side of the assignment can be a complex path

C

```
myRec.arrayField [otherRec.someIndex] += 1;
```

is obviously more convenient than

C

```
myRec.arrayField [otherRec.someIndex] =
        myRec.arrayField [otherRec.someIndex] + 1;
```

Eiffel lacks such shortcut assignment operators, but the need isn't as pressing, as the left-hand side can refer only to a field in the current class—you cannot assign to fields in external objects and therefore cannot have long paths as targets of assignments.

ALGOL has another form of this convenience that does not need a plethora of operators

ALGOL

```
<lhs> := * <operator> <expression>
```

where the * stands for "itself" and occurs in the natural place in the expression where you would repeat the lhs identifier. The only small niggle with this form is that * is also the multiplication operator; however, no ambiguity occurs, because the multiplication operator cannot appear as the first element in an expression—that is, as a unary operator—as can + and -.

We should note at this point that the operators >=, <=, !=, and == are not assignment operators, despite their syntactic similarity.

14.18 Defines

The define declaration

    #define d(<parameters>)   C

has a different effect than

    #define d (<parameters>)   C

The second form defines d as (<parameters>). Extra white space between tokens should not affect semantics of constructs.

#defines are poorly integrated with the language. The #define must be in column 1, and is not subject to scope rules. Defines can lead to obscure errors because the preprocessor does not detect them, but leaves them for the compiler. Programmers must be familiar with the particular preprocessor implementation on their systems, because preprocessor implementations are different, particularly between Classic C and ANSI C.

#define also exhibits a multiple update problem.

```
#include <stdio.h>                                                   C
#include <string.h>

#define dfn(x,y)  ((x)<(y)?(x)(y))

main ()
{
    int i, j, k;

    k = dfn (i++, j);

    printf ("i = %d j = %d k = %d\n", i, j, k);

    i = 0;  j = -1;
    k = dfn (i++, j);

    printf ("i = %d j = %d k = %d\n", i, j, k);

    i = 0;  j = 5;
```

```
            k = dfn (i++, j);

            printf ("i = %d j = %d k = %d\n", i, j, k);
    }
```

The results are

```
    i = 1       j = 0       k = 0
    i = 1       j = -1      k = -1
    i = 2       j = 5       k = 1
```

This is even worse if the actual parameter you pass is a function that updates other variables. All the variables will be updated the number of times the formal argument appears in the body of the define.

C++ at least reduces the need for defines by having inline functions. We discussed the problems with inlines in chapter 4.

Java and Eiffel have no such preprocessing facilities. Where #defines are used as cheap functions, i.e., the code of the define is expanded inline in the invoking code, Eiffel and Java expand inline routines that meet certain criteria, without the side effects of #define.

C #defines also have another ugly syntax feature, in that they do not split across lines without adding the \ line continuation character:

C

```
    #define dfn(x,y) \
        xx = x; \
        yy = y
```

These syntactic problems with defines are fixed in Unisys A Series ALGOL, where defines are better integrated with the language

ALGOL
(A Series)

```
    define
        one = 1 #,
        two = 2 #,
        three = 3 #,

        dfn (x, y) =
            xx = x;
            yy = y#;
```

#defines have often been used to provide a form of unrestricted genericity. In languages where genericity and templates are provided, this use for #defines disappears. With this form of define, along with another form in A Series ALGOL called compile-time defines for even more sophisticated compiler control, you can almost invent your own language. Thus it cannot be denied that defines are very powerful and often extremely useful. An example of how defines can be used for templates is

ALGOL
(A Series)

```
define
    declare_twice (r, t) =
        t procedure r (n);
            value n; t n;
        begin
            r := n * 2;
        end #;

    declare_twice (integer_twice, integer);
    declare_twice (real_twice, real);
    declare_twice (double_twice, double);
```

Even though these are a much nicer form of define than C's defines, by using appropriate language constructs you can mostly do without defines; you can get benefits from compiler checks, which defines can often subvert. Stroustrup says he would like to see the preprocessor abolished. "The character and file orientation of the preprocessor is fundamentally at odds with a programming language designed around the notions of scopes, types, and interfaces." [Stroustrup 94] (18.1)

14.19 Case Sensitivity

Now we come to one of those trivial issues that stirs up a lot of passion—case sensitivity. If you passionately feel that languages should be case sensitive, I recommend you skip this section.

It is good to adopt typographic conventions for names—this makes a program more readable, but should not affect semantics. Distinguishing between upper- and lowercase in names can cause confusion, which leads to errors and systems that are difficult to maintain and modify. Case distinction is based on the implementation paradigm of how character codes work. Why do we have names? To give entities identity, and to help us remember that identity. Case distinction introduces another form of overloading, the disambiguating mechanism being the underlying character codes. This undermines the fundamental purpose of names.

Case distinction makes names harder to remember, so it is contrary to the purpose of a memory aid. Remembering command mnemonics or file names is difficult enough, let alone the exact letter case. Your brain remembers the **sound** *fred*, not the characters used in spelling. In a case-sensitive system, you must remember the letter case, whether it was fred, Fred, or fRed, greatly complicating the memory process. If you want fRed to be read "f red," then it is probably better to spell the identifier f_red. As an aside, you might notice that this introduces the unpronounced underscore character in names where spaces would naturally go. Consider this identifier

usingUnderscoresInLongNamesMakes_the_names_easier_to_read

Some Java programmers have pointed out that a good style in this language is to name types beginning with an uppercase letter, as in Fred, but you should be able to name a variable of type as fred. This rather neat style is not in fact enabled by case distinction—it is enabled by the fact that the type name and the variable name are in distinct namespaces and are therefore not confused. Eiffel gives us proof of this, as Eiffel is a case-insensitive language, and yet you can declare variables to be the same name as classes.

Names are easier to remember than addresses. If we did not have names, we would have to retrieve files by addresses, access all machines on the Internet by their TCP address instead of host name, or call people by their social security number.

Case distinction is a poor user interface in interactive systems, because it adds an extra motion to continually use the shift key, slowing typing speed. Case sensitivity is one of the worst features of UNIX shell interfaces.

Consider the paradigm of letters and words. Words are spelled by assembling letters in a certain order. There are 26 distinct letters. With the addition of digits 0 to 9 and the underscore character, we have a complete lexical definition for identifiers. Letters can be written in a number of styles. They can be bold, italic, or upper- or lowercase. Such typographic representations, however, do not change the meaning of a word. Thus, if we write ALGOL, Algol, algol, **Algol**, or, *Algol*, we recognize the word to represent a computer language (or if you are an astronomer, a star). The case or type style of the letters does not change the semantics.

Case distinction is based on the low-level paradigm of character codes, such as ASCII used internally in the computer. This weakens the purpose of using names to replace addresses, as names are reduced to a string of character codes.

Case distinction also contributes to errors, introducing ambiguity, which as we have mentioned, weakens the purpose of names because identity is lost. As every programmer will have experienced, one-character errors are more difficult to find than you might think. For example, if an identifier is declared Fred, another one can be declared fred; these two identifiers can easily be mistyped and confused.

We are generally poor proofreaders. The psychological reason for this is the the brain tends to straighten out errors for our perception automatically. The human brain is an excellent instrument for working out what was intended, even in the presence of radical error. (This makes us good at difficult tasks like speech recognition.) Programmers must use their powers of concentration to override the natural tendency of the brain.

Case distinction adds cognitive difficulty. Good language design takes into account such psychological considerations in these small but important details, being designed toward the way humans work, not the way computers work. Such considerations of cognitive science make a big difference in the effectiveness of people, but they do not have any impact at all on the efficiency of code generated for the computer. What is more important, people or computers? With C the answer is often computers, since case distinction saves a few compiler processor cycles.

Case distinction provides a form of name overloading that is a double-edged sword because it leads to ambiguity, confusion, and error. Name overloading, as we suggested in chapter 5, should be provided only in controlled and expected ways, where overloading provides a useful function such as module independence or polymorphism. Where a name is overloaded in the same scope, the compiler should report an error.

An example of name overloading error is

```
class obj                                                    C++
{
    int Entry;

    void set_entry (int entry)
    {
        entry = Entry;
    }
}
```

If you have not spotted the error here, what does the example mean?

A common practice in C is to represent constants in uppercase. This is actually bad practice because a calling programmer should invoke a constant as a function that returns a value and so not use case to distinguish constants. The calling programmer does not need to know whether a class has implemented a feature as a constant, a variable, or a value-returning routine. This means that the class is free to change the implementation of the feature later, without having to bother all programmers to change the case of all occurrences of the identifier in order to follow some style rule.

In Java, Unicode adds another dimension. Java uses Unicode instead of ASCII. The typographic form a and a could be different identifiers if one represents LATIN small letter a and the other CYRILLIC small letter a, so the situation is even more complicated. Unicode does have one nice feature however—mathematical symbols can be used for identifiers. You can use the symbol π as the semiotic representation of the mathematical ratio of a circle's circumference to its diameter instead of `pi`. One implementation problem with this is that most Java programs will be written in ASCII because that is what most editors handle.

In Eiffel all words are case insensitive.

Some people argue that case sensitivity forces programmers to be consistent in style—in other words, if an identifier is declared as `fRed`, it must be represented this way when it is referenced; `fred`, even though the spelling is the same, is unacceptable. Case-insensitive languages could also enforce such consistency. However, most programmers would find this overfinicky because inconsistency would not lead to any error. On the other hand, because fred and fRed can declare two different identifiers in the same scope, this can lead to error, meaning that case insensitivity is to be preferred.

A very common argument in favor of case sensitivity is that it has a precedence in some natural languages such as German, where nouns are written with a capital letter to distinguish them from verbs spelled the same way. However, this argument is entirely invalid—many things in programming languages do not follow natural language because the precedences set in natural language are imprecise.

[Stroustrup 97] (4.9.3) A last word from Stroustrup: "It is unwise to choose names that differ only by capitalization."

14.20 Semicolons

This section also discusses another trivial issue that many feel passionate about disproportionate to its importance. You can also skip this section if you wish.
[Stroustrup 94] (14.1) Stroustrup makes a very good observation on such debates: "Curiously enough, the volume of interest and public debate is often inversely proportional to the importance of a feature. The reason is that it is much easier to have a firm opinion on a minor feature than on a major one; minor features fit directly into the current state of affairs, whereas major ones – by definition – do not."

I am not overly concerned whether the semicolon is defined as a terminator or a separator. Arguments that languages defining the semicolon as a terminator are superior to those defining it as a separator are, however, baseless. Many argue vehemently that C's semicolons being terminators are superior to Pascal's separators. However, C++'s use of semicolons has some inconsistencies, particularly in regard to declarations since all declarations are terminated by semicolons, except for functions and namespaces, which do not need a semicolon because they are terminated by a final brace.

The semicolon as separator is really quite logical, viewing the semicolon as a statement sequencing or concatenation operator. It is therefore a binary operator, requiring both a left- and a right-hand side. Some people claim to find this concept difficult to understand, but if we consider it in the context of a mathematical expression, it would be silly to expect that an addition be written as

```
a + b +
```

Another way to look at a separator is to consider the structure of a program. A program is a list of elements. The executable part of a program is a list of sequentially executed instructions. Elements in a list must be separated, and the semicolon is syntax to separate elements in a list. The semicolon is therefore part of the syntax of the list, not part of the syntax of the individual instructions. Languages such as FORTRAN separate instructions by requiring that they be placed on different lines or cards. If an instruction overflows a line, a continuation character is required, like the backslash in C. Syntactically well-defined languages do not require continuation characters because line breaks are unimportant and have no effect on semantics. Languages should have very regular grammars so that the semicolon could be an entirely optional typographic separator.

In natural language both the comma and semicolon are separators; only the full stop (period) is a terminator. If the comma were an expression terminator rather than a separator, function invocations would look like

```
fn (a, b+c, d, e,);
```

It is often argued that the semicolon as separator leads to irregularities. C's handling of the grammar of semicolons leads to an irregularity in if/elses.

```
if (condition)
    statement1; /* Semicolon required */
else
```

C

```
        statement2;
if (condition)
{
    statement1;
} /* Semicolon must be omitted */
else
    statement2;
```

This is an irregularity, as a parser will reduce both if statements to the grammatical form

```
"if" <condition> <statement>
"else" <statement>
```

In fact, why do conditions in C's if and while statements have to have parentheses around them? Also, why must a semicolon follow the closing brace of a class, but not the closing brace of a function?

Java, being C based, retains the semicolon as a terminator. Eiffel views the semicolon as a separator, but has one advantage—semicolons are optional. The semicolon can be used to visually emphasize the separation between two commands, for example, where two commands are placed on one line.

14.21 Comments

GWS 94]   The following example comes from [GWS 94]

C
```
main ()
{
    int *i, *j;
    int k;

    k = *i/*j;
}
```

as they point out what a good character combination /* is for delimiting comments.

14.22 Cpaghe++i

There are three kinds of *spaghetti* that occur in programs—gotos, globals, and pointers. Spaghetti is the introduction of dependencies between many parts of a program. While dependencies are necessary, the overuse of them complicates programs and makes them susceptible to certain kinds of error. Furthermore, dependency overuse makes a program more difficult to maintain. This is why most research efforts have concentrated on reducing the number of dependencies in programs. We have already noted the problems with pointers and globals—we reiterate them quickly here to emphasize that the problem is a problem of dependency.

Cpaghe++i Gotos

Most people know about spaghetti *code* that is present in programs that use gotos in an undisciplined fashion. As Knuth has pointed out, it is entirely possible to produce well-structured programs with gotos. The *well-tempered* goto emulates high-level structured statements such as conditionals, loops, and switch or case statements in higher-level languages.

Where a language provides the correct control structures and the programmer programs into that paradigm, gotos are not needed. The reverse argument could also be made if gotos cover all uses of high-level control structures and, even more, if we ask why we should have the high-level control structures at all. Why not just use gotos? The problem with gotos is that they are *too* powerful. They are too powerful in the same way assembler language is too powerful.

You can do everything with assembler or gotos, but it takes more work, and the result is often less than structured, difficult to understand, and unmaintainable. The more work you do, the less efficient you are. It is not working harder that makes you more efficient, it is working smarter. I'm a great fan of laziness!

Consider what you must do to construct a loop with gotos. You must declare a label, then place the label and the goto somewhere; you also have to think about identifiers for labels that are nonambiguous. For label identifiers, some languages use names, others use numbers. With a high-level loop construct, labels are implicit, meaning the programmer does not have this extra bookkeeping overhead. With gotos making changes becomes a lot more difficult, because you must create new labels, move them around, and delete others.

One legitimate use for gotos is to avoid overly complex nesting. Complex nesting usually occurs where there are many checks that result in multiply nesting **if**...**then**s, which often arise because of error checking. Proponents of gotos legitimately defend them for this situation. However, where the control structures are right, even this use of gotos is not needed.

Both Java and Eiffel abandon gotos. Java provides an extension to control structures which allows control structures to be named, and multilevel break and continue statements can be used to jump to an outer-level conditional or loop.

In Eiffel the philosophy is to program in sufficiently small atomic routines, so that multilevel control structures are avoided. Thus Eiffel's solution to the nesting problem is integrated with its routine mechanism and the way programmers are expected to use routines. In OO programming, it is good practice to keep routines small, with only one operation in a routine, as this enhances the possibility of reuse. Some programmers will object to small routines because there is an overhead to routine calls, particularly in register-based machines, where environments and registers must be saved. However, an Eiffel compiler will automatically inline small, nonpolymorphic routines.

The high-level-language concept that removes the need for gotos altogether for error checking is exception handling. In this mechanism, the error condition triggers an exception. When an exception is raised, a search for its handler occurs. This search progresses down the run-time stack until an embedded exception handler is found. In Eiffel, exception handlers are specified in **rescue** clauses. Note that, in an environment where exceptions can interrupt the flow of the code, garbage collection is even more important; in a system with manual memory management, it is very difficult to determine where to clean up and which objects to dispose of.

If exception raising and handling sounds expensive, you should realize that it often works out to be cheaper in the long run. Most of the time, the code runs normally, and an exception being raised *is* the *exception*. Only then is the stack search for the handler performed. Consider, for example, divide by zero—in most systems, the processor detects this error and raises an exception. If you don't have exception handling, you must test that the divisor is not zero before a divide operation. With exception handling, you assume that the division will work in most cases and so do not have to test. If the divisor is zero, you simply clean up in the exception handler. Only if there is no exception handler does the software fail, but this will happen in only a small minority of cases, thereby making exception handling the cheaper strategy.

Goto has a legitimate use when you are translating from one language to another. Very few languages' control structures match each other exactly, and in this case gotos provide sufficiently low-level control to emulate any control structure. While they might be used by an automatic source code generator, they are not necessary for source-level programming.

The bottom line is that, with the common high-level language constructs of **if…then**, loops, and cases, you can avoid *most* uses of goto. Add a high-level construct for exception handling, and you can avoid gotos altogether.

Cpaghe++i Globals

The second kind of spaghetti is globals. Where two or more objects access the same set of globals, interdependencies arise between those objects. This makes it far more difficult to determine the correctness of a program—even more so in concurrent environments. These interdependencies should be viewed as strands of spaghetti worming their way through a system—they are going to make maintenance, extension, and reuse difficult in the future.

Globals can be abandoned. Objects are to globals as control structures are to gotos.

Again Java and Eiffel abandon globals and thus ease the problems of maintenance, extension, and reuse. Note that I use the word *ease*, not *solve*. Even though Java and Eiffel make significant improvements, there are no silver bullets to solve the problems involved in programming.

Cpaghe++i Pointers

The third kind of spaghetti is pointers. The problems with pointer-based programming are well known. The kind of spaghetti you get worming through the system is undisciplined pointers pointing to other elements, bypassing the whole concept of interfaces and OO. Pointers introduce dependencies that would not be there otherwise. Furthermore, this can of worms results in dangling references and memory leaks. To do away with the problems of pointers, garbage collection is necessary. To implement good garbage collection, pointers must be abandoned. C++ is caught in this catch-22.

Neither Eiffel nor Java have pointers. Both have garbage collection built in from scratch.

Bibliography

[ter 69]

It is the custom to ornament every scientific work with a bibliography, a list of earlier books on the same subject. The aim may be to test the reader's competence by laying out for him an awe-inspiring course of reading; it may be to prove the author's competence by showing the mountain of dross he has sorted to win one nugget of truth.

[Marco and Lister 87]

This quote is from the milestone book on organizational incompetence, *The Peter Principle*. Perhaps I can appease Dr. Peter for my own incompetence by including his book here. I don't recommend reading all the books in this bibliography, but *The Peter Principle* is well worth the effort, along with De Marco and Lister's *Peopleware: Productive Projects and Teams*.

[Adams 96]
SCOTT ADAMS *The Dilbert Principle*, Harper Collins, New York, 1996.

[Aho 92]
ALFRED V. AHO and JEFFREY D. ULLMAN *Foundations of Computer Science*, Computer Science Press, New York, 1992.

[Bach 97]
JAMES BACH, ST LABS "The Hard Road from Methods to Practice," *IEEE Computer*, Volume 30, Number 2, February 1997.

[Ben-Ari 90]
   M. BEN-ARI *Principles of Concurrent and Distributed Processing*, Prentice Hall, Upper Saddle River, New Jersey, 1990.

[BOSW 98]
   GILAD BRACHA, MARTIN ODERSKY, DAVID STOUTAMIRE, PHILIP WADLER "Making the Future Safe for the Past: Adding Genericity to the Java Programming Language," *OOPSLA 98 Conference Proceedings ACM SIGPLAN Notices*, Volume 33, Number 10, October 1998.

[Bracha and Cook 90]
   GILAD BRACHA and WILLIAM COOK "Mixin-based Inheritance," *ECOOP/OOPSLA Proceedings ACM SIGPLAN Notices*, Volume 25, Number 10, October 1990.

[Brooks 95]
   FREDERICK P. BROOKS *The Mythical Man-Month*, 20th Anniversary Edition, Addison-Wesley, Reading, Massachusetts, 1995.

[Brown 98]
   ALAN W. BROWN and KURT C. WALLNAU "The Current State of CBSE," *IEEE Software*, Volume 15, Number 5, September/October 1998.

[Bruce 96]
   KIM B. BRUCE "Progress in Programming Languages," *ACM Computing Surveys*, Volume 28, Number 1, March 1996.

[C++ ARM]
   MARGARET A. ELLIS and BJARNE STROUSTRUP *The Annotated C++ Reference Manual*, AT&T Bell Telephone Laboratories, Murray Hill, New Jersey, 1990.

[Cardelli 88]
   LUCA CARDELLI *"A Semantics of Multiple Inheritance," Information and Computation*, Volume 76, 1988, 138–164.

[Cardelli 93]
   LUCA CARDELLI "Typeful Programming," *SRC Research Report* 45, May 24, 1989. Revised January 1, 1993.

[Cardelli 96]
   LUCA CARDELLI *A Theory of Objects*, Springer Verlag, New York, 1996.

[Cardelli 97]
   LUCA CARDELLI "Type Systems," in *Handbook of Computer Science and Engineering*, CRC Press, 1997.

[Cartwright and Steele 98]
ROBERT CARTWRIGHT and GUY L. STEELE JR "Compatible Genericity with Run-time Types for the Java Programming Language," *OOPSLA Proceedings SIGPLAN Notices*, Volume 33, Number 10, October 1998.

[Castagna 97]
GIUSEPPE CASTAGNA "Covariance and Contravariance: Conflict without a Cause," in *Object-Oriented Programming: A Unified Foundation*, Birkhäuser, Boston, Massachusetts, 1997.

[CD2 96]
X3J16 COMMITTEE *C++ International Standard Committee Draft 2, Registered December1996*, ISO SC22/WG21 ANSI X3J16, December 1996.

[Cline]
MARSHALL CLINE *C++: Frequently Asked Questions*, comp.lang.c++ newsgroup.

[CPN 98]
DAVID CLARKE, JOHN POTTER, and JAMES NOBLE "Ownership Types for Flexible Alias Protection," *OOPSLA 98 Conference Proceedings ACM SIGPLAN Notices*, Volume 33, Number 10, October 1998.

[DDH 72]
O. -J. DAHL, E. W. DIJKSTRA, and C. A. R. HOARE *Structured Programming*, Academic Press, New York, 1972.

[DeMarco and Lister 87]
TOM DEMARCO and TIMOTHY LISTER, *Peopleware: Productive Projects and Teams*, Dorset House, New York, 1987.

[Deming 82]
W. EDWARDS DEMING *Out of the Crisis*, Cambridge University Press, Cambridge, 1982.

[Digre 98]
TOM DIGRE "Business Object Component Architecture," *IEEE Software*, Volume 15, Number 5, September/October 1998.

[Dijkstra 76]
E. W. DIJKSTRA *A Discipline of Programming*, Prentice Hall, Englewood Cliffs, New Jersey, 1976.

[Ege 96]
STUART HIRSHFIELD and RAIMUND K. EGE "Object-Oriented Programming," *ACM Computing Surveys*, Volume 28, Number 1, March 1996.

[Ellemtel 92]

Programming in C++ Rules and Recommendations, Ellemtel Telecommunication Systems Laboratories, Sweden, 1992.

[Emery 86]

GLYN EMERY *BCPL and C*, Blackwell Scientific Publications 1986.

[Flanagan 96]

DAVID FLANAGAN *Java in a Nutshell*, O'Reilly & Associates, Sebastopol, California, 1996.

[Flew 89]

ANTONY FLEW *An Introduction to Western Philosophy*, Thames and Hudson, London, 1989.

[GWS 94]

SIMSON GARFINKEL, DANIEL WEISS, and STEVEN STRASSMANN *The Unix-Hater's Handbook*, IDG Books Worldwide Inc., Foster City California, 1994.

[Hext 90]

J. B. HEXT *Programming Structures: Machines and Programs,* Volume I, Prentice Hall of Australia, Sydney, 1990.

[Hoare 89]

C. A. R. HOARE *Hints on Programming Language Design.* In [Hoare and Jones 89].

[Hoare and Jones 89]

C. A. R. HOARE and C. B. JONES (editors) *Essays in Computer Science.* Prentice Hall, Upper Saddle River, New Jersey, 1989.

[Ince 92]

D. C. INCE "Arrays and Pointers Considered Harmful," *ACM SIGPLAN Notices*, January 1992.

[Java 96]

JAMES GOSLING, BILL JOY, and GUY STEELE, *The Java Language Specification*, Addison-Wesley, Reading, Massachusetts, 1996.

[Jones and Lins 96]

RICHARD JONES and RAFAEL LINS, *Garbage Collection Algorithms for Automatic Dynamic Memory Management*, John Wiley and Sons, Chichester, West Sussex, 1996.

[JVM 97]

TIM LINDHOLM and FRANK YELLIN, *The Java Virtual Machine Specification*, Addison-Wesley, Reading, Massachusetts, 1997.

[K&R 88]

BRIAN W. KERNIGHAN and DENNIS M. RITCHIE, *The C Programming Language*, Prentice Hall, Englewood Cliffs, New Jersey 1988.

[Kilov and Ross 94]

HAIM KILOV and JAMES ROSS, *Information Modelling: An Object-Oriented Approach*, Prentice Hall, Englewood Cliffs, New Jersey, 1994.

[Latzko and Saunders 95]

WILLIAM J. LATZKO and DAVID M. SAUNDERS, *Four Days with Dr. Deming: A Strategy for Modern Methods of Management*, Addison-Wesley, Reading, Massachusetts 1995.

[Macquarie 81]

MACQUARIE UNIVERSITY *The Macquarie Dictionary*, Macquarie University, North Ryde, New South Wales, 1981.

[Madsen 93]

O. L. MADSEN, MØLLER-PEDERSEN, and NYGAARD, *Object-Oriented Programming in the BETA Programming Language*, Addison-Wesley 1993.

[Madsen 95]

O. L. MADSEN "Open Issues in Object-Oriented Programming—A Scandinavian Perspective," *Software Practice and Experience*, Volume 25, 1995.

[Meyer 88]

BERTRAND MEYER *Object-Oriented Software Construction*, Prentice Hall, Hemel Hempstead, Hertfordshire, 1988.

[Meyer 90]

BERTRAND MEYER *Introduction to the Theory of Programming Languages*, Prentice Hall, Hemel Hempstead, Hertfordshire, 1990.

[Meyer 92]

BERTRAND MEYER *Eiffel: The Language*, Prentice Hall, Hemel Hempstead, Hertfordshire, 1992.

[Meyer 94]

BERTRAND MEYER *Reusable Software: The Base Object-Oriented Component Libraries*, Prentice Hall, Hemel Hempstead, Hertfordshire, 1994.

[Meyer 95]

BERTRAND MEYER *Object Success*, Prentice Hall, Hemel Hempstead, Hertfordshire, 1995.

[Meyer 96]

BERTRAND MEYER "A Taxonomy of Inheritance," *IEEE Computer*, Volume 29, Number 5, May 1996.

[Meyer 97]

BERTRAND MEYER *Object-Oriented Software Construction*, 2d edition, Prentice Hall, Upper Saddle River, New Jersey, 1997.

[Meyers 92]

SCOTT MEYERS *Effective C++: 50 Specific Ways to Improve Your Programs and Designs*, Addison-Wesley, Reading, Massachusetts, 1992.

[Meyers 96]

SCOTT MEYERS *More Effective C++: 35 New Ways to Improve Your Programs and Designs*, Addison-Wesley, Reading, Massachusetts, 1996.

[Mody 91]

R. P. MODY "C in Education and Software Engineering," *ACM SIGCSE Bulletin*, Volume 23, Number 3, September 1991.

[Morgan 90]

CARROLL MORGAN *Programming from Specifications*, Prentice Hall, Hemel Hempstead, Hertfordshire, 1990.

[Palsberg and Schwartzbach 94]

JENS PALSBERG and MICHAEL I. SCHWARTZBACH *Object-Oriented Type Systems*, John Wiley and Sons, Chichester, West Sussex, 1994.

[Peter 69]

DR. LAWRENCE J. PETER and RAYMOND HULL *The Peter Principle: Why Things Always Go Wrong*, William Morrow & Co. Inc., New York, 1969.

[Petitpierre 98]

CLAUDE PETITPIERRE "Synchronous C++: A Language for Interactive Applications," *IEEE Computer*, Volume 31, Number 9, September 1998.

[Plauger 93]

P. J. PLAUGER "Programming Language Guessing Games: If C++ Is the Answer, What's the question?" *Dr. Dobb's Journal*, October 1993.

[PST 91]

BEN POTTER, JANE SINCLAIR, and DAVID TILL *An Introduction to Formal Specification and Z*, Prentice Hall, Hemel Hempstead, Hertfordshire, 1991.

[RBPEL 91]

RUMBAUGH, BLAHA, PREMERLANI, EDDY, LORENSEN *Object-Oriented Modeling and Design*, Prentice Hall, Englewood Cliffs, New Jersey, 1991.

[Reade 89]

CHRIS READE *Elements of Functional Programming*, Addison-Wesley, Workingham, England, 1989.

[Rémy and Vouillon 98]

DIDIER RÉMY and JÉROME VOUILLON *On the (un)reality of Virtual Types*, November, 1998.

[Sakkinen 92]

MARKKU SAKKINEN *Inheritance and Other Main Principles of C++ and Other Object-Oriented Languages*, University of Jyväskylä, 1992. (Also published as selected papers in ECOOP 88, Computing Systems, Volume 5, Number 1, and Structured Programming, Volume 13, (1992).)

[Shang 95]

DAVID SHANG "Are Cows Animals?" *SIGS Publications*, 1995. (see WEBliography).

[Shaw 96]

MARY SHAW and DAVID GARLAN *Software Architecture: Perspectives on an Emerging Discipline*, Prentice Hall, Upper Saddle River, New Jersey, 1996.

[SJE 91]

SAAKE, JUNGCLAUS, EHRICH "Object-Oriented Specification and Stepwise Refinement," *IFIP Workshop on Open Distributed Processing,* Berlin, 1991.

[Solorzano and Alagić 98]

JOSE H. SOLORZANO and SUAD ALAGIĆ "Parametric Polymorphism for Java: A Reflective Solution," *OOPSLA Proceedings ACM SIGPLAN Notices*, Volume 33, Number 10, October 1998.

[Stevens 97]

AL STEVENS "The Proposed C++ Standard: Evolution, Revolution, Innovation, Invention, Convolution," *Dr. Dobb's Journal*, 269, September 1997.

[Strachey 67]

C. STRACHEY "Fundamental Concepts in Programming Languages," *Lecture Notes for the International Summer School in Computer Programming*, Copenhagen, August 1967.

[Stroustrup 94]

BJARNE STROUSTRUP *The Design and Evolution of C++*, Addison-Wesley, Reading, Massachusetts, 1994.

[Stroustrup 97]

BJARNE STROUSTRUP *The C++ Programming Language*, 3d edition, Addison-Wesley, Reading, Massachusetts, 1997.

[Sun 95]

The Java Language Environment: A White Paper, Sun, 1995 (http://java.sun.com).

[Sun 96]

The Java Language Specification, Sun, 1996. (http://java.sun.com).

[Szyperski 98]

CLEMENS SZYPERSKI *Component Software: Beyond Object-Oriented Programming*, Addison-Wesley Longman/ACM Press, Harlow, Essex, 1998.

[Tanenbaum 95]

ANDREW S. TANENBAUM *Distributed Operating Systems*, Prentice Hall, Upper Saddle River, New Jersey, 1995. (Also ANDREW S. TANENBAUM *Modern Operating Systems*, Prentice Hall, 1992, has almost the same chapter on concurrency and threads.)

[Torgersen 98]

MADS TORGERSEN *Virtual Types are Statically Safe*, Computer Science Department, Århus University 1998.

[TTW 61]

WARREN TAYLOR, LLOYD TURNER, and RICHARD WAYCHOFF "A Syntactical Chart of ALGOL 60," *Communications of the ACM*, Volume 4, Number 9, September 1961.

[Waychoff 79]

RICHARD WAYCHOFF "Stories about the B5000 and People Who Were There," unpublished paper (occasionally available on comp.sys.unisys), 1979.

[Wayner 96]
PETER WAYNER "Better Java Programming," *Byte*, Volume 21, Number 9, September 1996.

[Wegner 91]
PETER WEGNER "Concepts and Paradigms of Object-Oriented Programming," *ACM SIGPLAN OOPS Messenger*, Volume 1, Number 1, August 1990.

[Weisert 97]
CONRAD WEISERT "C++ Toolbox," *ACM SIGPLAN Notices*, Volume 31, Number 11, November 1997.

[Wiener 95]
RICHARD WIENER *Software Development Using Eiffel: There Can Be Life Other than C++*, Prentice Hall, Englewood Cliffs, New Jersey, 1995.

[Wilson 21]
JOHN DOVER WILSON *The Complete Works of William Shakespeare*, Cambridge University Press, 1921. (From *Macbeth*, Act 4, Scene 1.)

[Wirth 90]
NIKLAUS WIRTH *From Modula to Oberon*, 1990.

[X3J16 92]
X3J16 Working Group on Extensions "How to Write a C++ Language Extension Proposal for ANSI-X3J16/ISO-WG21," *ACM SIGPLAN Notices*, Volume 27, Number 6, June 1992.

WEBliography

Ada 95

    Home Page
    http://www.adahome.com/

    Ada vs. C++ Comparison
    http://www.adahome.com/articles/1997-03/ada_vs_cpp.html

Ada and Steelman

    Original Steelman DoD Language Requirements
    http://www.adahome.com/History/Steelman/intro.htm

    David Wheeler's Application of Steelman to Ada 95, C, C++, and Java
    http://www.adahome.com/History/Steelman/steeltab.htm

Beta

    http://www.daimi.aau.dk/~beta/

C++

    FAQ
    http://www.cs.bham.ac.uk/~jdm/CPP/index.html

    ISO SC22/WG21 Standards (X3J16)
    ftp://research.att.com/dist/c++std/WP

http://www.cygnus.com/misc/wp/index.html
http://www.maths.warwick.ac.uk/c++/pub

STL
http://www.sgi.com/Technology/STL/

Comments on Critique
http://www.cs.oberlin.edu/students/jbasney/critique/critique.html

Cardelli, Luca
(Many seminal papers)
http://www.luca.demon.co.uk/

Castagna, Giuseppe
(Many seminal papers)
http://www.ens.fr/~castagna/

Components
Trusted Components Effort
http://www.trusted-components.org/

Dilbert
The Dilbert Zone
http://www.unitedmedia.com/comics/dilbert/

Eiffel
VENDORS
Halstenbach
http://www.halstenbach.com/

Interactive Software Engineering
http://www.eiffel.com/

Object Tools: Visual Eiffel and Eiffel for Macintosh
http://www.object-tools.com/

SmallEiffel (GNU)
http://smalleiffel.loria.fr/

VENDOR INDEPENDENT PAGES
Eiffel Liberty—A website dedicated to exposing the Eiffel Method and Language
http://www.elj.com/

http://www.cm.cf.ac.uk/CLE/
http://www.eiffel.tm/

RESOURCES
Eiffel Forum—an Eiffel User Group
http://www.eiffel-forum.org/

Everything Eiffel Home Page
http://www.eiffel.tm/gustave/resource/org/eveeif.htm

Eiffel Grammar Online and Gobo Project
http://www.gobo.demon.co.uk/

Freeware Eiffel Programs and Libraries
http://www.altsoft.demon.co.uk/free/

Books on Eiffel
http://www.eiffel.com/doc/documentation.html

Eiffel Daily News
http://www.elj.com/new/

Brighton University
http://burks.bton.ac.uk/burks/language/eiffel/

Eiffel "Gotchas"
http://www.eiffel.tm/gustave/gotcha/

An Evaluation of Eiffel in the Context of Wegner's OOSE Goals and Design Dimensions for Inheritance
http://www.elj.com/elj/v1/n1/gew/

Java

Main page
http://java.sun.com/

Demonstration Applets
http://www.gamelan.com/index.shtml

Java Language Specification
http://java.sun.com/doc/language_specification/

Doug Lea's Concurrency Pages (*see also* Lea, Doug)
http://gee.cs.oswego.edu/dl/classes/EDU/oswego/cs/dl/util/concurrent/
                                                             intro.html

GJ Downloads
http://www.cis.unisa.edu.au/~pizza/gj

http://wwwipd.ira.uka.de/~pizza/gj
http://www.math.luc.edu/pizza/gj
http://www.cs.bell-labs.com/~wadler/pizza/gj

Lea, Doug

Many Excellent Java Resources
http://gee.cs.oswego.edu/

Oberon

The Oberon Reference Site
http://www.math.tau.ac.il/~guy/oberon/

The Oberon Home Page
http://www.oberon.ethz.ch/oberon/

From Modula to Oberon
ftp://ftp.inf.ethz.ch/pub/software/Oberon/OberonV4/Docu/ModToOberon.pz.gz

Sakkinen, Markku

References to Other Papers on C++ and Other Topics by Dr. Sakkinen
http://www.cs.jyu.fi/~sakkinen/

Shang, David

http://www.transframe.com/

Bibliographic Index

[Adams 96] 7
[Aho 92] 7
[Bach 97] 298
[Ben-Ari 90] 261, 262
[BOSW 98] 183, 184
[Brooks 95] 20, 304
[Brown 98] 60
[Bruce 96] 15
[C++ ARM] 92, 103, 104, 114, 149, 156, 176, 177, 249, 251, 273, 274, 306, 327, 338, 348
[Cardelli 88] 125, 145, 198
[Cardelli 93] 25, 163
[Cardelli 96] 19
[Cardelli 97] 13, 14
[Cartwright and Steele 98] 182, 184
[Castagna 97] 244, 333
[CD2 96] 71, 95, 126, 127, 149, 204, 236, 325, 326
[CPN 98] 135, 203, 269
[DeMarco and Lister 87] 7, 365
[Deming 82] 7, 13
[Digre 98] 61
[Dijkstra 76] 149

[Ege 96] 15, 176
[Ellemtel 92] 317, 338
[Emery 86] 35
[Flanagan 96] 97, 176
[Flew 89] 108
[GWS 94] 327, 361
[Hext 90] 331
[Hoare 89] 33
[Ince 92] 329
[Java 96] 233, 324
[Jones and Lins 96] 268
[JVM 97] 278
[K&R 88] 344
[Kilov and Ross 94] 26
[Latzko and Saunders 95] 7
[Macquarie 81] 21
[Madsen 93] 124, 135, 301
[Madsen 98] 180
[Meyer 88] 313
[Meyer 90] 47
[Meyer 92] 47, 48, 287, 312, 313, 317, 327
[Meyer 94] 118
[Meyer 95] 317
[Meyer 96] 118
[Meyer 97] 24, 26, 49, 56, 67, 118, 171, 177, 182, 236, 264, 270, 313, 317
[Meyers 92] 50, 128, 130, 131, 159, 199, 211, 268, 309, 310, 339, 342
[Meyers 96] 220, 281, 326
[Mody 91] 321
[Morgan 90] 3
[Palsberg and Schwartzbach 94] 171, 178, 228, 247

[Peter 69] 299, 365
[Plauger 93] 315, 318
[PST 91] 47, 109
[RBPEL 91] 157
[Reade 89] 3, 4, 162, 267
[Rémy and Vouillon 98] 182
[Sakkinen 92] 124, 153, 317, 319
[Shang 95] 180, 239
[Shaw 96] 27
[SJE 91] 117
[Solorzano and Alagi´c 98] 186
[Stevens 97] xvi, 319
[Strachey 67] 163
[Stroustrup 94] 70, 90, 93, 127, 140, 161, 176, 178, 215, 225, 229, 231, 232, 271, 273, 274, 313, 314, 315, 333, 338, 340, 344, 356, 359
[Stroustrup 97] 21, 48, 49, 50, 58, 61, 66, 73, 75, 99, 100, 103, 150, 196, 198, 271, 330, 359
[Sun 95] 20, 49, 68, 271, 305, 317, 324
[Sun 96] 196
[Szyperski 98] 60, 61
[Tanenbaum 95] 256
[Torgersen 98] 180
[TTW 61] 47
[Waychoff 79] 32
[Wayner 96] 97
[Wegner 91] 117
[Weisert 97] 218
[Wiener 95] 164, 317
[Wilson 21] 288
[Wirth 90] 27, 71
[X3J16 92] 317

Index

Symbols
-- 216, 287, 348–350
#define 102, 354–356
#include 69, 316
&& 217, 326
() 341–343
++ 216, 348–350
. 212
.* 215
/* 361
/* ... */ 286
/** ... */ 287
// 286
-> 212
->* 215
?= 229
|| 217, 326

Numerics
4GLs 34

A
A Series. *See* Unisys A Series
abstract 45, 158, 161
abstract data types 15, 58, 226
abstract grammar 47
abstract windows toolkit 316
abstraction 6–7, 108
AbstractMethodError 278
access control 191–206
activate 258
activation record 33
ad hoc polymorphism 163
Ada 69, 171, 304, 312, 315
Ada 95 124, 308
Adams, Scott 7, 298
adapter classes 136
Aho, Alfred 7
ALGOL 32, 37, 104, 291, 327, 341, 343–344
ALGOL 60 47, 224
ALGOL 68 36, 171
aliases 79
ambiguity 147
analysis 63, 107, 298
anchored types 166
and 217, 326
and then 217, 326
anonymous methods 137
ANSI 312
ANY 195, 335–336
Apple Computer 3
architecture 27
arguments 331–332
arrays 327–330
assembler 21, 31
assignment 350–352
assignment attempt 229
assignment expressions 352–353
assignment operator 211
auto_ptr 270
awt. *See* Abstract Windows Toolkit

B
B 35
Babel, Tower of 302, 304
Bach, James 298
Backus-Naur Form 32
bad deletions 274–275
BCPL 34
Beck, Harold 7
Beethoven, Ludwig van 298
Bell Laboratories 35
best viable function 219
BETA 33, 124, 178, 180, 301, 315
bitwise operators 326
block structure 33
BNF 47
BNF. *See* Backus-Naur Form
BON. *See* Business Object Notation
bookkeeping 2, 5–6, 72, 267
bool 325

boolean 146
booleans 324–326
bound variables 151
bounded polymorphism 187–188
bounded type quantification 188
bounding type 183
Brooks, Fred 20, 304
Burroughs B1000 23
Burroughs B20 254
Burroughs B205 32
Burroughs B5000 32
Burroughs Corporation 32, 47
Business Object Notation 301

C

C preprocessor 356
call 257
Cambridge University Mathematical Laboratory 34
cancel 258
Capability Maturity Model 301
cascaded deletes 269
case sensitivity 356–359
case statements 142
CASE Tools 301–303
Castagna, Giuseppe 244
casts 225–245, 333
catcall 120, 236–237, 244
catch 280–281, 283
Cfront preprocessor 248
Challenger disaster 249
changing availability or type 236
char 339
class files 307
class substitution 178
ClassCastException 233
ClassCircularityError 278
classification 118
Clearpath. *See* Unisys A Series
client-server 255
CLOS 162, 315
Close to the Edge 332
closed-world analysis 250
closed-world assumption 247
cluster 63
clusterfall model 300
clusters 67–68

CMM. *See* Capability Maturity Model
COBOL 23, 32, 37, 140, 341
    Object-COBOL 34
code bloat 177, 186
code refactoring 311
code repositories 53
collect_now 272
collect_off 272
comments 8, 285–287, 361
communication 6, 108, 303–304
compatibility 305
compatibility wars 314
compile-time checks 10
complexity 314–318
component-oriented operating systems 249
components 295
compromises 2
computer science 7
CONCURRENCY 265
concurrency 51, 253–266
CONDITION_VARIABLE 261–262
conditional expressions 224
const correctness 331
const_cast 204, 232
constants 100–103
constrained genericity 188
constructors 207–224
contravariance 233–245
convenience 25
CORBA IDL 295
coroutines 254
correctness 9–13, 16–19
correctness vs. cleverness 305
courtesy 25–26
courtesy concern 303–304
covariance 166, 233–245
Cox, Brad 3
CPL 34
Cpp 70
creation 208–209
critical region 261
cycle detection 69

D

dangling pointers 267
data hiding 21–25
De Marco, Tom 7
dead code elimination 70
deadlock 255

Declaration_body 79
declarations 19, 82, 98
declarative approach 5
declarators 82
default arguments 90–92
default constructor 208
deferred 158, 161, 223
defines 354–356
definition 82
definitions 98
delete 215
Deming, W. Edwards 7
deployment 26
deprecated 55
descriptors 323
design 293–320
    bottom up 107
    top down 107
design by contract 26, 293, 295, 304
destructors 207–224
detach 257
diamond inheritance 130
Dijkstra, Edsger W. 29, 149, 261
Dilbert 298
Dilbert Principle 7
direct repeated inheritance 128
dispose 211, 272
distributed computing 51
distributed systems 255
DLE. *See* Dynamic Linking in Eiffel
documentation 8, 285
documentation comment 54, 287
DoD 312
DOUBLE 288
Double 288
double 288
DOUBLE_REF 288
DYNAMIC 278
dynamic binding 158, 231
dynamic linking 277–278
Dynamic Linking in Eiffel 249, 277
dynamic schemata 210
dynamic_cast 230–231
DYNAMIC_CLASS 278

E

EBNF. *See* Extended Backus-Naur Form

Index

editors 21
efficiency 23, 310–312
egoless programming 26
EiffelBench 251
EiffelS 313
employee reviews 300
encapsulation 21–25, 202
ensures 294
enumerations 143–146
equivalences 140
exception handling
    13, 279–283
EXCEPTIONS 265, 283
exceptions 363
execute 260
expanded 209, 214, 276
expected comment 287
export 111, 192
Extended Backus-Naur Form
    (EBNF) 38, 41, 47, 78
extendible 277
external assignment 201

F

fairness property 256
false alarms 12
fault reporting 12
F-bounded polymorphism
    184, 187–188
feature 88
features 77–106
FieldModifier 85
final 156, 205
finalize 272
finally 281
flags 250
flat 74, 251
Flavors 124
flexibility 16–19, 26
fork () 265
formal design 57
formalisms 47
FORTRAN 31, 37, 140, 291,
    341, 360
fragile superclass
    problem 68
free comment 287
free variables 151
friends 120, 193–200
frozen 79, 156, 196, 291
function 79
function variables 34
functional access 24

functional programming 35,
    52
functional vs. nonfunctional
    52
functions 256
    mathematical 225, 341
    partial 226
functions vs. operations 24
functions vs. procedures 340

G

gannt charts 299
garbage collection
    140, 266–272, 314
    adding to C++ 270
    and exception
        handling 270
    and threads 272
    optional 272
GENERAL 231
genericity 15, 164, 166, 233,
    241, 312
    constrained 176
    heterogeneous
        instantiation 186
    homogeneous
        instantiation 186
    textual substitution 187
generics 171–190
GJ 182–183
global analysis 68, 158, 247,
    249
global variables 104, 257
globals 43, 64, 151, 364
gotos 362–364
grep 52

H

handles 323
hardware abstraction
    layer 309
header comment 287
header files 43, 50, 63, 68–72
Header_comment 78
hexadecimal literals 287
Hext, Jan 331
hold 258

I

idiomatic programming
    308–309
ignore 283
implementation 26
implementation hiding

21–25
implicit conversions 219
import 72
index clause 53
inheritance 15, 107–169
inheritance anomaly
    265–266
inlines 93–97, 194
inlining 93
    virtuals and 168
inner 223
inner class 136
inspect 346
interface 23
interfaces 45, 73–76,
    191–206
Internet 201
introspection 186
invariant 202
invariant schemata 210
invariants 296–297
ISO 312
ISO 9000 319

J

Java Virtual Machine 183,
    278, 307
java.lang.reflect 186
javadoc 54
join 261

K

Kay, Alan 33
keywords 52, 129
Knuth, Donald 32, 286, 362

L

LACE 67, 72–73, 316
lambda calculus 16–17, 19,
    151
launch 260
Lea, Doug 261
left values 34, 322
libraries 325
like Current 239
LINC 34
Lisp 315
Lister, Timothy 7
Literate Programming 286
liveness property 255
load-balancing 255
lock 262
logical operators 326
London Underground 7

longjmp 280
loosely-coupled 255
lvalue. *See* left values

M

M 36
Macintosh 254, 313, 323
main() 276
maintainability 305
make 2, 67–68, 316
management
   hierarchical
     structures 298
management policy 299
manifest array 102
mathematics 28
MCP 250
melting-ice technology 250
members 77, 88–106
MEMORY 211, 265, 272
memory allocation 139
memory leaks 267
metadata 24, 347
method overloading 166
methodologies vs. skill 298
methodology gap 298, 300
Meyer, Bertrand 24, 36
  and Z 301
mixins 118, 122–124
Modula 27, 35, 69, 143
Modula-2 329
module calculus 63
modules 63–76
Monadology of Leibniz 108
monitor 262
Moore's Law 253
Morgan, Carroll 3
Mozart, Wolfgang
  Amadeus 297
multiple interfaces 74, 200
multiprocessing 255
multiprogramming 256
mutable 204
MUTEX 261–262

N

name clashes 65
namespaces 43, 50, 63–66,
  74, 150, 152, 201
naming 89, 146
nested classes 132–137
nesting 202–204
NeXT 3
NextGen 182, 184

NICE 312
NoClassDefFoundError 278
NONE 195, 334, 339
NoSuchMethodError 278
notation 8
NT 29
NULL 338–339
null 161, 334, 339

O

Oberon 15, 27, 71
Object 259, 335
Object Pascal 156, 158, 248,
  323
Object success 317
Object Tools 313
Objective-C 3, 159
Object-Oriented Software
  Construction 317
obscure failures 10
Odersky, Martin 183
OLE 250
OMT 303
once function 101, 104
once routine 104
once routines
  and threads 263
one definition rule 99
OOA 300
OOD 300
OpenDoc 250
OpenStep 3
open-world assumption 247
operator = 211–212
operator features 218
operator overloading 218
operators 207–224
optimization 8, 155,
  310–312
or 217, 326
or else 217, 326
O-ring failure 249
overloaded functions 152
overloading 162–168, 219
own 104
own variables 34

P

P(S) 261
packages 63, 68
parameterized classes 171
parameters
  anonymous 88
  positional 89

parametric polymorphism
  107, 162, 171, 187
partial functions 226
Pascal 12, 15, 32, 36, 47, 69,
  140, 291, 316, 329, 344,
  347
passivate 258
patterns 33
peer-to-peer processing 255
performance profiling 96
perpetual change 155
Peter Principle 299–300, 320
Peters, Tom 7, 319
pipes 250
Pizza 182–183
PL/I 37, 315
Plauger, P. J. 315
pointers 198, 322–324, 364
polymorphism 158, 187–188
  ad hoc 163
  parametric 162
portability 26, 307–308
post 262
postconditions 294
Potter, John 333
precision 6–7
precondition paradox 264
preconditions 294, 296–297
  ADTs 226
  and concurrency 264
Precursor 221
preemptive multitasking 256
Principle of Uniform
  Access 162
Principle of Uniqueness
  317, 327
private 81, 191–206, 251,
  342
private inheritance 120, 199
procedure 79
process 255–256
process class 257
process classes 254
processes vs. threads 256
processor 255
Procrustean structures 23
Procrustes 23
Programming 3–6
project organization 2
project failure 6
projects 293–320
PROLOG 35
protected 81, 191–206, 251,
  342

Index

protected inheritance 120, 199
PROXY 263
public 81, 191–206
public inheritance 120, 199
pure virtual 158

Q

QoS. *See* Quality of Service
quality 13, 25
Quality of Service (QoS) 52

R

race conditions 255
railroad diagrams 47
raise 280
rapid application development 27
raw types 183
Reade, Chris 3, 267
records 32
redefine 112
REDEFINEs 140
redundancy 19–21
reference 288
references 98
reflection 186
reinterpret_cast 232
rename 111, 152
renames 65
requires 294
rescue 231, 282, 363
Result 345
resume 257
résumés 299
retry 282
return 344–345
reusability 51, 303–304
reuse 16–19
reverse assignment. *See* assignment attempt
reverse engineering 301
right values 322
Ritchie, Dennis 35
role-based security 201
routines 79
    small 308
RTTI. *See* run-time type information
rule-based languages 35
run () 258
Runnable 258
run-time checks 10
run-time type information 228
rvalues. *See* right values

S

SA/SD 302
safety 25–26
safety concerns 304
safety property 255
Sakkinen, Markku 153
schema 14, 20, 35
SCOOP 259, 263–265
scope 50, 100, 138, 148
scope resolution operator 126, 150–151
security 22, 201
SEI. *See* Software Engineering Institute
select 112
semantic gap 8, 298, 300
semantics checking 14
SEMAPHORE 261
semaphore
    binary 261
    general 261
semicolon 39
semicolons 359–361
separate 263
    call rule 264
separation of concerns 2, 4, 75, 95, 155, 309, 316
setjmp and 280
shadowed variables 151
Shang, David 180, 239
short 74, 162, 251, 260, 287, 294, 304
shortcut operators 217
signal 280
signal(S) 261
signature variance 233–245
signed char 339
Silver Bullet 20
Simple Concurrent Object-Oriented Programming 259
Simula 33, 37, 104, 157, 223, 254, 312
    concurrency in 257
skill vs. methodologies 298
slicing 275–276
small routines 92
SmallEiffel 313
Smalltalk 3, 14, 33, 159, 172, 225, 230, 267, 278, 312, 315, 318, 325
smart pointers 270
SML 342
SNOBOL 37
Software Engineering Institute 301
software life cycle 297–301
specification 3, 6
Standard Template Library 171
standardization 312–314
start () 258
static 103
static schemata 209
static typing 230
static variables 34
static_cast 232
Strachey, C. 162
Stradivarius violins 305
strcpy 350
strings 347–348
Stroustrup, Bjarne 2, 15, 21, 74
struct 43
subsumption 117, 121
subtype polymorphism 107, 171
super 222
switch 346–347
switch statements 231
synchronization 254
synchronized 259
Synchronous C++ 265
syntax 303
syntax charts 47
syntax checking 14
syntax diagrams 47
synthesis 63, 107
System.gc () 272
system-level validity 248, 250

T

Taylor, Warren 47
templates 171–190, 241
temporaries 219, 267
    and constructors 273–274
testing 297
    reliance on 13
thin clients 255
Thompson, Ken 35
THREAD 259–260

Thread 258
thread 256
THREAD_CONTROL 260
threads 258
three-tier 255
throw 280
tight coupling 93
tightly coupled 255
tool integration 9
transitive dependencies 70
trust 304
try 280–281
try_lock 262
try_wait 262
Turing machine 140
Turner, Lloyd 47
turn-of-the-century 29
type calculus 108
type casts 171, 225
type safety 225
type system
    fundamental purpose 14
type theory 43, 139
Type_mark 79
typedef 43, 49
typeid 231
types 14–15, 225, 296–297
    primitive 288–290
type-safe linkage 249–250

U
Ullman, Jeffrey 7
UML 315

UML. *See* Unified Modeling
    Language
unchecked warning 183
undefine 111
unexpected() 281
Unicode 359
Unified Modeling Language 303
uninitialized 345
union 43, 49, 139
unique 101, 144
Unisys 32
    A Series 32, 198, 250, 323
University of London
    Institute of Computer
    Science 34
UNIX 29, 32
unlock 262
URL 214

V
V(S) 261
validity 296
variance 233–245
variant records 139
variant types 140
viable functions 219
Vintage 95 Kernel Library 166
virtual 248
virtual binding 178
virtual functions 152–159

virtual memory 32
virtual tables 248
virtual types 180
Visual Eiffel 313
VNCC validity rule 189
Void 334, 339
void 332–338, 344
void * 332–338

W
Wadler, Philip 183
wait 262
wait(S) 261
Waychoff, Richard 47
Wilner, Wayne 23
Wirth, Niklaus 15, 27, 36, 38, 47, 71
workplace 7
write once, run anywhere 307

X
X3J16 313

Y
year 2000 problem xii, 23
Yes 332
yield 261

Z
Z 35–36, 47, 109, 295, 301

Keep Up-to-Date with
PH PTR Online!

We strive to stay on the cutting-edge of what's happening in professional computer science and engineering. Here's a bit of what you'll find when you stop by **www.phptr.com**:

@ Special interest areas offering our latest books, book series, software, features of the month, related links and other useful information to help you get the job done.

Deals, deals, deals! Come to our promotions section for the latest bargains offered to you exclusively from our retailers.

$ Need to find a bookstore? Chances are, there's a bookseller near you that carries a broad selection of PTR titles. Locate a Magnet bookstore near you at www.phptr.com.

! What's New at PH PTR? We don't just publish books for the professional community, we're a part of it. Check out our convention schedule, join an author chat, get the latest reviews and press releases on topics of interest to you.

Subscribe Today! **Join PH PTR's monthly email newsletter!**

Want to be kept up-to-date on your area of interest? Choose a targeted category on our website, and we'll keep you informed of the latest PH PTR products, author events, reviews and conferences in your interest area.

Visit our mailroom to subscribe today! **http://www.phptr.com/mail_lists**